RETRIEVING THE
American Past

A CUSTOMIZED U.S. HISTORY READER

Prof. Peter Karsten
U.S. History, 1865 - present
HIST 0601
University of Pittsburgh

Pearson Learning Solutions

New York Boston San Francisco
London Toronto Sydney Tokyo Singapore Madrid
Mexico City Munich Paris Cape Town Hong Kong Montreal

Senior Vice President, Editorial and Marketing: Patrick F. Boles
Senior Sponsoring Editor: Natalie Danner
Development Editor: Mary Kate Paris
Assistant Editor: Jill Johnson
Operations Manager: Eric M. Kenney
Production Manager: Jennifer Berry
Rights Manager: Jillian Santos
Art Director and Cover Designer: Renée Sartell

Cover Art: Courtesy of Library of Congress and the Chicago History
Museum.

Printed in the United States of America.

Please visit our websites at *www.pearsoncustom.com*.

Attention bookstores: For permission to return any unsold stock, contact
us at *pe-uscustomreturns@pearson.com*.

Pearson Learning Solutions, 501 Boylston Street, Suite 900, Boston,
MA 02116
A Pearson Education Company
www.pearsoned.com

ISBN 10: 0-558-09441-4
ISBN 13: 978-0-558-09441-6

CONTRIBUTORS

Senior Editor
Mitch Lerner

Managing Editor
David Staley

Copy Editor
Ann Heiss

Assistant Managing Editor
William Sturkey

Contributing Editors

Tyler Anbinder
Kenneth J. Andrien
Jean Harvey Baker
Michael Les Benedict
Mansel Blackford
Paul C. Bowers
Rowland Brucken
John D. Buenker
John C. Burnham
Joan E. Cashin
William R. Childs
Albert J. Churella
Steven Conn
Saul Cornell
Nick Cullather
Jeanette Davis
Merton L. Dillon
Daniel Feller
Charles Coleman Finlay
Emily Greenwald
Mark Grimsley
Bernard N. Grindel
Peter L. Hahn
James Hansen
Susan M. Hartmann
Mary Ann Heiss
Earl J. Hess
Michael J. Hogan
R. Douglas Hurt

Bruce Karhoff
Michael Kazin
Terence Kehoe
K. Austin Kerr
Frank Lambert
Valerie Mendoza
James McCaffrey
Allan R. Millett
Pamela J. Mills
Daniel Nelson
Margaret E. Newell
Josef Ostyn
Carla Gardina Pestana
Patrick D. Reagan
Randolph A. Roth
Hal K. Rothman
John A. M. Rothney
Leila J. Rupp
Richard D. Shiels
David Sicilia
C. Edward Skeen
Amy L. S. Staples
David L. Stebenne
David Steigerwald
Marshall F. Stevenson, Jr.
Warren R. Van Tine
Christopher Waldrep
J. Samuel Walker

Your *Retrieving the American Past* purchase includes access to online resources designed to complement your readings. This Companion Website is located at the following URL:

http://www.pearsoncustom.com/dbrtap/rtap/student

When prompted, enter the User Name: **rtapstudent** and Password: **rtaplearn**

(*Note:* The User Name and Password are case-sensitive, so be sure to use upper and lower case characters exactly as shown above.)

Once logged in, you will have access to the following resources:

- *Link Library.* A collection of vetted web links, organized by key terms and historical figures, which offer you background and context for many of the selections you'll be reading.

- *Documents.* Access (via links) to the full text of historical documents, which can furnish a backdrop to events that might have preceded, or followed, their drafting.

- *The Writing Process.* Advice that can aid you during the writing process. Included are guidelines and suggestions for each phase of writing, from start to finish.

- *Plagiarism.* Suggestions to help you maintain academic honesty, with illustrative examples.

- *Style Guide.* A brief guide to help you follow either MLA or Chicago Manual styles in citing your sources. The Modern Language Association style is widely used for papers in English composition, literature, and foreign languages. History, the fine arts, and some fields in the humanities (but not literature) use traditional footnotes or endnotes, which should conform to standards set by *The Chicago Manual of Style.*

We invite you to explore!

Contents

Race Relations, 1890-1915: Booker T. Washington and W.E.B. Du Bois

Christopher Waldrep

The Rise of the New Right

Michael Kazin

The Environmental Movement

Austin Kerr and Terence Kehoe

The Struggle for Black Rights during Reconstruction

Michael Les Benedict

INTRODUCTION

The Civil War and Reconstruction era witnessed a desperate fight for equal civil and political rights for African Americans. The legal position of black Americans had deteriorated in the first part of the nineteenth century, with racism actually growing in the North and South as slavery was rejuvenated by the development of cotton agriculture. The growth of the antislavery movement in the 1840s and 1850s, however, led some Northerners to argue that African Americans were entitled to the rights of citizenship. The Supreme Court's Dred Scott decision was a watershed that dashed black Americans' claims to citizenship. Black hopes and expectations brightened with the passage of the Thirteenth Amendment, but they were dimmed once more by the adoption of restrictive southern Black Codes. Seeing the codes as an attempt to salvage key aspects of slavery, Republicans urged the passage of the Civil Rights Act of 1866 to ensure that all Americans, regardless of color, received the basic rights of citizenship. Congress passed the bill, only to be rebuffed by President Andrew Johnson's veto. Overriding the president's veto, Republicans then passed the Fourteenth Amendment in an effort to secure African-American citizenship and rights beyond constitutional doubt.

While blacks embraced their new citizenship, they continued to demand suffrage. Among the most eloquent was Frederick Douglass, one of the greatest orators of his day. The clamor for black enfranchisement aroused apprehension among southern whites that black voters might overturn the traditional social order. The white people of Alabama were among those who voiced their fears of black dominance in a petition to Congress. Nonethe-

less, Congress imposed black suffrage on the South in the Recon-
struction Act of 1867, and in 1870 the requisite number of states
ratified the Fifteenth Amendment, which extended the change
throughout the nation and made it permanent.

But Republicans proved unable to secure equal civil and po-
litical rights for African Americans over bitter southern white
resistance. A series of Supreme Court decisions narrowed the
definition of federal citizenship and limited Congress's power to
protect these rights. The court proclaimed that the postwar consti-
tutional amendments authorized the federal government to pro-
tect rights only against violations by state authorities, leaving
African Americans to rely on unsympathetic state and local offi-
cials to protect them against all other invasions of their rights.

SECURING EQUAL RIGHTS: THE DOCUMENTARY RECORD

As slaves, most African Americans had been denied nearly all fundamental rights. But for much of the time before the Civil War, the civil status of free African Americans was uncertain. Many Northern states considered them citizens entitled to basic rights; most of the New England states conceded them political rights as well. Other states denied or limited the basic rights of free blacks to travel, to associate with others, and to sue and testify in court, without making clear whether they were citizens or not. It was uncertain how state citizenship related to United States citizenship. Not until the case of Dred Scott v. Sandford did the Supreme Court answer that question. In this case, the Supreme Court distinguished United States citizenship from state citizenship and held that African Americans were not citizens of the United States, whether they were citizens of individual states or not.

White southerners refused to accept the legitimacy of state governments elected by black voters, and they engaged in systematic violence to resubordinate African Americans and to paralyze the Republican state officials in the South. From 1868 to 1871 much of the violence was instigated by the Ku Klux Klan, loosely organized gangs of white terrorists that sprang up in various southern localities. From 1874 to 1876 the Democratic party organized "White Leagues," "Red Shirts," and less formal armed auxiliaries to break up the Republican party. Both white and black Republicans were victimized.

Most of the southern states passed vagrancy laws that prohibited freedpeople from buying or leasing land or homes, except in towns, and then authorized towns to make their own regulations.

The following documents will introduce you to the legislation and arguments associated with the effort to secure equal rights after the Civil War, as well as to the practical effect on the lives of ordinary people. Read them in light of the questions that follow this section, particularly considering how far Republicans intended to change the American system of government in order to protect citizens' rights.

The Thirteenth Amendment

Congress passed the Thirteenth Amendment in January 1865 and it was ratified by December of that same year. The amendment abolished slavery throughout the United States.

Section 1 - Neither slavery nor involuntary servitude, except as a punishment for crime whereof the party shall have been duly convicted, shall exist within the United States, or any place subject to their jurisdiction.

Section 2 - Congress shall have power to enforce this article by appropriate legislation.

The Black Codes

Under President Andrew Johnson's plan of reconstruction, southern state governments, elected by white men who had taken an oath pledging loyalty to the United States, passed laws specifying the rights of the freedpeople. Some were more restrictive than others. All gave freedpeople the right to make contracts and to buy, own, and sell property. Some subjected them to the same criminal laws and punishments that covered white people; others subjected them to the harsher criminal laws that had covered free black people before the war. None of the codes extended political rights or the right to serve on juries. Local communities also passed regulations that limited freedpeople's rights. The following are examples of restrictive state and local provisions that convinced Republicans to intervene.

Selections from the Mississippi Black Code conferring civil rights on freedmen and defining vagrancy are from Laws of the State of Mississippi . . . *(1866), 82-84, 91 92.*

Mississippi Black Code

An Act to confer Civil Rights on Freedmen . . .

Section 1. . . . [A]ll freedmen, free negroes and mulattoes may sue and be sued . . . in all the courts of law and equity of this State, and may acquire personal property . . . by descent or purchase, and may dispose of the same, in the same manner, and to the same extent that white persons may: Provided that the provisions of this section shall not be so construed as to allow any freedman, free negro or mulatto to rent or lease any lands or tenements, except in incorporated towns or cities in which places the corporate authorities shall control the same. . . .

Sec. 5. . . . [E]very freedman, free negro and mulatto, shall . . . have a lawful home or employment, and shall have written evidence thereof. . . .

Sec. 7. . . . [E]very civil officer shall, and every person may arrest and carry back to his or her legal employer any freedman, free negro or mulatto, who shall have quit the service of his or her employer before the expiration of his or her term of service without good cause. . . .

Mississippi Vagrancy Law

Sec. 2. . . . [A]ll freedmen, free negroes and mulattoes in this State, over the age of eighteen years, found on the second Monday in January, 1866, or thereafter, with no lawful employment or business, or found unlawfully assembling themselves together either in the day or night time, and all white persons so assembling with freedmen, free negroes or mulattoes, or usually associating with freedmen, free negroes or mulattoes on terms of equality, or living in adultery or fornication with a freedwoman, free negro, or mulatto, shall be deemed vagrants, and on conviction thereof, shall be fined in the sum of not exceeding, in the case of a freedman, free negro, or mulatto, fifty dollars, and a white man two hundred dollars, and imprisoned at the discretion of the court, the free negro not exceeding ten days, and the white man not exceeding six months. . . .

Sec. 5. . . . [I]n case any freedman, free negro or mulatto, shall fail . . . after the imposition of any fine . . . to pay the same, . . . it shall be, and is hereby made the duty of the sheriff of the proper county to hire out said freedman, free negro or mulatto, to any person who will, for the shortest period of service, pay said fine . . . .

Debate over African American Rights: The Civil Rights Act

Republicans insisted that all Americans, regardless of color, were entitled to the basic rights of citizenship. In response to the black codes and other deprivations of rights in many states, North and South, they proposed a civil rights act.

Congress passed the Civil Rights bill on 15 March 1866, with southern congressmen still not permitted to take their seats. The bill made it a crime for anyone acting "under the color of law" or "custom" to deny the rights specified in Section 1. It also allowed those denied their rights in the states to transfer civil and criminal cases to the federal courts.

President Johnson vetoed the Civil Rights bill, giving his reasons in the message excerpted below from The Congressional Globe, 39th Congress, 1st Session, 1679-81 (27 March 1866).

To the Senate of the United States:

I regret that the bill which has passed both Houses of Congress . . . contains provisions which I cannot approve, consistently with my sense of duty to the whole people and my obligations to the Constitution of the United States. . . .

By the first section of the bill, all persons born in the United States, and not subject to any foreign Power, excluding Indians not taxed, are declared to be citizens of the United States. This provision comprends the Chinese of the Pacific States, Indians subject to taxation, the people called Gypsies, as well as the entire race designated as blacks, people of color, negroes, mulattoes, and persons of African blood. . . .

The right of Federal citizenship thus to be conferred on the several excepted races before mentioned, is now, for the first time, proposed to be given by law. If, as is claimed by many, all persons who are native-born already are, by virtue of the Constitution, citizens of the United States, the passage of the pending bill cannot be necessary to make them such. If, on the other hand, such persons are not citizens, as may be assumed from the proposed legislation to make them such, the grave question presents itself, whether when eleven of the thirty-six States are unrepresented in Congress, at this time it is sound policy to make our entire colored population and all other excepted classes citizens of the United States? Four millions of them have just emerged from slavery into freedom. Can it be reasonably supposed that they possess the requisite qualifications to entitle them to all the privileges and immunities of citizens of the United States? . . .

Thus a perfect equality of the white and black races is attempted to be fixed by Federal law in every State of the Union, over the vast field of State jurisdiction covered by these enumerated rights. . . . In the exercise of State policy over matters exclusively affecting the people of each State, it has frequently been thought expedient to discriminate between the two races. By the statutes of some of the States, northern as well as southern, it is enacted, for instance, that no white person shall intermarry with a negro or mulatto. . . .

Hitherto every subject embraced in the enumeration of rights contained in this bill has been considered as exclusively belonging to the States. They all relate to the internal policy and economy of the respective States. . . .

In all our history, in all our experience as a people living under Federal and State law, no such system as that contemplated by the details of this bill has ever before been proposed or adopted. They establish, for the security of the colored race, safeguards which go infinitely beyond any that the General Government has ever provided for the white race. In fact, the distinction of race and color is, by the bill, made to operate in favor of the colored and against the white race. They interfere with the municipal legislation of the States, with the relations existing exclusively between a State and its citizens, or between inhabitants of the same State_an absorption and assumption of power by the General Government which, if acquiesced in, must sap and destroy our federative system of limited powers, and break down the barriers which preserve the rights of the States. It is another step, or rather stride, towards centralization and the concentration of all legislative powers in the national Government. The tendency of the bill must be to resuscitate the spirit of rebellion, and to arrest the progress of those influences which are more closely drawing around the States the bonds of union and peace.

Senator Trumbull's Response

Republican senator from Illinois Lyman Trumbull, managing the bill in the Senate, successfully argued for passage of the Civil Rights Act of 1866 over the president's veto. Taken from The Congressional Globe, *39th Congress, 1st Session (4 April 1866), 1756-58, 1760-61.*

What is the bill? It declares that there shall be no distinction in civil rights between any other race or color and the white race. It declares that there shall be no different punishment inflicted on a colored man in consequence of his color than that which is inflicted on a white man for the same offense. Is that a discrimination in favor of the negro and against the foreigner—a bill the only effect of which is to preserve equality of rights?

. . . Why, sir, the very object . . . is to prevent discrimination, and language, it seems to me, could not more plainly express that object and effect. It may be said that it is for the benefit of the black man because he is now in some instances discriminated against by State laws; but that is the case with all remedial statutes. They are for the relief of the persons who need the relief, not for the relief of those who have the right already; and when those needing the relief obtain it, they stand upon the precise footing of those who do not need the benefit of the law.

. . . The bill neither confers nor abridges the rights of any one, but simply declares that in civil rights there shall be an equality among all classes of citizens. . . . Each State, so that it does not abridge the great fundamental rights belonging, under the Constitution, to all citizens, may grant or withhold such civil rights as it pleases; all that is required is that, in this respect, its laws shall be impartial.

. . . This bill in no manner interferes with the municipal regulations of any State which protects all alike in their rights of person and property. . . . How preposterous, then, to charge that unless some State can have and exercise the right to punish somebody, or to deny somebody a civil right on account of his color, its rights as a State will be destroyed.

The Fourteenth Amendment

To secure African-American citizenship and rights beyond constitutional doubt, Congress passed the Fourteenth Amendment later in 1866.

Section 1. All persons born or naturalized in the United States, and subject to the jurisdiction thereof, are citizens of the United States and of the State wherein they reside. No State shall make or enforce any law which shall abridge the privileges or immunities of citizens of the United States; nor shall any State deprive any person of life, liberty, or property, without due process of law; nor deny to any person within its jurisdiction the equal protection of the laws....

Section 5. The Congress shall have power to enforce, by appropriate legislation, the provisions of this article.

Frederick Douglass Argues in Favor of Black Suffrage

Even before the Civil War ended, African-American leaders and radical Republicans were insisting that the national government secure the freedmen the right to vote. By 1867 most Republicans agreed, and by 1869 they were considering a constitutional amendment to bar racial tests for voting. Frederick Douglass, the great African-American orator and newspaper editor, explained "What the Black Man Wants" to a Boston audience in 1865. Note Douglass's allusion to the fact that women did not have the right to vote at this time. Note also his brief appeal to the anti-Irish prejudices of his Republican audience.

Excerpted from The Frederick Douglass Papers—Series One: Speeches, Debates, and Interviews, Volume 4: 1864-80, *ed. John W. Blassingame and John R. McKivigan (New Haven, 1991), 62-63, 66-68.*

I have had but one idea for the last three years to present to the American people.... I am for the "immediate, unconditional and universal" enfranchisement of the black man, in every State of the Union. (Loud applause.) Without this, his liberty is a mockery; without this, you might as well almost retain the old name of slavery for his condition; for, in fact, if he is not the slave of the individual master, he is the slave of society, and holds his liberty as a privilege, not as a right....

It may be asked, "Why do you want it? Some men have got along very well without it. Women have not this right." Shall we justify one wrong by another? That is a sufficient answer. Shall we at this moment justify the deprivation of the negro of the right to

A photograph of Frederick Douglass, ex-slave and prominent African-American political activist. (Courtesy the Library of Congress)

vote because some one else is deprived of that privilege? I hold that women as well as men have the right to vote (applause), and my heart and my voice go with the movement to extend suffrage to woman. But that question rests upon another basis than that on which our right rests. We may be asked, I say, why we want it. I will tell you why we want it. We want it because it is our right, first of all. (Applause.) No class of men can, without insulting their own nature, be content with any deprivation of their rights. We want it, again, as a means for educating our race. Men are so constituted that they derive their conviction of their own possibilities largely from the estimate formed of them by others. If nothing is expected of a people, that people will find it difficult to contradict that expectation. By depriving us of suffrage, you affirm our incapacity to form an intelligent judgment respecting public men and public measures; you declare before the world that we are unfit to exercise the elective franchise, and by this means lead us to undervalue ourselves, to put a low estimate upon ourselves, and to feel that we have no possibilities like other men. . . . [H]ere, where universal suffrage is the rule, where that is the fundamental idea of the government, to rule us out is to make us an exception, to brand us with the stigma of inferiority, and to invite to our heads the missiles of those about us. Therefore I want the franchise for the black man.

. . . It is said that we are ignorant; I admit it. But if we know enough to be hung, we know enough to vote. If the negro knows enough to pay taxes to support the Government, he knows enough to vote—taxation and representation should go together. If he knows enough to shoulder a musket and fight for the flag, fight for the Government, he knows enough to vote. If he knows as much when he is sober as an Irishman knows when drunk, he knows enough to vote, on good American principles. (Laughter and applause.)

. . . What have you asked the black men of the South, the black men of the whole country to do? Why, you have asked them to incur the deadly enmity of their masters, in order to befriend you and to befriend this government. You have asked us to call down, not only upon ourselves, but upon our children's children, the deadly hate of the entire Southern people. You have called upon us to turn our backs upon our masters, to abandon their cause and espouse yours; to turn against the South and in favor of the North; to shoot down the Confederacy and uphold the flag—the American flag. . . . And now, what do you propose to do when you come to make peace? To reward your enemies, and trample in the dust your friends? . . . Do you mean to give your enemies the right to vote, and take it away from your friends? . . . In time of trouble we are citizens. Shall we be citizens in war, and aliens in peace? Would that be just?

. . . What I ask for the negro is not benevolence, not pity, not sympathy, but simply justice.

The Nation Supports Black Suffrage

The weekly journal The Nation *was founded in 1865 to support radical solutions to the problem of restoring the Union. The journal endorsed black suffrage.*

Excerpted from "Universal Suffrage And Universal Amnesty," The Nation *(29 November 1866), 430.*

[T]he Federal Government is bound by every consideration of justice, honor, and decency either to see that the freedmen enjoy complete security or to furnish them with the means of protecting themselves. In other words, we are bound either to give the freedmen a police—to see that every man of whom we claim allegiance can eat or sleep in peace—or we are bound to see that he enjoys a fair share in the making of the laws and the selection of the officers who are to execute them. . . . The former of these courses is not strictly in accordance with the spirit of our institutions; the latter is. . . .

[T]he ballot will do for the negro what it does for the poor ignorant Irishman, or German, or Englishman, but no more. It will secure him against flagrant class legislation, or cruel or unusual punishments, and against all oppression which is on its face oppressive. It will do more than this; it will cause politicians and public men—sheriffs, policemen, and the whole race of functionaries, actual and expectant—to treat him with civility, even with deference. It will put a stop to outrages and assaults of various kinds on negroes, and to all open expressions of contempt for them or dislike of them. . . .

But more than this the ballot will not do for the negro. It will not make him a good judge of the value or importance of measures not bearing directly and patently on his personal comfort or convenience; it will not enable him to tell the difference between statesmen and demagogues; between honest public men and knavish public men; between his own real friends and his real enemies; to distinguish laws contrived by scoundrels for his spoliation, under a show of immediate benefit, and schemes contrived by statesmen for his permanent advantage.

Opposition to Black Suffrage

The Reconstruction Act of 1867 enfranchised both black and white southerners, with the exception of those whites who as officeholders had sworn to uphold the Constitution of the United States and then joined the rebellion. It

*put the southern states back under military control temporarily. In ex-
change for restoration to normal relations in the Union, the Reconstruction
Act required each southern state to frame a new constitution that would
secure equal civil and political rights regardless of race. In the following
document, a number of white Alabamans protested against the process.*

*Excerpted from the Petition and Memorial File, Records of the
House of Representatives, 40th Cong., Record Group 233, National
Archives, Washington, D.C.*

The White people of Alabama send this their humble petition.

We beseech your Honorable Bodies to withdraw yourselves
from the influence of the passions and contests of the hour, and
contemplate for a brief period, our miserable condition . . . .

. . . [I]t is well known by all who have knowledge on the
subject,—that while the negroes of the South may be more intelligent and of better morals than those of the same race in any other
part of the world . . . —yet they are in the main, ignorant generally,
wholly unacquainted with the principles of free Governments, im-
provident, disinclined to work, credulous yet suspicious, dishonest,
untruthful, incapable of self-restraint, and easily impelled by want
or incited by false and specious counsels, into folly and crime. . . .

Are these the people in whom should be vested the high gov-
ernmental functions of establishing institutions and enacting and
enforcing laws, to prevent crime, protect property, preserve peace
and order in society, and promote industry, enterprise and civilization in Alabama, and the power and honor of the United States?
Without property, without industry, without any regard for reputation, without controul over their own caprices and strong passions,
and without fear of punishment under laws, by courts and through
juries which are . . . created by and composed of . . . themselves, or of
those whom they elect,—how can it be otherwise than that they will
bring, to the great injury of themselves as well as of us and our
children,—blight, crime, ruin and barbarism on this fair land? . . .

Will you, nearly three years after the war has ended, . . . suffer
a whole State full of your kindred civilized white inhabitants, not
only those who had opposed the Government, but women, children, and loyal men who had adhered to it,—to be thus consigned
over to the horrid rule of barbarian negroes! . . .

. . . [D]o not, we implore you, abdicate your own rule over us,
by transferring us to the blighting, brutalizing and unnatural
dominion of an alien and inferior race: A race which has never
shown sufficient administrative capacity for the good govern-

ment of even the tribes, into which it has always been broken up in its native seats; and which in all ages, has itself furnished slaves for all the other races of the earth.

The Fifteenth Amendment

To make black enfranchisement permanent and to extend it to the north, Congress passed the Fifteenth Amendment in 1869 and sent it to the states for ratification. The required number of states ratified it in 1870.

Section 1. The right of citizens of the United States to vote shall not be denied or abridged by the United States or by any

The Fifteenth Amendment gave African Americans the right to vote for the first time; however, the end of Reconstruction, followed by the rise of Jim Crow laws in the South, largely marked the end of black suffrage until the Civil Rights movement almost a century later. (Courtesy of HarpWeek.)

State on account of race, color, or previous condition of servitude.

Section 2. The Congress shall have power to enforce this article by appropriate legislation.

Violent Resistance to Equal Rights in the South

The following documents describe Klan activities from several perspectives. Amzi Rainey, a black South Carolina sharecropper, described how the Klan terrorized his family in testimony excerpted from Proceedings in the Ku Klux Trials, at Columbia, S. C. in the United States Circuit Court, November Term, 1871 *(Columbia, S.C., 1872) 279-80.*

Former Senator James Chesnut of South Carolina testified before a congressional committee investigating the Klan. Simpson Bobo, a white lawyer and jack-of-all-trades, testified before the same committee. Their testimony is excerpted from Testimony Taken by the Joint Select Committee to Inquire into the Condition of Affairs in the Late Insurrectionary States, *vol. 1 and 2, South Carolina (Washington, D.C., 1872) 1:446, 449, 2:796-97.*

[Amzi Rainey's Testimony]

I looked out of the window, and I see some four or five disguised men coming up, and I ran up in the loft, and they came on; come to the door; and when they come to the door, they commenced beating and knocking. "God damn you, open the door! open the door! open the door!" . . . and my wife run to one of the doors and they knocked the top hinges off of the first, and she run across the house to the other, and agin that time they got the two hinges knocked off the other door, and the bolt held the door from falling, and she got it open . . . and when they come in, they struck her four or five licks before they said a word . . . .

They asked her who lived here. She said, "Rainey—Amzi Rainey." "What Amzi Rainey? What Amzi Rainey?" And she said, "Amzi Rainey," and he struck her another lick, and says: "Where is he? God damn him, where is he?" And she says: "I don't know."

The chief organization violently opposed to equal rights for African Americans was the Ku Klux Klan, which began in 1866 and relied on intimidation, terror, and murder to enforce white supremacy. (Courtesy the Library of Congress.)

And one said: "O, I smell him, God damn him; he has gone up in the loft." He says: "We'll kill him, too," and they come up then. . . .

I was in a box, and they said: "Oh, he is in this box, God damn him, I smell him; we'll kill him!" and the other says: "Don't kill him yet;" and they took me down. This man that struck my wife first, ran back to her and says: "God damn her, I will kill her now; I will kill her out;" and the one that went after me, he says: "Don't kill her;" and he commenced beating her then; struck her some four or five more licks, and then run back and struck me; he run back to her then, and drawed his pistol, and says: "Now, I am going to blow your damn brains out;" and the one by me threw the pistol up, and says: "Don't kill her." He aimed to strike me over the head, and struck me over the back and sunk me right down. Then, after he had done that, my little daughter—she was back in the room with the other little children—he says: "I am going to kill him;" and she runs out of the room, and says: "Don't kill my pappy; please don't kill my pappy!" He shoved her back, and says; "You go back in the room, you God damned little bitch; I will blow your brains out!" and fired and shot her . . . .

. . . [A]nd then they took me . . . [o]ff up the road, about a hundred and fifty yards; and they wanted to kill me up there, and one said, "No, don't kill him, let's talk a little to him first." Then, he asked me which way did I vote. I told him I voted the Radical [Republican] ticket. "Well," he says, "now you raise your hand and swear that you will never vote another Radical ticket, and I will not let them kill you." And he made me stand and raise my hand before him and my God, that I never would vote another Radical ticket . . . .

[Ex-Senator Chesnut's Testimony]

There is a deep dissatisfaction . . . in the hearts of the people of this State. . . . Three hundred thousand white people here around us, who had been accustomed to self-government, who had had an orderly government and had participated in that government, whose property had been taxed only by those who paid the taxes, beheld the whole thing suddenly subverted and themselves placed at the mercy of ignorance and of corruption . . . . These people are under an absolute despotism, and you will find that the countries where governments are most despotic are precisely those in which secret associations appear; small associations of parties ardent and seeking redress for real or fancied wrongs which they think cannot be avenged through the government. That is the true secret of this thing.

[Simpson Bobo's Testimony]

We have gone through one of the most remarkable changes in our relations to each other that has been known, perhaps, in the history of the world. The negro that was our slave has become our master suddenly . . . ; the bottom rail has got on top . . .—any one living here and knowing all about it, will be surprised that there has been as little disturbance as there has been. If the Government had give us a good government; if it had let us remain under a military government, none of these troubles would have been in this country. . . . There have been a great many . . . cases of the whipping of negroes in this county and some of the adjoining counties, some for one purpose and some for another. I think some of them have been political, and some of them have been with a view of answering special ends. . . . [T]he lower class of white people have a great prejudice against the negro, because he is a competitor for common labor, and wherever they come into collision, these fellows form themselves into a Klan, and take up negroes that come in their way, and punish them. . . . [F]or instance, a white man rents a tract of land to a negro. Some white man wants to get the land. The owner prefers giving it to the negro. For the purpose of punishing the negro, he will then get up a parcel of neighbors, and in disguise they will go and whip the negro half to death.

The Supreme Court Limits the Ability of the Federal Government to Protect Rights

In a series of cases interpreting the Fourteenth Amendment, the justices of the Supreme Court made it difficult for the federal government to protect the rights of American citizens in the south. In the Slaughter-House Cases, the Court distinguished between the rights people held as citizens of the United States and those they held as citizens of their states. The rights Americans thought of as basic to citizenship were those they held as state citizens, not as citizens of the United States. The Fourteenth Amendment, the justices said, only authorized the federal government to protect the latter.

Abridged from the Slaughter-House Cases, 83 U.S. 36, at 72-78 *(1873).*

The Slaughter-House Cases

The first section of the fourteenth article . . . opens with a definition of citizenship—not only citizenship of the United States, but citizenship of the States. . . . It declares that persons may be citizens of the United States without regard to their citizenship of a particular State, and it overturns the Dred Scott decision by making all persons born within the United States and subject to its jurisdiction citizens of the United States. . . .

It is quite clear, then, that there is a citizenship of the United States, and a citizenship of a State, which are distinct from each other, and which depend upon different characteristics or circumstances in the individual.

We think this distinction and its explicit recognition in this amendment of great weight in this argument, because the next paragraph of this same section . . . speaks only of privileges and immunities of citizens of the United States, and does not speak of those of citizens of the several States. . . .

The language is, "No State shall make or enforce any law which shall abridge the privileges or immunities of citizens of the United States." It is a little remarkable, if this clause was intended as a protection to the citizen of a State against the legislative power of his own State, that the word citizen of the State should be left out when it is so carefully used, and used in contradistinction to citizens of the United States, in the very sentence which precedes it. It is too clear for argument that the change in phraseology was adopted understandingly and with a purpose.

Of the privileges and immunities of the citizen of the United States, and of the privileges and immunities of the citizen of the State, . . . it is only the former which are placed by this clause under the protection of the Federal Constitution . . . .

The latter must rest for their security and protection where they have heretofore rested . . . .

[The Court then quoted an earlier lower court decision that defined the privileges and immunities of state citizenship:]

"What are the privileges and immunities of citizens of the several states? We feel no hesitation in confining these expressions to those privileges and immunities which are fundamental; which belong of right to the citizens of all free governments, and which have at all times been enjoyed by citizens of the several states which compose this Union. . . . They may all . . . be comprehended under the following general heads: protection by the government, with the right to acquire and possess property of every kind, and to pursue and obtain happiness and safety, subject, nevertheless, to such restraints as the government may prescribe for the general good of the whole."

. . . Was it the purpose of the 14th Amendment, by the simple declaration that no state should make or enforce any law which shall abridge the privileges and immunities of citizens of the United States, to transfer the security and protection of all the civil rights which we have mentioned, from the states to the Federal government? And where it is declared that Congress shall have the power to enforce that article, was it intended to bring within the power of Congress the entire domain of civil rights heretofore belonging exclusively to the states?

. . . We are convinced that no such results were intended by the Congress which proposed these amendments, nor by the legislatures of the states, which ratified them.

Civil Rights Cases

In the Civil Rights Cases, the Court ruled that the Fourteenth Amendment only authorized the federal government to protect people against deprivations of their rights by state officials or people acting under color of state authority.

Abridged from Civil Rights Cases, *109 U.S. 3, at 10-11 (1883).*

The first section of the Fourteenth Amendment . . . is prohibitory in its character, and prohibitory upon the States. It declares that:

"No State shall make or enforce any law which shall abridge the privileges or immunities of citizens of the United States; nor shall any State deprive any person of life, liberty, or property without due process of law; nor deny to any person within its jurisdiction the equal protection of the laws."

It is State action of a particular character that is prohibited. Individual invasion of individual rights is not the subject-matter of the amendment. . . . [T]he last section of the amendment invests Congress with power to enforce it by appropriate legislation. To enforce what? To enforce the prohibition. . . . This is the legislative power conferred upon Congress, and this is the whole of it. It does not invest Congress with power to legislate upon subjects which are within the domain of State legislation; but to provide modes of relief against State legislation, or State action, of the kind referred to. It does not authorize Congress to create a code of municipal law for the regulation of private rights. . . .

The Effect of "Redemption" on Black Southerners

The Supreme Court's narrow interpretation of the Fourteenth Amendment made it difficult to prosecute southern violence. Between 1873 and 1875, the resolve of the federal government to protect the rights of citizens in the south waned. By 1877, southern white Democrats regained control of southern state governments. Southern whites referred to their success as "redemption," and they used fraud in many states to prevent Republicans from regaining power. The following plea from

The return of control of state government to southern white Democrats resulted in conditions that, according to this Thomas Nast cartoon, were worse than slavery for American blacks. (Courtesy of the Library of Congress.)

22

Wilson H. Williams for help from the national government suggests how the change affected African Americans in the South. It had been illegal to teach slaves to read or write, so Williams's literacy, with all its spelling errors, was quite an accomplishment.

From Wilson H. Williams to Senator John Sherman, care of Rev. John D. Haynes, 15 January 1879, John Sherman papers, Manuscript Division, Library of Congress, Washington, D.C.

We poor coul[ored] men have got no more show then a good Dog. The White people is tareing all over the land picking up the poor coul men acreing [forcing] them back to thar old Homes giving them no triel but butchering them up for things that [got] don in 20 and 30 years a go. God hoe [who] made the wourld knows that it is not rite and we know you all ought to do sum thing for ous for we are healpletts cant do eney thing nor say eney thing [P]lease you all stop that thing for it has been going on long anuffe. . . .

Questions

---

1. *Describe the issues of social justice that affected the lives of free African Americans at the time the Civil War broke out.*
2. *Why did President Andrew Johnson oppose the Civil Rights Act? Did it discriminate in favor of African Americans, as he charged?*
3. *What reasons did proponents of African-American suffrage give for supporting it? Aside from the racism of the petition, did the petitioners have a point about enfranchising former slaves so soon after emancipation? How would Frederick Douglass have answered? Given the hostility of white southerners toward equal civil rights for African Americans, what would you have done to secure their rights?*
4. *To what degree were the Supreme Court decisions interpreting the Fourteenth Amendment consistent with the spirit in which they were passed?*
5. *Over all, to what degree did the civil status of African Americans change during the era of Reconstruction? How much did their status improve? What were the limitations of the change?*

Further Reading

The standard, prize-winning work on Reconstruction in general, providing a wealth of information about the effort to restore the Union on the basis of equality of rights, is Eric Foner's *Reconstruction: America's Unfinished Revolution, 1863-1877* (New York, 1988). A briefer and more focused work is Foner's "Rights and the Constitution in Black Life during the Civil War and Reconstruction," *Journal of American History* 74 (December 1987): 863-83. Herman Belz addresses constitutional questions more directly than Foner in *Emancipation and Equal Rights: Politics and Constitutionalism in the Civil War Era* (New York, 1978). Peyton McCrary offers another argument for the radicalism of Republican Reconstruction policy in "Republican Ideas about Politics and Social Change," *Civil War History* 30 (December 1984): 330-50. Robert J. Kaczorowski criticizes the Supreme Court for retreating from the Republican commitment to rights in *The Politics of Judicial Interpretation: The Federal Courts, Department of Justice, and Civil Rights, 1866-1876* (New York, 1985).

The Temperance and Prohibition Movement

K. Austin Kerr

INTRODUCTION

This unit raises three important questions. What was the temperance and prohibition movement? Why was there a temperance and prohibition movement? What did the temperance and prohibition movement accomplish?

A reform movement arose in American life in the 1830s that responded to drunkenness and the problems of what later generations called alcohol abuse. This reform movement preached temperance, urged Americans to "take the pledge" and abstain from consuming alcoholic beverages, and developed fraternal societies to provide social support for temperance behavior. The reform movement was remarkably successful, attracting thousands of followers and helping reduce drinking.

But it was not enough, some temperance reformers came to realize, simply to persuade individuals to abstain. Victory over the scourges of alcohol abuse seemed to require coercive measures, prohibition laws to make it illegal to manufacture and sell alcoholic beverages. In short, it seemed necessary to go beyond the individual and to change part of the social system in order to build a more perfect society of abstaining citizens. Between 1846 and 1855 every northern state, except Pennsylvania and New Jersey, enacted some form of prohibition.

The coercive aspect of this reform was always controversial, and the state prohibition laws generally fell into disfavor during and after the Civil War. The individual and social problems of alcohol abuse remained, however. The temperance and prohibition movement revived in 1869 when the Prohibition Party formed to offer candidates for president and other offices committed to enforcing prohibition. Then, in the winter of 1873-74 a mass move-

ment of women arose, the largest mass movement of American women yet, in a crusade to persuade drinkers to stop drinking and saloonkeepers to stop serving liquor. The women formed the Woman's Christian Temperance Union to keep the ideas of the crusade alive. The WCTU continued to press for prohibition, and a wide range of other reforms, including woman suffrage. During the 1880s the revived prohibition movement achieved a few local and state victories, but, overall, the results were disappointing. The businesses, especially breweries, that supplied liquor were expanding, and the problems associated with alcohol abuse seemed also to be enlarging.

The Anti-Saloon League organized in 1893 in a new attempt to bring reformers together and pass prohibition laws. The league, without too much success before 1900, worked to enact "local option" laws allowing neighborhoods to forbid "the liquor traffic" from plying its trades in specified communities. As more and more areas became "dry" under these measures, the league promoted state prohibition laws, winning initial victories in Oklahoma and Alabama in 1907. In 1913 the league announced its campaign to achieve national prohibition through a constitutional amendment. With the 1916 elections, and with much help from a revived WCTU, the drys elected the two-thirds majorities required in both houses of Congress to initiate their amendment. Congress submitted an amendment to the states in 1917, and by 6 January 1919, three-quarters of the states had ratified the eighteenth or prohibition amendment, to take effect one year hence.

Prohibition lasted nationally until 1933 when the twenty-first amendment repealed it. During those years—as well as the decades it took to pass prohibition—the reform was very controversial. Although prohibition received widespread support, with dry majorities in Congress peaking with the 1928 elections, and the consumption of alcoholic beverages dropped dramatically, many Americans complained that prohibition was an improper imposition on their personal liberty. Opposition centered in the cities, where many immigrant groups especially viewed prohibition as an attack on their cultural norms and religious practices. In New York City and Hollywood, important centers of the production *and dissemination of popular culture, and of the news, opponents of prohibition held sway.*

Wealthy Americans funded the repeal campaign, which carried the day after the onset of the Great Depression in 1929 changed American political attitudes. The wealthy hoped that taxes on liquor would replace taxes on their incomes, and other persons believed that the restoration of the liquor businesses would provide sorely needed employment opportunities. And newer immigrant groups, now more powerful politically than ever before, viewed repeal as an affirmation of the acceptance of their cultural traditions, which commonly included using drink in religious and other rituals.

In the end prohibition left little permanent mark on the American people. To be sure, the consumption of alcoholic beverages subsided, as did the individual and social problems associated with alcohol misuse. Drinking rates did not recover to pre-prohibition levels for about forty years, when Americans again saw the problems of alcohol abuse as widespread as to require renewed exhortations to refrain from overindulgence and government support for prevention and treatment programs for "problem" drinkers. Perhaps the most lasting impact of prohibition was the propagation of the myth that laws and public policy cannot change people's behaviors.

HISTORIANS VIEW PROHIBITION

Even before its repeal, prohibition attracted the attention of historians. Victors write history, and for several decades scholars essentially agreed with the propaganda of repeal advocates. Generations of history students learned about the "failure" of prohibition and read caricatures of dry advocates. As time passed, however, historians began to view the century-long debate over prohibition differently, and to understand the prohibition reformers as part of broader impulses for political change. When a new generation of Americans began to address the policy problems associated with alcohol misuse in the 1970s, historians also learned that prohibition sharply reduced beverage alcohol consumption. Some writers even saw prohibition in retrospect as a public health "success."

Prohibition and the American Progressive Reform Tradition

Historians have disagreed about what the prohibition movement was, and what and who it represented. Personal views toward the reform, and toward drink, sometimes color scholars' perceptions. Richard Hofstadter, whose book won a Pulitzer Prize and remains influential, took a dim view of the movement. Excerpted from Richard Hofstadter, The Age of Reform: From Bryan to F.D.R. *(New York, 1955), 287–91.*

Prohibition . . . *was* a major issue. . . . Prohibition, in the twenties, was the skeleton at the feast, a grim reminder of the moral frenzy [Progressive reform] that so many wished to forget,

Many Americans celebrated the end of prohibition. (Courtesy of AP/Wide World Photos.)

a ludicrous caricature of the reforming impulse, of the Yankee-Protestant notion that it is both possible and desirable to moralize private life through public action.

To hold the Progressives responsible for Prohibition would be to do them an injustice. Men of an urbane cast of mind, whether conservatives or Progressives in their politics, had been generally antagonistic, or at the very least suspicious, of the pre-war drive toward Prohibition; and on the other side there were many advocates of Prohibition who had nothing to do with other reforms. . . . Prohibition was a pseudo-reform, a pinched, parochial substitute for reform which had a widespread appeal to a certain type of crusading mind. It was linked not merely to an aversion to drunkenness and to the evils that accompanied it, but to the immigrant drinking masses, to the pleasures and amenities of city life, and to the well-to-do classes and cultivated men. It was carried about America by the rural-evangelical virus: the country Protestant frequently brought it with him to the city when the contraction of agriculture sent him there to seek his livelihood. Students of the Prohibition movement find it easy to believe that the majority sentiment of the country stood in favor of Prohibition at the time the amendment was passed and for some years before; for even many drinking people were sufficiently persuaded by the note of moral uplift to concede that Prohibition might, after all, be a good thing. And even if the desire for Prohibition was a minority sentiment, it was the sentiment of a large minority, one whose intensity and insistency gave its members a power disproportionate to their numbers. Politicians, at any rate, catered to their demands, and there were among them some . . . who unquestionably believed that the conquest of the demon rum was one of the important tasks of political life.

. . . The demand for liquor reform, long familiar in American politics, seems to have quickened during the Progressive era, notably after about 1908, and the final victory of the amendment was the culmination of five years of heightened agitation by the Anti-Saloon League. The alcohol issue had been approached with the usual Populist-Progressive arguments: it was one of the means by which the interests, in this case the "whiskey ring," fattened on the toil of the people. Drinking was pre-eminently a vice of those classes—the plutocrats and corrupt politicians and ignorant immigrants—which the reformers most detested or feared. The saloon, as an institution pivotal to the life of vice on one side and of American urban politics on the other, fell under particular reprobation. . . .

George Kibbe Turner . . . probably went to the heart of the Prohibition sentiment when he wrote an article attacking the city saloon in which he pointed out that city people constituted each year a larger and larger portion of the whole population and insisted that the first thing to be done in the movement for city reform was "to remove the terrible and undisciplined commercial forces which, in America, are fighting to saturate the populations of cities with alcoholic liquor." During the war the alleged need to conserve materials and the Germanic names of the leading brewers added some force to the prohibitionist propaganda; but what stood the drys in the best stead was the same strong undercurrent of public self-castigation, the same reaction against personal and physical indulgence and material success that underlay the Progressive tirades against the plutocracy. . . . The sense that others were fighting battles and making sacrifices in which one somehow *ought* to share was greatly heightened by the war; and the dry agitation, with its demand for self-denial, struck an increasingly congenial note. . . . Of course this sort of thing could not last forever, but while it was at its pitch the dry lobbyists struck, and when they were finished the Prohibition mania was fixed in the Constitution; and there it remained for almost fifteen years, a symbol of the moral overstrain of the preceding era, the butt of jokes, a perennial source of irritation, a memento of the strange power of crusades for absolute morality to intensify the evils they mean to destroy.

But Prohibition was more than a symbol—it was a means by which the reforming energies of the country were transmuted into mere peevishness. All through the period . . . when the dry crusade spoke the language of social and humanitarian reform, leading Prohibitionists had often been leading reformers, and the churches that gave the strongest support to the Social Gospel movement in American Protestantism were all by the same token supporters of the dry cause. The victory of Prohibition, the transformation of the drinker from a victim of evil to a lawbreaker, the necessity of defending a law that was widely violated, drew many one-time reformers toward the camp of the conservatives, while the circumstances of American politics led them into Catholic-baiting and city-baiting in 1924 and 1928. Prohibition became a low grade substitute for the old Social Gospel enthusiasms.

The Popularity of Prohibition in the Progressive Tradition

Some historians disagree with Hofstadter. Based in part on research into popular political attitudes, they realized that prohibition reformers, and their opponents, expressed widely held cultural and religious outlooks. Prohibition was popular in every region and social class, in city and country alike. Taken from Jack S. Blocker, Jr., American Temperance Movements: Cycles of Reform *(Boston, 1989), xi–xv.*

During the years of national Prohibition . . . a stereotype grew up. . . . The stereotypical prohibitionist was a dour, cadaverous, puritanical fellow who was obviously not enjoying life very much because of his single-minded devotion to preventing other people from enjoying theirs. Misanthropy, not altruism, drove him; to his fellow human beings he offered a police club, not a helping hand. From his misguided efforts flowed violence and crime. The repeal of national Prohibition added to this stereotype the label of losers, a sour minority who tried but inevitably failed to deflect Americans from full enjoyment of the fruits of their abundant economy. For many years popular stereotype and historical perception coincided, as historians found inconceivable the notion that alcoholic damage could have any place in the causal chains they constructed to explain reform and reformers. Loss of status, loss of deference, loss of the certainty of sin, loss of traditional work habits, loss of order, virtually any lack but the lack of sobriety in the world around them was imaginable as motivation for reformers.

In truth, temperance folk have been such a varied lot that any attempt to put them into a single suit of clothes necessarily makes an awkward fit. Let us begin with the most basic of social distinctions. Although men led the reform in its early days, from the beginning women saw temperance as a woman's issue, one that allowed them to address important problems in their daily lives. In 1873 temperance crusaders launched the largest mass movement of women to that point in American history, and for the next quarter century women provided the reform's most creative and dynamic leadership. From Quaker women in the eighteenth century through the Woman's Christian Temperance Union (WCTU) of the nineteenth century to Mothers Against Drunk Driving (MADD). . . , women have entered temperance reform. . . .

Temperance was clearly a middle-class reform. . . . [I]t articulated most forcefully and forced upon the public most articulately the theme of self-control that lay at the core of middle-class identity in the nineteenth century. Even so, temperance reform has never been solely a mirror for the middle class. During much of the reform's long history . . . it received substantial infusions of support from working-class men and women. From an early point in temperance history manufacturers' desires for sober and therefore (they thought) productive workers brought powerful recruits to the cause, and during the Progressive period of the early twen-

---

From Author's Introduction to *American Temperance Movements: Cycles of Reform* by Jack S. Blocker, Jr. Copyright © 1989 by Jack S. Blocker, Jr. Excerpted with permission of Twayne Publishers an imprint of Simon & Schuster Macmillan.

tieth century a segment of the corporate elite provided crucial backing. . . .

Like other early-nineteenth-century reforms, the temperance ethos and organization originated in the Northeast. . . . By the late nineteenth century the Midwest became the prohibitionist heartland. Even during the years of northeastern hegemony a significant number of southerners gave their support to the cause, and the final wave of enthusiasm for statewide prohibition before the Eighteenth Amendment began in 1907 in Oklahoma and Alabama. That wave finally spread from the South through the West and Midwest to isolate the Northeast, which had changed in a hundred years from a temperance stronghold to the last redoubt of the antiprohibition forces.

Because rural states led the final march to national Prohibition, temperance has long been considered essentially an expression of rural values. We now know better. In the late eighteenth century the new ideology of temperance appeared first in Philadelphia, the metropolis of the infant Republic. . . .Voluntary associations . . . to promote the temperance ideology . . . found ready support in burgeoning industrial cities such as Worcester, Massachusetts, and Rochester, New York. Women's mass action against saloons later in the century sprang from small towns. Today . . . the temperance cause still flourishes in new forms in its cities and suburbs.

In the pages of the *Dictionary of American Temperance Biography* one finds few names that suggest other than English origins, and in this respect the leadership seems to have reflected faithfully the backgrounds of most temperance folk. Nevertheless, other groups have embraced temperance reform to control drinking within or outside their own group. During the antebellum period some blacks organized their own temperance societies while others joined white-dominated associations. Scandinavian-Americans during the late nineteenth and early twentieth centuries were overrepresented in the temperance ranks. Hibernian Total Abstinence Societies were not unknown, and Irish-Americans took the lead in organizing the Catholic Total Abstinence Union in 1872. . . . [T]emperance reform must shape its strategies to the reality of a multicultural nation.

A similar point might be made about religion. Evangelical Protestant lay people and clergy have usually provided the bulk of temperance leadership and grass-roots support. At times, however, nonevangelical Protestants have played key roles, and the existence of the Catholic Total Abstinence Union and other Roman Catholic temperance associations indicates the persistent presence of non-Protestant temperance folk. . . . [R]eformers learned that they would have to deploy more than biblical arguments if they were to succeed in a materialistic and pluralistic society. Accordingly, they pictured their reform as indispensable to individual health and social welfare as well as necessary to salvation and attainment of the millennium. By framing their arguments in secular terms temperance reformers helped to undermine the churches' claims for divine sanction as the basis for social action. Recognizing the threat, most churches maintained arm's length distance between themselves and the zealous drys. That temperance reformers were evangelical Protestants does not mean that their relations with their churches were either simple or stable.

Time, of course, changed the composition of temperance support along most of the dimensions we have considered. New generations of men and women came to the reform, bringing with them new experiences and ideas. Within a single generation the turnover in some organizations was massive. . . . Changes in movement policy, such as . . . the WCTU's alliance with the Prohibition party in the 1880s, drove out many. Experience, policy, and membership danced an intricate dance, to a tune called by none of the dancers alone, but improvised by all three together.

In pursuit of their reform, temperance reformers argued, pleaded, cajoled, confessed, denounced, and declaimed; they produced articles, stories, poetry, plays, songs, and novels; published books and pamphlets; and posted advertisements. They conducted surveys, prayed and sang, marched on saloons, marched in parades, marched in demonstrations, and attended meetings and conventions. They destroyed the contents of saloons with axes, hatchets, hammers, rocks, and metal bars. They formed associations at every level from the neighborhood to the nation; they appeared in courts as prosecutors, plaintiffs, informers, and defendants; they created pressure groups and political parties, petitioned, circularized candidates, canvassed, voted, and watched the polls. They served in lawmaking bodies from village councils to the U.S. Congress. They were harassed, mocked, beaten, hosed down, hung in effigy, shot at, and shot down.

Temperance advocates repeated the message that the saloon and drinking too often harmed families and the lives of children. (Courtesy of The New York Public Library.)

. . . The scale most commonly employed by historians of temperance reform . . . is a spectrum between persuasion and coercion. At one end lies the tactic known in the nineteenth century as "moral suasion," which assumes a symmetrical relationship between individuals of equal power and presumed rationality. Its essence is dialogue, in which the reformer appeals to the intellect and emotions of his or her listener in an attempt to convince the person of the rightness and goodness of the reformer's position. In contrast, coercion requires an asymmetrical relationship between individuals or groups of unequal power, involves only the crudest form of communication, and considers intellect and emotions peripheral to the outcome. The rightness and goodness of the reformer's position are not at issue; the only question is whether the reformer can mobilize enough force to compel acquiescence. Between these polar extremes lie many gradations encompassing many combinations of moral suasion and coercion. . . .

Temperance reform began . . . with methods more suasionist than coercive, but its history reveals no simple progression toward coercion. . . . [T]he Anti-Saloon League, among the most coercive of temperance organizations, made a strong commitment to "education," turning out from its presses at Westerville, Ohio, millions of pages of propaganda. Even after the passage of national Prohibition, the most coercive of temperance measures, a significant faction within the Anti-Saloon League argued for renewal of an educational campaign. Time and again frustration pushed temperance reformers toward coercion, but again and again moral suasion found ways to assert its claims.

The Saloon and Drinking

Students of the saloon, and of drinking customs, have concluded that the prohibition reformers were acting in response to very real human problems. Excerpted from Mark Edward Lender and James Kirby Martin, Drinking in America: A History, *rev. ed. (New York, 1987), 102-4, 106.*

The dramatic social changes inherent in rapid industrialization and urbanization placed traditional dry worries over alcohol and such civil maladies as poverty, vice, crime, disease, and violence in a new and more visible context. Poverty . . . was a major fact of urban life. Late nineteenth century economic fluctuations, language barriers among immigrants, and limited work skills kept thousands periodically unemployed or locked into poorly paid jobs. Equally worrisome, many people spent too much of what little they earned on liquor, and through drinking they often lost their jobs, thus impoverishing not only themselves but also their families. Even dispassionate studies of the matter—by urban reformers, municipal officials, and newly professionalized social workers—put alcohol at the root of a minimum of 20 percent of urban poverty cases. Such personal tragedy, of course, was not confined to the industrial poor; yet the relative novelty of seeing so many instances of drinking-related poverty made a distinct impression on the middle-class public. Indeed, by the turn of [the] century many students of urban affairs . . . and Progressive reformers . . . agreed that the liquor question must be tackled if the urban-industrial order were to be a fit, safe environment. . . .

Along with the skid row bum [popular stereotype of the alcoholic], the most ominous symbol of the dangers of drink became the urban saloon. Not that temperance workers liked

---

rural or Western saloons any better, but the city version was more visibly associated with the ills of an industrializing society and thus seemed to be more immediately threatening. Most urban saloons were a far cry from . . . any of the elegant establishments . . . recalled so fondly. The majority were neighborhood bars, and too many were simply ginmills. The worst were dives serving as centers of drunkenness, crime, profanity, prostitution, gambling, and political corruption. Their patrons, frequently immigrants and unskilled industrial workers, held few values in common with those of the temperance movement.

In most major cities, political bosses used saloons as their headquarters and employed regular patrons to stuff ballot boxes (these same bars often served as polling places) or to terrorize opponents. Similarly, the rise of organized prostitution paralleled the growth of the urban ginmills. In Philadelphia, for instance, an 1876 canvass found 8,037 legal and illegal drinking establishments in the city: At least 3,782 of them had direct or indirect connections with "houses of ill fame." . . . The saloon, then, seemed to mock temperance conceptions of public virtue and stood starkly at odds with traditional American mores. . . .

But the [liquor] traffic did not worry very much about its image. In fact, it insolently faced down complaints. Large brewers owned most of the local saloons and used them as outlets for their beers. Breweries were highly competitive, and they openly encouraged heavy drinking. . . .

. . . Techniques kept liquor flowing. Many saloons lured customers with offers of a "free lunch"—usually well salted to inspire drinking (the saloon "bouncer" was generally on hand to discourage hearty appetites). New patrons also were given free drinks. As one Brewers' Association spokesman explained, this tactic extended even to children: A few cents spent on free drinks for boys was a good investment; the money would be amply recovered as these youths became habitual drinkers! At the time, many Americans, and by no means just temperance workers, regarded such practices much the same as our own generation would consider a modern drug-pusher giving children "free samples."

The saloons nevertheless scoffed at reform efforts. They had plenty of money for political wars and plenty of votes, which, as the *Liquor Man's Advocate* noted in 1874, they were ready to use. "Every saloon averages eighty regular customers," the paper observed, "and these eighty customers have eighty votes, and, if properly managed, every bartender might influence these eighty votes to a given point, decided by bartenders *en masse.*" The saloon thus accorded temperance workers a perfect target.

The Success and Failure of Prohibition

Conventional wisdom in the United States holds that prohibition was a failure. In this view, Americans did not stop drinking, organized crime mushroomed to slake thirsts, and a generation matured disrespectful of law in general. The selection that follows is a summary of this viewpoint. Taken from Samuel Eliot Morison, The Oxford History of the American People *(New York, 1965), 900-902.*

Orderly progress in temperance was rudely interrupted by the Volstead Act of 28 October 1919, . . . [which prohibited the manufacture, transportation, and sale of beverages] containing over one-half of one per cent alcohol; and by Amendment XVIII, which . . . went into effect in . . . 1920. The reasons for so precipitate an enlargement of the federal government's power over the citizenry were many. The dry states complained that they could not enforce Prohibition when adjacent states were wet; the war induced a "spirit of sacrifice," and the German-American Alliance . . . made drinking seem faintly treasonable. Wives of workingmen wanted their husbands to bring home their pay instead of spending half of it with "the boys" in a saloon; the liquor industry had been proved a major factor in political corruption and was tied in with prostitution, gambling, and other vices. Many business men and manufacturers favored Prohibition, hoping it would eliminate "blue Monday" absenteeism. The Anti-Saloon League printed some 100 million flyers, posters, and pamphlets, mostly to further the idea that alcohol was mainly responsible for poverty, disease, crime, insanity and degeneracy, and that national Prohibition would empty the jails, the asylums, and the poorhouses. . . .

Prohibition enforcement received much attention. Prohibition reformers sought to move beyond mere enforcement to education and persuasion. (Courtesy of Corbis-Bettmann.)

No sooner had national prohibition become law than the country seemed to regret it, and a new occupation, bootlegging, sprang up to quench the public thirst. The federal government in ten years made over half a million arrests for breaking the Volstead Act, and secured over 300,000 convictions; but smuggling increased. The Canadian and Mexican borders were full of "leaks." Small craft easily ran cargoes from Cuba into Florida and the Gulf states; mountain moonshiners multiplied; . . . carloads of grapes went to Italian- and Greek-Americans to be trodden out in a traditional winepress and allowed to ferment. Off every seaport from Maine to Miami, outside the three-mile limit, rode a fleet of ocean-going ships loaded with every variety of wine and liquor. Motor launches, too fast for coast guard or enforcement agents to catch, ran these cargoes ashore, where they were transferred to trucks and cars owned by bootleggers; but the truckloads often got "hijacked" by other criminals, and in any case the strong liquor was "cut" with water before being sold. Millions of gallons of industrial alcohol . . . were converted into bootleg whisky or gin, and bottled under counterfeit labels; poisonous wood alcohol, inexpertly "converted," caused numerous deaths. Liquor and wine imported under license for "medicinal purposes," easily found its way to the stomachs of healthy citizens. Every city became studded with "speakeasies" to replace the saloon, almost every urban family patronized a local bootlegger, and in defiant states like Rhode Island . . . one could buy a bottle of British gin right off the shelves of a grocery store for ten dollars. Those who did not care to patronize bootleggers and so contribute to crime and political corruption, made their own "bathtub" gin at home or got along with home-brewed beer and cider. Bravado induced numerous young people to drink who otherwise would not have done so; restaurants which refused to break the law themselves provided "set-ups" of ice, soda water, and ginger ale to be energized by whatever the patrons brought.

There were many social effects of Prohibition, apart from the encouragement of lawbreaking and the building up of a criminal class that turned to gambling and drugs [after the repeal of Prohibition in] . . . 1933. The high point in the Chicago gang war that was fed by bootlegging was the "St. Valentine's Day Massacre" of 1929. Al Capone ran one gang; George Bugs Moran, the other. In four years there had been 215 unsolved murders in the Windy City. The Capone hoods, disguised as policemen, machine-gunned six of the Moran gang in a garage where they were waiting to buy a truckload of liquor from hijackers. Nobody was punished for this multiple murder; it took the federal government to get the planner, Capone, for evasion of income taxes. . . .

Since beer and wine did not pay bootleggers like strong liquor, the country's drinking habits were changed from the one to the other. College students who before Prohibition would have in a keg of beer and sit around singing the "Dartmouth Stein Song," and "Under the Anheuser Busch," now got drunk quickly on bathtub gin and could manage no lyric more complicated than "How Dry I Am!" Woman . . . now helped her husband to spend on liquor the savings that formerly went to the saloon. Hip-flask drinking certainly helped the revolution in sexual standards. . . . And it encouraged hypocrisy in politics.

Both major parties successfully blinked the issue for a decade. The Republicans, strongest in the rural communities and the middle classes, in general stood behind what President Hoover called "an experiment noble in motive and far-reaching in purpose." The Democrats were torn between Southern constituencies which were immovably dry because Prohibition was supposed to help "keep the Negroes in order," and Northern cities, full of Irish-, German- and Italian-Americans who were incurably wet. This division almost split the party in 1924 when the drys supported McAdoo and the wets Alfred E. Smith. The wets, having gained the upper hand by 1928, then nominated Al Smith, who proposed to abandon national prohibition and return the alcohol problem to the States. This stand was partly responsible for his spectacular success in the urban centers of the North, as well as for his defeat in the solid South and West.

President Hoover, who really tried to enforce the Volstead Act, appointed a commission to investigate the question of law enforcement. This Wickersham Commission submitted, in January 1931, a confused report to the effect that federal prohibition was unenforceable but should be enforced, that it was a failure but should be retained! By 1932 the "noble experiment" was so palpable a failure that the Republican party favored a "revision" of Amendment XVIII: the Democrats demanded outright repeal.

Assessing Prohibition

Scholars who have studied the impact of prohibition carefully dispute the conventional wisdom that the policy was a failure. Theirs is a mixed assessment, with obedience to the law uneven across time and place. In any event, organized crime flourished prior to prohibition and thereafter, while drinking dropped dramatically under the policy, and consumption rates took about four decades to recover to pre-prohibition levels. Excerpted from Norman H. Clark, Deliver Us from Evil: An Interpretation of American Prohibition *(New York, 1976), 140-49.*

Some intriguing legends to the contrary, the beginnings of Prohibition did not seem so grim. Several states had been dry for six years, several others for more than a decade. . . . [T]he dry morning of January 17 [1920, the morning the Volstead Act took effect] brought no national trauma. In major cities not already dry,

Wealthy Americans championed the repeal of prohibition, which they hoped would shift their tax burden to beer drinkers. (Courtesy of AP/Wide World Photos.)

the barrooms of most larger hotels had closed weeks before, and there was no great guzzle at the final hour, no ultimate orgy of binges. . . . [C]ontemporary writers stressed that in hotels, clubs, and private homes they found people who wanted to obey the law and usually did. . . .

There were others, however, who were totally unprepared for even a delicate passage into a new era. John Allen Krout, then a young history instructor in New York City, observed that to many Americans, "prohibition came with something of a shock." Though they were vaguely aware that somewhere out in the tall grass of the Bible Belt were people called "drys," and that these people were interested in politics, "they had not realized that the reformers were so near the goal.". . . Their immediate response . . . was "to cry fraud, since it seemed impossible that the people of a great nation could be fairly persuaded to write into their fundamental law so radical a change in social custom." . . .

More than a few were not impressed, and their cries of *fraud* enlivened the early Volstead era. Their anguish was regularly enflamed by the more mindlessly impassioned nativists and Prohibitionists—both of which groups, in an age of frivolous journalism, were given inordinate newspaper publicity—whose sanctimonious platitudes and downright perversities did indeed darken the lives of men who shared the liberal persuasion. . . . [Some drys] applauded every raid of federal agents on private homes and every wiretapped telephone, demanded that the army patrol the Canadian border, asked the government to sterilize drinkers, and urged that violations . . . be made a capital offense. In this atmosphere it is no wonder that many broad-minded urbanites came to fear for their own security and that, in their anxiety, they began to explain their misfortunes in what became a legacy of conventional legends.

Such legends held that Puritans from the Corn Country and lady school teachers from the Rocky Mountains had deviously manipulated honest patriotism to force the 18th Amendment into the Constitution while the attention of all right-minded citizens was fixed on the war. . . . Then, suddenly, in . . . post war society . . . they discovered a grave crisis: The malignant repressions of the wicked Puritans were actually eroding the moral fiber of a free and creative America. Prohibition, by distorting the role of alcohol in civilized life, allegedly caused Americans to drink more rather than less, and to do so with increasing morbidity. . . .

There are today few reasons to believe that these legends [of prohibition's failure] . . . are more than an easy and sentimental hyperbole crafted by men whose assumptions about a democratic society had been deeply offended. To suppose, for example, that the principle of the 18th Amendment was generated by wartime hysterias . . . is . . . to ignore temperance legislation across a century of American history. To suppose, further, that the Volstead Act caused Americans to drink more rather than less is to defy an impressive body of statistics as well as common sense. The common sense is that a substantial number of people wanted to stop both their own and other people's drinking, and that the saloons where most people had done their drinking were closed. There is no reason to suppose that the speakeasy, given its illicit connotations, more lurid even than those of the saloon, ever . . . replaced the saloon. In fact, there is every reason to suppose that most Americans outside the larger cities never knew a bootlegger, never saw a speakeasy, and would not have known where to look for one.

The statistical evidence to support this takes more than a footnote. The most recent figures are those assembled by the task force of scholars from the Department of Health, Education and Welfare who prepared for Congress the special report entitled *Alcohol and Health* (1971). This report shows that the annual per capita consumption of alcoholic beverages in the United States—conveniently converted to gallons of absolute alcohol—stood at 2.60 for the period 1906-1910, which was the period before the state dry laws had any national impact and the period which must be regarded as "before Prohibition." After Prohibition, in 1934, the figure stood at 0.97. In 1940, by which time the effects of repeal had surely pervaded the national drinking habits, the figure was only 1.56. It would be difficult to overemphasize the significance of this change: Americans after Prohibition were drinking less than at any time since they had learned the technology of distillation, and the marked change had surely taken place during the 1920s. . . .

. . . Joseph Gusfield has . . . concluded that "Prohibition was effective in sharply reducing the rate of alcohol consumption in the United States. We may set the outer limit of this at about 50 percent and the inner limit at about one-third less alcohol consumed by the total population [than] that had been the case . . . [before Prohibition] in the United States." . . .

There is, furthermore, an abundance of evidence in social statistics from the 1920s indicating that Prohibition could not have encouraged drinking among most Americans. . . . [A]rrests for drunkenness fell off remarkably during the Volstead era, as did the public expenses for jailing drunks. There were marked decreases in the incidence of diseases associated with alcoholic psychoses, and for several years . . . articles on alcoholism simply disappeared from the periodicals of American medicine. . . .

. . . [There is] also a refutation of the "almost universal public belief" in a crime wave during the 1920s. The best studies in criminology . . . give no evidence of any "wave," though across the decade there probably was a slowly rising level of criminal activity. People believed the "wave" was real because of impressions left by journalists who saw a lot of crime, reported a lot, and—in the age of instant communication—were irresistibly tempted to romanticize it. Among competing newspapers, crime became the most welcome kind of "hot news," and it was eagerly fastened on the front pages. This is not to deny that there has always been a great deal of crime in the United States to see and to publicize; it is only to suggest that Prohibition did not make it any easier than it had been before to bribe a policeman, or commit a murder, or corrupt a friend of the President.

Questions

---

1. *What was the source of prohibitionists' actions? Were they responding to real or imagined problems?*
2. *Prohibition was about social values. Who were the prohibitionists? Who were their opponents?*
3. *Was prohibition a success or a failure? How does one decide? Is the question itself appropriate?*

The Long, Grueling Dispute Over The Liquor Traffic and Prohibition

The use of beverage alcohol (liquor) has provoked disputes over private behavior, community norms, and public policy for most of the nineteenth and twentieth centuries. For much of the nineteenth century, dedicated, zealous "drys" fought to change behavior, affirm community norms of sobriety, and enforce public policies that denied the right to do business in the liquor trades. Dry sentiment and political power increased in the first quarter of the twentieth century, only to recede in the early 1930s. The prohibitionists always fought well-funded enemies who were zealous in their "wet" position.

The Woman's Crusade of 1873-74

The Woman's Crusade of 1873-74 culminated many years of women taking direct action against the saloon and the liquor traffic. Women in the United States then enjoyed no direct political power, and direct action—prayer vigils, petition campaigns, demonstrations, hymn-singing—were among the few means at their disposal for seeking change. The crusade sought to persuade saloonkeepers to destroy their beverages, close their doors, and enter some other line of business.

Eliza Daniel Stewart (she referred to herself as "Mother Stewart") was active during the Woman's Crusade and enjoyed a notable career as a temperance speaker thereafter. Taken from Mother Stewart, Memories

of the Crusade: A Thrilling Account . . . *(Columbus, Ohio, 1888),*
215-16.

    I had just returned to the hotel . . . when I heard a great shout
in the street, and soon after all the bells in the city commenced
ringing. At the same time there arose a prolonged cheer from the
Granger's Convention just across the street from the hotel, and it
was evident that something unusual had happened.

    Going out I saw crowds of people thronging towards
Whitman street, and heard on every hand in joyful accents, "The
Shades of Death [a saloon] has surrendered!" The good news
proved true, and I found Whitman street thronged with people. A
little before 3 o'clock, as it appeared from the general account, Mr.
Steve Phillips, of the "Shades of Death," invited the ladies to enter,
and announced that he gave up everything to them, and would
never sell anything intoxicating in Xenia again. Then the ladies,
joined by the spectators, sang "Praise God from whom all bless-
ings flow," while the liquors were rolled into the street. A half-
barrel of blackberry brandy, the same of high-wines, a few kegs of
beer, and some bottles of ale and whisky were soon emptied into
the street, amid the shouts of the enthusiastic multitude. The
leading lady then announced that if Mr. Phillips went into any

*This twentieth century artist captured some of the spirit of the woman's
crusade of 1873–74. (Courtesy of The Library of Congress.)*

other business in Xenia, they should feel it a duty to support him. A dispatch was sent to the Grangers (the State Grange was in session in Xenia at the time,) eliciting three cheers, and all the bells were set ringing in honor of the first victory. When I arrived the liquor had mostly collected in one depression in the street, and such a stench went up—"a rank offense that smelt to heaven,"—as made me think it a very fortunate thing for somebody's stomach that the liquor had been poured out. Of the women around, some were crying, some were laughing, a few alternatly [alternately] singing and returning thanks. One elderly lady in the edge of the crowd was almost in hysterics, but still shouting in a hoarse whisper, such as one often hears at camp-meeting: "Bless the Lord! O, bless the Lord !" She had the appearance of a lady in good circumstances, and a citizen informed me that she is ordinarily one of the quietest, most placid of women. One of her sons died of intemperance, and another is much addicted to liquor.

On every side nothing was witnessed but smiles, laughter, prayers, hand-shaking, and congratulations. The "Shades of Death" was considered by the temperance people as the "back-bone of the rebellion," and within twenty-four hours four more saloons surrendered. The movement continues with unabated vigor, and only twelve more saloons remain. Twenty-nine have been closed.

The Saloon Observed

The Anti-Saloon League, founded in 1893, proved the most successful of the dry political organizations. It focused attention on the saloon and "the liquor traffic"—the businesses that supplied and sold liquor. By choosing to focus on the evils of the saloon, the league was in the tradition expressed by the woman's crusade; it was also opposing an institution widely seen as undesirable.

The saloon won the attention of muckrakers, reform-minded journalists in the early twentieth century who exposed vice, corruption, and other social and political sores. Excerpted from George Kibbe Turner, "The City of Chicago: A Study of the Great Immoralities," McClure's Magazine 28 (April 1907): 576–79.

The sale of dissipation is . . . a great business . . . in Chicago. The leading branch . . . is the sale of alcoholic liquor. . . . [T]he liquor interests are vastly more extended in Chicago than any other. There are 7,300 licensed liquor sellers in Chicago, and . . . about a thousand places where liquor is sold illegally. The only business which approaches this in number of establishments . . . is the grocery trade, which has about 5,200. The city spends at least half as much for what it drinks as for what it eats. . . .

The great central power in the liquor business in America is the brewery. . . . [T]he breweries own or control the great majority of the saloons of American cities. They have a distinct policy:—If there are not as many saloons as there can be, supply them. This is what has been done in Chicago. Fully ninety per cent of the Chicago saloons are under some obligation to the brewery; with at least eighty per cent, this obligation is a serious one.

The business of the brewery is to sell beer. . . . The brewery, under present conditions . . . must sell beer at all cost, or promptly die. This is because the brewing business has been over-capital-ized and overbuilt there for at least ten years. There has been furious competition. . . . [A]t the present time a full third of the capital invested in the forty companies and fifty plants is not earning dividends. Under these circumstances, the breweries of Chicago can have but one aim—to fill Chicago with beer to the point of saturation.

Each brewer disposes of his product by contracting with spe-cial saloon-keepers to sell his beer and no other. The more saloons he has, the better. . . . The brewers employ special agents to watch continually every nook and cranny in Chicago where it may be possible to pour in a little more beer. If a rival brewery's saloon-keeper is doing well, his best bartender is ravished from him and set up in business alongside. If a new colony of foreigners ap-pears, some compatriot is set at once to selling them liquor. Ital-ians, Greeks, Lithuanians, Poles . . . have their trade exploited to the utmost. . . . [N]o man with two hundred dollars [capital] . . . need go without a saloon in Chicago. . . . [T]he brewery sorts him out a set from its stock of saloon fixtures, pays his rent, pays his license, and supplies him with beer. He pays for everything in an extra price on each barrel of beer. . . .

Under this system . . . Chicago has four times as many saloons as it should have, from any standpoint whatever, except, of course, the brewers' and the wholesalers'. . . . There is . . . one retail liquor dealer to every two hundred and eighty-five people, disregarding, of course, the one thousand unlicensed dealers. In the laboring wards the licensed saloons run as many as one to every one hundred and fifty. Take the stock-yards. Around that long and dismal stockade, at every hole from which a human being can emerge, a shop or group of shops sits waiting. At the main entrance they lie massed in batteries. . . .

The Chicago market is thoroughly saturated with beer, and incidentally with other liquor. Reckoning it out by population, every man, woman, and child in Chicago drank, in 1906, two and one-quarter barrels of beer,—that is, seventy gallons,—three and one-half times the average consumption in the United States. . . .

Now, if the competition is red-handed among the breweries, it is simply ravenous among the saloon-keepers. There is a popular fallacy that there is great profit in the retail saloon business. The saloon-keepers themselves believe this when they go into it. . . .

All this means one thing—a premium on the irregular and criminal saloon-keeper. . . . A place is popular, or it is nothing. . . . There are two general business methods of attracting it [a good trade]: By giving unusually large measures and big bonuses of free lunch; or by carrying illegitimate and illegal side lines. The first . . . does not leave large margins of profit; the second does. A year ago the license fee was raised [to] . . . wipe out the criminal saloon. It did, of course, nothing of the sort. The poor, miserable little dives in the working-man's ward, each snatching a starvation living from the lips of the dwellers of the dozen smoke-befouled frame tenements about it, staggered down—a few hundred of them—and died. The man with the side-line of prostitution and gambling naturally survived and had the benefit of the others' failure.

Some Brewers Seek Saloon Reform

Some leaders in the brewing industry recognized that saloon conditions abetted the dry cause, and they sought to reform retail liquor businesses. One focus of the brewers' reform was to reduce the number of saloons to no more than one per five hundred people so that each establishment could operate profitably without resort to prostitution, gambling, and other vices. The following is an excerpt from a report done by brewers who sought to get the industry's house in order. Taken from "Summary of Replies to Inquiries Regarding the Causes of Opposition to Saloons," Brewing and Liquor Interests and German and Bolshevik Propaganda, Report and Hearings of the Subcommittee on the Judiciary, U.S. Senate, *65th Cong.,1919,1070.*

Replies were received from 118 representative brewers. . . . [T]heir replies do not constitute an indictment against all saloons, or even any considerable proportion of the saloons, but that the evils they speak of are found to exist in a sufficient number of cases to cast discredit upon the business as a whole.

Over half of the replies refer to the bad character of certain saloon-keepers and bartenders, and of the careless way in which some of the saloons are conducted. Special reference is made in a large number of the replies to the noise and profanity which takes place, not only inside the saloon, but in front of it. Over forty references are made to gambling in saloons, and fifty-five brewers speak of the use of the dive-saloon as a rendezvous for loafers, gangsters, prostitutes and criminals. No less than sixty-seven brewers state that the selling to known drunkards and intoxicated persons is one of the serious evils, while forty-eight brewers cite the selling of intoxicants to boys and girls.

Arguments For and Against Prohibition

The arguments for and against prohibition occurred all across the United States, in churches and political caucuses, town meetings and legislative sessions. Congress first debated the issue near the end of 1914. Each side advanced more than one argument; the four documents that follow represent core views.

For Prohibition

Richmond P. Hobson, a representative from Alabama, voiced his support for a prohibition amendment on the floor of the House of Repre-

sentatives on 22 December 1914. The proposed amendment received a majority of votes, but not the necessary two-thirds majority to proceed with the process. Excerpted from Richmond P. Hobson, "The Prohibition Amendment," in The Politics of Moral Behavior: Prohibition and Drug Abuse, *ed. K. Austin Kerr (Reading, Massachusetts, 1973), 97-100, 102.*

What is the object of this resolution? It is to destroy the agency that debauches the youth of the land and thereby perpetuates its hold upon the Nation. How does the resolution propose to destroy this agent? In the simplest manner. . . . It does not coerce any drinker. It simply says that barter and sale, matters that have been a public function from the semicivilized days of society, shall not continue the debauching of the youth. Now, the Liquor Trust are wise enough to know that they can not perpetuate their sway by depending on debauching grown people, so they go to an organic method of teaching the young to drink. Now we apply exactly the same method to destroy them. We do not try to force old drinkers to stop drinking, but we do effectively put an end to the systematic, organized debauching of our youth through thousands and tens of thousands of agencies throughout the land. Men here may try to escape the simplicity of this problem. They can not. Some are trying to defend alcohol by saying that its abuse only is bad and that its temperate use is all right. Science absolutely denies it, and proclaims that drunkenness does not produce one-tenth part of the harm to society that the widespread, temperate, moderate drinking does. Some say it is adulteration that harms. Some are trying to say that it is only distilled liquors that do harm. Science comes in now and says that all alcohol does harm; that the malt and fermented liquors produce vastly more harm than distilled liquors, and that it is the general public use of such drinks that has entailed the gradual decline and degeneracy of the nations of the past.

[The wets] have no foundation in scientific truth to stand upon, and so they resort to all kinds of devious methods.

Their favorite contention is that we can not reach the evil because of our institutions. This assumes that here is something very harmful and injurious to the public health and morals, that imperils our very institutions themselves and the perpetuity of the Nation, but the Nation has not within itself, because of its peculiar organization, the power to bring about the public good and end a great public wrong. They invoke the principle of State rights. As a matter of fact, we are fighting more consistently for State rights than they ever dreamed of. . . .

Neither can they take refuge about any assumed question of individual liberty. We do not say that a man shall not drink. . . . We do not say that a man shall not have or make liquor in his own home for his own use. . . . We only touch the sale. A man may feel he has a right to drink, but he certainly has no inherent right to sell liquor. A man's liberties are absolutely secure in this resolution. The liberties and sanctity of the home are protected. The liberties of the community are secure, the liberties of the county are secure, and the liberties of the State are secure. . . .

Little Less of a Man After Each Drink

Thus a man is little less of a man after each drink he takes. In this way continued drinking causes a progressive weakening of the will and a progressive growing of the craving, so that after a time, if persisted in, there must come a point where the will power can not control the craving and the victim is in the grip of the habit.

Slaves in Shackles

When the drinking begins young the power of the habit becomes overwhelming, and the victim might as well have shackles. It is estimated that there are 5,000,000 heavy drinkers and drunkards in America, and these men might as well have a ball and chain on their ankles, for they are more abject slaves than those black men who were driven by slave drivers.

Present-day Slave Owners

These victims are driven imperatively to procure their liquor, no matter at what cost. A few thousand brewers and distillers, making up the organizations composing the great Liquor Trust, have a monopoly of the supply, and they therefore own these 5,000,000 slaves and through them they are able to collect two and one-half billions of dollars cash from the American people every year. . . .

There can be but one verdict, and that is this great destroyer must be destroyed. The time is ripe for fulfillment. The present generation, the generation to which we belong, must cut this millstone of degeneracy from the neck of humanity. . . .

The Final Conclusion

To cure this organic disease we must have recourse to the organic law. The people themselves must act upon this question. A generation must be prevailed upon to place prohibition in their own constitutional law, and such a generation could be counted upon to keep it in the Constitution during its lifetime. The Liquor Trust of necessity would disintegrate. The youth would grow up sober. The final, scientific conclusion is that we must have constitutional prohibition, prohibiting only the sale, the manufacture for sale, and everything that pertains to the sale, and invoke the power of both Federal and State Governments for enforcement.

Against Prohibition

Richard Bartholdt, a Republican member from Missouri, was a principal speaker on the wet side. "There is, of course, no doubt about the final outcome," he told the House. "A nation which has thrown off the shackles of despotism will not, for any length of time, tyrannize over itself." Taken from Richard Bartholdt, "Ten Reasons Against Prohibition," in The Politics of Moral Behavior: Prohibition and Drug Abuse, *ed. K. Austin Kerr (Reading, Massachusetts, 1973), 112–13*

Prohibition is a deathblow to the liberty of the individual because it prohibits what is not wrong in itself. No despot in history has ever dared to prohibit what is morally right, and the attempt to do so would have cost him his head. The exercise of rights which concern persons individually, and whose exercise does not injure the neighbor, is a basic condition of freedom which prohibition violates. The right to eat and drink what we please is an inalienable human right of which even a majority can not deprive us without at the same time robbing us of our liberty. But let us go to the bottom of this matter. It has ever been the aim of the friends of liberty to wrest the scepter of Government from the hands of individual rulers and place it in the hands of the people. Since this has been achieved in America the problem of liberty was believed to have been solved for all time, for no one dreamed that the Nation would ever need protection against its own will or would ever tyrannize over itself. The prohibition movement teaches us, however, that such tyranny after all is possible under self-government by the majority misusing its political liberty or its right to govern for the purpose of restricting personal liberty. In other words, we are dealing in this case with what John Stuart Mill called "the tyranny of the majority," an evil against which the Nation must protect itself if it desires to remain free; for individual liberty, the right of personal conduct, is an inalienable human right which should never be taken away either by majorities or by law or constitution. From this we can see how much larger than the mere drink problem this question really is, for if it were right in one respect to take away from the individual the privilege of self-control it would be right in all other respects, and the final outcome could be nothing less than a condition of complete slavery.

Our opponents say, "We do not propose to prohibit drinking, but merely the manufacture and sale of beverages," but remember that this hypocritical and insidious subterfuge is the very means by which despots always robbed the people of their liberties.

The Liquor Trade

The arguments for and against prohibition occupied hundreds of thousands of pamphlets, books, speeches, broadsides, and other publications. Percy Andreae was the liquor trade's most able political strategist before the First World War. He viewed the drys as simply intolerant, religious zealots. Excerpted from Percy Andreae, "A Glimpse behind the Mask of Prohibition," in The Prohibition Movement in its Broader Bearings upon Our Social, Commercial, and Religious Liberties *(Chicago, 1915), 9-19.*

It means that government by emotion is to be substituted for government by reason, and government by emotion . . . is, according to the testimony of all ages, the most dangerous and pernicious of all forms of government. It has already crept into the legislative assemblies of most of the States of the Union, and is being craftily fostered by those who know how easily it can be made available for their purposes—purposes to the furtherance of which cool reason would never lend itself. Prohibition is but one of its fruits, and the hand that is plucking this fruit is the same hand of intolerance that drove forth certain of our forefathers from the land of their birth to seek the sheltering freedom of these shores.

What a strange reversal of conditions! The intolerants of a few hundred years ago are the upholders of liberty to-day, while those they once persecuted, having multiplied by grace of the very liberty that has so long sheltered them here, are now planning to impose the tyranny of their narrow creed upon the descendants of their persecutors of yore.

Let the greater public, which is, after all, the arbiter of the country's destinies, pause and ponder these things before they are allowed to progress too far. Prohibition, though it must cause, and is already causing, incalculable damage, may never succeed in this country; but that which is behind it, as the catapults and the cannon were behind the battering rams in the battles of olden days, is certain to succeed unless timely measures of prevention are resorted to; and if it does succeed, we shall witness the enthronement of a monarch in this land of liberty compared with whose autocracy the autocracy of the Russian Czar is a mere trifle.

The name of this monarch is Religious Intolerance.

Jack London

Jack London was a popular writer and a heavy drinker who supported prohibition. In this letter he explains his willingness to make a personal sacrifice on behalf of the larger social good. Excerpted from The Letters of Jack London, *vol. 3, ed. Earle Labor, Robert C. Leitz, III, and I. Milo Shepard (Stanford, California, 1988), 1583-84.*

To W. H. Geystweit

Glen Ellen, California,
October 6, 1916.

Never had much experience with wine-grape growing. The vineyards I brought were old worked out worthless so I pulled out the vines and planted other crops. I still work a few acres of profitable wine grapes. My position on alcohol is absolute nation-wide prohibition.

I MEAN ABSOLUTE. I HAVE NO PATIENCE IN HALF-WAY MEASURES. HALF-WAY MEASURES ARE UNFAIR ARE TANTAMOUNT TO CONFISCATION AND ARE PROVOCATIVE OF UNDERHAND CHEATING LYING AND LAW-BREAKING. WHEN THE NATION GOES IN FOR NATIONWIDE PROHIBITION THAT WILL BE THE END OF ALCOHOL AND THERE WILL BE NO CHEATING LYING NOR LAW-BREAKING. PERSONALLY I SHALL CONTINUE TO DRINK ALCOHOL FOR AS LONG AS IT IS ACCESSIBLE. WHEN ABSOLUTE PROHIBITION MAKES ALCOHOL INACCESSIBLE I SHALL STOP DRINKING AND IT WONT BE ANY HARDSHIP ON ME AND ON MEN LIKE ME WHOSE NAME IS LEGION. AND THE GENERATION OF BOYS AFTER US WILL NOT KNOW ANYTHING ABOUT ALCOHOL SAVE THAT IT WAS A STUPID VICE OF THEIR SAVAGE ANCESTORS.

JACK LONDON

The Success and Failure of Prohibition

Once prohibition was enacted, the arguments about it persisted. Although it appears that the popularity of prohibition increased through the 1928 elections (which produced the largest dry majorities yet and in Hoover the first president committed to the reform), the wets' attacks were ongoing. The arguments in the 1920s echoed those expressed earlier; they also involved a dispute over the success and failure of prohibition.

The College Student and Prohibition

Senator James Reed of Missouri was a dedicated enemy of prohibition. During hearings on law enforcement, he arranged testimony from a Yale University student, Russell Lee Post, who reported that a pool of Yale students indicated overwhelming approval for an easing of prohibition enforcement and that drinking on campus was rampant. Taken from The National Prohibition Law, Hearings before the Subcommittee of the Committee on the Judiciary, U.S. Senate, *69th Cong., 1st sess., 1926, 1410–11.*

Senator REED of Missouri. What are the facts with reference to the ability of students to obtain liquor?

Mr. POST. Why, it is obtainable, sir; the greater the attempts at enforcement the stronger the sentiment against it.

Senator REED of Missouri. Do bootleggers ply their trade among the students?

Mr. POST. Well, it is the reverse; the students go to the bootleggers.

Senator REED of Missouri. The students go to the bootleggers?

Mr. POST. Yes; they do not enter the university campus. . . .

Senator REED of Missouri. Is there any difficulty of any student of ordinary intelligence—and I presume they are all that at Yale University—getting all the whisky he wants to buy, or alleged whisky at least?

Mr. POST. No, sir.

Senator REED of Missouri. Is this liquor drunk on the campus or in the quarters of the students?

Mr. POST. Yes, sir.

Senator REED of Missouri. And is it drunk elsewhere?

Mr. POST. Yes, sir.

Senator REED of Missouri. That is all.

There were observations to the contrary. Taken from "The 'Old Days' and the New Among American Students," The International Student 26 *(November 1928): 21.*

Robert E. Reinow, dean of men [at the University of Iowa], "recalls the period before the saloons were outlawed when it was considered a collegiate accoutrement to be able to drink large quantities of liquor. . . . Now, despite some bootlegging, the problem of drinking is almost solved on the University of Iowa camps. . . ."

[Irving Fisher, a distinguished professor of economics at Yale University:] "The amount and evils of drinking among college students have been enormously exaggerated in the press. . . . There is certainly nothing like as much alcoholic liquor consumed by college students today as there was in pre-prohibition days."

A Mayor Speaks Out

Fiorello H. LaGuardia was a prominent New York City Republican politician who served several terms in the House of Representatives before being elected mayor. An outspoken critic of prohibition, he testi-

fied to the policy's failure. Taken from The National Prohibition Law, Hearings before the Subcommittee of the Committee on the Judiciary, *U.S. Senate, 69th Cong., 1st sess., 1926, 649–51.*

It is impossible to tell whether prohibition is a good thing or a bad thing. It has never been enforced in this country.

There may not be as much liquor in quantity consumed to-day as there was before prohibition; but there is just as much alcohol.

At least 1,000,000 quarts of liquor is consumed each day in the United States. In my opinion such an enormous traffic in liquor could not be carried on without the knowledge, if not the conniv-ance of the officials entrusted with the enforcement of the law. . . .

I believe that the percentage of whisky drinkers in the United States now is greater than in any other country of the world. Prohibition is responsible for that. . . .

At least $1,000,000,000 a year is lost to the National Govern-ment and the several States and counties in excise taxes. The liquor traffic is going on just the same. This amount goes into the pockets of bootleggers and in the pockets of the public officials in the shape of graft. . . .

I will concede that the saloon was odious but now we have delicatessen stores, pool rooms, drug stores, millinery shops, pri-vate parlors, and 57 other varieties of speak-easies selling liquor and flourishing.

I have heard of $2,000 a year prohibition agents who run their own cars with liveried chauffeurs.

It is common talk in my part of the country that from $7.50 to $12 a case is paid in graft from the time the liquor leaves the 12-mile limit until it reaches the ultimate consumer. There seems to be a varying market price for this service created by the degree of vigilance or the degree of greed of the public officials in charge.

It is my calculation that at least a million dollars a day is paid in graft and corruption to Federal, State, and local officers. Such a condition is not only intolerable, but it is demoralizing and dan-gerous to organized government. . . .

The Government even goes to the trouble to facilitate the financing end of the bootlegging industry. In 1925, $286,950,000 more of $10,000 bills were issued than in 1920 and $25,000,000 more of $5,000 bills were issued. What honest business man deals in $10,000 bills? Surely these bills were not used to pay the salaries of ministers. The bootlegging industry has created a demand for bills of large denominations, and the Treasury Department accommodates them.

The drys seemingly are afraid of the truth. Why not take inventory and ascertain the true conditions. Let us not leave it to the charge of an antiprohibition organization, or to any other private association, let us have an official survey and let the American people know what is going on. A complete and honest and impartial survey would reveal incredible conditions, corruption, crime, and an organized system of illicit traffic such as the world has never seen.

Prohibition a Success

The widespread claims that prohibition was a failure prompted the National Federation of Settlements to commission a study, surveying social workers across the United States about the policy's effects. The following document is from the report of Estelle Jamison of the County and City Welfare Association. Excerpted from Martha Bensley Bruère, Does Prohibition Work?: A Study of the Operation . . . *(New York, 1927), 18-22, 273.*

In Sioux Falls there were two liquor cures doing a thriving business. Both cures went out of business for lack of patronage with the advent of prohibition. . . .

We have more crime now than in the days of the saloon, but much less disorder, due to the absence of drunken people on the streets and in public places. Police records show a tremendous falling off in the arrests for intoxication.

Since the advent of prohibition the red-light district and the disorderly houses have passed out of existence. The necessity for a red-light district seemed to pass away when the saloon went out of business.

. . . Since the closing of the saloons there has been very little trouble with the colored population. Prostitution and drunkenness among the colored people in this city have dropped to next to nothing; at any rate, the police do not seem to have the trouble. . . . they used to have in the days of the saloon.

There is but very little bootlegging and illicit manufacture of liquor. The majority of the people are in favor of enforcing the liquor laws, and the sheriff and the chief of police are very active in running down bootleggers and stills.

The poverty obtaining now can be ascribed wholly to the industrial situation and other causes outside of the use of alcohol.

. . . The activity of the bootleggers in this city is so limited that the amount of liquor sold does not appear to have any effect on the community. Bootleggers do not remain in business very long, however. There is not enough illicit liquor consumed in this city to make any noticeable change in the general health of the community.

Of 22 men who were formerly saloon keepers or bartenders in Sioux Falls, 1 is dead, 1 has moved away, 1 is sick at home, 2 have retired on their incomes, 2 are packing-house laborers, 3 are in the real-estate business, and there is also a day laborer, a waiter in a café, an auctioneer, a janitor of a church, a baker, an operator of a lakeside resort, a truck farmer, a butcher, a grocer, a salesman of electric apparatus, and a secretary of a club.

There is much complaint about the prevalence of drinking among young people of high-school age, but an investigation of such rumors always results in finding that such drinking is confined to a very few young people. In no instance has it been found that the young people are acquiring the drink habit; even if they should wish to, the source of supply is too limited. People will start rumors that drinking is more common now among young people than in the days of the saloon, that young women will not go with a young fellow unless he carries something on his hip; but the moment that the names of specific young women are demanded, at once comes the reply that, 'It is common talk; everyone knows the young people are drinking. I am only repeating what everyone is talking about.' . . .

The bootleggers and moonshiners have no political pull in this state whatever; not even the Democrats will get mixed up in any way favoring the relaxing of our state liquor laws. Our city and county officials, from the highest to the lowest, are all elected on dry platforms.

There are some hold-over liquor addicts who insist on becoming intoxicated on canned heat, flavoring extracts and similar impossible drinks, but these people are as a rule the derelicts left over from the days of the saloon. They are rapidly passing and leaving no successors.

Weeks pass by now in Sioux Falls without a single arrest for intoxication; while during the days of the saloons on Monday morning there would sometimes be as high as thirty cases of intoxication to be tried by the Municipal Court.

George W. Burnside, who was mayor of Sioux Falls twenty-one years, calls attention to the disappearance of the old-time saloon 'clean up.' Men who were down and out because of the drink habit, are no longer to be seen. . . .

Dean Woodruff of the Episcopal Church says that since the outlawing of the use of liquor there is not the squalid poverty in this city that obtained before prohibition.

The Hon. Mr. Gunderson, member of the legislature and candidate for United States Senator on the Democratic ticket, who lives at Vermilion, where the state university is located, says that there is not the drinking among the young people; you do not see any drunken people; you do not hear the boisterous and loud talk. . . .

The people to whom the social workers are neighbors throughout the great Atlantic port cities are not taking the prohibition law very seriously. Nowhere in their . . . history have they had any preparation for it. It is not a law which came upon them because they felt the need for it, but because another people . . . wanted it for them. Nothing could be more different than the way the fifth or sixth generation of Americans in the cities of the Northwest and the new citizens of the Atlantic ports are reacting to the law. But the fact remains that the social workers do see improved conditions even under this imperfect observance.

Questions

---

1. *What values were at the root of the disagreement over prohibition? What was the core of the disagreement between wets and drys before the enactment of national prohibition?*

2. *What conditions in the liquor trades fueled the prohibition movement? Why would women organize and march—lead a "crusade"—against the saloon?*
3. *What were the arguments that prohibition was a failure? What was the evidence that prohibition was a failure? a success?*

FURTHER READING

In addition to the books from which these readings were drawn, there are several important works. Jack S. Blocker, Jr. has written several books on the subject, including Retreat from Reform: The Prohibition Movement in the United States, 1890-1913 *(Westport, Connecticut, 1976).* Ruth Bordin, Woman and Temperance: The Quest for Power and Liberty, 1873-1900 *(Philadelphia, 1981) is important. Jed Dannenbaum,* Drink and Disorder: Temperance Reform in Cincinnati from the Washingtonian Revival to the WCTU *(Urbana, Illinois, 1984) and Robert Smith Bader,* Prohibition in Kansas: A History *(Lawrence, Kansas, 1986) are excellent local and state studies, respectively. Richard F. Hamm,* Shaping the Eighteenth Amendment: Temperance Reform, Legal Culture, and the Polity, 1880-1920 *(Chapel Hill, North Carolina, 1995) and K. Austin Kerr,* Organized for Prohibition: A New History of the Anti-Saloon League *(New Haven, Connecticut, 1985) explore the organization and politics of prohibition.*

Pictures and more texts are available on the World Wide Web at http://www.history.ohio-state.edu/projects/prohibition

The Rise of Big Business and the Persistence of Small Business in American Industry, 1850–1920

Mansel G. Blackford

INTRODUCTION

In 1901, J. P. Morgan, America's best-known and most powerful investment banker, combined Carnegie Steel with other firms to form United States Steel, capitalized at over $1.4 billion. The establishment of the world's first billion-dollar corporation was a signal that big business had achieved a permanent institutional status on the American scene. Morgan organized United States Steel from firms that had earlier competed in the marketplace. Now those firms could cooperate; and through their combined size, control of iron ore, and efficiencies of production, Morgan expected that they would dominate the nation's steel industry, reducing price competition. A key element in modern America had been created: in 1860 no single American company was valued at $10 million, but by 1904 some three hundred were.

Giant firms clustered in just a few fields. Nearly all were in industry. Of the 278 American companies with assets of $20 million or more, in 1917, some 236 were manufacturing companies. By way of contrast, only five were agricultural firms (one each in ranching, the growing of sugar cane, and the harvesting of crude rubber, and two diversified multinationals, the United Fruit Company and its competitor, the Atlantic Fruit and Sugar Company). Of the manufacturing businesses, 171 firms, or nearly three-quarters, were in just six groups: 39 in primary metals, 34 in food processing, 29 in transportation equipment, 24 in manufacturing machinery, 24 in oil refining, and 21 in chemicals. These companies shared certain characteristics. Most had combined production with distribution—previously, these two business functions had been carried out by separate companies—by the time of World War I. Nearly all were multi-unit enterprises with factories spread across the United States.

The share of America's industrial output coming from small businesses dropped as large manufacturing ventures rose to prominence. Corporations—the legal form assumed by most big businesses, but relatively few small businesses (most small firms were single-owner proprietorships or partnerships)—accounted for three-quarters of America's industrial production by 1904. Small businesses also became less important as employers. By 1914, nearly a third of all industrial workers found employment in plants with 500 or more in their labor forces, and another third in those with 100 to 499. As large companies arose in manufacturing, a growing share of industrial workers found employment in companies operating more than one plant; at least a third of the nation's workers did so by 1923.

Small businesses did not, however, disappear from the industrial scene in the United States. The same set of census statistics alluded to above show that in 1914 a third of America's industrial workforce found employment in firms with 100 or fewer laborers. If small businesses are defined as those with 250 or fewer workers, 54 percent of those employed by manufacturing concerns worked for small firms. Moreover, some fifty-four thousand little businesses, those with six to twenty workers, were still in operation on the eve of the First World War. Those small businesses that survived and prospered in manufacturing did so by following several strategies. In some fields—such as leather working, furniture making, and lumber milling—few economies of scale existed, and big businesses did not develop. That is, the cost of production per number of goods made did not decline as the number of products turned out increased. In these areas, small manufacturers continued to make goods much as they had in earlier years. In those realms in which big businesses did emerge, small industrialists had to adapt to the presence of their larger counterparts, and many small firms were quite successful in doing so. [Portions of this introduction have been previously published in Mansel G. Blackford, A History of Small Business in America *(New York, 1991), 28–37.]*

RAILROADS:
PIONEERS IN BIG BUSINESS

As business historian Alfred D. Chandler, Jr., wrote, railroads were "pioneers in big business" in America. Railroads developed new management techniques later used by a wide variety of industrial firms. By uniting America economically, railroads created a national market for industrial goods, setting the stage for the more general growth of big business in the United States.

Railroads: The First Big Businesses

As the first emerging big business, railroads faced management challenges unknown by previous, much smaller enterprises; they, however, also could generate much larger profits, if those challenges could be met. In solving their problems, railroads developed basic management techniques still used in the United States and abroad. Excerpted from Mansel G. Blackford and K. Austin Kerr, Business Enterprise in American History, 3d ed. (Boston, 1994), 126–35, 137–39, 141–42, 147–48, 165.

By the 1850s, individual railroads had become the biggest businesses of their day. Even before the Civil War, the trunk-line railroads [major routes handling long distance through traffic] controlled about 500 miles of track each and employed hundreds,

Excerpts reprinted from *Business Enterprise in American History* by Mansel G. Blackford and K. Austin Kerr, published by Houghton Mifflin Company, 1994. Copyright © 1994 by Houghton Mifflin Company.

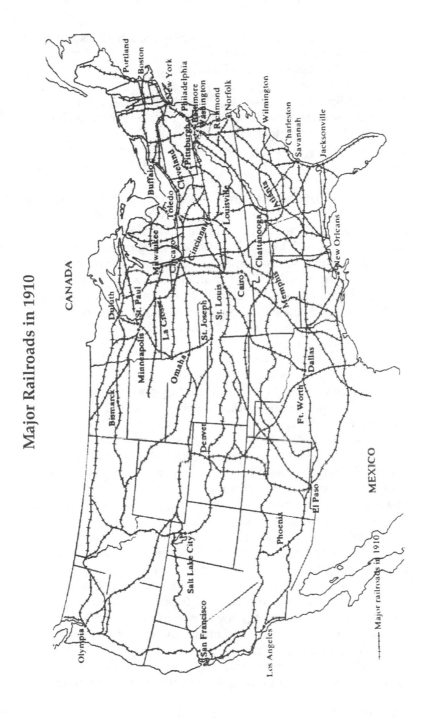

Major Railroads in 1910

sometimes thousands, of workers. During the late 1860s and early 1870s, trunk-line railroads such as the New York Central and the Pennsylvania established control over through routes to the West, and entrepreneurs completed America's first transcontinental lines. Building these lines was an expensive task; the trunk-line railroads connecting the East with the Midwest were capitalized at from $17 million to $35 million each. Other pre-Civil War businesses paled by comparison. Even the largest textile mills employed fewer than a thousand people, and only a handful were capitalized at more than $1 million.

Railroads continued to grow in size and complexity after the Civil War. Hungry for capital before the war, they [the railroads] became voracious after it. . . . In the 1880s, Americans built an annual average of 8,000 miles of track, so that by 1890, the nation had 166,000 miles of track, and a growing number of large cities were linked by a national transportation network. The construction of more than 254,000 miles of track finished the system by 1916, but even by the end of the 1880s, an integrated, nationwide railroad network was available to farmers, manufacturers, merchants, and passengers. . . .

Because of their rapid expansion, railroads faced unprecedented managerial problems. They were much larger in terms of people employed, regions served, and capital invested than any other companies of the period, even the biggest textile mills. Moreover, their operations were more complex and much faster than those of other businesses. . . . Decisions that affected the lives of people over ever-larger regions needed to be made quickly and accurately in the railroad business, and suitable ways of making such decisions had to be developed. . . . Even more complex were strategic problems: problems of financing expansion and problems in meeting competition. . . .

Clearly, business executives could not run railroads in haphazard ways and hope to survive very long. The complexities of both the operating and the strategic problems called for systematic management methods. Railroad executives solved their problems through the establishment of business bureaucracies, the first in American history. For the most part, railroad officers acted as innovators in setting up new management systems in response to specific business problems. . . .

. . . [Benjamin] Latrobe [chief engineer of the Baltimore & Ohio Railroad] set up an administrative structure that separated the responsibility for activities into two parts: a finance department to handle the internal and external financing of the line and to take care of other matters of grand strategy, and an operations department to run the trains. The operations department was separated into geographic divisions. Each geographic division, in turn, possessed three managers—one in charge of transportation (scheduling and running the trains), a second in charge of constructing and repairing the roadbed, and a third in charge of repairing machinery. All three functional managers reported to their respective functional superiors in the central office, where the railroad's general superintendent coordinated the work of the different managers. . . .

The Pennsylvania Railroad became known as the "standard railroad of the world" because of its good management. Herman Haupt, a West Point graduate, helped develop its bureaucratic organization during the 1840s and 1850s in his position as the railroad's superintendent of transportation and as its general superintendent. This structure was then more fully developed by J. Edgar Thomson, the railroad's president. In 1857, Thomson enlarged the central office of the line by separating the accounting from the treasury department and by creating a secretary's office and a legal department. Thomson also clarified relations between the head office and the railroad's operating divisions and began moving in the direction of fully demarcating the duties of its officers. In the 1860s and 1870s, he completed the task of separating the responsibilities of the executives in the central office from those of the managers in the railroad's three regional divisional offices, and he installed financial controls by which the executives in the central office could monitor and coordinate work throughout all of the divisions.

Three hallmarks of modern business management stand out in the steps taken by these railroad executives. First, they began to separate policy making from operations—that is, they began to divide strategy and tactics. Different groups of executives were in charge of overall planning and of operational details. It came to be the job of top management to plan for the future of the lines and to coordinate the functions of different parts of the lines. Second, and directly related to the first point, the railroads began to build bureaucratic organizations staffed by middle managers. These middle managers were essential to the development of the railroads as big businesses. While the top management in the central office concentrated on grand strategy, the middle management in the divisional offices attended to the operational details. These middle managers received reports from conductors, station managers, and the like, digested them, and then made their own reports to the top management, forming a chain that connected the various levels of the railroad bureaucracy. And if they were the chain, better financial reporting—the third hallmark of modern business management—was one of the major links. Railroad executives developed new types of accounting methods to hold together and analyze the work of their complex business empires. . . .

. . . [Of specific interest,] railroad executives developed *cost accounting*. They divided their companies' costs into various categories of fixed costs (such as those of roadbeds and tracks) and variable costs (such as that of labor). Because their fixed costs were much higher than their variable costs, railroad managers sought to run as many fully laden cars as possible. And they used cost accounting to pinpoint problems in their companies' operations and to aid in setting profitable railroad rates. The men responsible for railroad accounting thus pioneered in administering prices, as opposed to allowing invisible market forces to determine them.

The adoption of bureaucratic methods by railroads marked a fundamental shift in how American business people conducted their affairs. The personal business world of the merchant [in earlier times] gave way to the more highly organized and impersonal world of modern big business, a trend that continued in the late nineteenth and twentieth centuries and that came to characterize many firms beyond the railroad industry.

The changes occurring in railroad management were important not only for the railroad industry but also for a vast array of other businesses and industries in the United States. As their companies grew in size and complexity during the 1870s and 1880s, America's industrialists sought new management methods and structures by which they might control them. They found these methods and structures, in part, in their nation's railroads. The general idea of bureaucratic rather than personal management and specific methods of accounting and statistical controls spread from the railroads to other industrial ventures.

As railroads increased in size [the subsequent rise of big business and] . . . [e]conomic growth created new opportunities for businesses to expand the scope of their operations, and the building of America's railroad network lay at the heart of this business expansion. [This allowed for the exploitation of the resources in America's interior and permitted industrial enterprises to tap the growing domestic market.] . . .

The Spread of Big Business

The growth of the U.S. population and its concentration into cities linked by the railroads [and the telegraph] was an important change that allowed entrepreneurs to construct big businesses. The population of the United States rose from 31 million people in 1860, to 63 million in 1890, to 106 million in 1920, and most of that growth occurred in the cities. . . . The growth in population combined with the railroad system to create unprecedented business opportunities.

Not everyone favored the development of large railroads. Safety problems prompted broadsides like this one condemning the railroads. (Courtesy of The Library of Congress.)

The story of Andrew Carnegie and the steel industry illustrates the importance of railroads and expanding cities to the rise of big business. Carnegie benefited directly from the example of the railroads in organizing his steel business; the railroads and urban construction projects provided significant markets for his steel mills. A Scottish émigré who moved with his family to Pittsburgh in 1848, Carnegie owed much of his success to what he learned in the railroad business. In Pittsburgh,

Carnegie held several low-paying menial jobs, including that of bobbin boy in a textile mill, before becoming one of the city's leading telegraph operators. While he was working as a telegrapher in 1852, Carnegie was hired by Thomas Scott, the superintendent of the western division of the Pennsylvania Railroad, as his personal telegrapher and secretary. When Scott became a vice president of the line seven years later, Carnegie succeeded him as superintendent of the railroad's western division, a position he held until he resigned in 1865 to pursue other business interests. . . .

When Carnegie entered the steel business in 1872, he brought with him several important lessons from his railroad experience. He was aware of the large and expanding market for steel that railroads were creating with their requirements for track, bridges, and locomotives. In fact, one of his first major sales was steel track to the Pennsylvania Railroad. Moreover, in managing his steel company Carnegie took to heart the obsession of railroad executives with low-cost, high-volume operations. Like the railroads, steel was a capital-intensive business, and Carnegie sought always to lower the costs and increase the volume of production of his steel mills. Like the executives of the Pennsylvania Railroad, he installed sophisticated cost-accounting and recordkeeping systems in his company, systems he used both to locate production inefficiencies and to reward (or penalize) his plant managers. Take care of the costs, Carnegie believed, and the profits would take care of themselves.

Carnegie's policies proved successful. He created the largest steel company in the world and, with bankers and other American steelmakers, established the United States as the leading steel-producing nation. By 1900, America's output of pig iron had risen to 15 million tons, surpassing Great Britain's. The output of steel in the United States soared from 70,000 tons in 1870 to more than 4 million tons just twenty years later, as steel went into America's expanding railroad network and into skeletons for the buildings of the nation's growing cities. By 1900 American steel production had leaped to nearly 12 million tons, and in 1920 it reached 47 million tons. By the latter date, the United States was producing about 60 percent of the world's steel. . . .

. . . [As the example of Carnegie Steel shows, mass production was one of the keys to the development of big business.] The opening of the national market enticed manufacturers into boost-

An unlikely combination: steel king Andrew Carnegie, William Jennings Bryan, railroad magnate James J. Hill, and John Mitchell of the UMW. (Courtesy of The Library of Congress.)

ing their production, and the development of new technological processes made increased output feasible.

Mass production first appeared in industries processing liquids, where the application of new heat and chemical processes made it possible to turn out more product in less time with fewer workers. The use of enlarged stills, superheated steam, and catalytic cracking permitted the development of large-batch or continuous-process production in the oil, sugar, fats, and alcohol industries during the 1870s and 1880s.

Breakthroughs in machinery designs brought mass production to a number of mechanical industries at a slightly later date. The use of a machine to make cigarettes transformed that industry in 1881. By the mid-1880s, one machine made 120,000 cigarettes per day, many more than the 3,000 that could be made by hand. The adoption of similar continuous-process machinery also remade the match, soap, and grain-milling industries, bringing mass production to them in the 1880s and 1890s.

Finally, the establishment of mass production in the metalmaking and metalworking industries occurred in several steps. First, more complex and expensive machinery was installed to make and work the metal. Using new steel alloys as cutting edges on machine tools greatly sped metalworking processes. Even more important, entire plants were designed to ensure as continuous a flow as possible from the suppliers of raw materials through the various production processes to the shipment of goods to market. Inefficiencies and bottlenecks in production were eliminated. . . .

As they grew larger, the big businesses of the late nineteenth and early twentieth centuries developed internal structures different from those of most earlier enterprises. These structures evolved in response both to the opportunities of the new national market and to the increasing complexity of manufacturing processes and goods. The national market offered glittering possibilities to American business people, but it also presented them with previously unknown perils. The nationwide transportation network broke down local monopolies, intensifying competition across the United States and demanding changes in business methods. At the same time, the tremendous increase in the output of their factories and the growing complexity of goods their factories produced raised additional difficulties for industrialists, giving rise especially to problems in marketing the increasing numbers of technologically sophisticated products.

In an attempt to reestablish control over their economic destinies, business executives restructured their companies. Vertical integration was one common response to the problems and opportunities of the new national market and became a hallmark of big business in America. In vertical integration a company that initially engages in only one stage of the production and sale of its goods may acquire control of its sources of raw materials and/or the making and sale of its finished products.

Andrew Carnegie's desire to control fully his costs of production while taking advantage of the opportunities offered by the national market for steel led him to construct a self-contained, vertically integrated business empire. Initially, the Carnegie Steel Company depended on other firms for many of its raw materials—iron ore, coking coal, limestone, and the like. This situation displeased Carnegie, because he thought he was being charged too much for the raw materials and, even more important, because he could not always secure enough of them during times of peak production. To lower his costs and ensure adequate supplies, Carnegie moved to control his sources of raw materials. In the 1880s and 1890s, Carnegie gained control of the Frick Coke Company (a producer of coking coal), the Mesabi iron-ore range, and numerous limestone quarries. Moreover, to carry the raw materials to his smelters near Pittsburgh, Carnegie acquired a fleet of Great Lakes ore ships and put together a railroad system of about a thousand miles of track. He also took steps to control the making and sale of finished steel products. In the 1890s, Carnegie began production of a wider variety of finished goods than in early times, and he set up his own sales offices in major cities in the United States and Canada. . . .

Horizontal integration provided a second mechanism by which industrialists tried to restructure their companies. In horizontal integration, a number of companies combined forces to control one step in the production or sale of their products. As in vertical integration, the goal of horizontal integration was to bring order to an unstable, highly competitive business situation. Horizontal integration sought to lessen competition, thus reducing the risks to the capital invested in America's new industrial enterprises. John D. Rockefeller's Standard Oil Company was a classic example of horizontal integration, as Rockefeller and other oil magnates sought to control their rapidly expanding industry.

The growth of the oil industry, like that of the steel industry, was explosive. In Pennsylvania in 1859, E. L. Drake sank the first commercial oil well in America. This strike led to oil booms throughout the East and Midwest during the late nineteenth century, as Americans substituted kerosene for whale oil and candles. Oil discoveries in Oklahoma, Texas, and California in the 1890s and early 1900s further expanded the petroleum industry. In the early twentieth century, oil began gradually supplanting coal as a source of energy for railroad locomotives and some industrial plants. And with the development of the automobile, gasoline emerged as the major oil product in the 1910s and later. . . .

Rockefeller was a pioneer in the oil industry. Born in Richford, New York, in 1839, he had moved to Cleveland, Ohio, by the time he was sixteen years old. There he entered the business world as a bookkeeper in the firm of a commission merchant, earning a salary of fifty cents per day. Using his own savings and a gift from his father, Rockefeller became a jobber of hay, grain, and meat in 1859. Rockefeller took his work very seriously. "Don't be a good fellow," he later warned people. "It is my firm conviction that every downfall is traceable directly or indirectly to the victim's goodfellowship, his good cheer among his friends." Not surprisingly, he was viewed as solemn and humorless. "Oh, young Rockefeller—he's a stick!" noted the son of the Cleveland merchant who first hired Rockefeller. But Rockefeller was successful, and he soon used the earnings made in trade to go into the oil business.

Rockefeller entered oil refining in 1863, just four years after Drake drilled his well. By 1867, he owned a large refinery in the Cleveland area and purchased oil for it from well-owners in Pennsylvania and other eastern states. Needing capital for further growth, he incorporated his company in 1870 as the Standard Oil Company. The anticipated expansion occurred. However, oil refining was a very competitive industry, and Rockefeller and his rivals soon found themselves battling fiercely over the national market for kerosene and other oil products. No one really wanted to engage in this competition, which threatened to disrupt operations and lower profits.

To lessen competition, the owners of the Standard Oil Company and forty other oil-refining companies entered into a trust agreement in 1882. They turned over the common stock in their companies to nine trustees. The nine trustees then operated the companies in ways that avoided competition among them. In return for the stock in their original companies, the shareholders received trust certificates, and each year the nine trustees distributed what they thought were equitable shares in the earnings of the refining companies to the shareholders. By the 1890s, Standard Oil controlled more than 90 percent of the petroleum refining capacity of the United States. . . .

Additional changes soon took place in Standard's structure. In 1889, New Jersey amended its incorporation law to become the first state allowing one company to own stock in another company—to become a "holding company." Many large corporations took advantage of this provision to become holding companies by incorporating in New Jersey. Standard Oil was one of these firms. In 1899, Standard incorporated under New Jersey law and purchased the stock of the other members of the trust. In the early 1900s, Standard emerged as a single operating company. Its management sold or closed inefficient plants and rationalized the work of the corporation by uniting offices, such as sales offices, previously operated separately. Once horizontally integrated,

Standard turned to vertical integration. In the 1880s, Standard had begun securing its own supplies of crude at a reasonable cost. Somewhat later, Standard began operating long-distance pipelines to transport its oil and sales outlets to market it. . . .

As their companies grew in size and became fully integrated enterprises, the decisions of the managers of big businesses played ever-larger roles in determining how the business system of the United States functioned. In those parts of the nation's industrial economy dominated by big businesses, the visible hand of management replaced the invisible hand of market forces in controlling production and distribution of industrial goods and services. Decisions once made in thousands of independent market transactions became concentrated in the hands of managers of relatively few big businesses. By the opening decade of the twentieth century, in fact, key segments of U.S. industry were characterized by oligopoly. That is, in some fields of manufacturing, a handful of companies dominated their markets. Oligopoly was particularly characteristic of the metal, oil, rubber, chemical, tobacco processing, electrical machinery, transportation equipment, and sugar refining industries. As early as 1904, a few major companies controlled at least half the output of seventy-eight industries in the United States. During the opening decade of the twentieth century, the structure of much of American industry assumed its modern form: oligopolist and concentrated.

The emergence of big businesses in some fields, combined with the vigorous persistence of small businesses in other fields, illustrates a key fact about America's business system in this period: it was fast becoming a dual system. The big businesses, "center firms," were at the center of the nation's new business system. Center firms were capital-intensive companies, such as Standard Oil and Carnegie Steel. They often used continuous-processing or large-batch production methods to achieve important economies of scale. Center firms were also usually vertically or horizontally integrated (or both) and frequently exercised some degree of control over their markets. As large ventures in manufacturing, communications, and transportation, the center firms were of tremendous importance to America's emergent industrial economy; the fortunes of a single center firm often had a ripple effect on the nation's economy as a whole. "Peripheral firms," on the other hand, were smaller, for no production efficiencies resulted from increasing their scale of production. They were likely to be labor-intensive rather than capital-intensive and usually had no control over their markets. Small businesses in the aggregate remained very important to the American economy, but what happened to any single peripheral firm had little impact upon the national economy. . . .

Although American business executives may have had a difficult time understanding the economic changes occurring in the late nineteenth and early twentieth centuries, the actions they took to deal with those changes permanently altered the nature of business in the United States. Big businesses with managerial bureaucracies replaced many small businesses run directly by their owners. Vertically and horizontally integrated companies supplanted single-unit firms, thus leading to concentration in industry and to the creation of oligopoly in many fields of manufacturing. These developments, in turn, influenced the nature of economic decision making in the United States. With the rise of big business, decisions about the production and distribution of goods that had previously been made by the free interplay of market forces came to be internalized within the business firm. The visible hand of management replaced the invisible hand of the market in determining the functioning of part of the American economy.

Small Business Persists:
Specialty Products and Niche Markets

Small manufacturing firms remained an important part of America's economy despite the development of large industrial corporations. Rather than competing head-to-head with their larger counterparts, smaller industrial firms pursued a strategy of developing specialty products for niche markets—a strategy successfully used by textile, steel, and other small industries throughout the twentieth century. Selected from Mansel G. Blackford, A History of Small Business in America *(New York, 1991), 38–43, 45.*

Most small businesses that succeeded in manufacturing . . . succeeded by differentiating their products from those of their larger counterparts. Doing so often meant producing a wide range of goods for rapidly changing regional and seasonal markets. Part of the ability to accomplish this task lay in the possession of intelligent, innovative work forces; another part lay in the flexible use of the most advanced (not primitive) technologies. In short, by carving out market niches, and by developing new production methods, small businesses could remain as independent enterprises in successful coexistence with larger firms. Among the fields in which small firms prospered well into the twentieth century were textiles and metal making.

As the nineteenth century progressed, the textile industry divided into two segments. In Waltham and Lowell in New England, large factories employed unskilled workers to turn out standardized goods for the mass market. The mills quickly became fully integrated in the production of textiles, with all the steps—preparation, spinning, weaving, and dyeing—carried out on different factory floors linked by elevators. These milling companies were among the largest businesses of the antebellum period. As early as 1832, eight of them were capitalized at at least $600,000 apiece. They each employed hundreds of workers, and their physical plants were large. In 1849 one company possessed five mills, each of which was five stories tall, with each story taken up by one room measuring 40 by 151 feet. By the 1830s and 1840s, all the companies had adopted the corporate form of organization, and most were run through rudimentary managerial hierarchies. Few small textile firms developed in Waltham or Lowell, for the large businesses controlled the available plant sites and sources of waterpower, denying access to others. By 1850, 12 corporations employed 12,000 textile workers in Lowell. . . .

The textile business developed differently in Philadelphia. In 1850, 326 firms employed 12,400 textile workers. Two-thirds possessed 25 or fewer workers, and 28 of the largest 32 employed only between 102 and 225 workers. Though employing as many workers in the aggregate as their counterparts in Waltham and Lowell, the Philadelphia firms were capitalized at much less—$4.7 million, about a third of the amount invested in the Lowell and Waltham companies. Most of the Philadelphia companies were organized as single-owner proprietorships. Only about 17% were partnerships, and even fewer—a scant 3%—were corporations.

The Philadelphia firms competed successfully throughout the nineteenth century with the much-larger mills of New England by stressing specialization and flexibility in production and marketing. Few Philadelphia firms tried to master all aspects of textile production; most specialized in one or two steps, which they then did very well indeed, using the most up-to-date machinery and employing skilled workers, often men, at high wages. Their productivity levels were high. In their labor practices as in their management methods, the Philadelphia mills differed from the larger mills in Lowell and Waltham. The Lowell and Waltham mills employed young, unskilled farm women as workers and treated them very paternalistically, housing them in company dormitories and strictly supervising their morals. Turnover rates were probably higher in Lowell and Waltham than in Philadelphia, thus probably making productivity lower in the northern mills. With skilled work forces and modern machinery, the Philadelphia mills could also more rapidly switch to various types of cotton, wool, and other fabrics as needed.

For the most part, the owners of the Philadelphia textile establishments did not become members of their city's social elite—in sharp contrast to the situation in New England, where mill owners became influential figures in cities like Boston. Instead, the Philadelphia mill owners remained close to their work, and a commercial elite of merchants long dominated Philadelphia's affairs. This circumstance paid an unexpected dividend. Although Philadelphia was not immune to labor unrest, disturbances were mitigated by bonds uniting managers and workers. Workers and managers knew each other personally through work on the plant floor and through membership in the same churches and social organizations. Moreover, many mill owners had started as skilled artisans, often renting space for their nascent ventures and only later expanding their enterprises. Workers and owners "talked the same language" and respected each other, even when they disagreed.

The flexibility of the Philadelphia firms served them well during the crises of the 1860s and the 1870s. Most adjusted better than their counterparts in Lowell and Waltham to the cotton shortage and the wartime demands of the Civil War by shifting to the production of woolen goods and other items. Similarly, their flexibility allowed the Philadelphia mills to prosper and expand even during the hard times of the mid-1870s, a period in which many New England mills encountered severe difficulties. By the early 1880s, Philadelphia possessed 849 textile establishments employing 55,000 workers, the largest such concentration of firms and workers in the nation. These were mostly profitable firms. The return on capital in Philadelphia's cotton textile companies averaged 23% in 1890, compared with 6% in the Lowell and Waltham companies and 8% in cotton textile firms nationwide. Most of the Philadelphia companies remained what they had been in the antebellum years—small, family firms in which the owner-manager personally supervised every aspect of his firm's operations. As a spokesman noted with pride, Philadelphia's textile community was "composed almost exclusively of individuals and individual firms . . . no corporations."

Small size and versatility continued to be hallmarks of the Philadelphia textile firms into the twentieth century. Not even the depression of the 1890s, which ushered in merger movements in many industries, led to concentration in Philadelphia's textile industry. Economic factors militated against mergers—the flexible, batch system of production; the ease of entry into the industry; and the near-absence of scale economies—but more important was the character of the men owning the mills. They identified personally with their businesses, which they often viewed as extensions of their families. Philadelphia remained the domain of small firms. In 1905, 728 textile companies capitalized at a total of $100 million employed 60,000 workers within the city of Philadelphia (there were additional firms in the suburbs and nearby areas). As before, these were flexible, specialized companies attuned to making rapid production changes as markets altered (in 1910, for example, a carpet maker celebrated its twenty-fifth anniversary by bringing out its 25,000th pattern). . . .

. . . [I]n America's iron and steel industries . . . large companies, such as Carnegie Steel and later the United States Steel Corporation, did come to dominate important segments of their industries. By using new, large-batch production methods, they turned out vast quantities of homogeneous steel products, mainly rails and structural steel, for America's expanding national market. Nonetheless, smaller iron and steel mills continued to thrive alongside the giants, even in Pittsburgh, the heart of the nation's iron and steel industry, well into the twentieth century.

Pittsburgh's iron and steel industries took form as collections of relatively small businesses. As late as 1870, the typical firm was capitalized at just $210,000, produced 3,000 tons of iron and steel annually, and employed only 119 workers. Like their counterparts elsewhere in America, Pittsburgh's iron and steel mills were unintegrated enterprises. They engaged in only one or two, not all, of the steps involved in turning out iron and steel products. The companies were for the most part family businesses, with about 40 families dominating the industries. The owners lived in Pittsburgh or nearby areas and ran their businesses themselves, eschewing the use of managerial hierarchies.

The switch from iron to steel, and with this change the use of the capital-intensive Bessemer and open-hearth methods, altered the situation in Pittsburgh, but only somewhat. Despite the expansion of new methods of steel making, iron production continued to grow as well, and older methods of steel making, such as the crucible process, continued to enjoy popularity. Many mills did become larger, but few approached the enormous size of the Carnegie operations. By the late 1880s, the average Pittsburgh iron and steel firm was capitalized at $805,000, produced 14,000 tons of iron and steel, and had a work force of 332. Many of these firms continued to be run by well-established Pittsburgh families (Carnegie was considered an outsider). The rise of a few giant firms, such as Carnegie Steel, should not obscure the continuing importance of the many smaller companies, for there remained 58 independent iron and steel mills in Pittsburgh in 1894.

The independent Pittsburgh mills (those not part of the expanding Carnegie empire) survived and indeed prospered by specializing. Rather than compete with Carnegie Steel in the large-batch production of rails and structural steel, most coexisted side by side with the Carnegie enterprises by producing specialized goods for niche markets. In pursuing this strategy Pittsburgh's independent iron and steel producers closely resembled the approach to business taken by Philadelphia's textile makers in their competition with the larger companies of New England. Oliver and Phillips, the Sable Rolling Mill, Vesuvius Iron, Juniata Iron, Crescent Steel, Hussey Wells and Company, and LaBelle Steel were some of the firms that successfully specialized. Oliver and Phillips, for instance, went into the making of nuts and bolts, wagon hardware, and barbed wire, while Vesuvius engaged in the production of bar and sheet iron, rods, hoops, and nails. . . .

Throughout the nineteenth century and into the twentieth, the independent mill owners composed much of the social elite of Pittsburgh, in marked contrast to the lesser social role played by the textile makers in Philadelphia. From the 1840s through the 1890s, 141 families owned and operated iron or steel mills in Pittsburgh. About half of these families were considered to be among the city's upper class. This situation continued into the middle twentieth century, as many iron and steel families entered banking. It was this social elite—based on iron, steel, and finance—that largely controlled Pittsburgh's political and cultural life for many years, losing its hegemony only after World War II.

Their positions as leaders in their community influenced how the independent iron and steel mill owners dealt with their labor forces. Perhaps both because they were close to their workers in relatively small plants and because they cared deeply for the welfare of Pittsburgh, most tended toward a grudging acceptance of unions and a pragmatic willingness to try to work with them. More so than the operators of the much-larger Carnegie mills, the owner-operators of the small independent facilities sought to achieve a harmonious relationship with their workers, especially in the 1870s and 1880s. In the 1890s and later, following the lead of the larger firms, the independent mill owners became less tolerant of labor. As they adopted more capital-intensive equipment and were influenced by the examples of violence against labor at Carnegie Steel, they turned more of their attention to breaking unions. . . .

. . . Common themes run through the successes of those small companies which proved capable of coexisting with big businesses in manufacturing. Consciously or unconsciously, the small manufacturers adopted a growth strategy that would remain one of the keys to success in small business into the late twentieth century: they developed specialty products that they then sold in niche markets, thereby often avoiding direct competition with their larger counterparts. To make this growth strategy work, the firms usually adopted (or developed themselves) the most advanced production technologies available. These small companies were not backward workshops using obsolete equipment but were instead among the most advanced industrial establishments of their day.

Running the companies were managers deeply committed to their success. Most of the companies, even those organized as corporations, continued to be operated as family enterprises. The businesses remained single-unit enterprises devoid for the most part of managerial hierarchies (though some of the independent Pittsburgh mills did develop simple hierarchies in the late nineteenth century). More than a quest for profits animated their owners. A sense of personal satisfaction, almost a sense of craftsmanship, remained a primary motivating factor for their executives and workers.

Questions

1. *Why were railroads so important to the development of big business in America? Why do historians call railroads "pioneers in big business"? What did manufacturing firms learn from railroads in terms of new management methods?*
2. *Why did big businesses develop in American manufacturing in the late nineteenth and early twentieth centuries? What was vertical integration and why was it so important for large manufacturing firms in America?*
3. *How did smaller companies persist in some areas of industry? How did they compete (or coexist) with their larger counterparts? What is meant by "niche markets" and "specialty products"?*

THE SEARCH FOR ORDER, THE STRUGGLE TO SURVIVE

The selections below offer contemporary perspectives on major trends in American business during the late nineteenth and early twentieth centuries. The first two sources provide first-hand explanations of specific organizational innovations in big business: bureaucratic management, pioneered by the nation's railroads, and vertical integration, exemplified by Andrew Carnegie's steel empire. The concluding documents present contrasting accounts of how smaller companies fared in the era of big business. The first business failed when it attempted to compete directly with the powerful Standard Oil trust. The experience of the second, however, illustrates how some smaller businesses flourished by finding a "niche" in the market, by utilizing advanced technology, and by adopting some of the accounting and managerial techniques perfected by their larger counterparts.

Railroads Change Their Management Methods

The New York & Erie Railroad and the Chicago, Burlington & Quincy were among America's leading trunk-line railroads of the mid- and late-nineteenth century. As they grew in size and complexity, railroads developed modern bureaucratic management methods, as this report from the superintendent of the New York & Erie Railroad illustrates. Selected from The Railroads: The Nation's First Big Business, Sources and Readings, *ed. Alfred D. Chandler, Jr. (New York, 1965), 101–3, 108, 118–20.*

Superintendent's Report

OFFICE GENERAL SUP'T N. Y. & ERIE R. R.
NEW YORK, March 25, 1856

HOMER RAMSDELL, ESQ.
PRESIDENT OF THE NEW YORK AND ERIE RAILROAD COMPANY:

SIR:

. . . *Theoretically,* other things being equal, a long road should be operated for a less cost per mile than a short one. This position is so clearly evident and so generally admitted, that its truth may be assumed without offering any arguments in support of it; and, notwithstanding the reverse so far as *practical* results are considered, has generally been the case, we must look to other causes than the mere difference in length of roads for a solution of the difficulty.

A Superintendent of a road fifty miles in length can give its business his personal attention, and may be almost constantly upon the line engaged in the direction of its details. . . . In the government of a road five hundred miles in length a very different state of things exists. Any system which might be applicable to the business and extent of a short road, would be found entirely inadequate to the wants of a long one; and I am fully convinced, that in the want of a system perfect in its details, properly adapted and vigilantly enforced, lies the true secret of their failure; and that this disparity of cost per mile in operating long and short roads, is not produced by *a difference in length,* but is in proportion to the perfection of the system adopted. . . .

In my opinion a system of operations, to be efficient and successful, should be such as to give to the principal and responsible head of the running department a complete daily history of details in all their minutiae. Without such supervision, the procurement of a satisfactory annual statement must be regarded as extremely problematical. . . . [I]t will scarcely be expected that we can at once adopt any plan of operations which will not require amendment and a reasonable time to prove its worth. A few general principles, however, may be regarded as settled and necessary in its formation, amongst which are:

1. A proper division of responsibilities.
2. Sufficient power conferred to enable the same to be fully carried out. . . .

3. The means of knowing whether such responsibilities are faithfully executed.

4. Great promptness in the report of all derelictions of duty, that evils may be at once corrected.

5. Such information, to be obtained through a system of daily reports and checks that will not embarrass principal officers, nor lessen their influence with their subordinates.

6. The adoption of a system, as a whole, which will not only enable the General Superintendent to detect errors immediately, but will also point out the delinquent.

Organization

The following comprises a list of the principal officers acting directly under the General Superintendent, with powers and duties arranged with reference to obtaining the results proposed.

1. Division and Branch Superintendents.
2. Masters of Engine and Car Repairs.
3. Car Inspectors.
4. General Freight Agent.
5. General Ticket Agent.
6. General Wood Agent.
7. Superintendent of Telegraph.
8. Foreman of Bridge Repairs.

For the more convenient working of the road it is now separated into Divisions. . . . The several Divisions and Branches are in charge of Superintendents, who are held responsible for the successful working of their respective Divisions, and for the maintenance of proper discipline and conduct of all persons employed thereon, except such as are in the employment of other officers acting under directions from this office. . . . They possess all the powers delegated by the organization to the General Superintendent, except in matters pertaining to the duties of General Ticket Agent, General Freight Agent, General Wood Agent, Telegraph management, and Engine and Car Repairs. . . .

All that is required to render the efforts of railroad companies in every respect equal to that of individuals, is a rigid system of personal accountability through every grade of service.

[DANIEL C. MCCALLUM]

Organization of Railroads (1885)

[A memorandum from Charles E. Perkins, president of the Chicago, Burlington & Quincy Railroad]

IN DECIDING the question of organization it will be necessary to consider two stages, so to speak, of railroad development. The first stage where the volume of traffic is not sufficient to make necessary or to warrant the highest degree of physical efficiency; and the second stage where the volume of traffic is so great as not only to warrant the expenditure, but also to make it economical to maintain the physical efficiency at the highest point.

Ordinarily the second stage will come only with increased mileage and while there are exceptional cases where roads of small fixed mileage acquire a large business by reason of their forming a link in a through line, or being in direct competition with one or more other roads between two commercial centers, they are so rare that it is best in considering the general question of organization to assume that a road in the second stage will be one of 500 miles or more in length. . . .

The responsible head of the operations of a road in the first stage is usually the general superintendent, a general manager only becoming necessary when the road has grown and business has so increased as to make it desirable to confine the general superintendent to the care of the machine alone. In the first stage he can and will himself look closely after his track and rolling stock as well as the traffic. In the second stage with the increase of traffic he will find his time and mind largely occupied with business questions, and also that he can draw the straight line of perfection to work to, and can safely trust to educated experts most of the questions relating to the efficient maintenance of the machine. The proper economical maintenance of a road in the first stage is not an exact science, while that of a road in the second stage is, and scientific methods which would be unnecessary and extravagant on the one may become necessary and economical on the other.

An organization for the management of a road in the first stage is comparatively simple. The duties of the president will be to advise the chief financial and accounting officer and the chief operating officer and also the purchasing and supply agents, to supervise and execute all important contracts, to conduct the most important negotiations, to specifically approve all expenditures chargeable to capital account before they are incurred, to supervise and direct the most important purchases of material and equipment, and to watch closely the results by means of reports from the heads of the two great departments of accounts and operations. . . .

An organization for the management of a large road in the second stage is on the other hand more complex. Here the duties of the president will be the same as in the first stage of development, but the amount of expenditure, the number of contracts, negotiations, reports, interviews, new schemes, etc., will have so largely increased that the president may require the aid of one vice president to assist him generally and possibly two or three personal assistants with fixed duties besides.

The departments of accounts and finances will also have grown so that a second vice president may be needed to look after the treasurer, the auditor and the secretary, three offices which in the first stage would be so combined as to be held by one, or at the most two, persons.

So of the departments of operation and construction. If the mileage is large it will be found expedient probably to put a third vice president at the head of this great department, which controls so largely the income and outgo. Under him again will be a general manager in direct charge of the daily details and taking the position occupied by the general superintendent in the first stage. The purchasing agent will act under the 3rd vice president and also especially in making large purchases of rails, rolling stock etc. directly under the president.

Andrew Carnegie and Carnegie Steel

Carnegie Steel was the largest industrial enterprise in the world in its day and formed the basis for the establishment of United States Steel. Vertical integration—the linking of all the steps in making steel in one company—gave Carnegie Steel production cost advantages over its less-well-integrated rivals. In his autobiography, Carnegie discussed how he organized his firm and some of the reasons he was successful. He stressed the importance of vertical integration, especially owning his own supplies of raw materials and his own pig iron furnaces (pig iron was then made into steel). Excerpt from Autobiography of Andrew Carnegie *(Boston, 1920), 220–22, 226–27.*

THE one vital lesson in iron and steel that I learned in Britain was the necessity for owning raw materials and finishing the completed article ready for its purpose. Having solved the steel-rail problem at the Edgar Thomson Works, we soon proceeded to the next step. The difficulties and uncertainties of obtaining regular supplies of pig iron compelled us to begin the erection of blast furnaces. Three of these were built. . . .

. . . We were the second firm in the United States to manufacture our own spiegel [a combination of iron, magnesium, and carbon], and the first, and for years the only, firm in America that made ferro-manganese. We had been dependent upon foreigners for a supply of this indispensable article, paying as high as eighty dollars a ton for it. . . .

We continued to develop our blast-furnace plant, every new one being a great improvement upon the preceding, until at last we thought we had arrived at a standard furnace. . . . The blast-furnace department was no sooner added than another step was seen to be essential to our independence and success. The supply of superior coke was a fixed quantity—the Connellsville field being defined. We found that we could not get on without a supply of the fuel essential to the smelting of pig iron; and a very thorough investigation of the question led us to the conclusion that the Frick Coke Company had not only the best coal and coke property, but that it had in Mr. Frick himself a man with a positive genius for its management. He had proved his ability by starting as a poor railway clerk and succeeding. In 1882 we purchased one half of the stock of this company, and by subsequent purchases from other holders we became owners of the great bulk of the shares.

There now remained to be acquired only the supply of iron stone. If we could obtain this we should be in the position occupied by only two or three of the European concerns. We thought at one time we had succeeded in discovering in Pennsylvania this last remaining link in the chain. We were misled, however, in our investment in the Tyrone region, and lost considerable sums as the result of our attempts to mine and use the ores of that section. . . .

To make a ton of steel one and a half tons of iron stone has to be mined, transported by rail a hundred miles to the Lakes, carried by boat hundreds of miles, transferred to cars, transported by rail one hundred and fifty miles to Pittsburgh; one and a half tons of coal must be mined and manufactured into coke and carried fifty-odd miles by rail; and one ton of limestone mined and carried one hundred and fifty miles to Pittsburgh. How then could steel be manufactured and sold without loss at three pounds for two cents? This, I confess, seemed to me incredible, and little less than miraculous, but it was so.

Opposition to Standard Oil

Not all Americans favored the development of big business; many saw large firms as threats to economic and political independence in the United States. Standard Oil, one of the first large industrial concerns, became the butt of much criticism. Independent refiners feared the competition from Standard Oil, whose costs of production were lower, resulting in lower consumer prices for goods such as kerosene. No independent producer was more outspoken than George Rice, who refined crude oil in Marietta, Ohio. Rice believed Standard Oil was using unethical means to destroy his business. In particular, Rice thought railroads colluded with Standard against him—charging less to carry Standard Oil's products than they charged him. Rice also accused Standard of undercutting his prices in an unethical fashion. Selected from "Testimony of George Rice, November 11, 1899" in the Industrial Commission: Preliminary Report on Trusts and Industrial Combinations *(Washington, 1900), 1:687, 704.*

"I am a citizen of the United States, born in the State of Vermont. Producer of petroleum for more than 30 years, and a refiner of same for 20 years, but my refinery has been shut down during the past 3 years, owing to the powerful and all-prevailing machinations of the Standard Oil Trust, in criminal collusion and conspiracy with the railroads to destroy my business of 20 years of patient industry, toil, and money in building up, wholly by and through unlawful freight discriminations. I have been driven from pillar to post, from one railway line to another, for 20 years, in the absolutely vain endeavor to get equal and just freight rates with the Standard Oil Trust, so as to be able to run my refinery at anything approaching a profit, but which I have been utterly unable to do. I have had to consequently shut down, with my business absolutely ruined and my refinery idle. . . .

Outside of rebates or freight discriminations I had no show with the Standard Oil trust, because of their unlawfully acquired monopoly, by which they could temporarily cut only my custom- ers' prices, and below cost, leaving the balance of the town, nine- tenths, uncut. This they can easily do without any appreciable harm to their general trade, and thus effectually wipe out all competition, as fully set forth. Standard Oil prices generally were so high that I could sell my goods 2 to 3 cents a gallon below their prices and make a nice profit, but these savage attacks and cuts upon my customers' goods, and their consequent loss, plainly showed to them their power for evil, and the uselessness to con- tend against such odds. . . ."

A Smaller Manufacturer:
The Buckeye Steel Castings Company

The success of small firms in the iron and steel industries was not limited to the Pittsburgh region. Buckeye Steel Castings Company of Columbus, Ohio, was formed as a partnership in 1881. It was one of some two hundred companies producing a variety of cast-iron goods for the local market in central Ohio. Buckeye did not produce a specialty product, which might have given it an advantage over its competitors, and it came very close to failing during the hard times of the mid-1880s. Buckeye Steel, however, was saved by the development of a specialty product for a niche market—an automatic railroad car coupler. Originally made out of cast iron in the 1890s, and later out of stronger cast steel, this technologi- cally sophisticated coupler gave Buckeye an edge over its competitors and allowed the company to break into the national market. New manage- ment techniques, especially new cost accounting practices, also made Buckeye more competitive.

In his approach to cost accounting, Buckeye's plant superintendent was among the most advanced managers of his day, pioneering in the inclusion of indirect and overhead expenses as part of his costs of produc-

tion, as illustrated by the following April 1905 financial report. Taken from Mansel G. Blackford, A Portrait Cast in Steel: Buckeye International and Columbus, Ohio, 1881–1980 *(Westport, Connecticut, 1982), 56–57.*

Costs of Production for April 1905

Metal in mould	$ 49,266
Moulding	17,730
Core-making	4,873
Annealing and cleaning	3,419
Fitting and finishing	15,725
Patterns and drafting	414
Repairs to plant and equipment	5,266
Locomotive service, heat, light, and power	2,779
Selling expense	2,755
Shipping expense	989
Office expense	698
Superintendence	527
Miscellaneous expenses	2,691
Salary of officers	838
Advertising	250
Insurance and taxes	350
Freight	2,347
Testing	259
Total	$ 111,179
Add for defective castings	2,241

. . . While not engaging in true capital accounting (few businesses had reached this level of sophistication), Buckeye's superintendent was figuring monthly charges for furnace repairs, building repairs, machinery repairs, and building depreciation as production costs as early as 1903. He explained his accounting methods in that year:

> For instance, we produced 18,500 tons of castings from the beginning of operations to Dec. 31, 1903. Total cost furnace repairs $12,129 = 70¢ per ton. Repairs of buildings about $3,000 = 20¢ per ton. Repairs of machinery about $6,000 = 35¢ per ton. Depreciation of buildings figures at 3% per year. Buildings are worth $200,000. Depreciation is $5,000 or 35¢ per ton.

Depreciation of machinery is figured at 10% per year. Machinery is worth $250,000. So depreciation comes to $25,000 or $1.40 per ton.

Questions

1. *What unique problems did managing a large railroad network entail? How did the New York & Erie Railroad attempt to meet these challenges?*
2. *How did Andrew Carnegie pursue vertical integration in his steel empire? In what ways did such a policy bring "order" and "efficiency" to Carnegie's operations?*
3. *Why, according to George Rice, did his oil refining business fail? Do you think his judgment of Standard Oil's business practices is fair? Why or why not? What specific techniques and strategies used by Buckeye Steel Castings allowed that company to survive? Explain.*

FURTHER READING

Alfred D. Chandler, Jr., Visible Hand: The Managerial Revolution in American Business *(Cambridge, 1977), examines the emergence of big businesses. Two good studies of Andrew Carnegie are Harold Livesay,* Andrew Carnegie and the Rise of Big Business *(Boston, 1975); and Joseph Frazier Wall,* Andrew Carnegie *(New York, 1970). Allan Nevins,* John D. Rockefeller: The Heroic Age of American Enterprise *(New York, 1940), and Ralph and Muriel Hidy,* Pioneering in Big Business, 1882–1921 *(New York, 1955), look at the history of Standard Oil. John N. Ingham,* Making Iron and Steel: Independent Mills in Pittsburgh, 1820–1920 *(Columbus, Ohio, 1991), and Philip Scranton,* Proprietary Capitalism: The Textile Manufacture at Philadelphia, 1800–1885 *(Cambridge, 1983), present industry studies emphasizing the roles smaller firms played in manufacturing.*

The Emergence
of the Modern
Labor Movement

Pamela J. Mills and Warren R. Van Tine

INTRODUCTION

The years between the Civil War and World War I witnessed the emergence of the modern American labor movement in response to the explosion of industrialism and the rise of big business. Yet the form and philosophy that the labor movement ultimately took was not preordained. Rather, three different "consciousnesses" competed for dominance during these years.

The first was a "community consciousness" best articulated by the Noble and Holy Order of the Knights of Labor in the 1870s and 1880s. Broadly speaking, the goal of the Knights was to return the worker to a position of equal citizenship and to restore social harmony within the community through a program of education and a range of reforms, the most radical of which was to temper competitive capitalism through the creation of producer cooperatives, in which workers could also be owners.

The second current seeking to represent workers during these years was that of "class consciousness" as articulated by the Socialist Labor Party beginning in the 1870s, the Socialist Party from the turn of the century, and most stridently the Industrial Workers of the World (IWW) from its founding in the 1900s through World War I. Unlike the Knights of Labor, such class-conscious workers thought that no degree of social harmony could exist as long as the capitalist system prevailed. To them, the working class's salvation would come through victory in the class war—either through electoral success at the polls or by physically driving the bosses out of their offices—followed by the creation of a worker-controlled cooperative commonwealth.

In the end, the labor organization that became the dominant voice of workers by 1910, the American Federation of Labor

(AFL), rejected the community vision of the Knights of Labor and the class struggle rhetoric of the IWW for a much more cautious "craft consciousness." The AFL shunned the efforts of the Knights and IWW to organize all workers regardless of race or gender and built a closed structure of largely white, male, skilled craftsmen. Its goal was not community rejuvenation or social revolution, but simply gaining shorter hours, better working conditions, and higher pay for its members. Dubbed "business unionism" or "pure and simple" unionism, the AFL avoided extensive political involvement or entangling links with social reformers. Basically, it accepted the American social and economic system as it was with all of its disparities and simply sought a bigger piece of the pie for those it represented.

ESTABLISHING A PHILOSOPHY
FOR AMERICAN LABOR

The three perspectives about what a labor movement should be or do were not just philosophical speculations, but were deeply rooted in the adherents' own life experiences. John H. M. Laslett links the three forms of unionism competing for dominance in the late nineteenth and early twentieth centuries to the lives of their three most articulate advocates, Terence Powderly of the Knights of Labor, "Big Bill" Haywood of the IWW, and Samuel Gompers of the AFL. Laslett is quick to point out that such an approach, while illuminating the social basis for each outlook, does not explain why the "craft conscious" AFL prevailed over the "community conscious" Knights of Labor or the "class conscious" IWW. For the answer to that question one must turn to the role of the state, the activities of business, and the texture of American culture and society. Abridged from John H. M. Laslett, "Establishing a Philosophy for American Labor," in Men, Women, and Issues in American History, *eds. Howard H. Quint and Milton Cantor (Homewood, Illinois, 1975), 2:67–87.*

Historians have frequently puzzled over just why and when it was that the dominant labor ideology in America, unlike that in most European countries, became limited to the narrow, pragmatic, job-conscious form of trade unionism exemplified in the history of the American Federation of Labor and in the life of its most famous leader, Samuel Gompers, who was President with

Excerpts from "Establishing a Philosophy for American Labor" by John H. M. Laslett reprinted from *Men, Women and Issues in American History,* Volume 2, Howard H. Quint and Milton Cantor, editors, published by Dorsey Press, Inc., 1975. Copyright © 1975 by the Dorsey Press. Reprinted by permission of Wadsworth Publishing Co.

only one year's interruption from 1886 (the year of its founding) to his death in 1924. They have generally attributed the growth of the AF of L's hegemony to broad national developments that took place in the United States during the last quarter of the 19th century. These developments, which in themselves had little to do with the labor movement, were initially accomplished by a supposed psychology of abundance, induced by widespread opportunities for self-employment and the presence of an open frontier. Later there was a shift to a psychology of scarcity induced by urbanization, mass immigration, and the declining independence of the skilled artisan. Only relatively recently have historians troubled to ask themselves whether any other form of labor ideology existed in America, still less inquired as to its extent or popularity. . . .

. . . [T]he job-conscious philosophy of the American Federation of Labor won out over both that of the Knights of Labor and the IWW [Industrial Workers of the World], at least until the 1930s. The Federation's membership also became much larger than either of its rivals. The Knights of Labor tumbled from its peak of 750,000 in 1886 to relative insignificance by 1900; and the IWW . . . never acquired more than approximately 50,000 members at any one time. The AF of L, on the other hand, had organized two million workers by 1917, four million by 1921; and thereafter its numbers never fell below two and a half or three million, rising rapidly to more than six million in the 1930s under the competitive stimulus of the CIO [Congress of Industrial Organizations]. But these developments had far more to do with specific events taking place both within the labor movement and in American society at particular points in time . . . than they did with any overarching or readily predictable historical design. Neither the individual lives of [Terence V.] Powderly, Gompers, or [William D. "Big Bill"] Haywood, nor even a brief survey of the organizations they led, can of course tell us anything absolutely conclusive about the reasons for these historical developments. Nevertheless, they can point to some highly important trends.

Although the broad, producer-oriented tradition of the Knights of Labor was both older and more deeply embedded in the history of American reform movements than either the revolutionary syndicalism of the IWW or the narrow business unionism of the AF of L, institutionally speaking it was the AF of L that appeared first. . . .

Samuel Gompers, principal founder of the American Federation of Labor, . . . was born on January 27, 1850, in the impoverished Spitafields [Spitalfields] silk-weaving district of east London. . . . Gompers at the age of ten was apprenticed to his father's own trade of cigarmaking. . . .

. . . [In 1863] the Gompers family, oppressed by poverty and a growing number of children, . . . migrated from London's east end to its equivalent on the lower East Side of New York. . . . For 18 months young Samuel helped his father roll and cut cigars in the combination kitchen, living room and workshop which, aside from a single bedroom, was all that the Gompers family could afford. At the age of 17 Gompers married Sophia Julian, another London-born Jewish immigrant, moved out of his parents' home to start a family of his own, and began to look about him. Employed now in a larger cigar factory instead of in a tenement workshop—and avidly studying history, science, and economics at night school—Gompers attended debates at Cooper Union on the nature and purposes of the labor movement. He sat around the long cigarmaking tables discussing them with his friend Sam Prince and his mentor Ferdinand Laurell, and in the winter of 1874 joined the great Tompkins Square demonstration of the unemployed. Six months later he was elected president of the largest Cigarmakers International Union [CMIU] local in New York City, Local 144.

The ensuing five years were fateful ones for Gompers, for the CMIU and, as it later turned out, for the American labor movement as a whole. During the depression of the mid-1870s, employers in New York's cigar industry had transferred much of their production from the larger shops to tenement houses, which were much more difficult to organize and where near-starvation wages were usually paid. In response Gompers, Adolph Strasser, and Sam Prince among others led a general strike of New York cigarmakers in the fall of 1877. Their goal was to abolish the tenement house system. From seven to ten thousand men walked out, supported by cigarmakers across the country. Gompers, dismissed from his job, pawned everything but Sophie's wedding ring and moved into even cheaper quarters in Brooklyn. But still the strike was lost. Leaders of Local 144 were finally convinced of the need to reform the CMIU along English lines.

Up to this point the union had admitted rollers and bunchers as well as skilled cigarmakers. There was no uniformity in dues or initiation fees, and strike benefits were paid only when there happened to be money available. At the 1879 convention of the CMIU, Gompers with Strasser in support, secured adoption of a wide range of changes designed to transform the union from a confederation of loose, sovereign locals into a tightly knit, financially sound, and stable institution primarily serving the interests of the skilled. The changes were most significant and suggestive: high dues to build a financial reserve during depressions; strike, sick, and death benefits that would provide a financial incentive for permanent membership; centralized control, especially in authorizing strikes; and, perhaps most important of all, the English principle of equalization of funds making money from one local available to others in time of stress. . . .

. . . Most of the craft unions that were later to establish the AF of L had suffered severely during the depression of the mid-1870s. . . . Moreover, in the early 1880s knowledgeable observers of the labor movement were understandably more impressed with the rapidly rising star of the Knights of Labor—already recognized then as a broadly-based national labor federation embracing unskilled workers, small town employees and even some farmers, as well as skilled artisans—than they were with the weak, fragmented Federation of Organized Trades and Labor Unions (the AF of L's immediate predecessor), which could boast the support of only a few, scattered east coast unions. Equally promising, at this early stage at least, was the short, but dignified and scholarly-looking figure of the man who would become the Knights's second and most famous Grand Master Workman, Terence V. Powderly. In three short years he had risen from the obscurity of a blacklisted employee on the Delaware, Lackawanna and Western Railroad to become Mayor of Scranton, Pennsylvania and then, in 1879 at the astonishingly young age of 30, he was chosen national leader of the Knights of Labor.

Although born on January 27, 1849, only 12 months before Samuel Gompers, and experiencing much of the same poverty and deprivation in his early years, this difference of one year symbolized a gap of at least a generation in terms of the overall development of the American labor movement. Gompers'[s] formative years had been spent amid urban craftsmen struggling to defend their skills; and the solutions he advocated to the labor problem, although narrow and ultimately stulifying [stultifying] in their social consequences, appeared essentially modern and forward-looking at the time they were first advocated. Powderly's youth, by contrast, was spent in the rural atmosphere of the small, isolated, railroad town of Carbondale, Pennsylvania. . . .

Land and currency reform, temperance, third-party politics, and a deep but essentially utopian and backward-looking commitment to rescuing the "independent producer" from the onrush of post-Civil War capitalism were thus the dominating influences in Terence V. Powderly's early life. He had left home at the age of 13 to become a railroad machinist, a member of the Machinists and Blacksmiths Union and, in 1877, Corresponding Secretary of District Assembly 5 in the Scranton-Reading area. In varying degree these ideas were also reflected in the national policies of the Knights of Labor. So, too, was a broad ecumenicalism with regard to organizing the great mass of working people, irrespective of race, occupation, and skill. The K of L made far greater efforts to implement ideals of social equality among its members than most American labor organizations, either before or since. . . . Also a far wider variety of occupations—among them farmers and small tradesmen as well as semi-skilled and unskilled laborers—were encouraged to join both the "mixed" and the "trade" Local Assemblies of the Knights. Few of the aforementioned were permitted to enter into the skilled unions of the AF of L. For Powderly, as for many Knights, the slogan "An injury to one is an injury to all" was taken more seriously than either before or since in the American labor movement.

The corollary to this broad, humanitarian approach—and probably the most important ingredient in Powderly's social philosophy—was his hostility toward the wages system. "The aim of the Knights of Labor—properly understood—is to make each man his own employer," Powderly repeatedly stated. But this antipathy toward capitalism had no Marxism in it. Indeed Powderly was contemptuous of most socialists. . . . Unlike Haywood, Powderly was opposed to strikes or revolutionary violence as a means of solving labor disputes. And unlike Gompers (who was also strongly anti-Marxist, although for very different reasons), he had little understanding of or sympathy with a purely economic analysis of society.

Accompanying Powderly's antipathy to class conflict and his belief in education as a panacea for numerous social ills went an abiding faith in both producers' and consumers' cooperation, and this despite repeated practical disappointments. Such cooperation was a means of subverting the wage system and of returning to an economy more consistent with the human scale. . . . Thus at the first General Assembly after his election as Grand Master Workman . . . , Powderly insisted that the delegates eschew such relatively "petty questions" as higher wages and shorter hours, and embark instead "on a system of cooperation, which will make every man his own master, and every man his own employer." Almost none of the cooperatives established by the K of L succeeded. . . . By the end of the decade inefficiency, lack of money, and the strong opposition of many elements in the business community had forced the Knights's leadership to abandon cooperation as the major tool of social reconstruction. Instead, they placed their hopes on organization, education, and third-party politics, and in particular on the program of the People's Party.

. . . The ethos of the Knights prompted resistance to the idea that American workers had become permanent wage earners who needed full-time labor leaders to guide them. Certainly it was no discredit to Powderly that he sought to maintain in his own life a position as an "independent producer." Less easy to condone, however, was his quixotic policy toward strikes. . . . Powderly, it is true, personally disapproved of the use of the strike weapon. . . . But his naive belief in arbitration as the only proper means for settling industrial disputes led him to ignore the fact that employers, then as now, rarely concede anything to the workers unless forced to do [so]. Finally, his extremely ill-timed attempt to discipline the strikers in the middle of the 1886 walkouts brought grass-roots anger and resentment. . . .

In turn, these losses greatly strengthened the hand of those skilled workers in the Order who had never approved the Knights's policy of encouraging Mixed Assemblies (enrolling all of the workers in a given area into one local irrespective of occupation or skill). Having joined the Knights only because their own craft unions had been temporarily overwhelmed by the mid-1870s depression, these skilled workers now seized upon the opportunity presented by the defeat of the Gould and Chicago stockyard strikes to demand the establishment of Trade Assemblies (groups of workers defined occupationally rather than geographically) and to reject the larger organizational philosophy of the Knights. With the sudden rise in K of L membership early in 1886, numerous craft unions . . . accused the Knights of stealing their members. Although accounts of such raiding were undoubtedly exaggerated on both sides, one such incident led to open warfare between them and ultimately to the downfall of the Knights. The main protagonist in the struggle was none other than Samuel Gompers'[s] Cigarmakers Local 144.

. . . In the ensuing fight for control over the labor movement the tide ran quickly against the Knights. Employer hostility, the Order's virtually uniform lack of strike success after 1886, and the attempt by Mixed Assemblies to prevent their members from joining the craft unions alienated many of the skilled. Long-standing organizational weaknesses, the unwarranted assumption by the public that the K of L had supported the Haymarket riot of May 1886, and the depression of the mid-1890s did the rest. By 1895 the once-proud Knights had been reduced to less than 75,000 members, the bulk of them coming from the hard core of small-town mechanics, shop-keepers, petty employers and farmers to whom the organization's all-inclusive producer philosophy had made its first and most forceful appeal.

. . . Faced by rising criticism of his authoritarian handling of the Knights's internal affairs and by his inability or unwillingness to delegate responsibility to other officials, Powderly was forced out of office in 1893 by an alliance of western agrarians and eastern socialists. . . .

With Powderly out of the way and the Knights of Labor in rapid decline, President Gompers of the AF of L . . . proceeded to institutionalize at the national level the principles of high-dues-high-benefits, pure-and-simple, craft unionism that Gompers had first developed during his years with Local 144 in New York. . . .

Soon after Gompers'[s] confirmation as President of the AF of L in 1886, he began that stream of articles, speeches, and addresses to labor conventions that would be reiterated continually over the next 30 years. All upheld the virtues of craft unionism. . . . Gompers accepted the inevitability of conflict between employers and employees owing to their divergent economic interests, and he vigorously upheld the necessity for strikes. Indeed, . . . as a young man he was in many respects a Marxist. . . .

. . . [T]he radical implications in Gompers'[s] class view of American society were progressively whittled down by two basic considerations. The first of these was a growing preoccupation with dividing up control over the terms of employment of the purely urban labor force between the AF of L and the employers. . . . This preoccupation evolved into a view of the labor movement as defensive and job-conscious rather than militant and class-conscious. Such a view not only ignored farmers and other petty-bourgeois elements but also made no attempt to challenge capitalist ownership of the means of production. Gompers'[s] second consideration was based on the changes in technology, which increasingly threatened the position of industry's hand-skill workers. In response to this development, the AF of L limited its interests still further, ignoring not only farmers and petty-bourgeois elements but semi-skilled and unskilled workers as well. The reasons for these changes . . . derive essentially from the fact that the AF of L was born out of a reaction against the broad and inclusive character of the Knights of Labor, which was understandably unwilling to devote more than a limited share of its resources to defending the interests of the skilled worker.

. . . Labor lost one strike after another in the 1890s. These disputes involved both unskilled and semi-skilled workers as well as craftsmen—steelmen at Homestead in 1892, railroad workers at Pullman in 1894, and coal miners nationwide in the same year. Numerous other critics joined Socialists in attacking the AF of L's exclusive preoccupation with the interests of skilled workers as narrow, self-serving, and ultimately futile. The introduction of mass-production techniques, they argued, with its attendant destruction of craft lines, had already placed the unskilled into competition with the skilled for a wide range of jobs. The influx of new immigrants from southern and from eastern Europe that took place in the 1880s simply worsened matters. The proper answer was to open up the unions to the entire labor force and not, incidentally, on the basis of the Mixed Assemblies of the old Knights of Labor. Rather there should be modern industrial unions—with each incorporating all of the wage workers in an industry into a single, coherent, and militant mass union. . . .

It was in this context that a second great labor leader arose to challenge the hegemony of pure-and-simple trade unionism— William D. Haywood of the Industrial Workers of the World. . . . On June 27, 1905, at Brand's Hall in Chicago, the 36-year-old Haywood—a tall, powerful figure of a man, of ample girth but with a handsome face set off by a patch over his right eye (the result of a childhood accident)—brought the IWW's 200 founding delegates to their feet in a ringing denunciation of the labor philosophy of the AF of L. "The American Federation of Labor," he argued, "which presumes to be the labor movement of this country, is not a working class movement." "It includes organizations which prohibit the initiation of a . . . colored man; that prohibit the conferring of the obligation of foreigners." And, he continued, "The Industrial Workers of the World will be formed, based, and founded on the class struggle, having but one object and purpose and that is to bring the workers of this country into the possession of the full value of the product of their toil." Following Haywood's advice the IWW adopted a form of organization . . . in which all American workers—skilled and unskilled, native and immigrant, black and white, and even Orientals, an earlier target of labor's hostility in the western metal mines—were to be grouped into five main "industrial departments," with low dues and free, universal union transfer cards. The whole organization would be under the general aegis of a central IWW administration in Chicago.

Bill Haywood had taken a considerable time to come to this revolutionary position. Born in Salt Lake City, Utah, in 1869—20 years after either of our other two labor leaders and less susceptible, therefore, to labor ideologies that had been fashionable before the Civil War—Haywood's early life nevertheless bore more resemblance to Powderly's than it did to that of Gompers. . . .[He] acquired his first knowledge of the labor movement from Pat Reynolds, an Irish fellow-worker who had earlier been a member of the Knights. Like Powderly, Haywood was a brilliant orator, while at the same time being more direct in his language and much more forceful. Although well-read, Haywood was in many respects anti-intellectual. Essentially a man of action, he was at his best when addressing a crowd, debating with opponents, or leading a strike demonstration, as in the famous Lawrence textile strike of 1913. There was no air of the effete intellectual about him, still less that of the pompous labor bureaucrat.

And yet, like Gompers, Haywood was also a good administrator. The period between 1914 and 1917, when he was working full time for the IWW, was one of the few in which the organization achieved a modicum of stability. To be sure, he also had qualities that would have shocked the Victorian moral code of his elders in the labor movement. An unhappy marriage to Nevada Jane, a crippled, care-worn, frontier woman, frequently drove him to the solace offered by saloons and brothels. Indeed, in January 1906, when he was arrested—along with President Charles A.

Moyer and Charles A. Pettibone of the Western Federation of Miners [WFM]—on trumped-up charges of murdering ex-Governor Steunenberg of Idaho, Pinkerton detectives found him in a Denver house of prostitution, virtually within walking distance of his family home. Despite these lapses as well as an often-exaggerated reputation as a no-good layabout and as a sinister subversive, Haywood at his best was a hero to ordinary working people in a way that Powderly and Gompers never were. . . .

. . . [I]t is paradoxical that he first came to the fore as an efficient trade union administrator. . . . What in fact turned the moderate Socialist reformer into a militant and a rebel was the ruthless, bitter, and—from the WFM point of view—disastrous 1903-1904 Cripple Creek strike. Before walking out, over a matter that in its origin was nothing more alarming than the eight-hour day, the WFM locals had offered to negotiate with the gold mine owners. But the Colorado Mine Owners Association, in conjunction with state Governor James H. Peabody and numerous Citizens Alliances, were determined not only to categorize the WFM as an un-American, seditious and even as a criminal organization but also to smash it. In a naked display of power the State sent in militia, made illegal searches and seizures, and forcibly deported over 400 miners from Colorado. Deputies openly attacked Haywood himself on the streets of Cripple Creek. He wounded one of them severely, but was freed soon afterward since the deputies were clearly to blame.

The Cripple Creek strike represented the culmination of a long series of bitterly fought struggles that had all the characteristics of class war. It was a turning point in Haywood's career just as the 1877 general strike of cigarmakers in New York City had been for Samuel Gompers. . . . Cripple Creek prompted Haywood to reject conventional labor tactics in favor of militant industrial unionism as the only proper form of labor organization. . . . It also caused him—and many of those who would join him in founding the IWW 18 months later—to doubt even the value of Socialist political action as a means of affording protection to the worker. Again, interestingly enough, Haywood, like Gompers, rejected Socialist politics. . . . [Haywood] had come to see the union not as providing a substitute for the liberal state, but as offering the means for fashioning a revolutionary alternative to it. The only direct experience of state power for many Wobblies [nickname of the IWW] had been at the receiving end of a policeman's club; but they nonetheless feared that even members of their own class, if elected to political office would become corrupted by participation in capitalist politics. Hence direct action in the form of strikes, demonstrations, sit-downs, and even sabotage (although the degree to which the IWW actually practiced violence was predictably exaggerated by the press) was preferred to voting as the only sure means of asserting economic control over the means of production. In theory at least, the culmination was the general social strike.

The character of its membership influenced the IWW's hostility towards political action. Before 1908 its members were largely western metal miners or disaffected AF of L members working in industrial occupations. Following the withdrawal of the WFM from the IWW in 1908, IWW membership came to be drawn, with some exceptions, from a sub-proletariat of lumbermen, wheat farmers, migratory fruit pickers, unnaturalized immigrants or southern Negroes. Since many of these workers could not vote, the IWW's ideological move towards syndicalism was thereby reinforced and encouraged.

. . . President Gompers and other AF of L leaders . . . denounced the IWW as a dual union. . . . The IWW's goal, they charged, was not to promote industrial unionism, but "to direct, pervert and disrupt the whole labor movement." If the trade union movement were to be based on the fatuous "scheme" of industrial organization, Gompers told a Pittsburgh audience in August 1905, "the tinker, tailor, and the candlestick maker would legislate upon every minute detail affecting the interests of the workers." In other words, the labor movement would revert back to nothing more than "the old K of L idea." . . .

Gompers'[s] assertion . . . that success for the IWW would have simply meant a reversion to the "old K of L idea" was wide of the mark. True, the IWW reasserted the Knights's old spirit of solidarity among all the workers, its antipathy towards craft-union exclusiveness, and its hostility toward capitalism as an institution. But it looked forward to a revolutionary general strike as the ultimate means of changing capitalist society and not backward to the recreation of a pre-industrial order. It upheld direct action and even violence as the catalysts of change, rather than arbitration and political action. And although its membership was organized into general unions that were more like the Mixed Assemblies of the K of L than the industrial unions later organized by the CIO, it accepted fundamental Marxist notions concerning the inevitability both of industrialization and of revolution. It did *not* seek to resurrect utopian ideas of a cooperative universe.

Bill Haywood's leadership may be measured by his degree of responsibility for the IWW's progressive retreat into the fringes of the labor force. . . . Nonetheless, it is less easy to assess the role of leadership in contributing to the IWW successes and failures than it is about either the Federation or the Knights. First of all, it was far more of a grass-roots kind of organization than either of the other two, thus tending to reduce the role of national leaders. Moreover, the IWW, almost from the first, was subject to such hostility from the press, from employers, from state agencies, and from Gompers and the AF of L itself (the AF of L willingly joined in the federal government's wartime persecution of the organization as subversive), that it is dubious whether any leader could have significantly altered the IWW's place in history.

And yet in Haywood's very first speech to the 1905 founding convention, he himself appeared to reflect the Wobblies' ambivalence about their role which was to dog the IWW in its subsequent development. "We are here for the purpose of organizing . . . an organization broad enough to take in all the working class," he asserted, a purpose which, had the IWW been allowed to carry it out successfully, might perhaps have generated a mass labor movement of industrial unionists two generations before the CIO appeared. "What I want to see from this organization," however, Bill Haywood added, "is an uplifting of the fellow that is down in the gutter." Organizing fellows down in the gutter is what the IWW came largely to be remembered for. It was a noble ideal, but it certainly did not make for organizational stability.

. . . Biographical sketches such as these can illuminate the movements out of which the dominant labor ideology in America ultimately came. But they do not, of course, tell why the conservative AF of L officials, despite the increasingly anachronistic character of many of their views, managed to retain control of the labor movement of this country until the 1930s. History after all, especially the history of social movements, is more than a record of the actions of great men. . . .

. . . [P]rofound internal developments in the nature of American society also determined labor's choices. The creation and preservation of a form of labor aristocracy was central to Gompers'[s] efforts. . . . [Organized challenges from common workers] did not succeed in America—at least insofar as such can be seen in the efforts of the leaders of the Knights of Labor and the IWW. This failure can be attributed partly to Gompers'[s] own good fortune and astuteness, and partly to weaknesses of leadership displayed by Powderly and Haywood. But it was due more to the presence of other factors—government and big business preference for AF of L unionism; the suppression of left-wing alternatives; and, perhaps most importantly of all, the ethnic and racial fragmentation of the labor force.

Questions

1. *How did the differing backgrounds of Gompers, Powderly, and Haywood shape their consciousness about what a labor movement should be?*
2. *Which approach to unionism—community, class, or craft—do you think would have best met the workers' needs? Why?*
3. *What reasons does Laslett give for the AFL becoming the dominant voice of the American labor movement by World War I?*

THREE APPROACHES TO UNIONISM

In the late nineteenth and early twentieth centuries, workers in America's mines, mills, and shops sought ways to protect themselves from the forces unleashed by the rise of industrial capitalism. On the job, they found their skills diluted, their work routinized, the workplace impersonalized, their security ravaged by frequent layoffs and unemployment, and themselves alienated from the products of their own labor. In the community, workers confronted poor housing, sanitation, and recreational facilities. They also experienced increased marginalization as a solidifying class structure transferred an even greater share of political, economic, and social power to the hands of the upper class and its middle-class allies.

Workers responded to these changes in a myriad of ways. Many took individualistic action, most notably moving from job to job or place to place hoping to find a better situation. Thus, the rates of both job turnover and geographic mobility were every bit as high for working-class people in the Gilded Age and Progressive Era as they are today. At times, individualistic-minded workers would temporarily band together out of frustration and strike an employer. (Most strikes before the 1930s were not initiated by labor unions.) Far more often than not, however, such efforts would fail. Any nascent organization would collapse, leaders would face employer blacklists, and the followers would as likely as not move on to another job in another place.

A small but significant minority of workers, however, recognized that the only meaningful way to improve their lot was to form permanent labor unions. (Until the 1930s, union members never represented more than ten percent of the nation's workforce.) Yet these workers were not united on what the focus and purpose of unions should be. Broadly speaking, three perspectives on unionism competed for dominance from the 1870s to the 1920s, each nominally represented by a national organization.

The Noble and Holy Order of the Knights of Labor, founded in 1869, was the most significant organization of workers until the 1890s. The order clearly sought to perpetuate the more egalitarian, producer-oriented society that supposedly existed in the pre-Civil War era. To do this, it sought to change the hearts and minds of the people—to establish a counterculture to the emerging material culture linked to the rise of industrial capitalism. The Knights sought to replace competitiveness with cooperation, strife with harmony, denigration with character (thus its emphasis on temperance). Believing that "An injury to one is the concern of all," it opened its doors to all producers—skilled as well as unskilled, black as well as white, women as well as men. The Knights' vision of a cooperative alternative to competitive capitalism and the Knights' inclusiveness, however, were not accepted by all who flocked into their ranks, particularly during the turbulent times of the mid-1880s. Whereas the Knights offered a dream of a better world, many members only wanted better conditions in this one and abandoned the organization and resumed their individualistic strategy when higher pay, shorter hours, and improvements on the job were not forthcoming.

Skilled workers, particularly in the building and printing trades but also in other crafts such as cigarmaking, were never very comfortable with the Knights' inclusiveness or idealistic vision. Skilled workers had been among the first workers to form unions for the purpose of addressing specific issues—wages, hours, working conditions—rather than broad social reform. In 1886, this approach gained a national forum when several national craft unions formed the American Federation of Labor as an umbrella organization to challenge the Knights' intrusive recruitment of skilled workers.

Under the leadership of Samuel Gompers, the AFL sought to advance the interests of skilled craftsmen, both against technological changes and de-skilling brought on by industrial capitalism and against competition from less-skilled workers whose ranks were surging because of the forces of immigration and urbanization. Gompers accepted industrialization as a given and simply wanted to gain a larger share of the benefits from that system for the AFL's membership. He had no desire to restructure society, to reach out to the truly marginalized and dispossessed. Indeed, he tried to keep the AFL from getting too tied to various reform movements or politics. Such an approach has been labeled "job conscious unionism," "pure-and-simple unionism," and even "business unionism." In 1893, quizzed by a congressional committee over what labor wanted, Gompers's answer was simply, "More!" This was a vision held by most skilled workers (and probably most workers not even affiliated with the AFL), thus, providing a framework that allowed the American Federation of Labor to survive.

Just as the idealism and inclusiveness of the Knights brought the AFL forward as a challenger, the pragmatism and exclusiveness of the AFL also brought forth the challenge of the Industrial Workers of the World. The IWW was born in the Rocky Mountain West in the midst of an era in which silver, copper, and lead miners were reduced to working for giant industrial concerns. It was nurtured in the East among unskilled immigrant steel, textile, and rubber workers. The IWW matured amidst the western lumber and agricultural laborers, as an inclusive organization that shunned the pretenses of skilled craftsmen and sought to organize all workers as a class.

Sparked to life by employer violence such as the Coeur d'Alene strike and the Colorado Labor Wars, the IWW saw workers trapped in a class conflict with industrial capitalists. Only when workers united as a class, took control of the factories and mines from the capitalists, and instituted a cooperative commonwealth would a truly egalitarian society be established. Like the Knights, the IWW was both visionary and inclusive, opening membership to anyone regardless of their sex, ethnicity, or job. Unlike the Knights, however, the IWW advocated confrontation and strife (and walked a hazy line around the issue of violence). The IWW rejected the idea that conditions could be changed through electoral politics, not only because so many of its members were disenfranchised but also because it saw the political process as firmly controlled by the hidden hand of capitalism. Rather, it advocated that workers directly confront the boss at the job site and in the pocketbook, through strikes and sabotage. Such militant rhetoric—which far exceeded the IWW's actual deeds—provided the justification needed for both private business and local, state, and federal repression, particularly during World War I and its immediate aftermath. Moreover, the radical rhetoric and the general disapproval by mainstream society of the IWW deterred most workers from joining the organization or staying with it too long. Although the IWW lingered on after 1920, its importance to the American labor movement, like that of the Knights of Labor, which faded from the scene after 1900, had ended. The main organization claiming to speak for American workers during the 1920s was the least representative of all, the American Federation of Labor.

Different Visions:
The "Rule of Perfect Equality
Among Men"—The Knights of Labor

Terence V. Powderly was the Grand Master Workman of the Knights of Labor during its heyday in the 1880s and early 1890s. As leader of the Knights, he felt his primary task was to educate the membership on the true purpose of the Order. In his autobiography, Powderly discusses some of the practices and rituals of the Knights, hinting at the broader religious and social values that underlay the Knights's perspective. Abridged from The Path I Trod: The Autobiography of Terence V. Powderly, *ed. Harry J. Carman, Henry David and Paul N. Guthrie. (New York, 1940) 47, 49–57, 59–60.*

From 1869 up to 1878, the Knights of Labor had no platform, preamble or declaration of principles, and the extreme secrecy surrounding its movements gave to organizers a latitude of expression in explaining the purposes of the order that was limited only by the imagination of the organizer.... [The early organizers' goal was to establish] the "rule of perfect equality among men" when that organization became strong enough to successfully champion the cause of oppressed humanity. . . .

To the Knights of Labor, all who toiled might find entrance and a welcome. The scavenger doing his work on the street was admitted on exactly the same terms of equality as the highest priced or most skilled artisan. The name of the Order was never printed and seldom spoken. Only in the assembly was it mentioned and then only that the newly initiated might know the name of the Order he had joined. . . .

When a candidate was presented for initiation, he was asked three questions. First: "Do you believe in God, the Creator and Universal Father of all?" Second: "Do you obey the Universal Ordinance of God, in gaining your bread by the sweat of your brow?" Third: "Are you willing to take a solemn vow binding you to secrecy, obedience, and mutual assistance?" . . .

The Worthy Foreman [presiding officer of the local assembly] when the candidate came before him would say:

> In the beginning God ordained that man should labor, not as a curse, but as a blessing; not as a punishment, but as a means of development, physically, mentally, morally, and has set thereunto his seal of approval in the rich increase and reward. By labor is brought forth the kindly fruits of the earth in rich abundance for our sustenance and comfort; by labor (not exhaustive) is promoted health of body and strength of mind, labor garners the priceless stores of wisdom and knowledge. . . .
>
> In all the multifarious branches of trade, capital has its combinations, and whether intended or not, it crushes the manly hopes of labor and tramples poor humanity in the dust. We mean no conflict with legitimate enterprise, no antagonism to necessary capital, but men in their haste and greed, blinded by self-interest, overlook the interests of others and sometimes even violate the rights of those they deem helpless. We mean to uphold the dignity of labor, to affirm the nobility of all who live in accordance with the ordinance of God, "in the sweat of thy brow shalt thou eat bread." We mean to create a healthy public opinion on the subject of labor (the only creator of values or capital), and the justice of its receiving a full, just share of the values or capital it has created. We shall with all our strength support laws made to harmonize the interests of labor and capital for labor alone gives life and value to capital, and also those laws which tend to lighten the exhaustiveness of toil. We shall use every lawful and honorable means to procure and retain employ for one another, coupled with just and fair remuneration, and should accident or misfortune befall one of our number, render such aid as lies within our power to give without inquiring his country or his creed. Without approving of general strikes among artisans, yet should it become justly necessary to enjoin an oppressor, we will protect and aid any of our number who thereby may suffer loss and as opportunity offers, extend a helping hand to all branches of honorable toil. . . .

It was one of the aims of the Order to cause every member to know how to "write his name in full" [on a membership card] ... instead of being obliged to make his mark in the presence of witnesses who might deceive him as to the purport of the instrument he signed. I had the evidence of over one hundred men in Scranton that the lesson taught by that card, one of the first card systems, influenced them to take a course in writing so that they could not only write but read their names and other things beside.

... [I]n this organization we were to understand that while we had rights to battle for, we owed duties to our fellow men as well. We could claim no right for self that did not carry with it an obligation and a call to do our duty by and to others.

... We admitted all men and taught them the significance and value of organized, coöperative effort. Workers who up to that time dreamed that their callings could not be classed as skilled were taught to know that there is no unskilled labor.... All trades, all callings came into the Knights of Labor, and, catching the inspiration born of touching elbows in a common cause, they called their fellow toilers together to meet with them at the dawn of the day of specialty. We believed one man to be as good as another and entitled to the same "rights, privileges, and benefits" in life. Maybe we placed a too implicit faith in what the Declaration of Independence held out to us. Perhaps some lingering, belated wind from the scenes of the early days of the French Revolution carried to our minds the thought that equality could be won, so far as rights and duties went, without reddening our record with a single drop of human blood....

When we vitalized and gave to the world the declaration of principles of our old Industrial Brotherhood we held out the chart of truth as we saw it. For doing so we were derided, sneered at, ridiculed, laughed at, and when we caused this nation to stop and think, those who were aiming at making everything subservient to wealth and corporate power changed their attitude and began to abuse us.

... We had no organizers, paid or otherwise. Every member carried a message to his fellows, and in a short time assemblies began to grow and flourish....

I tell you of this happening [a railroad strike in 1877] that you may know something about the hardships endured by the pioneers of the labor movement. We walked, daylight and dark. We ate, not when we were hungry, but when and where we could get it. We shared our homes, tables, and beds with each other. I often had two or three Knights of Labor with me over night. We slept in shanties, ash pits, freight cars, or wherever night caught us after our work. Why did we do it? Because it was necessary and we wanted to be of use. . . .

We have been compared to the early crusaders, but I cannot think of a comparison less fitting. A crusader is, or was, a fellow who dressed himself up in a suit of sheet iron clothing, pulled an iron skillet over his head, drew on a pair of steel, knuckle-jointed gloves, climbed up on a horse that always looked too fat to run, set a crowbar-looking thing called a lance into a metal-lined pocket in the saddle, and, in company with a lot of other animated hardware stores rode out of town "on their gaily caparisoned steeds" in the direction of the Holy Land to rescue the tomb of the Saviour. . . .

The Knights of Labor aimed at rescuing man himself from a tomb, the tomb of ignorance. The aim was to roll away the stone from that tomb that he might know that moral worth and not wealth should constitute individual and national greatness.

. . . The great strike of 1877 in Pennsylvania made victims of hundreds of Knights of Labor, who left the state and went in all directions carrying with them no murderous lance; neither were they dressed in garments of steel. They were clothed in righteousness, and bore in their hearts and minds God's high and holy command: "Love your neighbor." Perhaps we did not always give the public to understand that love of neighbor was our aim for we had to strike, boycott, and do other things not supposed to be in accord with the Ten Commandments. But remember that for the first time in human history labor, in the last quarter of the nineteenth century, stood at least partially solidified, partially organized, and partially united in opposition to a power that had its origin in the first lockout, on the day that Adam and Eve were locked out of that rather exclusive garden in which fruit was grown with apples a specialty. That power was greed, century-fortified, steel-armored greed, and you must not blame us for striking against it now and then or for using other harsh methods.

Different Visions:
"A Permanent Constructive and Conserving Force"—The American Federation of Labor

Samuel Gompers was president and the leading publicist of the American Federation of Labor from the organization's founding in 1886 to his death in 1924. Gompers offers a brief description of the philosophy of "pure-and-simple" unionism and the social values underlying it. Abridged from Samuel Gompers, Seventy Years of Life and Labor: An Autobiography, *ed. Nick Salvatore (Ithaca, New York, 1984), 53–54, 103, 105.*

Our union was a great deal more than a militant organization. As we studied our trade problems and tried out policies for bettering conditions for cigarmakers, we soon found that we had to understand our industry as a whole. Trade agreements were made early in the cigar industry. The procedure was very simple. Our union drew up a bill of prices and submitted it to the employer. If he accepted, the transaction was complete; if he refused, we undertook to negotiate an agreement. If we failed, a strike or lockout resulted.

A problem which demanded our thought from the beginning was how to stabilize the union and retain progress achieved. I saw clearly that we had to do something to make it worthwhile to maintain continuous membership, for a union that could hold members only during a strike period could not be a permanent constructive and conserving force in industrial life. The union must develop within itself cohesive forces that would make for continuous effort. I gathered all the information I could get on the benefits provided by the British trade unions. I saw that our problem was different from that with which the English had to deal, in that militancy must dominate until we established our right to represent the workers of our craft in making trade agreements. An out-of-work benefit, provisions for sickness and death appealed to me. Participation in such beneficent undertakings would undoubtedly hold members even when payment of dues might be a hardship.

. . . I proposed that we consider providing for uniform dues and benefits for all members. These motions were referred to the Committee on Constitution of which I was the chairman. Our Committee recommended to the convention constitutional changes providing uniform dues of ten cents a week and initiation fee, traveling benefits, annual equalization of funds among all unions, a sinking fund on the basis of fifteen cents for each member and twenty-five cents for each newly initiated member, a traveling loan system. . . .

My job as the president of the A. F. of L. was coveted by no one in the early days. There was much work, little pay, and very little honor. Though the Federation had been created by agreement, it had to be given reality by making it a force in industrial affairs. The necessary first step was to win for the Federation the good will of the wage-earners. The Federation was the unified activity of the trade union men. It was dependent upon good will and understanding of economic power. So I became a seeker of men. I wanted to win them for a labor movement which was sound philosophically, competent economically, and inspiring spiritually. At times I was well-nigh consumed with zeal, so that I gave little thought to anything else. My work was my life. So in recording the events of my life the labor movement is the controlling purpose.

. . . The nineties brought no spectacular growth for the A. F. of L. There was steady progress, but it seemed painfully slow to my ardent hopes and boundless aspiration. Between 1890 and 1900, obviously the primary thing to do first was sustained effort to gather into the folds of the Federation national labor organizations that were eligible to membership.

Different Visions:
"Abolition of the Wage System"—
The Industrial Workers of the World

A number of prominent radicals were associated with the Industrial Workers of the World, but unlike the Knights of Labor or the American Federation of Labor, the IWW had a much more diffuse leadership structure. While speeches and pamphlets played a role in getting the IWW's message out, far more important were the popular art forms used to educate an often illiterate—at least in English—audience. In 1908, the IWW issued one of the most revolutionary statements ever made in its "Preamble of the Industrial Workers of the World." To popularize their message and motivate the masses, the IWW also utilized songs, such as, "Workers of the World, Awaken!" by Joe Hill (who wrote hundreds of such pieces, mostly to familiar religious music), and artwork that graphically drove home their point. Taken from Rebel Voices: An I.W.W. Anthology, *ed. Joyce L. Kornbluh (Ann Arbor, Michigan, 1964), 12–13, 143, 25, 33.*

PREAMBLE
of the Industrial Workers of the World

The working class and the employing class have nothing in common. There can be no peace so long as hunger and want are found among millions of working people and the few, who make up the employing class, have all the good things of life.

Between these two classes a struggle must go on until the workers of the world organize as a class, take possession of the earth and the machinery of production, and abolish the wage system.

We find that the centering of management of the industries into fewer and fewer hands makes the trade unions unable to cope with the ever growing power of the employing class. The trade unions foster a state of affairs which allows one set of workers to be pitted against another set of workers in the same industry, thereby helping defeat one another in wage wars. Moreover, the trade unions aid the employing class to mislead the workers into the belief that the working class have interests in common with their employers.

These conditions can be changed and the interest of the working class upheld only by an organization formed in such a way that all its members in any one industry, or in all industries if necessary, cease work whenever a strike or lockout is on in any department thereof, thus making an injury to one an injury to all.

Instead of the conservative motto, "A fair day's wage for a fair day's work," we must inscribe on our banner the revolutionary watchword, "Abolition of the wage system."

It is the historic mission of the working class to do away with capitalism. The army of production must be organized, not only for the every-day struggle with capitalists, but also to carry on production when capitalism shall have been overthrown. By organizing industrially we are forming the structure of the new society within the shell of the old.

Joe Hill composed the words and the music to this song, which appeared in the ninth edition of the I.W.W. songbook.

WORKERS OF THE WORLD, AWAKEN!

By Joe Hill

Workers of the world, awaken!
Break your chains, demand your rights.
All the wealth you make is taken
By exploiting parasites.
Shall you kneel in deep submission
From your cradles to your graves?
Is the height of your ambition
To be good and willing slaves?

Refrain:

Arise, ye prisoners of starvation!
Fight for your own emancipation;
Arise, ye slaves of every nation
In One Union Grand.
Our little ones for bread are crying,
And millions are from hunger dying;
The means the end is justifying,
'Tis the final stand.

If the workers take a notion,
They can stop all speeding trains;
Every ship upon the ocean
They can tie with mighty chains;
Every wheel in the creation,
Every mine and every mill,
Fleets and armies of the nation
Will at their command stand still.

Join the union, fellow workers,
Men and women, side by side;
We will crush the greedy shirkers
Like a sweeping, surging tide.
For united we are standing,
But divided we will fall;
Let this be our understanding—
"All for one and one for all."

Workers of the world, awaken!
Rise in all your splendid might;
Take the wealth that you are making,
It belongs to you by right.
No one will for bread be crying,
We'll have freedom, love and health
When the grand red flag is flying
In the Workers' Commonwealth.

[*The following appeared in* Solidarity, *June 30, 1917.*]

The Hand That Will Rule the World—One Big Union

[*This illustration of the Wobblies' belief that only the IWW could save the workers from the woes of industrial capitalism was printed in* One Big Union Monthly *in July 1920.*]

Union Inclusiveness—
Attitudes Toward Women
Paternalism: Samuel Gompers and the AFL

One approach to a better understanding of the various currents of unionism is to look at the treatment of subgroups of marginalized workers, such as women. Samuel Gompers and the AFL were rather reluctant recruiters of women. Heading an organization composed overwhelmingly of skilled, white male workers who were interested in limiting access to a discrete number of high-paying jobs, Gompers did little to open up to women the trades covered by his organization. Rather, he dealt with the women's question in broad, posturing generalizations, as examples from his self-serving autobiography illustrate. Selected from Samuel Gompers, Seventy Years of Life and Labor: An Autobiography, *ed. Nick Salvatore (Ithaca, New York, 1985), 126–29.*

I have known a number of remarkable women both within and without the labor movement. Nothing has been more essential to the sustained progress of the labor movement than the conscious and unconscious co-operation of the womenfolk of union men. My daily observation taught me the meaning of the sacrifices made by the wives of men who have devoted themselves to the labor movement. Not only did the wife share privations and actual want, but she lived the spiritual sacrifice of being helpmate to a man who gives an absorbing cause first demand on his life. . . .

There have been within the labor movement, in addition to those who sustained this sort of auxiliary relationship to the labor movement, wonderful women trade unionists, for the labor movement, like all primary human movements, is neither male nor female—it is the instrumentality of unity. So I have never felt that there was properly a sex phase to the fundamentals of trade unionism. Trade unionism is to protect all who work for wages, whether male or female.

Devotion to trade unionism leads to interest in movements for freedom in all relations of life; consequently, I was early interested in the movement for equal suffrage. Equal rights for all brought me logically to endorse the women's struggle for equal political and legal rights. At that early day, the cause was at the height of its greatest unpopularity. I was one of the early advocates of woman's suffrage. . . .

While the large number of women were advocating equal suffrage, but few of them devoted any attention or activity to a movement in which I was deeply interested—that is, the movement to secure to women and girls equal pay with men and boys who were engaged in the same work. It was one of the principles for which I strongly contended within the labor movement. I believed, and as time goes on, I have become more fully convinced, that political equality without some degree of industrial independence would be more of a fantasy than a practical reality. . . .

It was the beginning of the twentieth century when the Women's Trade Union League was launched—a somewhat different type of working-women's organization—for the purpose of organizing women into trade unions. . . . [T]he leaders in this movement were largely social workers. I was in sympathy with the movement and gave it my cordial co-operation because I hoped it would lead to genuine trade union work.

. . . Some of the staunchest workers in the labor movement have been women. Some few of them . . . have been rewarded by official position in unions whose membership is composed of both men and women.

Union Inclusiveness—
Attitudes Toward Women Romanticization:
The Industrial Workers of the World

The IWW actively recruited women and had a number of notable female leaders, including Elizabeth Gurley Flynn and Mary "Mother" Jones. Still, its depiction of women in its pamphlets, songs, and pictures was highly idealized—replacing a very popular bourgeois stereotype of the

"True Woman" with one of the "Rebel Girl." This vision is revealed in the song "The Rebel Girl," written by the IWW's most famous songster, Joe Hill, in 1915. Taken from Songs of the Workers: To Fan the Flames of Discontent *(Popularly known as* The Little Red Songbook.)*, 34th ed. (Chicago, n.d.), 38–39.*

THE REBEL GIRL

(words and music written by Joe Hill in jail, February 1915)

There are wo - men of man - y de - scrip - tions—
Yes, her hands may be hard-en'd from la - bor — —

— In this queer world as eve - ry - one knows— Some are
— And her dress may not be ver - y fine — — But a

liv - ing in beau - ti - ful man-sions— And are wear-ing the
heart in her bos - om is beat-ing— — That is true to her

fin - est of clothes — — —There are blue blood - ed
class and her kind — — —And the graft - ers in

queens and prin-cess - es— Who have charms made of
ter - ror are tremb-ling— When her spite and de-

dia - monds and pearl— But the on - ly and tho-rough-bred
fi - ance she'll hurl — — For the on - ly and tho-rough-bred

la - dy Is the Reb - - el Girl. - - - -
la - dy Is the Reb - - el Girl. - - - -

CHORUS

That's the Reb - el Girl, That's the Reb - el Girl, To the

work - ing class she's a pre - cious pearl She brings cour - age

pride and joy - - - To the fight - ing Reb - el Boy - - We've had

girls be - fore but we need some more in the In - dust - rial

Work - ers of the World - - - For it's great to fight for free - dom

With a Reb - - el Girl. - - - - -

Union Inclusiveness—
Attitudes Toward Women
Separatism: The Knights of Labor

In the area of recruiting women, the Knights of Labor were far more progressive than the AFL and far more successful than the IWW. Estimates are that ten percent or more of the Knights' membership was female. Some organized in mixed assemblies with men, but many more organized in separate women's assemblies, which numbered 113 at the Knights' high point in 1886. The Knights established a Women's Department headed by Leonora Barry to coordinate the Order's work with women. While her appointment and the accomplishments of the Knights were a milestone for the labor movement, in the end she was frustrated with the results. As the following passages from her annual reports reveal, Barry found the policy of separatism and its underlying male attitudes to be barriers to true equality for women within the movement. Excerpted from America's Working Women, *ed. Rosalyn Baxandall, Linda Gordon and Susan Reverby. (New York, 1976), 120–25.*

1887

. . . Upon the strength of my observation and experience I would ask of officers and members of this Order that more consideration be given, and more thorough educational measures be adopted on behalf of the working-women of our land, the majority of whom are entirely ignorant of the economic and industrial question which is to them of such vital importance; and they must ever remain so while the selfishness of their brothers in toil is carried to such an extent as I find it to be among those who have sworn to demand equal pay for equal work. Thus far in the history of our Order that part of our platform has been but a mockery of the principles intended.

1888

My understanding of the duties implied in my office was that I was to do everything in my power that would in my judgement have a tendency to educate and elevate the workingwomen of America and ameliorate their condition. Therefore, when I spoke to a public audience of American citizens, exposing existing evils and showing how, through the demands of Knighthood, they could be remedied, I felt that I was fulfilling the duties of my office. . . . When I found an opportunity of laying before other organizations of women the cause of their less fortunate sisters and mold a favorable sentiment, I felt I was doing that which is an actual necessity, as woman is often unconsciously woman's oppressor. . . .

It has been intimated that the Woman's Department was started on sentiment. Well, if so, it has turned out to be one of the most thoroughly practical departments in the Order. Without egotism I can safely say it has done as much effective work in cheering, encouraging, educating and instructing the women of this Order in the short year of its existence as was done by the organization in the whole time of women's connection with it previous to its establishment.

As you will all doubtless remember, I instituted a Beneficial Department for women, of our Order by way of encouragement and that they might have some tangible proof of the benefits of our organization. Owing to the lack of business methods and selfishness of others, and a general apathy with which comfortably-situated women are afflicted, it did not become the universal success I had hoped. . . .

1889

My work has not been confined solely to women and children, but to all of earth's toilers, as I am of the opinion that the time when we could separate the interests of the toiling masses on sex lines is past. If it were possible, I wish that it were not necessary for women to learn any trade but that of domestic duties, as I believe it was intended that man should be the bread-winner. But as that is impossible under present conditions, I believe women should have every opportunity to become proficient in whatever vocation they choose or find themselves best fitted for.

A few words about the Woman's Department. When I took a position at its head I fondly hoped to weld together in organization such a number of women as would be a power for good in the present, and a monument to their honor in the relief it would establish for the women of the future. I was too sanguine, and I am forced to acknowledge that to fulfill my best hopes is a matter of impossibility; and I believe now we should, instead of supporting a Woman's Department, put more women in the field as Lecturers to tell women why they should organize as a part of the industrial hive, rather than because they are women. There can be no separation or distinction of wage-workers on account of sex, and separate departments for their interests is a direct contradiction of this, and also of that part of our declaration which says "we know no sex in the laws of Knighthood." Therefore, I recommend the abolition of the Woman's Department, believing, as I now do, that women should be Knights of Labor without distinction, and should have all the benefits that can be given to men—no more, no less—thereby making it incumbent upon all to work more earnestly for the general good, rather than for sex, Assembly or trade.

Questions

---

1. *What three or four words used by Powderly do you feel best reveal the social values underlying his view of unionism?*
2. *What key words and phrases used by Gompers best delineate his perspective on unionism that is different from Powderly's viewpoint?*
3. *In what ways does the IWW rhetoric differ from and/or compliment the rhetoric of Gompers and Powderly?*
4. *Despite their limitations, which approach do you think offered the most promising avenue for advancement for female workers— Gompers's, Powderly's, or the IWW's perspective on women?*

FURTHER READING

For a fuller treatment of the lives and ideas of Terence V. Powderly, Samuel Gompers, and William D. "Big Bill" Haywood, see the respective essays by Richard Oestreicher, John H. M. Laslett, and Joseph R. Conlin in Labor Leaders in America, *ed. Melvyn Dubofsky and Warren Van Tine (Urbana, Illinois, 1987). Two still viable treatments of the differences between the Knights of Labor and the American Federation of Labor can be found in Norman J. Ware,* The Labor Movement in the United States, 1860–1895 *(New York, 1964); and Gerald N. Grob,* Workers and Utopia: A Study of Ideological Conflict in the American Labor Movement, 1865–1900 *(Chicago, 1961). The best history of the IWW is Melvyn Dubofsky's* We Shall Be All: A History of the Industrial Workers of the World *(Chicago, 1969). For a wonderful collection of IWW songs, poems, pictures, and essays, see* Rebel Voices: An I.W.W. Anthology, *ed. Joyce L. Kornbluh (Ann Arbor, Michigan, 1964).*

The First
Sexual Revolution

Leila J. Rupp

INTRODUCTION

In the decades before and after 1900, profound changes in American society constituted what historians have called a "sexual revolution." By this they mean a transformation of sexual behavior and attitudes, in particular an increase in sexual contact outside of both marriage and prostitution among some groups in society and a new openness about sexuality, especially women's sexuality. As more white working and middle-class women moved out of the home and into the factories, offices, department stores, and college classrooms of a rapidly industrializing society, the nineteenth-century separation of male and female spheres began to erode. As the economy shifted from the stage of heavy industrialization to the production of consumer goods, the societal emphasis on thrift gave way to the glorification of spending and pleasure. In the newly respectable world of commercialized entertainment— consisting of dance halls, amusement parks, and the movies— young men and women socialized freely with strangers, setting the stage for what commentators came to call the "revolution in manners and morals."

Urban areas served as the crucible for change. Here the massive wave of immigration from southern and eastern Europe and the northward trek of African Americans introduced different sexual attitudes and practices to the white native-born population. In addition, an influx of young, white, rural men and women contributed to the growth of urban working-class subcultures where changes in social and sexual behavior flourished. In traditional rural communities, young people socialized on the front porch or at church, under the watchful eyes of family or community, but in the cities "women adrift"—young women living apart from their families—mingled with strange men in public places. The automobile, too, for those who could afford one, provided privacy that facilitated greater intimacy. The phenomenon of dating, including various kinds of sexual activity, came to replace the more serious "courting" signified by the pairing off of a couple.

As social barriers between men and women crumbled, the nineteenth-century notion of women as "passionless" in contrast to men as inherently lustful came under attack. Women, too, were recognized as sexual beings, a perception underscored by their adoption of shorter skirts, bobbed hair, and makeup. Although a large gap remained between the sexual experience of men and women, both faced new societal demands for "sex appeal." Couples increasingly came to expect sexual satisfaction and fun in marriage. Sexuality separated from the demands of reproduction necessitated access to birth control, a battle originally fought by "emancipated" and radical women in the first decades of the century.

In accordance with the breakdown of social barriers between women and men, sexologists and psychologists emphasized the naturalness of heterosexuality, thereby stigmatizing the same-sex "romantic friendships" that had been widely accepted in the nineteenth century. The usage of the terms "heterosexual" and "homosexual" in the U.S. dates from the turn of the century, when the idea that sexual behavior defined categories of people first developed. Commentators began to notice subcultures of what they termed "inverts"—a description that associated "reversed" gender characteristics with same-sex sexual behavior—in American cities. The sexual revolution both sexualized relationships that had previously seemed non-sexual and categorized people by the sexual acts in which they engaged.

At the heart of all these transformations, then, lay a sexualizing of society. People talked more openly about sexuality, ironically spurred by the social hygiene movement that sought to fight the spread of venereal disease by controlling sexual behavior. People engaged more openly in sexual activity outside the confines of marriage and beyond the world of prostitution. Changes that began in the working-class urban subcultures attracted the attention of a bohemian vanguard in such places as Greenwich Village and Harlem, who then spread the word through their novels, paintings, and music. The "flapper" style of the 1910s and 1920s represented the acceptance by young middle-class women, particularly on college campuses, of styles of behavior pioneered by their working-class sisters. American society would never be the same again.

DATING AND PETTING

Historians often tend to assume that changes in behavior percolate down from the upper or middle classes. The sexual revolution of the early twentieth century first came to light in investigations of middle-class youth. But social historians investigating the working-class subcultures of cities such as New York and Chicago have discovered changes in sexual mores even before those that swept the middle class in the 1920s. Young single women and men, living in boarding houses or furnished rooms, pioneered many of the changes in sexual attitudes and behavior previously associated with college youth.

Paula Fass details the changing sexual norms among native-born, white, middle-class college students in the 1920s, a group that left readily accessible sources by which we can chart new attitudes and behavior. Certainly they played an important role in the transformation of modern American sexuality. But they were not as pioneering as we once thought, as Kathy Peiss's work makes clear. Her interpretation of working-class life in turn-of-the-century cities is based on a careful reading of the reports of middle-class observers—reformers, social workers, and journalists—who often reacted with alarm to what they saw as violations of decent morality. Peiss "reads against the grain" in order to try to understand, through the filter of middle-class minds, how working-class men and women viewed their own sexuality. Both Fass and Peiss are interested in the development of peer subcultures that challenged, to a lesser and greater extent, traditional understandings of morality.

Sexuality on Campus in the 1920s

Paula S. Fass, in a commentary on sexuality among white college youth, argues that young people "appeared suddenly, dramatically, even menacingly on the social scene" in the 1920s. By that she means that the stage of youth became increasingly significant for young people themselves and for the setting of trends in society as a whole. Excerpted from Paula S. Fass, The Damned and the Beautiful: American Youth in the 1920's *(New York, 1977), 260–68, 271–72.*

Students of modern sexual behavior have quite correctly described the twenties as a turning point, a critical juncture between the strict double standard of the age of Victoria and the permissive sexuality of the age of Freud. Too often, however, the sexual revolution of the twenties has been described exclusively in terms of scattered data suggesting an increase in premarital sexual intercourse on the part of women. One is tempted to picture investigators hunting for that special morning between 1919 and 1929 when 51% of the young unmarried women in America awoke to find that they were no longer virgins. Instead, of course, investigators are forced to deduce revolutionary changes from small, though important, increases in what remained a minority pattern of behavior. This kind of thinking, not unlike the Victorian concept of all or nothing, overlooks the fact that changes in sexual habits, as in most other areas of social relations, are evolutionary and take place through a gradual accretion of behavioral and value changes. These changes must be located not in sudden reversals of traditional beliefs and habits but in adaptations to new circumstances and in a reorientation to new social groups that set the standards and establish the patterns which most individuals imitate.

By concentrating so exclusively on the incidents of premarital coitus, analysts have overlooked the most fruitful area for understanding the changes in sexual patterns among the majority of the middle-class population. For it is to the behavior and attitudes of young men and women in the twenties, who had to deal with emerging sexual impulses and had the least vested interest in maintaining older norms, that one must look for the readjustments that underlay the process of change. From this perspective the post-war decade was indeed critical for the evolution of modern sexual patterns. The young, reared in a moral standard in which all sex was taboo, redefined that standard according to their own needs and laid the basis for a change in the standard itself. The college campus, especially, provided a fertile social environment for the new mores concerning the relationships between men and women. On the coeducational campuses of the 1920's (matrimonial bureaus, they were sometimes called), sex was a perpetual peer concern.

College youth of the 1920's redefined the relationship between men and women. In good part this resulted from a simple rediscovery—love is erotic. The remainder drew on an old assumption—that the goal of relations between men and women was marriage. Together the new insight and the old tradition resulted in a significant restructuring of premarital forms of sexual behavior as relationships were charged by a new sexual dynamism and a vigorous experimentalism. Sex for middle-class youths of the 1920's had become a significant premarital experience, but it continued to be distinctly marriage-oriented and confined by stringent etiquettes and sharply etched definitions. In the process of defining their future roles in the new society and within the context of already potent changes, the young helped to create the sexual manners of the twentieth century.

The norms established by college youths had a dual purpose. They provided room for the exploration of immediate sexual interests, and they facilitated mate selection for future marriage. The result was a sexual revolution: not, however, as often implied, a revolution erupting in a sudden and drastic increase in sexual intercourse among the unmarried young, but a revolution growing out of new patterns of sexual play. The young evolved a code of sexual behavior that was, in effect, a middle ground between the no-sex-at-all taboo officially prescribed by the adult world and inculcated by their families, and their own burgeoning sexual interests and marital aspirations. To this dual purpose, youths elaborated two basic rituals of sexual interaction—dating and petting. These behavior patterns accompanied and emphasized several important value changes: more tolerance for non-norma-

In the dance halls; painting by Thomas Hart Benton, "City Activities with Dance Hall." (Courtesy of The Equitable Life Assurance Soceity of the United States.)

tive sexual behavior, the recognition and approval of female sexuality, and a positive evaluation of emotional response and expression in relations between men and women. This nexus of behavior and value was the heart of the sexual revolution of the 1920's.

Dating was something definitely new in the ritual of sexual interaction. It was unlike the informal get-togethers that characterized youth socializing in the village or small town of the nineteenth century, for at such events there was no pairing early in an acquaintance. It was also unlike courting, which implied a commitment between two people. Dating permitted a paired relationship without implying a commitment to marriage and encouraged experimental relations with numerous partners. Dating emerged in response to a modern environment in which people met casually and irregularly, and in response to new kinds of recreations like movies, dance halls, and restaurants, where pairing was the most convenient form of boy-girl relation. . . . The lack of commitment permitted close and intimate associations and explorations of personality, and isolation and privacy laid the ground for sexual experimentation, both as a means for testing future compatibility and as an outlet for present sexual energies.

With the isolation of relations, the young were forced to rely on their own judgment in determining the degree and limits of permissible eroticism. It was this latitude for self-determination that produced the haunting fear of sexual promiscuity in the jeremiads of the twenties. The fear was unfounded. The young were thrown back on their own resources, but they were not free, either from the influence of childhood training or, more immediately, from the controls and sanctions of their peers. Basing their actions on an unyielding taboo against sexual intercourse and an elaborate network of peer norms and standards, they proceeded to open up the possibilities of sexual play without overstepping the bounds of family prohibition and peer propriety. . . .

"Petting" described a broad range of potentially erotic physical contacts, from a casual kiss to more intimate caresses and physical fondling. Even such limited eroticism would have automatically defined a woman as loose and disreputable in the nineteenth century. To the Victorians, who divided good women from bad, revered ideal purity, and were suspicious of female sexuality, all forms of eroticism on the part of women could be equated with total submission. Even in the twenties, it was not unknown for reformers to introduce legislation that would prohibit petting and define it along with fornication as illegal as well as immoral. But the young drew distinct boundaries between what was acceptable erotic behavior and what was not. Petting was the means to be safe and yet not sorry, and around this form of sexual activity they elaborated a code of permissible eroticism. As a result, while there remained two kinds of women among college students in the twenties, the difference was not between sexual women and non-sexual women but between sexual women who lived by the rules and those who did not. A Trinity College editor put it well when he asserted, "There are only two kinds of co-eds, those who have been kissed and those who are sorry they haven't been kissed." And he later added just the right note about the group norms that carefully tailored female behavior: "Although a girl will not always let you kiss her when you ask her, she usually appreciates your asking her, often so much that she has to tell her friends." . . . [T]he youth of the twenties were incorporating dating and petting into a wholly new ritual of graded relationships. A casual first date might thus entail a good-night kiss, but greater intimacies and a certain amount of erotic play were permitted and expected of engaged couples. . . . The young first sanctioned eroticism and then imposed degrees and standards of acceptability.

College youths were fully aware of, and highly sensitive to, the criticism that petting evoked from their elders. But the editors of college papers were quick to deny any widespread evil in the behavior or intentions of the young. They did not, however, deny the existence of petting or its importance in the social relations between the sexes. What they denied was the adult evaluation of such behavior as promiscuous or immoral, as in fact it was by an earlier standard. Peer norms, which deviated from adult attitudes, were now legitimate criteria for evaluating conduct. By the standards of the young, petting was not immoral. It was inappropriate when abused and when the rigid boundaries the young imposed on their own behavior were overstepped. In decrying the inordinate amount of attention that youth's morals were receiving from the public, the *Daily Illini*, for example, illustrated how out of touch older people were with the life of the young by referring to a recent questionnaire where the term "spooning" had been used. A sure way of antagonizing youth, the *Illini* noted, was to be so removed from the realities of their lives as to use an expression as archaic and wholly unreal as "spooning."

In view of the strength of peer-group influence, youth were unlikely to bypass the restrictions and staged ritual associated with sexual behavior. But neither was petting restricted to only a small minority of wildly experimental youths, for petting had become a convention and a necessary demonstration of conformity. One investigation of coed behavior found that 92% of all women admitted petting at one time or another. . . . One observed the restrictions on petting in order to remain respectable to peers, but given the occasion and the desire, one could and did pet because it was commonly accepted behavior. There was undoubtedly also considerable pressure to pet at least a little in order to remain in good standing in the eyes of peers and to assure that future dates would be forthcoming. One result of this peer compulsion was that experimental erotic exploration was often a group phenomenon. The petting party was probably the major contribution of the twenties to group sex, and it was in such groups that the first hesitant initiations into erotic play were often made. . . .

The rating system by which social connections were made and by which eligibility was established and maintained worked within a tight system of gossip, reference, bull-session discussions, and careful conformity to standards. A correspondent to the *Daily Illini* . . . asked pointedly, "At what fraternity house will you not find sooner or later just such a discussion of 'Girls Who Pet'?" If a woman could be criticized for the way she wore her hair, for excessive reliance on the paint box, or for overly suggestive dancing, and when it was generally known whether she was "a first-night petter," how much more would her reputation be affected by an imputation of officially and unofficially proscribed behavior? One study of undergraduate life noted, "Men are very dependent on one another's estimate of a girl. Some fraternities blacklist a girl for being obviously 'a speed,' too giddily dressed, or lacking sex attraction." There was a very clear differentiation between positive sex appeal and offensive behavior. For the majority, "a petting party is the right thing to do," but a really "fast woman" was disreputable. Sexual irregularity on the part of coeds, as one investigator of campus ethics discovered, was universally condemned by men and women as the worst of all possible offenses on the campus. Significantly, women still condemned such irregularities more consistently than men, and since it was women who usually regulated sexual behavior, there was still a tight lid on intercourse with campus women. Despite an easing of the double standard and an erosion of distinctions between virtuous women and sexual women, students still clung to a double standard in their own behavior and described illicit sexual behavior as far worse for women than for men. . . .

Dating and petting were, moreover, distinctly marriage-oriented in the twenties. Since mating was one of the chief aims of both rituals, immediate sexual satisfactions had to be carefully weighed in view of long-term goals. And while virginity in a bride was no longer an absolute prerequisite for most men, it was still considered desirable. For men, female chastity appears to have taken a back seat to considerations of compatibility, but there was still some ambiguity on this point, and the devaluation of virginity in the bride was probably related to a growing acceptance of intercourse among engaged couples rather than to a tolerance of casual promiscuity. Women too continued to display considerable anxiety about the consequences of lost virginity. These multiple ambivalences reinforced the sense of acceptable limitations on sexual indulgence. . . .

The controlled ritual of petting had opened up the possibilities of intimacy and response in the relationship between young men and women. At the same time, it also restricted complete spontaneity and laid the basis for the emotionally inhibiting cat-and-mouse game of staged seductions and "scoring" that continued to govern sexual relations among the young throughout the first half of the twentieth century. It was a first and necessary step toward modern patterns of sexual behavior, for the youths of the twenties redefined sexuality in erotic and emotional terms. But in ritualizing a process of personal and cultural experimentation, the youth of the twenties had also placed bonds on individual expression and behavior quite as real and determinate as those which ruled in the heyday of Victorian morals.

"Charity Girls" and City Pleasures

Beginning in the last decades of the nineteenth century, urban working-class youths created their own peer subculture that in many ways foreshadowed what would happen on campuses in the 1920s. Excerpted from Kathy Peiss, "'Charity Girls' and City Pleasures: Historical Notes on Working-Class Sexuality, 1880–1920" in Powers of Desire: The Politics of Sexuality, *ed. Ann Snitow, Christine Stansell, and Sharon Thompson (New York, 1983), 75–78, 81–84.*

My discussion focuses on one set of young, white working women in New York City in the years 1880 to 1920. Most of these women were single wage earners who toiled in the city's factories, shops, and department stores, while devoting their evenings to the lively entertainment of the streets, public dance halls, and other popular amusements. Born or educated in the United States, many adopted a cultural style meant to distance themselves from their immigrant roots and familial traditions. Such women dressed in the latest finery, negotiated city life with ease, and sought intrigue and adventure with male companions. For this group of working women, sexuality became a central dimension of their emergent culture, a dimension that is revealed in their daily life of work and leisure.

These New York working women frequented amusements in which familiarity and intermingling among strangers, not decorum, defined normal public behavior between the sexes. At movies and cheap theaters, crowds mingled during intermissions, shared picnic lunches, and commented volubly on performances. Strangers at Coney Island's amusement parks often involved each other in practical jokes and humorous escapades, while dance halls permitted close interaction between unfamiliar men and women. At one respectable Turnverein ball, for example, a vice investigator described closely the chaotic activity in the barroom between dances:

> Most of the younger couples were hugging and kissing, there was a general mingling of men and women at the different tables, almost everyone seemed to know one another and spoke to each other across the tables and joined couples at different tables, they were all singing and carrying on, they kept running around the room and acted like a mob of lunatics let lo[o]se.

As this observer suggests, an important aspect of social familiarity was the ease of sexual expression in language and behavior. Dances were advertised, for example, through the distribution of "pluggers," small printed cards announcing the particulars of the ball, along with snatches of popular songs or verse; the lyrics and pictures, noted one offended reformer, were often "so suggestive that they are absolutely indecent." . . .

Other forms of recreation frequented by working-class youth incorporated a free and easy sexuality into their attractions. Many social clubs and amusement societies permitted flirting, touching, and kissing games at their meetings. One East Side youth reported that "they have kissing all through pleasure time, and use slang language, while in some they don't behave nice between [sic] young ladies." Music halls and cheap vaudeville regularly worked sexual themes and suggestive humor into comedy routines and songs. At a Yiddish music hall popular with both men and women, one reformer found that "the songs are suggestive of everything but what is proper, the choruses are full of double

*Luna Park—Coney Island Amusement Park, site of the working-class
urban heterosocial subculture. (Courtesy of Culver Pictures, Inc.)*

meanings, and the jokes have broad and unmistakable hints of
things indecent." Similarly, Coney Island's Steeplechase amusement park, favored by working-class excursionists, carefully mar-
keted sexual titillation and romance in attractions that threw patrons into each other, sent skirts flying, and evoked instant intimacy among strangers. . . .

The heterosocial orientation of these amusements made
popularity a goal to be pursued through dancing ability, willingness to drink, and eye-catching finery. Women who would not
drink at balls and social entertainments were often ostracized by
men, while cocktails and ingenious mixtures replaced the five-
cent beer and helped to make drinking an acceptable female activity. Many women used clothing as a means of drawing attention
to themselves, wearing high-heeled shoes, fancy dresses, costume
jewelry, elaborate pompadours, and cosmetics. As one working
woman sharply explained, "If you want to get any notion took of
you, you gotta have some style about you." The clothing that such
women wore no longer served as an emblem of respectability.
"The way women dress today they all look like prostitutes,"

The dance craze. (Courtesy of The Library of Congress.)

reported one rueful waiter to a dance hall investigator, "and the waiter can some times get in bad by going over and trying to put some one next to them, they may be respectable women and would jump on the waiter."

Underlying the relaxed sexual style and heterosocial interaction was the custom of "treating." Men often treated their female companions to drinks and refreshments, theater tickets, and other incidentals. Women might pay a dance hall's entrance fee or carfare out to an amusement park, but they relied on men's treats to see them through the evening's entertainment. Such treats were highly prized by young working women; as Belle Israels remarked, the announcement that "he treated" was "the acme of achievement in retailing experiences with the other sex."

Treating was not a one-way proposition, however, but entailed an exchange relationship. Financially unable to reciprocate in kind, women offered sexual favors of varying degrees, ranging from flirtatious companionship to sexual intercourse, in exchange for men's treats. "Pleasures don't cost girls so much as they do young men," asserted one saleswoman. "If they are agreeable they are invited out a good deal, and they are not allowed to pay anything." Reformer Lillian Betts concurred, observing that the working woman held herself responsible for failing to wangle men's invitations and believed that "it is not only her misfortune, but her fault; she should be more attractive." Gaining men's treats placed a high premium on allure and personality, and sometimes involved aggressive and frank "overtures to men whom they desire to attract," often with implicit sexual proposals. One investigator, commenting on women's dependency on men in their leisure time, aptly observed that "those who are unattractive, and those who have puritanic notions, fare but ill in the matter of enjoyments. On the other hand those who do become popular have to compromise with the best conventional usage." . . .

The extent of the sexual culture . . . is particularly difficult to establish, since the evidence is too meager to permit conclusions about specific groups of working women, their beliefs about sexuality, and their behavior. Scattered evidence does suggest a range of possible responses, the parameters within which most women would choose to act and define their behavior as socially acceptable. Within this range, there existed a subculture of working women who fully bought into the system of treating and sexual exchange, by trading sexual favors of varying degrees for gifts, treats, and a good time. These women were known in underworld slang as "charity girls," a term that differentiated them from prostitutes because they did not accept money in their sexual encounters with men. As vice reformer George Kneeland found, they "offer themselves to strangers, not for money, but for presents, attention, and pleasure, and most important, a yielding to sex desire." Only a thin line divided these women and "occasional prostitutes," women who slipped in and out of prostitution when unemployed or in need of extra income. Such behavior did not result in the stigma of the "fallen woman." Many working women apparently acted like Dottie: "When she needed a pair of shoes she had found it easy to 'earn' them in the way that other girls did." Dottie, the investigator reported, was now known as a respectable married woman. . . .

The charity girl's activities form only one response in a wide spectrum of social and sexual behavior. Many young women defined themselves sharply against the freer sexuality of their pleasure-seeking sisters, associating "respectability" firmly with premarital chastity and circumspect behavior. One working woman carefully explained her adherence to propriety: "I never go out in the evenings except to my relatives because if I did, I should lose my reputation and that is all I have left." Similarly, shop girls guarded against sexual advances from co-workers and male customers by spurning the temptations of popular amusements. "I keep myself to myself," said one saleswoman. "I don't make friends in the stores very easily because you can't be sure what any one is like." Settlement workers also noted that women who freely attended "dubious resorts" or bore illegitimate children were often stigmatized by neighbors and workmates. Lillian

Betts, for example, cites the case of working women who refused to labor until their employer dismissed a co-worker who had born a baby out of wedlock. To Betts, however, their adherence to the standard of virginity seemed instrumental, and not a reflection of moral absolutism: "The hardness with which even the suggestion of looseness is treated in any group of working girls is simply an expression of self-preservation."

Other observers noted an ambivalence in the attitudes of young working women toward sexual relations. Social workers reported that the critical stance toward premarital pregnancy was "not always unmixed with a certain degree of admiration for the success with the other sex which the difficulty implies." According to this study, many women increasingly found premarital intercourse acceptable in particular situations: "'A girl can have many friends,' explained one of them, 'but when she gets a "steady," there's only one way to have him and to keep him; I mean to keep him long.'" Such women shared with charity girls the assumption that respectability was not predicated solely on chastity.

Perhaps few women were charity girls or occasional prostitutes, but many more must have been conscious of the need to negotiate sexual encounters in the workplace or in their leisure time. Women would have had to weigh their desire for social participation against traditional sanctions regarding sexual behavior, and charity girls offered to some a model for resolving this conflict. This process is exemplified in Clara Laughlin's report of an attractive but "proper" working woman who could not understand why men friends dropped her after a few dates. Finally she receives the worldly advice of a co-worker that social participation involves an exchange relationship: "Don't yeh know there ain't no feller goin' t'spend coin on yeh fer nothin'?" . . .

For . . . young working women, respectability was not defined by the strict measurement of chastity employed by many middle-class observers and reformers. Instead, they adopted a more instrumental and flexible approach to sexual behavior. Premarital sex *could* be labeled respectable in particular social contexts. Thus charity girls distinguished their sexual activity from prostitution, a less acceptable practice, because they did not receive money from men. Other women, who might view charity girls as promiscuous, were untroubled by premarital intimacy with a steady boyfriend.

This fluid definition of sexual respectability was embedded within the social relation of class and gender, as experienced by women in their daily round of work, leisure, and family life. Women's wage labor and the demands of the working-class household offered daughters few resources for entertainment. At the same time, new commercial amusements offered a tempting world of pleasure and companionship beyond parental control. Within this context, some young women sought to exchange sexual goods for access to that world and its seeming independence, choosing not to defer sexual relations until marriage. Their notions of legitimate premarital behavior contrast markedly with the dominant middle-class view, which placed female sexuality within a dichotomous and rigid framework. Whether a hazard at work, fun and adventure at night, or an opportunity to be exploited, sexual expression and intimacy comprised an integral part of these working women's lives.

Questions

1. *How similar and how different were the definitions of acceptable sexual behavior shaped by the college culture in the 1920s and the working-class subculture in the period from 1890-1920?*
2. *What class differences in attitudes toward sexuality do you see in comparing working-class and middle-class Americans, including both middle-class college students and middle-class observers of the working-class subculture?*
3. *How "revolutionary" was the first sexual revolution?*
4. *In what ways might the changes described by Paula Fass and Kathy Peiss have set the stage for contemporary relations between the sexes?*

PERSPECTIVES ON SEXUALITY IN THE EARLY TWENTIETH-CENTURY UNITED STATES

Dating and petting among white, urban, working class youth and college students represent an important sign of the first sexual revolution, but there were other manifestations of this important transformation in American society. Commentators from the 1910s on noticed the greater openness in discussions of sexuality, often linking them to public discourse about prostitution, venereal disease, and birth control. Perhaps nothing shocked the arbiters of traditional morality so much as young women—the "flappers" who revealed their boyish bodies, used cosmetics, and claimed the right to smoke and drink with men—who talked of "white slavery"—a term that implicitly contrasted involuntary prostitution to the enslavement of Africans and African Americans—without batting an eye. So, too, public discussion of birth control, pioneered by anarchist Emma Goldman and socialist Margaret Sanger, threatened the traditional order by validating sexuality apart from reproduction.

The changes associated with the sexual revolution also affected diverse groups of Americans. Alongside the cafes and dance halls catering to the heterosexual crowd, establishments for men (and to a far lesser extent women) attracted to members of the same sex grew up in urban areas. That the freer expression of sexuality—both heterosexual and same-sex—affected not just young white people is clear from the art, music, and social life that flowered during the Harlem Renaissance of the 1920s. Following the massive migration of African Americans from the rural South to the urban North, the vibrant mixed-class neighborhood of Harlem fostered both artistic and sexual experimentation. Novels, plays, poetry, and especially the blues celebrated sexuality and even fostered the recognition and grudging toleration of same-sex relationships. The fol-

lowing documents illustrate a range of perspectives on the widespread changes that comprised the sexual revolution.

"Sex O'Clock" in America

"Sex O'Clock in America," a much-cited article published in 1913, heralds the new openness about sexuality and discusses the views of a number of commentators who disagreed about what was going on and whether or not the new developments should be viewed as dangerous. This article appeared in Current Opinion, 55, no. 2 (August 1913): 113–14.

A WAVE of sex hysteria and sex discussion seems to have invaded this country. Our former reticence on matters of sex is giving way to a frankness that would even startle Paris. Prostitution, as *Life* remarks, is the chief topic of polite conversation. It has struck "sex o'clock" in America, to use [journalist] William Marion Reedy's memorable phrase. The White Slave appears in the headlines of our newspapers. . . . [Journalist] Witter Bynner in *The Forum* exploits the White Slave in blank verse. *Leslie's Weekly* points out her lesson in short stories. *The Smart Set* makes her the subject of a novelette. In the theater, "Damaged Goods," a play of which the action springs from venereal disease, marks an epoch of new freedom in sex discussion. . . . Vice reports leap into print. Vice commissions meet and gravely attempt to rebuild in a fortnight the social structure of the world. Is this overemphasis of sex a symptom of a new moral awakening or is it a sign that the morbidity of the Old World is overtaking the New? Does it indicate a permanent change in our temper or is it merely the concomitant of the movement for the liberation of woman from the shackles of convention that will disappear when society has readjusted itself to the New Woman and the New Man? Has it struck sex o'clock permanently or will time soon point to another hour?

One writer in the St. Louis *Mirror*, James F. Clark, asserts that we must grant to-day to woman the same promiscuity that society tacitly grants to the male. This statement has aroused a storm of discussion and protest. Mr. Reedy himself, tho a radical, strongly dissents from the attitude of his aggressive contributor. . . .

"The laxity in sex matters in this and other countries cannot be said to be due to the broadening of women's views. The women who have entered upon the life of civic and social enlargement are not those who 'go astray.' The sexually loose women are not the so-called advanced women. They are the parasite women, the indulged women, the women who do not think. And I want to say that I don't believe in the theory that the woman has the same passions as a man. I, too, have been to Cyprus, and the woman of passion, from Sappho to Catherine of Russia, is a fake or a physio-psychological freak. Woman's passion is mostly a pretence. The idea that women in any great number would resort to promiscuity is absurd. The removal of the fear of consequences won't count for much with an intelligent womanhood. Not intelligence, but igno-rance recruits the ranks of the social evil."

The brilliant Saint Louis editor has little use for the anti-vice crusades financed by Standard Oil money. There are, he says, and he speaks with the authority of a man of wide experience, plenty of women of evil life in all large cities. But these are not "White Slaves." The inmates of houses may be in debt to mistresses, but they are not held prisoners and cannot be. "But as young Rockefeller is putting up the money for the White Slave hunt, of course," Mr. Reedy goes on to say, somewhat cynically, "'White Slaves' have to be produced." Vice and crime, he insists, are the symptoms of poverty, which itself is a symptom of the disease known as privilege. We should strike at the root, not at the branches.

The vice crusade business in Chicago, New York, San Fran-cisco, everywhere, thinks Reedy, is being overdone. There is too much sensationalism in its campaigns. There is too much censor-ship of songs and dances. . . .

"No one is particularly in favor of vice. But most thinking people are in favor of liberty and there cannot prevail much liberty when the raiding plan of reform is so generally adopted. I have an idea that people have a right to go to hell in their own way. And that a good way to drive them to hell is to begin to coerce and drive them towards other people's ideals of righteous-ness. Raids are going to produce more harm than good. If society is going to hell by way of the tango and the turkey trot and the cabaret show, who started it in that direction? Why, 'the best people.' It is 'the best people' that have exalted vaudeville and girl shows above the genuine drama. It is the best people who have made the cabaret show and demanded that it be ever more and more highly spiced. When the habits and customs of the best people broaden down to the common people, lo, there is a wild cry for reform. And it is all done now in the name of the working girl. Balderdash! The working girl is a working girl, not a bawd at large. The working girl doesn't keep the hot joints in the big town running. That is done mostly by folks who think themselves in the know and in the swim. The prevalent looseness in society is not to be checked by sensational raids or slumming expeditions by legislative committees of investigation. We must begin farther back than the patrol-wagon."

Reedy places the blame for the sex hysteria upon the hedonistic materialistic philosophy that pervades American life. The poor, he says, learn their worst vices from the rich. Everybody lives for a good time in the upper world, and the infection spreads downward. "Is there," he asks, "anything of the spiritual left in education in America, broadly speaking? There is not."

"Education is now directed to the end of enabling a man to get money. Our youths study what they think will enable them to get there quickest. No classics. No arts and no metaphysics. No religion. And science—well, science is fallen into the hands of those who pursue it not to *know*, but to *get*. Education is not to draw a man out of himself, but to draw material things to himself. No one is concerned with eternal things. All that interests us is the immediate gratification. And some few of us have the idea that, because we think we are better than other people, we have a right to say what they shall sing or dance and whom they shall marry and whether they shall marry at all. We want to make people good by science." . . .

Dr. Cecile L. Greil, a Socialist writer, welcomes the fact that society is drawing its head out of the sand of prudery where it had hidden it, ostrich-like. But she, too, fears the hysteria of sex discussion. She especially warns the members of her own sex. The pendulum with women swings more rapidly to extreme degrees, she asserts. This may be because of her highly sensitized nervous organism, which fastens with almost hysterical tenacity to anything which produces an emotional appeal. And surely nothing that has come to her for study or reflection in all the ages has been as important to her, and through her to posterity, as is this freedom of sex knowledge, which guards the citadel of society and makes for a better, finer race of citizens. "But one danger lurks in her midst. Sex freedom is frequently hysterically interpreted into meaning sex license. And the science which shall give her the right to freer, happier motherhood entails all the responsibilities that freedom in any other sense does." The modern social system, the writer continues in *The Call*, is a terrific endurance test against the forces within ourselves and the forces that attack us without. Vanity and love and sport she admits, quoting a Judge of one of the Night Courts, make more prostitutes than economic pressure and exploitation.

"Youth is extravagant to prodigality with itself. It is drunk with its own intoxicating perfume. It looks down into the glass of life as did Narcissus into the brook, and like Narcissus falls in love with its own beauty. And we surround that young, passionate, bursting blossom with every temptation to break down its resistant power, lure it into sentient, pulsating desire and eroticism by lurid literature, moving pictures, tango dances, suggestive songs, cabarets, noise, music, light, life, rhythm, everywhere, until the senses are throbbing with leashed-in physical passion—everything done to lure, but nothing to instruct. So one day the leash snaps, and another boy or girl is outside the pale. We do much for the developing of the intellect and for the use of our hands so that we may send our young people out into the big battle that lies beyond the home, but for the battle against the physical forces, the law of the magnetic attraction of the sexes, at the dangerous period of puberty and adolescence, we do nothing. Education is the only thing that can save, rational libertarian education on the subjects pertaining to the laws of personal and social hygiene."

Society is apt to regard the fourteen-year-old adolescent as a little dreamy school-girl, ties pretty ribbons in her hair, and keeps her dresses well confined to knee length, forgetting that all the externals of the child mask the seething turbulent ocean underneath. In the child dwells a fully awakened woman. Nature goes through a vicarious process of sex awakening with all its stupendous morbid psychology and complexes. The position of the boy at puberty, contends Dr. Greil, is still worse. He has not even the hereditary instincts of inhibition that his little sister has.

"Society smiles on his acts, calls them 'sport,' sowing his wild oats, etc. He becomes a moral coward and sneak, conscious only of strong animal impulses that he need not curb, and these drive him early to secret vice, to the brothel, to dissipation and roguery. And the crop he reaps from the wild oats he sows fill our streets with prostitutes, fill our foundling asylums with nameless babies and give him a heritage of venereal disease to wreck his future usefulness and hand down as a sad legacy to his posterity. He fears no moral code! His mother and sisters live in a rarified atmosphere of imaginary purity that cuts him off from intimacy, and the understanding which his mother could impart to him if she were his friend instead of a transcendental ideal far up on a pedestal out of his reach. His father, perhaps the only human being who could save him at the crucial period, is his bitterest foe or at best a total stranger to him, shielding himself after exhausting all the phases of sex liberty for himself in an armor of virtue and respectability, which simply antagonizes the boy and widens the breach between himself and society.

"He becomes an alien in his own home, an outcast free to mingle with the world of vicious freedom that welcomes him with open arms, makes him the tool of lost souls and stains him with a smear of filth that ruins him utterly before he is old enough to learn that his much-prized sex freedom is a bondage that makes him pay exorbitant prices in loss of strength, ideals and health. Truly, life does teach as thoroly [thoroughly] as any academy, but how it makes us pay!"

The necessity of sex education is generally recognized. Yet there are also evidences of reaction. Thus the Chicago Board of Education rescinded the order issued by Mrs. Ella Flagg Young, in whose hands rests the school system of Chicago, providing for lectures on sex hygiene in the schools. *The Ecclesiastical Review*, a Roman Catholic publication, maintains that whatever warning and instruction may be necessary should be left in the hands of the priest. Nevertheless, the editor, tho grudgingly, prints a list of books on eugenics for the use of Roman Catholic teachers and priests to aid them in following intelligently the trend of public opinion. Another Roman Catholic publication, *America*, asks for the suppression of vice reports and of vice commissions, except for restricted particular investigations. The publication attacks Doctor Eliot's championship of the Society of Sanitary and Moral Prophylaxis. Eliot has no right, in the opinion of *America*, to declare that before the advent of the Society and its head, Dr. Morton, the policy of the world was "absolute silence" with regard to sex hygiene. "There is," we are told, "a world of difference between absolute silence and the wise and prudent discretion which bids father and mother and teacher refrain from handling the topic in public and without discriminating sense, whilst it at the same time inspires them to say at the fitting time the right word which shall safeguard their children, and to say it with a circumspection not likely to destroy the sense of shame, which is the best natural protection of the innocence of these little ones."

Radicals and conservatives, Free-thinkers and Catholics, all seem to believe in solving the sex problem by education, but as to the method that is to be followed there are abysmal differences of opinion.

The Flapper

This unsigned article written in 1915 by the renowned journalist and social critic H.L. Mencken caricatures the young upper- or middle-class woman who had embraced the flapper style and could discuss prostitution or venereal disease without blushing. Taken from H.L. Mencken, "The Flapper," in The Smart Set 45, no. 2 (February 1915): 1–2.

THE American language, curiously enough, has no name for her. In German she is *der Backfisch,* in French she is *l'Ingénue,* in English she is the Flapper. But in American, as I say, she is nameless, for Chicken will never, never do. Her mother, at her age, was a Young Miss; her grandmother was a Young Female. But she herself is no Young Miss, no Young Female. Oh, dear, no! . . .

Observe, then, this nameless one, this American Flapper. Her skirts have just reached her very trim and pretty ankles; her hair, newly coiled upon her skull,

Flapper fashions. (Courtesy of UPI/Corbis-Bettmann.)

has just exposed the ravishing whiteness of her neck. A charming creature! Graceful, vivacious, healthy, appetizing. It is a delight to see her bite into a chocolate with her pearly teeth. There is music in her laugh. There is poetry in her drive at tennis. She is an enchantment through the plate glass of a limousine. Youth is hers, and hope, and romance, and—

Well, well, let us be exact: let us not say innocence. This Flapper, to tell the truth, is far, far, far from a simpleton. An Ingénue to the Gaul, she is actually as devoid of ingenuousness as a newspaper reporter, a bartender or a midwife. The age she lives in is one of knowledge. She herself is educated. She is privy to dark secrets. The world bears to her no aspect of mystery. She has been taught how to take care of herself.

For example, she has a clear and detailed understanding of all the tricks of white slave traders, and knows how to circumvent them. She is on the lookout for them in matinée lobbies and railroad stations—benevolent-looking old women who pretend to be ill, plausible young men who begin business with "Beg pardon," bogus country girls who cry because their mythical brothers have failed to meet them. She has a keen eye for hypodermic needles, chloroform masks, closed carriages. She has seen all these sinister machines of the devil in operation on the screen. . . . She has followed the war upon them in the newspapers.

Life, indeed, is almost empty of surprises, mysteries, horrors to this Flapper of 1915. She knows the exact percentage of lunatics among the children of drunkards. . . . She knows exactly what the Wassermann reaction [a blood test for venereal disease] is, and has made up her mind that she will never marry a man who can't show an unmistakable negative. . . . She is opposed to the double standard of morality, and favors a law prohibiting it.

This Flapper has forgotten how to simper; she seldom blushes; it is impossible to shock her. She saw "Damaged Goods" without batting an eye, and went away wondering what the row over it was all about. The police of her city having prohibited "Mrs. Warren's Profession," [a novel about prostitution] she read it one rainy Sunday afternoon, and found it a mass of platitudes. . . . She slaved at French in her finishing school in order to read Anatole France. . . . She plans to read Havelock Ellis during the coming summer. . . .

As I have said, a charming young creature. There is something trim and trig and confident about her. She is easy in her manners.

She bears herself with dignity in all societies. She is graceful, rosy, healthy, appetizing. It is a delight to see her sink her pearly teeth into a chocolate, a macaroon, even a potato. There is music in her laugh. She is youth, she is hope, she is romance—she is wisdom!

Emma Goldman Lectures on Sex

Harry Kemp, a Bohemian writer known as the "Don Juan of Greenwich Village," relates part of the story of his life on the road as a tramp. Kemp, using the name "Johnnie," describes a lecture by the anarchist advocate of emancipation, Emma Goldman, here called "Emma Silverman." Goldman lectured widely on sex, birth control, and the emancipation of women. She was deported after the First World War for her radical views. Excerpted from Harry Kemp, Tramping on Life: An Autobiographical Narrative *(New York, 1922), 285–88. (Note: Kemp uses a modified form of ellipses in the text.)*

Emma Silverman, the great anarchist leader, came to Laurel, with her manager, Jack Leitman. I went to the Bellman House, the town's swellest hotel, to see her. I had never met her but had long admired her for her activities and bravery. . . .

Her first lecture was on Sex. The hall was jammed to the doors by a curiosity-moved crowd.

She began by assuming that she was not talking to idiots and cretins, but to men and women of mature minds—so she could speak as she

Emma Goldman, anarchist, birth control advocate, and apostle of sexual freedom. (Courtesy of UPI/Corbis-Bettmann.)

thought in a forthright manner. She inveighed against the double standard. When someone in the auditorium asked what she meant by the single standard she replied, she meant sexual expression and experience for man and woman on an equal footing . . the normal living of life without which no human being could be really decent—and that regardless of marriage and the conventions!

"The situation as it is, is odious . . all men, with but few exceptions, have sexual life before marriage, but they insist that their wives come to them in that state of absurd ignorance of their own bodily functions and consequent lack of exercise of them, which they denominate 'purity.' . . I doubt if there is a solitary man in this audience—a married man—who has not had premarital intercourse with women."

All the while I kept my eye on Professor Wilton, who sat near me, in the row ahead . . he was flushing furiously in angry, puritanic dissent . . and I knew him well enough to foresee a forthcoming outburst of protest.

"Yes, I think I can safely say that there is not one married man here who can honestly claim that he came to his wife with that same physical 'purity' which he required of her."

Wilton leaped to his feet in a fury . . the good, simple soul. He was so indignant that the few white hairs on his head worked up sizzling with his emotion. . .

"*Here's one!*" he shouted, forgetting in his earnest anger the assembled audience, most of whom knew him.

There followed such an uproar of merriment as I have never seen the like before nor since. The students, of course, howled with indescribable joy . . Emma Silverman choked with laughter. Jack Leitman rolled over the side table on which he had set the books to sell as the crowd passed out——

After the deafening cries, cat-calls and uproars, Emma grew serious.

"I don't know who you are," she cried to Professor Wilton, "but I'll take chances in telling you that you're a liar!"

Again Wilton was on his feet in angry protest.

"Shame on you, woman! have you no shame!" he shouted.

Excerpt from *Tramping on Life: An Autobiographical Narrative* by Harry Kemp, published by Boni and Liveright Publishers, New York, 1922. Copyright © 1922 by Boni and Liveright, Inc.

This sally brought the house down utterly. The boys hooted and cat-called and stamped again. . .

Emma Silverman laughed till the tears streamed down her face. . .

"I have something on my conscience," remarked Miss Silverman to me, "Johnnie, do you really think that old professor was speaking the truth?"

"I'm sure of it, Miss Silverman."

"Why, then, I'm heartily sorry . . and it was rough of me . . and will you tell the professor for me that I sincerely apologise for having hurt his feelings . . tell him I have so many jackasses attending my lectures all over the country, who rise and say foolish and insincere things, just to stand in well with the communities they live in—that sometimes it angers me, their hypocrisy—and then I blaze forth pretty strong and lay them flat!"

Same-Sex Subcultures

An excerpt from British sexologist Havelock Ellis's Sexual Inversion, *the second volume of a multi-volume work called* Studies in the Psychology of Sex, *describes the existence of same-sex sexual subcultures in U.S. cities. Most observers of such subcultures, like the middle-class reformers who described the heterosexual urban working-class world, expressed the kind of disapproval evident in Ellis's account. The term "invert," introduced by medical commentators at the turn of the century, reflected the assumption that men attracted to men were feminine and women attracted to women were masculine—their gender was "inverted." Taken from Havelock Ellis,* Studies in the Psychology of Sex, *vol. 2,* Sexual Inversion, *3d ed. (Philadelphia, 1933), 351–52, 299–300.*

As regards the prevalence of homosexuality in the United States, I may quote from a well-informed American correspondent:—

"The great prevalence of sexual inversion in American cities is shown by the wide knowledge of its existence. Ninety-nine normal men out of a hundred have been accosted on the streets by inverts, or have among their acquaintances men whom they know to be sexually inverted. Everyone has seen inverts and knows what they are. The public attitude toward them is generally a negative one—indifference, amusement, contempt.

"The world of sexual inverts is, indeed, a large one in any American city, and it is a community distinctly organized—words, customs, traditions of its own; and every city has its numerous meeting-places: certain churches where inverts congregate; certain cafés well known for the inverted character of their patrons; certain streets where, at night, every fifth man is an invert. The inverts have their own 'clubs,' with nightly meetings. These 'clubs' are, really, dance-halls, attached to *saloons*, and presided over by the proprietor of the saloon, himself almost invariably an invert, as are all the waiters and musicians. The frequenters of these places are male sexual inverts (usually ranging from 17 to 30 years of age); sightseers find no difficulty in gaining entrance; truly, they are welcomed for the drinks they buy for the company—and other reasons. Singing and dancing turns by certain favorite performers are the features of these gatherings, with much gossip and drinking at the small tables ranged along the four walls of the room. The habitués of these places are, generally, inverts of the most pronounced type, *i.e.*, the completely feminine in voice and manners, with the characteristic hip motion in their walk; though I have never seen any approach to feminine dress there, doubtless the desire for it is not wanting and only police regulations relegate it to other occasions and places. You will rightly infer that the police know of these places and endure their existence for a consideration; it is not unusual for the inquiring stranger to be directed there by a policeman." . . .

. . . [I]t is notable that of recent years there has been a fashion for a red tie to be adopted by inverts as their badge. This is especially marked among the "fairies" (as a *fellator* is there termed) in New York. "It is red," writes an American correspondent, himself inverted, "that has become almost a synonym for sexual inversion, not only in the minds of inverts themselves, but in the popular mind. To wear a red necktie on the street is to invite remarks from newsboys and others—remarks that have the practices of inverts for their theme. A friend told me once that when a group of street-boys caught sight of the red necktie he was wearing they sucked their fingers in imitation of *fellatio*. Male prostitutes who walk the streets of Philadelphia and New York almost invariably wear red neckties. It is the badge of all their tribe. The rooms of many of my inverted friends have red as the prevailing color in decorations. Among my classmates, at the medical school, few ever had the courage to wear a red tie; those who did never repeated the experiment."

"Prove It On Me Blues"

The blues played an important role as a cultural medium for the expression of sexuality, especially within African American culture. The lesbian lyrics of "Prove It On Me Blues," by bisexual blues singer Ma Rainey, is an example of the unconventional sexuality associated with the Harlem Renaissance. Written by Ma Rainey in 1928, the lyrics of this song are reprinted from Sandra R. Lieb, Mother of the Blues: A Study of Ma Rainey *(Amherst, 1981), 124.*

"Prove It On Me Blues"

Went out last night, had a great big fight,
Everything seemed to go on wrong;
I looked up, to my surprise,
The gal I was with was gone.

Where she went, I don't know,
I mean to follow everywhere she goes;
Folks said I'm crooked, I didn't know where she took it,
I want the whole world to know:

They say I do it, ain't nobody caught me,
Sure got to prove it on me;
Went out last night with a crowd of my friends,
They must've been women, 'cause I don't like no men.

Reprinted from *Mother of the Blues: A Study of Ma Rainey* by Sandra R. Lieb, published by the University of Massachusetts Press, 1981.

It's true I wear a collar and a tie,
Make the wind blow all the while;
They say I do it, ain't nobody caught me,
They sure got to prove it on me.

Say I do it, ain't nobody caught me,
Sure got to prove it on me;
I went out last night with a crowd of my friends,
They must've been women, 'cause I don't like no men.

Wear my clothes just like a fan,
Talk to the gals just like any old man;
'Cause they say I do it, ain't nobody caught me,
Sure got to prove it on me.

Questions

---

1. *What different perceptions of and attitudes about the sexualization of American society can you identify in these documents?*
2. *What different changes in sexual life can you identify from these documents?*
3. *Do you think the changes were greater for women or for men?*
4. *What evidence can you identify in these documents supporting the idea that urban life facilitated changes in sexual behavior?*

FURTHER READING

Intimate Matters: A History of Sexuality in America, *by John D'Emilio and Estelle B. Freedman (New York, 1988), provides a comprehensive overview of changes in sexual attitudes and behavior throughout the history of the U.S.* Kathy Peiss, Cheap Amusements: Working Women and Leisure in Turn-of-the-Century New York *(Philadelphia, 1986), and Joanne J.* Meyerowitz, Women Adrift: Independent Wage Earners in Chicago, 1880–1930 *(Chicago, 1988) discuss the lives of women in the urban working-class subcultures. Kevin White,* The First Sexual Revolution: The Emergence of Male Heterosexuality in Modern America *(New York, 1993), analyzes the impact of the sexual revolution on men.* Gay New York: Gender, Urban Culture, and the Making of the Gay Male World, 1890–1940, *by George Chauncey (New York, 1994), tells the story of changes in the male same-sex subculture of New York.*

Clash of Cultures
in the 1910s and 1920s

William R. Childs

INTRODUCTION

From the colonial times until the present, Americans have had a peculiar ability to look backward and forward at the same time. Tradition and progress have stood side-by-side in the American mind. In the 1910s and 1920s, this paradox interacted with a variety of economic, social, and intellectual forces in a manner that suggested that Americans, for the very first time, were really trying to define themselves as a culture, as a civilization distinct from others. Cultural tensions—conflicts between opposing views of how the world should be and how Americans should define themselves—more intensely and widely engaged Americans between 1915 and 1930 than ever before. The debates took place in the mass media and in the state and national legislatures. At times the conflicts resulted in violence. The next comparable period would be the 1960s and early 1970s.

The explosive nature of the 1910s and 1920s had been building for nearly one-half a century. Expansion of industrialism had by the 1910s set the stage for a number of conflicts. A consumer society that exalted immediate consumption undermined the older producer economy that was based on delayed gratification. Economic expansion attracted more and more immigrants from Eastern and Southern Europe, areas that had not sent many immigrants to the United States before, and that had languages, religions, and cultures different from the White Anglo-Saxon Protestant (WASP) culture that dominated American society in the nineteenth century. At the same time, "modern" ideas from science challenged religious truths that had been held for several centuries. Discoveries in biology, particularly the ideas of Darwinian evolutionism, joined new concepts from physics, such as

Einstein's relativity principles, to challenge older ideas. The new ideas stressed uncertainty and relativism and thus conflicted with older Victorian ideas of stability and predictability. Conflicts between old and new appeared to separate older generations from the younger one. New sexual mores challenged older Victorian beliefs.

The World War I experience enhanced the tensions between old and new. It sharpened Americans' awareness that they were different from Europe, even though many of the American traditions and peoples hailed from Europe. It stimulated more citizens to move from the country to the city, even though the city had a greater number of temptations and vices that challenged many rural beliefs. It showed that national advertising campaigns could stimulate sales of goods. (During the war, the government used national advertising to promote bond sales that financed much of the war effort.) It showed that technological change could greatly affect a war effort—with the result that more soldiers and civilians were affected.

Many Americans did not like the changes being wrought, and they challenged the emerging modern order. While it is too simplistic to say that country folk battled city folk for the power to define the American civilization, it is not too simplistic to argue that people who held traditionally rural values battled those who held modern values. This conflict between city and country appeared more directly in the evolving Democratic party than in the majority Republican party.

Between 1915 and 1930, with the World War I experience accelerating the trend, more and more a number of Americans challenged directly the move toward a modern world. Their challenges took on a variety of forms and encompassed a large number of issues. Some people promoted the idea of restricting the number of new immigrants and "Americanizing" those already here. The infamous Sacco and Vanzetti trial in Massachusetts reflected American fears of "outsiders." Immigration restriction laws targeted such outsiders specifically. Some Americans tried to force others to follow their value systems. Prohibition was in large measure an attempt to control the drinking habits of the working class, comprised mostly of immigrants from Eastern and Southern

Europe. The second Ku Klux Klan, while designed to be a money-making enterprise, also directly challenged the immorality of the cities. Prime targets of KKK violence included not only blacks and immigrants, but also those who participated in the new sexual mores. Much of the conflict of cultures centered around religion and science. Indeed, although the number of churches declined in the 1920s, the number of Americans participating in organized religion increased. The John Scopes trial of 1925—the "monkey trial"—became a national cause celebre, as fundamentalists battled modernists for the power to shape the education of young Americans.

By the early 1930s, the major manifestations of the clash of cultures—Prohibition, immigration restrictions, the KKK, the battle between fundamentalism and scientific inquiry—had decreased in intensity. Opponents of the new values had lost many of the battles. In fact, the Democratic party was clearly evolving away from its Southern and Western roots towards becoming a political organization with an urban base of supporters. But the older values were not totally lost. Later societal eras—the Depression, World War II, and the postwar era—continued to refine what it meant to be "American." And as the clashes of the 1960s and 1970s, and of the 1990s, illustrate, Americans are still capable of noisily debating—sometimes violently—the nature of their culture.

PROHIBITION AND IMMIGRATION RESTRICTION

Much of the clash of cultures focused on the perceived threats that the "new" immigrants posed to the then accepted American norms. In addition to economic competition, the new immigrants represented religious competition, for most of them were Catholics and Jews, religious followers who did not subscribe to the then dominant Protestant religion. Many, moreover, came from nation states that were not based on democracy, but rather on authoritarian statist regimes.

Americans attempted a variety of approaches to stem the tide of new immigrants and/or the changes they were supposedly bringing to society. Some believed the immigrants should be "Americanized." Private businesses and churches sponsored "Americanization" programs in which immigrants were taught the basics that would enable them to participate in American society. English-language instruction and studies of American-style democracy dominated these programs.

Other Americans, however, focused their efforts on directly changing the habits of immigrants or restricting their access to the United States entirely. Prohibition evolved into a program designed for the most part to eliminate from the urban scene the "immigrant saloon," and thus the vices associated with that institution (prostitution, gambling, corruption). Simultaneously, others worked to restrict the number of new immigrants arriving in the United States.

New Perspectives on the Prohibition "Experiment" of the 1920s

Prohibition reflected many of the forces involved in the clash of cultures that animated American society in the 1910s and 1920s. Religious arguments, scientific data, class differences, and urban-rural rivalries permeated the discussions leading to the enactment of national Prohibition during the war era and the law's eventual repeal in 1933. Controls over alcohol had been in place in America since the colonial era, but only at the local level. As industrialism knitted together a national marketplace, so too did it promote a national view on social problems. Indeed, the Progressive era underwent a general transformation from local to state to national attempts to change society. With passage of the Eighteenth Amendment in 1919, the federal government embarked on a more concerted attempt to regulate national drinking habits. Americans had decided that some of the cultural aspects of alcohol—mental disease, inefficient and dangerous workers—were consequences of industrialism that needed to be reformed. Just a little more than a decade after embarking on this reform, however, Americans reversed themselves and repealed the Eighteenth Amendment in 1933. Since then, most observers have labeled the Prohibition era a failure.

In the article that follows, historian John C. Burnham draws upon a variety of arguments and statistics to counter the perception that Prohibition was a failure. He shifts the focus from the 1919–1933 period to include most of the 1910s. He also alleges that the media incorrectly portrayed the consequences of prohibition reform. Given that the targeted groups—working class immigrants—reduced their alcohol consumption during the period, and that increased drinking by middle- and upper-class Americans has been exaggerated, Burnham argues that Prohibition should be viewed as more successful than heretofore believed. If his argument holds up, it may have applications to current discussions on drug laws. Abridged from J. C. Burnham, "New Perspectives on the Prohibition 'Experiment' of the 1920's," Journal of Social History, *2 (Fall 1968): 51–56, 58–68.*

[A] number of historians have shown that the temperance movement that culminated in national prohibition was central to

Excerpts from "New Perspectives on the Prohibition 'Experiment' of the 1920's" by John C. Burnham reprinted from *Journal of Social History*, Vol. 2, No. 1, Fall, 1968. Copyright © 1968 by Peter N. Stearns.

the American reform tradition. . . . [They] have demonstrated in detail how the Eighteenth Amendment was an integral part of the reforms of the Progressive movement. Yet we commonly refer to the "prohibition experiment" rather than the "prohibition reform." This characterization deserves some exploration. . . . One explanation may be that of all of the major reforms enacted into law in the Progressive period, only prohibition was decisively and deliberately repealed. . . .

We have been comfortable for many decades now with the idea that prohibition was a great social experiment. The image of prohibition as an experiment has even been used to draw lessons from history: to argue, for example, that certain types of laws—especially those restricting or forbidding the use of liquor and narcotics—are futile and probably pernicious. . . .

. . . [Other scholarship, however, suggests that] the prohibition experiment . . . can more easily be considered a success than a failure. While far from clear-cut, the balance of scholarly evidence has shifted the burden of proof to those who would characterize the experiment a failure. It is now becoming clear, moreover, how the myth of failure developed and why it flourished.

In order to understand how prohibition came to be a Progressive reform measure, it is necessary to take into account turn-of-the-century class structure among Americans, their drinking habits, and particularly their liquor-by-the-drink retailing institution, the saloon. At that time, typical middle class Americans did not drink, except sometimes wine. Respectable men were careful about being seen in or about a saloon. The saloon was for the most part a noxious institution, in fact inextricably bound up with prostitution, gambling, police corruption, and crime. The image of the respectable, old-fashioned saloon with its free lunch and manly conviviality was to a surprising extent the product of sentimental reminiscing. There were, it is true, many such delightful neighborhood institutions, but most saloons were disreputable places.

. . . [T]he saloon did serve social needs of the working class, especially the first generation immigrants . . . and when middle class reformers took it away from them, the deprived opposed the reform. . . . [But, their voting strength was ineffective.]

The Progressive movement represented an alliance of upper and middle class reformers with two different groups. Many reforms, such as workmen's compensation laws, were achieved by a combination of urban labor elements and the reformers. Other reforms, of which prohibition was the prototype, were achieved by the reformers only with the active aid of a part of the business community in its business capacity. For the Progressives, prohibition . . . was a means by which they could use law to change the personal habits of Americans in general in such a way that both the nation and the individual would profit. The viewpoint of the business elements was not so altruistic, but it was equally convincing. They believed that a sober, temperate worker was a more productive, a more stable, and a happier worker. . . .

. . . Beginning in 1907 a large number of state and local governments enacted laws or adopted constitutional provisions that dried up—as far as alcoholic beverages were concerned—a substantial part of the United States. The success of the anti-liquor forces, led by the Anti-Saloon League, was so impressive that they were prepared to strike for a national prohibition constitutional amendment. This issue was decided in the 1916 Congressional elections, although the Amendment itself was not passed by Congress until December 22, 1917. A sufficient number of states ratified it by January 16, 1919, and it took effect on January 16, 1920.

In actuality, however, prohibition began well before January, 1920. In addition to the widespread local prohibition laws, federal laws greatly restricted the production and sale of alcoholic beverages, mostly, beginning in 1917, in the guise of war legislation. . . . The Volstead Act of 1919, passed to implement the Amendment, provided by law that wartime prohibition would remain in effect until the Amendment came into force.

The Eighteenth Amendment prohibited the manufacturing, selling, importing, or transporting of "intoxicating liquors." It was designed to kill off the liquor business in general and the saloon in particular; but at the same time the Amendment . . . [and the local laws were] not designed to prohibit either the possession or drinking of alcoholic beverages. . . . The very limited nature of the prohibition experiment must, therefore, be understood from the beginning.

At the time, a number of union leaders and social critics pointed out that the Eighteenth Amendment constituted class legislation; that is, the political strength of the drys lay among middle class Progressives who wanted, essentially, to remove the saloon from American life. The Amendment permitted those who had enough money to lay in all the liquor they pleased, but the impecunious [almost penniless] workingman was to be deprived of his day-to-day or week-to-week liquor supply. The class aspect of prohibition later turned out to have great importance. [Although there was widespread support for Prohibition as early as 1916, enforcement of the laws by local and federal agencies was extremely lax. Unwillingness to spend vast sums for enforcement, lack of interest from local judges and juries, and other factors explain this. Only in 1929 did President Herbert Hoover work to increase enforcement.] . . .

With such extreme variations in the enforcement of prohibition over the United States, judging the over-all success of the experiment on the basis of enforcement records is hazardous. . . .

An easier basis for generalizing about the effectiveness of enforcement is the impact that prohibition had on consumption of alcohol. . . . [But a major complication] crops up: the availability of liquor varied greatly from time to time and specifically from an initial period of effectiveness in 1919–1922 to a later period of widespread violation of the law, typically 1925–1927.

. . . Many people, relying on their memories, have generalized from this later period, after about 1925, to all of the prohibition years and have come, falsely, to the conclusion that enforcement was neither real nor practical. Overall one can say that considering the relatively slight amount of effort put into it, enforcement was surprisingly effective in many places, and particularly in the early years.

Both so-called wet and dry sources agree that the amount of liquor consumed per capita decreased substantially because of prohibition. The best figures available show that the gallons of pure alcohol ingested per person varied widely over four different periods. In the period 1911–1914, the amount was 1.69 gallons. Under the wartime restrictions, 1918–1919, the amount decreased to .97. In the early years of national prohibition, 1921–1922, there was still further decrease to .73 gallons. In the later years of prohibition, 1927–1930, the amount rose to 1.14 gallons. . . . [These statistics show that "prohibition" began well before 1920.] The peak of absolute consumption of beer, for example, was reached in the years 1911–1914, not 1916–1918, much less 1919. . . .

The best independent evidence of the impact of prohibition can be found in the available figures for certain direct and measurable social effects of alcohol consumption. The decrease from about 1915 to 1920–1922 in arrests for drunkenness, in hospitaliza-

Several men dash bottles of alcohol to the ground in a dump during the Prohibition era in 1923. (Courtesy of The Library of Congress.)

tion for alcoholism, and in the incidence of other diseases, such as cirrhosis of the liver, specifically related to drinking was remarkable. The low point of these indexes came in 1918–1921, and then they climbed again until the late 1920's. . . . [Thus] there is clear evidence that in the early years of prohibition not only did the use of alcohol decrease but American society enjoyed some of the direct benefits promised by proponents of prohibition.

Undoubtedly the most convincing evidence of the success of prohibition is to be found in the mental hospital admission rates. There is no question of a sudden change in physicians' diagnoses, and the people who had to deal with alcohol-related mental diseases were obviously impressed by what they saw. . . . [Burnham cites one example: the admission rate for alcohol psychoses in New York state hospitals fell from 10 percent between 1909–1912 to 1.9 percent in 1920.] For many years articles on alcoholism literally disappeared from American medical literature.

In other words, after World War I and until sometime in the early 1920's, say, 1922 or 1923, when enforcement was clearly breaking down, prohibition was generally a success. Certainly there is no basis for the conclusion that prohibition was inherently doomed to failure. The emasculation of enforcement grew out of specific factors that were not organically related to the Eighteenth Amendment.

. . .[M]ost of the criticism of prohibition has centered around assertions not so much that the experiment failed but that it had two more or less unexpected consequences that clearly show it to have been undesirable. The critics claim, first, that the Eighteenth Amendment caused dangerous criminal behavior; and, second, that in spite of prohibition more people drank alcohol than before. If a candid examination fails to confirm these commonly accepted allegations, the interpretation of prohibition as a failure loses most of its validity. Such is precisely the case.

During the 1920's there was almost universal public belief that a "crime wave" existed in the United States. In spite of the literary output on the subject, dealing largely with a local situation in Chicago, there is no firm evidence of this supposed upsurge in lawlessness. Two criminologists . . . at the end of the decade reviewed the available crime statistics, and the most that they could conclude was that "there is no evidence here of a 'crime wave,' but only of a slowly rising level." These admittedly inadequate statistics emphasized large urban areas and were, it should be emphasized, *not* corrected to reflect the increase in population. Actually no statistics from this period dealing with crime are of any value whatsoever in generalizing about crime rates. Apparently what happened was that in the 1920's the long existent "underworld" first became publicized and romanticized. The crime wave, in other words, was the invention of enterprising journalists feeding on some sensational crimes and situations and catering to a public to whom the newly discovered "racketeer" was a covert folk hero.

Even though there was no crime wave, there was a connection between crime and prohibition, as Frederick Lewis Allen suggested in his alliterative coupling of "Alcohol and Al Capone." Because of the large profits involved in bootlegging and the inability of the producers and customers to obtain police protection, criminal elements organized and exploited the liquor business just as they did all other illegal activities. It would be a serious distortion even of racketeering, however, to emphasize bootlegging at the expense of the central criminal-directed activity, gambling. Since liquor-related activities were not recognized as essentially criminal in nature by substantial parts of the population, it is difficult to argue that widespread violation of the Volstead Act constituted a true increase of crime. Nevertheless, concern over growing federal "crime" statistics, that is, bootlegging cases, along with fears based on hysterical journalism, helped to bring about repeal.

We are left, then, with the question of whether national prohibition led to more drinking than before. It should first be pointed out not only that the use of 1920 as the beginning of prohibition is misleading but that much of the drinking during the 1920's was not relevant to the prohibition of the Eighteenth Amendment and Volstead Act. Private drinking was perfectly legal all of the time, and possession of liquor that had been accumulated by the foresighted before prohibition was entirely lawful. The continued production of cider and wine at home was specifically provided for also. Indeed, the demand for wine grapes was so great that many grape growers who in 1919 faced ruin made a fortune selling their grapes in the first years of the Amendment. . . .

We still face the problem of reconciling the statistics quoted above that show that alcohol consumption was substantially reduced, at one point to about half of the pre-prohibition consumption, with the common observation of the 1920's that as many or more people were drinking than before.

What happened, one can say with hindsight, was predictable. When liquor became unavailable except at some risk and considerable cost, it became a luxury item, that is, a symbol of affluence and, eventually, status. Where before men of good families tended not to drink and women certainly did not, during the 1920's it was precisely the sons and daughters of the "nice" people who were patronizing the bootleggers and speakeasies, neither of which for some years was very effectively available to the lower classes. This utilization of drinking as conspicuous consumption was accompanied by the so-called revolution in manners and morals that began among the rebellious intellectuals around 1912 and reached a high point of popularization in the 1920's when the adults of the business class began adopting the "lower" social standards of their children.

We can now understand why the fact was universally reported by journalists of the era that "everyone drank, including many who never did before." Drinking, and often new drinking, was common among the upper classes, especially among the types of people likely to consort with the writers of the day. The journalists and other observers did indeed report honestly that they saw "everyone" drinking. They seldom saw the lower classes and almost never knew about the previous drinking habits of the masses. . . .

The important point is that the "everyone" who was reported to be drinking did not include working-class families, i.e., the preponderant part of the population. . . . [Burnham then cites two studies that concluded that working-class families were consuming much less, perhaps as much as one-half less alcohol under Prohibition.] Even in its last years the law, with all of its leaks, was still effective in cutting down drinking among the workers, which was one of the primary aims of prohibition. . . . Taking together all of this evidence of the success of prohibition, especially in its class differential aspects, we are still left with the question of why the law was repealed. [Until about 1923, criticisms of Prohibition emanated from a small minority of contemporary observers in the cities. The notion of repeal did not exist.]

. . . In 1923–1924 a major shift in the attitudes of the mass circulation information media occurred so that acceptance was replaced by nearly universal outright criticism accompanied by a demand for modification of the Volstead Act. The criticism was based on the assumption that Volsteadism, at least, was a failure. The suggested solution was legalizing light wines and beers.

. . . [The drys counterattacked, and consequently claimed too much for the Prohibition movement. Their opponents, basing their arguments on the perceived "crime wave," argued that if] the most respectable elements of society . . . openly showed contempt for the Constitution, how could anyone be expected to honor a mere statute? Much of the leadership of the "anti's" soon came from the bar associations rather than the bar patrons.

Coincident with this shift in opinion came the beginning of one of the most effective publicity campaigns of modern times, led by the Association Against the Prohibition Amendment. At first largely independent of liquor money, in the last years of prohibition the AAPA used all it could command. By providing journalists with reliable information, the AAPA developed a virtual monopoly on liquor and prohibition press coverage. . . .

. . . [The AAPA targeted the Volstead Act for modification, and worked in the states to repeal local enforcement statutes. The AAPA did not expect to gain outright repeal of the Eighteenth Amendment.] But suddenly an overwhelming surge of public sentiment brought about the Twenty-First Amendment denouement.

The cause of this second sudden shift in opinion was the Great Depression that began about 1929. . . . These [post-Depression] rationalizations of repeal were masks for the fact that the general public, baffled by the economic catastrophe, found a convenient scapegoat: prohibition. (The drys had, after all, tried to credit prohibition for the prosperity of the 1920's.) . . .

Because the AAPA won, its explanations of what happened were accepted at face value. One of the lasting results of prohibition, therefore, was perpetuation of the stereotypes of the wet propaganda of the 1920's and the myth that the American experiment in prohibition (usually misunderstood to have outlawed personal drinking as well as the liquor business) was a failure. Blanketed together here indiscriminately were all of the years from 1918 to 1933. . . .

The concern now is not so much the destruction of myth, however; the concern is that our acceptance of the myth of the failure of prohibition has prevented us from exploring in depth social and especially sociological aspects of the prohibition experiment.

Out of Many, One: Immigration Restriction

Historian Carl Degler surveys the rationales behind the movement to restrict the number of immigrants coming to the United States. The centerpiece legislation, the 1924 National Origins Act, passed and became law as Americans continued to follow the Sacco and Vanzetti trial and its appeals. The questionable courtroom antics of both sides in that trial revealed the tensions of the clash of cultures. A majority in Congress believed it was easier and safer simply to prevent other Saccos and Vanzettis from entering the United States. Taken from Carl N. Degler, Out of Our Past: The Forces That Shaped Modern America, *rev. ed. (New York, 1970), 299–302.*

[There appeared in the late nineteenth century] a movement to restrict both the numbers and the kinds of people who could enter the United States—an approach to the immigrant which was new to American thought. The first concrete step in this direction was taken in 1882, when Congress, responding to the fears of

Californians and others, prohibited the future immigration of Chinese.

During the remaining years of the century, a number of broadly based groups and organizations displayed mounting concern over the possible changes and dangers the rising flood of immigrants would inflict upon American society. Businessmen, for instance, though torn between their economic self-interest in cheap immigrant labor and their worry over social disturbances sparked by foreigners, began to speak out in favor of some kind of restriction on immigration. Labor leaders were similarly of two minds on the subject, but by the late nineties organized labor was taking a stand in favor of cutting down on immigration. . . .

The whole movement was given intellectual underpinning by . . . [scholars from Columbia, Harvard, and M.I.T.]. For years these learned gentlemen and others like them preached the gospel of the Anglo-Saxon heritage of Americans, warning in elegant tones against the degradation which awaited the country if the immigrant tide—particularly that part of it originating in eastern and southern Europe—was left unchecked.

Anglo-Saxonism, moreover, was popular as well as academic. . . . [A labor organizer informed Congress] that he wanted to see that type of immigrant "to come from which we came . . . I glory in my kinship," he remarked. "My father on one side, was a German, my father upon the other was an Englishman. . . . That is the kind we can absorb. . . . They belonged to that independent race . . . who . . . came with the idea already imbedded in their hearts and minds of the beauties of self-government."

To achieve the dual purpose of limiting numbers and at the same time discriminating between desirable and undesirable peoples, the advocates of restriction hit upon the literacy test. . . .

Three times measures providing for a literacy test were driven through Congress by public concern over the ability of America to absorb so many different kinds of people. And each time they were vetoed. Woodrow Wilson spoke for his predecessors when he told the Congress in his veto of 1915 that the literacy tests represented a "radical change in the policy of the Nation." . . . But

---

Excerpts reprinted from *Out of Our Past: The Forces That Shaped Modern America* by Carl N. Degler. Copyright © 1959, 1970 by Carl N. Degler. Reprinted by permission of HarperCollins Publishers, Inc.

the vetoes were only temporary holding actions; the literacy test became law in 1917 over Wilson's second veto.

. . . Some leaders . . . injected the dangerous doctrine of race into the question of the immigrant. "Mental, spiritual and moral traits . . . are closely associated with the physical distinctions among the different European races. The Alpine race [i.e., eastern Europeans] is always and everywhere a race of peasants. . . . The Nordics are, all over the world, a race of soldiers, sailors, adventurers, and explorers, but above all, of rulers, organizers and aristocrats in sharp contrast to the essentially peasant character of the Alpines."

Racist views like . . . [this] were not confined to the study or select company; variants of them were a part of acceptable discourse at the seat of government. "Our capacity to maintain our cherished institutions stands diluted by a stream of alien blood, with all its inherited misconceptions respecting the relationship of the governing power to the governed," contended Congressman Albert Johnson, chairman of the House Committee on Immigration in 1927. Heretofore the Negro had been the primary target of racist thought, but under the impact of the new immigration such thinking was applied to the newcomers as well. . . .

The principal step in the restriction of immigration was taken in the twenties. . . . [A] severe reduction of numbers was provided for in the 1924 law; no more than 150,000 could enter the country within a single year, though as recently as 1921 over 800,000 had come in. But more significant than the large cut in numbers was the law's effort to deal with the question of western versus southern European immigration, always the central concern of restrictionists and racists. . . .

Superficially at least, a theory of American culture was evident here. It assumed that the people of the United States had attained the proper ethnic mixture and no further change was desirable; immigrants were to come into the country in proportion to the numbers already here. If examined a little more closely, the measure also revealed a decided ethnic bias against the eastern and southern Europeans. . . . For purposes of setting quotas, the total population of the United States was to be broken down into countries of origin, regardless of how far back the first generation came over. This was a procedure which obviously favored the northern and western Europeans, since they had been the earliest immigrants and by 1920 would count the most descendants. . . .

[T]he national origins approach to immigration remained American policy for over forty years.

Questions

---

1. *Generally, do you think Burnham proved his case that Prohibition should be considered a success? Who and what were the basic targets of Prohibition? How does this reflect the clash of values that animates this period of American history?*
2. *Are there any other factors that Burnham did not consider in explaining the drop in alcohol consumption by the working class? What factors, other than the Great Depression, could explain the movement for repeal? Could changing political alignments have had an effect? What other factors made old arguments more viable in the early 1930s?*
3. *Can you rank-order, from most important to least important, the main forces behind the movement to restrict the number of immigrants?*
4. *What lessons for the present can be gleaned from these analyses of the past?*

CONTEMPORARY ANALYSES OF THE KKK AND THE "MONKEY TRIAL"

Prohibition and immigration restriction were two aspects of the clash of cultures that manifested themselves in the national political arena. Both utilized the national government to promote the shaping of the American culture. Although two other movements—the second KKK and the Scopes trial—drew national attention, both took place for the most part in the local and state government arenas. Like prohibition, but unlike immigration restriction, both were momentary crusades that did not sustain government support for their causes. All four movements, however, reasserted themselves throughout the rest of the twentieth century.

The Second KKK

Ironically, the KKK used modern business techniques to stem the tide of modernism. The KKK drew on Americans' anxieties with the changes occurring in society to build membership and thus enhance the coffers of the institution. The Klan did try—and in a few cases succeeded for a short time—to use government to foster its goals of returning Americans to older values.

The following extract, written in 1931 by journalist Frederick Lewis Allen, presents, on one level, the facts behind the rise and decline of the Klan. On another level, however, the selections reveal where Allen stood

Excerpts reprinted from *Only Yesterday: An Informal History of the Nineteen-Twenties* by Frederick L. Allen. Copyright © 1931 by Frederick Lewis Allen. Copyright renewed 1959 by Agnes Rogers Allen. Reprinted by permission of HarperCollins Publishers, Inc.

in the clash of cultures that the Klan embodied. Only recently have historians begun to re-evaluate the Klan phenomenon in order to obtain a better understanding of why people joined the Klan. Taken from Frederick Lewis Allen, Only Yesterday: An Informal History of the Nineteen-Twenties *(New York, 1964), 54–57.*

The Klan had been founded as far back as 1915 by a Georgian named Colonel William Joseph Simmons, but its first five years had been lean. When 1920 arrived, Colonel Simmons had only a few hundred members in his amiable patriotic and fraternal order, which drew its inspiration from the Ku-Klux Klan of Reconstruction days and stood for white supremacy and sentimental Southern idealism in general. But in 1920 Simmons put the task of organizing the Order into the hands of one Edward Y. Clarke of the Southern Publicity Association. Clarke's gifts of salesmanship . . . were prodigious. The time was ripe for the Klan, and he knew it. Not only could it be represented to potential members as the defender of the white against the black, of Gentile against Jew, and of Protestant against Catholic, and thus trade on all the newly inflamed fears of the credulous small-towner, but its white robe and hood, its flaming cross, its secrecy, and the preposterous vocabulary of its ritual could be made the vehicle for all that infantile love of hocus-pocus and mummery, that lust for secret adventure, which survives in the adult whose lot is cast in drab places. Here was a chance to dress up the village bigot and let him be a Knight of the Invisible Empire. The formula was perfect. And there was another inviting fact to be borne in mind. Well organized, such an Order could be made a paying proposition.

The salesmen of memberships were given the entrancing title of Kleagles; the country was divided into Realms headed by King Kleagles, and the Realms into Domains headed by Grand Goblins; Clarke himself, as chief organizer, became Imperial Kleagle, and the art of nomenclature reached its fantastic pinnacle in the title bestowed upon Colonel Simmons: he became the Imperial Wizard. A membership cost ten dollars; and as four of this went into the pocket of the Kleagle who made the sale, it was soon apparent that a diligent Kleagle need not fear the wolf at the door. Kleagling became one of the profitable industries of the decade. The King Kleagle of the Realm and Grand Goblin of the Domain took a small rake-off from the remaining six dollars of the membership fee, and the balance poured into the Imperial Treasury at Atlanta.

... [In 1921] Simmons was succeeded as Imperial Wizard by a Texas dentist named Hiram Wesley Evans, who referred to himself, perhaps with some justice, as "the most average man in America"; but a humming sales organization had been built up and the Klan continued to grow. It grew, in fact, with such inordinate rapidity that early in 1924 its membership had reached ... the staggering figure of nearly four and a half millions. It came to wield great political power, dominating for a time the seven states of Oregon, Oklahoma, Texas, Arkansas, Indiana, Ohio, and California. Its chief strongholds were the New South, the Middle West, and the Pacific coast, but it had invaded almost every part of the country and had even reached the gates of that stronghold of Jewry, Catholicism, and sophistication, New York City. So far had Clarke's genius and the hospitable temper of the times carried it.

The objects of the Order as stated in its Constitution were "to unite white male persons, native-born Gentile citizens of the United States of America, who owe no allegiance of any nature to any foreign government, nation, institution, sect, ruler, person, or people; whose morals are good, whose reputations and vocations are exemplary ... to cultivate and promote patriotism toward our Civil Government; to practice an honorable Klanishess toward each other; to exemplify a practical benevolence; to shield the sanctity of the home and the chastity of womanhood; to maintain forever white supremacy, to reach and faithfully inculcate a high spiritual philosophy through an exalted ritualism, and by a practical devotion to conserve, protect, and maintain the distinctive institutions, rights, privileges, principles, traditions and ideals of a pure Americanism."

Thus the theory. In practice the "pure Americanism" varied with the locality. At first, in the South, white supremacy was the Klan's chief objective, but as time went on and the organization grew and spread, opposition to the Jew and above all to the Catholic proved the best talking point for Kleagles in most localities. Nor did the methods of the local Klan organizations usually suggest the possession of a "high spiritual philosophy." These local organizations were largely autonomous and beyond control from Atlanta. They were drawn, as a rule, mostly from the less educated and less disciplined elements of the white Protestant community. ("You think the influential men belong here?" commented an outspoken observer in an Indiana city. "Then look at their shoes when they march in parade. The sheet doesn't cover the shoes.") Though Imperial Wizard Evans inveighed against lawlessness, the members of the local Klans were not always content with voting against allowing children to attend parochial schools, or voting against Catholic candidates for office, or burning fiery crosses on the hilltop back of the town to show the niggers that the whites meant business. The secrecy of the Klan was an invitation to more direct action.

If a white girl reported that a colored man had made improper advances to her—even if the charge were unsupported and based on nothing more than a neurotic imagination—a white-sheeted band might spirit the Negro off to the woods and "teach him a lesson" with tar and feathers or with the whip. If a white man stood up for a Negro in a race quarrel, he might be kidnapped and beaten up. If a colored woman refused to sell her land at an arbitrary price which she considered too low, and a Klansman wanted the land, she might receive the K. K. K. ultimatum—sell or be thrown out. Klan members would boycott Jewish merchants, refuse to hire Catholic boys, refuse to rent their houses to Catholics. A hideous tragedy in Louisiana, where five men were kidnapped and later found bound with wire and drowned in a lake,

A parade of Ku Klux Klan members march along Pennsylvania Avenue in the nation's capital in 1926. (Courtesy of The Library of Congress.)

was laid to Klansmen. R. A. Patton, writing in *Current History*, reported a grim series of brutalities from Alabama: "A lad whipped with branches until his back was ribboned flesh; a Negress beaten and left helpless to contract pneumonia from exposure and die; a white girl, divorcée, beaten into unconsciousness in her own home; a naturalized foreigner flogged until his back was a pulp because he married an American woman; a Negro lashed until he sold his land to a white man for a fraction of its value."

Even where there were no such outrages, there was at least the threat of them. The white-robed army paraded, the burning cross glowed across the valley, people whispered to one another in the darkness and wondered "who they were after this time," and fear and suspicion ran from house to house. Furthermore, criminals and gangs of hoodlums quickly learned to take advantage of the Klan's existence: if they wanted to burn someone's barn or raid the slums beyond the railroad tracks, they could do it with impunity now: would not the Klan be held responsible? Anyone could chalk the letters K. K. K. on a fence and be sure that the sheriff would move warily. Thus, as in the case of the Red hysteria, a movement conceived in fear perpetuated fear and brought with it all manner of cruelties and crimes.

Slowly, as the years passed and the war-time emotions ebbed, the power of the Klan waned, until in many districts it was dead and in others it had become merely a political faction dominated by spoilsmen: but not until it had become a thing of terror to millions of men and women.

Rescued Self-Esteem

In this extract from sociologist John Moffatt Mecklin, we see a somewhat different approach to understanding the motivations behind the rise of the KKK. Extracted from John Moffatt Mecklin, The Ku Klux Klan: A Study of the American Mind *(New York, 1924), 107–8.*

He is tossed about in the hurly-burly of our industrial and so-called democratic society. Under the stress and strain of social competition he is made to realize his essential mediocrity. Yet according to traditional democratic doctrine he is born free and the equal of his fellow who is outdistancing him in the race. Here is a large and powerful organization offering to solace his sense of defeat by dubbing him a knight of the Invisible Empire for the small sum of ten dollars. Surely knighthood was never offered at such a bargain!

The Monkey Trial and the *New York Times*

The so-called "monkey trial" in Dayton, Tennessee, in mid-summer 1925, attracted a lot of media attention across the U.S. and in Europe. The New York Times included coverage every day during the month of July, sometimes including several stories. Although the New York Times included copy on both sides of the issue, the newspaper's editorial stance clearly favored one side: modernism over fundamentalism.

While there were many actors in this media event, several were central to the drama that unfolded in the hot summer of 1925. John Scopes was the teacher accused of violating the state's law that forbade the teaching of evolution in the schools. Clarence Darrow was a prominent civil liberties lawyer who led the defense. William Jennings Bryan, a candidate for president in 1896 and several times thereafter, Woodrow Wilson's secretary of state, and most recently a traveling fundamentalist preacher and huckster for Florida real estate, lent his prestige to the prosecution. For both Darrow and Bryan, the trial was not over whether or not Scopes violated the law, but rather over what values should define American culture. Darrow reflected "modernist" views that encompassed the new sciences and freedom of thought and speech. Bryan reflected some Americans' desires that Protestant religious principles should anchor American culture.

What follows is a chronological sampling of coverage from the New York Times. Often the headlines alone indicated the content of the story that followed. Other times the text filled in necessary detail. The presentation of these primary sources draws from a technique that the novelist John Dos Passos employed in his USA trilogy, three novels on the 1920s written in the 1930s. It is intended to convey the breadth, and sometimes

---

Excerpts from *The Ku Klux Klan: A Study of the American Mind* by John Moffatt Mecklin, Ph.D., published by Russell & Russell, 1924. Reprinted with the permission of Simon & Schuster.

Opposing attorneys Clarence Darrow and William Jennings Bryan chat during the Scopes Trial. (Courtesy of AP/Wide World Photos.)

depth(s), of the story that caught Americans' attention in 1925. The issues embraced include science versus religion; state versus national law; the separation of church and state; city versus country; and, always, the fight over who would define American culture. Students are encouraged to find the original stories (generally available in newspaper microfilm collections in university and public libraries) and read them for more detail.

JULY 4, 1925, PAGE 2

Scopes Attorneys Fight Dayton Trial

To Ask Federal Court Monday for Injunction Based on Law's Unconstitutionality.

SHUN CIRCUS ATMOSPHERE

Darrow Says Case Is Too Serious to Be Made a Jest, as Other States May Ban Evolution.

JULY 4, 1925, PAGE 10 (EDITORIAL PAGE)

More Than Scopes Is on Trial.

Being a man of ability, CLARENCE DARROW sees much more in the Scopes case than the trial of a young school teacher on the charge of breaking an absurd law. To MR. DARROW it is a much larger thing than that, and for him it is larger by the fact that two other States already have passed similar laws, while in two others like laws have been beaten by the narrowest of majorities, and in some twenty more the enemies of evolution are actively engaged in preaching to the ignorant and fanatical the taking of like action. This he sees as only a beginning of an effort to enslave the human mind and as something to be met and fought at once. . . .

But these questions are not at all involved in the indictment of MR. SCOPES, or they are involved only indirectly and in a way to which it seems impossible for a Judge ... to consider. And it will not be for them to decide whether the law is constitutional or not. Power to do that will lie in higher courts on appeal. . . .

It is to be regretted that the affair has so many amusing features and that it lies under some suspicion, probably unjust, of being an advertising dodge invented by the inhabitants of Dayton.

[The New York Times was incorrect in its assumption! Scopes had agreed to go on trial when business leaders of Dayton approached him to

Bible

Author of Tennessee Law Tells Motives That Led Him to Frame It.

Fears For The Children

Believes Statute, if Enforced, Will Prevent Them From Becoming Infidels.

HAS SPENT LIFE ON FARM

J. W. Butler Is a Primitive Baptist Who Believes Government Is Founded on Scripture.

. . . [John W. Butler:] "For some time it has been against the law of Tennessee to teach the Bible in the public schools or to allow the teaching of any system of religion, although the Bible can be read in such schools without comment. If this law can be upheld, I am satisfied that a law which, in my opinion and those of thousands of other Tennessee

institute a test court case.]

JULY 5, 1925, SECTION 4, PAGE 1 (MAGAZINE SECTION)

The Evolution Arena At Dayton

Circus Sideshows and Curious Visitors Descend Upon Tennessee Mountain Town, but Legal Struggle Will Involve Christian Faith, Science, Free Speech, and the Constitution

JULY 5, 1925, SECTION 2, PAGE 1

Fights Evolution To Uphold

Injunction; State Trial Friday

Judge Gore Rules Tennessee Officers Are Acting in the Only Way They Are Authorized.

Two Petitions Presented

Teacher Charges Violation of Liberty—Parent Asserts Right to Educate His Children.

Appeal To Be Taken Later

Darrow Says He Fears the State Court May Limit the Case to

Scopes Fails To Get Federal

JULY 7, 1925, PAGE 1

---

parents, would tend to prevent the making of infidels of our children can be equally enforced."

JULY 6, 1925, PAGE 2

Doubts Scopes Violated The Law

Chattanooga Bar Association Head Says It Doesn't Prohibit Teaching of Evolution.

Explains Act's Meaning

John C. Cantrill Disapproved Use of Court Proceeding as Background for Personal Publicity.

... "Many people outside the State who have become excited over the case of John T. Scopes, the Dayton teacher indicted for violation of the law prohibiting the teaching of evolution in the public schools, have expressed surprise that Tennessee lawyers, as a rule, have seemed to consider the case as of little importance.

... [The Tennessee lawyers] are justified in this ... because:

"First, the so-called anti-evolution law is very narrow in its scope, and does not prohibit the teaching of evolution as is generally supposed.

"Second, I do not believe ... that Professor Scope, or any other Tennessee teacher, has actually violated the act by affirmatively teaching 'that man has descended from a lower order of animals.' Any teacher may teach that there was no divine creation of anything, that everything in Nature happened by chance, and that the Bible teaching on every subject is false from Genesis to Revelation and he will not violate this law, unless he also affirmatively teaches 'that man has descended from a lower order of animals.' ["]

JULY 7, 1925, PAGE 1

199

JULY 9, 1925, PAGE 1

Bryan Threatens National Campaign To Bar Evolution

Warns That if Defeated in the Courts the Bible Will Be Put Into the Constitution.

Sees Morality Imperiled

He Declares There Is a Majority in Every State to Push Through Federal Amendment.

DAYTON READY FOR TRIAL

. . . Altogether, Mr. Bryan was in good humor. He had been met at the station by about 300 people, 50 of whom were reporters and photographers, had been paraded up the main street in an automobile, had shaken hands with all those on the side of the prosecution and some interested in the defense, had had a long talk with the lawyers with whom he will be associated, had been interviewed, had an ice cream soda in the drug store, and made a speech at a dinner in his honor. It was Bryan day, for there was no other distinguished visitor in town. He even looked at the court house where he will declaim against evolution, sitting far back from the road behind a green lawn and trees, and pronounced it good.

Whether Law Was Violated.

JULY 8, 1925, PAGE 1

Bryan In Dayton, Calls Scopes Trial Duel To The Death

If Evolution Wins, He Declares, Christianity Goes, for Both Cannot Survive.

Sees The Bible At Stake

Trying to Destroy It, He Asserts, on Evidence That Would Not Convict a Habitual Criminal.

CROWD CHEERS HIS ARRIVAL

200

July 10, 1925, page 1

Dayton Keyed Up For Opening

Today Of Trial Of Scopes

Intense Excitement Grips Town as Principals Reach Scene of Battle on Evolution.

JUDGE GIVES HIS ATTITUDE

Says He Wants Inquiry for "Eternal Truth" and Warns Against Personal Ambitions.

STATE'S CASE TO BE BRIEF

Defense Will Then Produce Scientists and Educators—Catholics Offer Help to Bryan.

Trial Attracts Many Cranks.

People have come from all over the South to Dayton. What they hope to get out of it is a problem. One negro drifted in from Georgia today, having got leave from his employer to come here and work for his employer's relatives for the duration of the trial. He wanted to see the show. One or two women, with obvious mental irregularities of a religious tendency, have come to town, and chatter volubly to any one who will listen to them.

A man who calls himself the greatest authority on the Bible, proclaimed by a large sign on his back on which is printed inversions of Bible phrases, trots up and down indefatigably. He is willing to exhort anybody at any time on any subject.

"Independent," the only proponent of evolution to appear so far, is James Pollock Kohler of 350 Fulton Street, Brooklyn. He announced he came "on his own hook to combat the influence of Bryan on the outside." He said he was ready to hire a hall and speak to the people on "evils of accepting the Bible literally."

"Monkey town" is the name of Dayton in the rest of Tennessee. Whatever the deep significance of this trial, if it has any, there is no doubt that it has attracted some of the world's champion freaks.

201

JULY 11, 1925, PAGE 1

Who's Who and What's What in Scopes Trial

Plaintiff—The People of the State of Tennessee through their legal officers, who have the aid of volunteer outside counsel.

Defendant—John Thomas Scopes, 24 years old, native of Paducah, Ky., teacher of biology in the Rhea County High School at Dayton.

The Charge—That Scopes taught his pupils that man descended from a lower order of animals, in violation of a State statute forbidding such teaching.

Penalty—A fine of not less than $100 nor more than $500 for each offense.

Counsel for Prosecution—William Jennings Bryan, ex-presidential candidate and ex-Secretary of State; General Ben McKenzie, ex-District Attorney of Dayton; J. Gordon McKenzie, his son; Sue and Herbert Hicks, young Dayton lawyers; E. T. Stewart, Circuit Attorney General; Walter White, Superintendent of Schools and County Prosecutor; W. C. Haggard, Dayton attorney; William Jennings Bryan Jr.

Counsel for Defense—Clarence Darrow of Chicago, noted criminal lawyer; John R. Neal, Knoxville, former acting Dean of the University of Tennessee Law School; Dudley Field Malone, New York attorney.

The Jury—W. F. Robertson, tenant farmer; J. W. Dagley, farmer; James Riley, farmer; W. J. Taylor, farmer; R. L. Gentry, farmer and teacher; J. R. Thompson, farm owner (retired); W. D. Smith, farmer; W. J. Day, retired farmer; Jesse Goodrich, shipping clerk; J. S. Wright, farmer; J. H. Bowman, farmer; R. L. West, farmer.

Trial before Judge J. T. Raulston of Winchester, Tenn., Judge of the Eighteenth Tennessee Circuit, in Rhea County Court House, Dayton.

The Law in the Case.

Be it enacted by the General Assembly of the State of Tennessee, That it shall be unlawful for any teacher in any of the universities, normals and all other public schools of the State which are supported in whole or in part by the public school funds of the State, to teach any theory that denies the story of the Divine creation of man as taught in the Bible, and to teach instead that man has descended from a lower order of animals.

Be it further enacted, That any teacher found guilty of the violation of this act, shall be guilty of a misdemeanor. * * *

JULY 11, 1925, PAGES 1-2

Europe Is Amazed By The Scopes Case

NOTED SCIENTISTS PROTEST

LONDON, July 10.—The Scopes trial at Dayton, Tenn., is attracting the widest attention of the British press, scientists and public men. All the published opinion strongly condemns the prosecution of the school teacher or expresses amazement that an American State should attempt to prevent the teaching of the known facts of evolution. . . .

Sir Arthur Shipley, Master of Christ College, Cambridge, one of the many prominent educators expressing views of the Dayton trial . . . says the average American of the Middle and Southern States is a very "naive mammal."

"As a prominent citizen tells us in the current number of the National Review," he says, "the United States is a nation of adult children and certainly some things they do seem to older and more mature countries decidedly childish. And after all thought is free in spite of William Jennings Bryan. If one likes to think that man is descended from animals resembling man it will be very difficult to stop it.". . .

The Rev. Frank Ballard, Christian Evidence lecturer for the Wesleyan conference, writes:

"The assumptions of Fundamentalism are so preposterous, alike in theory and practice, I am not altogether surprised when I called to mind my experiences in America twenty-five years ago. It was pitifully manifest then that both the science and theology of many of those who posed as authorities were half a century behind the times. But one did hope the intervening years would have opened their eyes. The notion of a Judge's charge to the Grand Jury beginning with the reading of the First Chapter of Genesis as an account of creation which Tennessee teachers must adopt savors of sixteenth rather than the twentieth century.". . .

"To those who think of the United States as the extreme expression of modern spirit, the man or ape trial in Tennessee must come as a severe shock. To a smaller number of Englishmen who judge America not by its movies or its millionaires or motor cars or its schemes for regeneration, on a strictly dividend paying basis, of the Old World, but by its attitude toward abstract ideas there is nothing surprising, though there is much that is curious in that heresy hunt.

July 11, 1925, PAGE 1

Scopes Jury Chosen With Dramatic Speed After Prayer Opens Picturesque Trial; State Fights Testimony By Scientists

FARMERS WILL TRY TEACHER

Jury Includes Ten, a Schoolmaster and a Shipping Clerk.

ONE IS UNABLE TO READ

None Believes in Evolution, but Darrow Says He Did Not Expect to Find Any Who Did.

July 12, 1925, PAGE 1

Hostility Grows In Dayton Crowds; Champions Clash

Bryan and Darrow Gird for Monday's Battle, Contending Over Testimony by Scientists.

Sectional Feeling Raised

Bryan Scores 'Invasion of Outsiders'—Defense Counsel Tilts at Commoner's 'Chinese Wall.'

JULY 13, 1925, PAGE 1

Dayton's One Pro-Evolution Pastor Quits As Threat Bars Dr. Potter From Pulpit; Bryan's Sermons Anger Scopes Defense

Trial Stirs Local Storm

Preacher Is Told Church Would Be Wrecked Over New York 'Infidel.'

3,000 Listen to Commoner

JULY 13, 1925, PAGE 15

CALLS DAYTON TRIAL A SILLY PERFORMANCE

Evolution Does Not Contradict Fact of Creation, Says the Rev. W. B. Kinkead.

JULY 13, 1925, PAGE 15

Says Bryan Group Betrays Freedom

Trying to Put the State Behind a Religion of Authority, Warns Dr. Dieffenbach.

EVOLUTION MINOR MATTER

Real Issue Is Whether We Shall Return to Medievalism, He Tells Unitarians Here.

Says Tennessee Ignores Progress

Christians Need Not Believe in Genesis Literally, Declares Dean Mathews.

SHOULD USE INTELLIGENCE

Dean Cites Beliefs of Biblical Age Which Have Been Discarded Without Harm to Religion.

JULY 14, 1925, PAGE 1

205

Darrow Scores Ignorance And Bigotry, Seeking To Quash Scopes Indictment; State Argues For Its Police Power

JULY 14, 1925, PAGE 3

Streets Of Dayton Deserted For Shade

Concessionaires Fare Poorly as People Gather Under Trees to Hear Trial by Radio.

SOME EVANGELISTS DEPART

Peace and Good-Will Are Displayed After Sunday's Religious Turmoil.

FLOOD OF SATIRE LOOSENED

Darrow Denounces the Statute as Unconstitutional and the Indictment as Faulty.

STEWART DEFENDS BOTH

He Contends That the Legislature, Supporting the Schools, Has Right to Fix Curriculum.

DECISION TODAY IS LIKELY

Judge Will Also Decide on Whether He Will Hear Scientists.

206

JULY 15, 1925, PAGE 1

Stormy Scenes In The Trial Of Scopes As Darrow Moves To Bar All Prayers; 'Leak' Delays Indictment Decision

INTENSE BITTERNESS SHOWN

Heated Words Are Passed as Defense Calls Prayers Argumentative.

JUDGE OVERRULES DARROW

Defense Then Fails in Plan to Have Alternate Modernist and Fundamentalist Prayers.

PRESS WARNED BY COURT

Contempt Action Threatened on Premature Publication of Ruling on the Indictment.

JULY 15, 1925, PAGE 1

TWO APES AND 'LINK' ARRIVE AT DAYTON

Wrath of Town Placated When It Is Said That They May Be Used to Disprove Evolution.

Bryan Visits Chimpanzee

'Wonderful!' He Exclaims, When Theory of Simian Degeneration From Man Is Explained to Him.

Special to The New York Times.

DAYTON, Tenn., July 14.—Two chimpanzees and a strange-appearing man who is called the "missing link" were brought today to Dayton. After flocking to view the monkeys, Dayton has decided that it was not man who evolved from the anthropoid, but the anthropoid which devolved from man; and it points now at the two chimpanzees and the "missing link" to prove the assertion. . . .

Bryan Meets the Chimpanzee.

. . . [William Jennings Bryan and scientist Hubbard Nye inspected the chimpanzee.] "I hate, even as Tennessee has already said, to think that we are descended from one of those beasts," said Mr. Nye. "I have studied them for years, and I have come to the conclusion, supported by scientific and demonstrable fact, that Darwin was wrong. We did not evolve upward from the anthropoid. Instead, the anthropoid is the product of man who went down—he devolved. It's devolution, and this chimpanzee is the refutation of the Darwinian theory."

Mr. Bryan's eyes sparkled as he gazed at the chimpanzee.

"Wonderful!" he said. "Wonderful!"

JULY 15, 1925, PAGE 2

Mr. Bryan Protests Against A Dispatch

Did Not Say That He 'Would Put the Bible In the Constitution.'

REPORTER CONDENSED IT SO

What Bryan Did Say Which Led to the Belief That He Contemplated Such a Campaign.

Darrow Puts First Scientist On Stand To Instruct Scopes Judge On Evolution; State Completes Its Case In An Hour

DEFENSE CASE IS OUTLINED

Malone Denies Any Conflict Between Evolution and Christianity.

"MILLIONS BELIEVE BOTH"

He Declares That His Side Will Prove That the Bible Teaches Various Theories of Creation.

QUOTES COMMONER'S WORDS

Bryan Declares He Will Reply in Full and Wants No Court Protection.

INDICTMENT IS SUSTAINED

Judge Also Upholds Constitutionality of the Tennessee Law.

STATE CALLS 4 WITNESSES

Puts Bible Into Record After Showing Scopes Taught Life Originated From One Cell.

MODERNIST PRAYER IN COURT

Decision Likely Today on Permitting the Jury To Hear Scientists' Testimony.

BRYAN NOW REGRETS BARRING OF EXPERTS

Says He Would Welcome Evidence, but That the Law Had to Be Obeyed.

DARROW TURNS ON HIM

Declares Commoner Did Not Dare to Test His Views In Court Against Scientists.

JULY 18, 1925, PAGE 12 (EDITORIAL PAGE)

The End In Sight At Dayton.

...It must not be forgotten that this prosecution was initiated by Tennessee citizens who do not believe in the anti-evolution law and who are confident that it will ultimately be declared null and void by the courts. A test case was deliberately made up for the express purpose of appealing from an expected conviction in the lower court to a higher tribunal.

JULY 19, 1925, SECTION 1, PAGE 2

JULY 18, 1925, PAGE 1

Judge Shatters The Scopes Defense

By Barring Testimony Of Scientists;

Sharp Clashes As Darrow Defies Court

[For purposes of appeal, Judge Raulston allowed the defense to read into the record scientific statements about evolution.]

JULY 18, 1925, PAGE 2

DAYTON HOSPITABLE TO CRITICAL GUESTS

Citizens Patiently Bear Intrusion of 'Foreigners' and Their 'Strange' Beliefs.

DAYTON, Tenn., July 18.—Rhea County's emotional stress during the anti-evolution trial has been impressive and remarked upon in the press of all the world. High religious feeling, intolerance, bigotry, fear, unfairness, ignorance, all these have been seen, felt and reported more or less accurately; but one of the most remarkable phases of this remarkable trial has been the courtesy shown by the people of East Tennessee to the writers and lawyers who have said to the world these things about them.

Dayton, an agricultural town of less than 500 families who for generations have never questioned the "literal inerrancy" of the Bible, was overrun in a day by a horde of persons whose ways and thoughts were strange; lawyers with a strange argument that the Bible was not revealed religion; free thinkers who insisted that the Bible was superstition; animal trainers with chimpanzees which they asserted were the fathers or the sons of men, and special writers who ridiculed them, their town, their habits and even their religion.

These have been trying days for a self-respecting independent people. Yet they have behaved with remarkable constraint and courtesy toward all who have criticized and ridiculed them and their beliefs so unrestrainedly.

...These persons who have called Dayton, Rhea County and Tennessee all these names have been living in the homes of the very people they criticized, but there has been no instance of where anything that has been said has been openly resented, no instance where a writer or a lawyer or a special advocate or a freak has been asked to desist save for his own safety among the irresponsible.

JULY 21, 1925, PAGE 1

[On Monday, July 20, 1925, the defense read into the record the evidence for evolution. In the afternoon the defense requested that Mr. Bryan take the stand for the purpose of showing that the Bible need not be taken literally; if that were so, then Mr. Scopes did not teach a theory that contradicted the Bible. The confrontation took place outside, for there were too many onlookers for the courthouse.]

. . . To the crowd spread under the trees watching the amazing spectacle on the platform the fight seemed a fair one. There was no pity for the helplessness of the believer come so suddenly and so unexpectedly upon a moment when he could not reconcile statements of the Bible with generally accepted facts. There was no pity for his admissions of ignorance of things boys and girls learn in high school, his floundering confessions that he knew practically nothing of geology, biology, philology, little of comparative religion, and little even of ancient history.

. . . These Tennesseans were enjoying a fight. That an ideal of a great man, a biblical scholar, an authority on religion, was being dispelled seemed to make no difference. They grinned with amusement and expectation, until the next blow by one side or the other came, and then they guffawed again. And finally, when Mr. Bryan, pressed harder and harder by Mr. Darrow, confessed he did not believe everything in the Bible should be taken literally, the crowd howled.

JULY 22, 1925, PAGE 1

Scopes Guilty, Fined $100, Scores Law; Benediction Ends Trial, Appeal Starts; Darrow Answers Nine Bryan Questions

FINAL SCENES DRAMATIC

Defense Suddenly Decides to Make No Plea and Accept Conviction.

BRYAN IS DISAPPOINTED

Loses Chance to Examine Darrow and His Long-Prepared Speech Is Undelivered.

HIS EVIDENCE IS EXPUNGED

Differences Forgotten in the End as All Concerned Exchange Felicitations.

[The $100 fine was about one-third of the court's cost in putting on the trial. The defense spent $25,000, even though the defense lawyers accepted no fee. The appeal was based on two considerations: First, the defense contended that the law was not constitutional. Second, even if it were constitutional, it was not violated by Mr. Scopes. The defense had been prevented during the trial from showing this.]

JULY 27, 1925, PAGE 1

W.J. Bryan Dies In His Sleep At Dayton, While Resting In Evolution Battle; Had Spoken Continuously Since Trial

APOPLEXY CAUSES HIS DEATH

Had Said He 'Never Felt Better' on His Return From Church.

SPOKE TO 50,000 SATURDAY

Full of Zeal to Take Cause to Country, He Was Thrilled by Crowds on Last Journey.

WIFE WAS APPREHENSIVE

Feared Anti-Evolution Fight Was Overtaxing His Strength, but Now Bears Loss Bravely.

JULY 22, 1925, PAGE 2

Crowd At The End Surges To Darrow

Tennessee Fundamentalists Pay a Spontaneous Tribute to His Courage.

ALL CONGRATULATE HIM

It Is Only Later That Thought Is Given to Bryan and the Other Figures in the Trial.

Special to The New York Times.

DAYTON, Tenn., July 21.—When John Thomas Scopes, the young school teacher, was found guilty today of teaching the theory of evolution, as every one had expected, a strange thing happened in the Rhea County Court House, where so many strange things have happened since the strange trial started.

The so-called Fundamentalists of Tennessee, who had seemed so overwhelming in favor of the law, who had cheered the utterances of counsel defending faith in the Bible against the "heresies" of scientists, stormed Clarence Darrow, the agnostic, to shake his hand.

Questions

1. *List the aspects of the KKK that reflect the clash of cultures. Can you rank-order these motivating factors in terms of significance? In what order?*
2. *KKK activities often turned violent. Except for a little rowdiness early on, the Dayton trial proceedings took place without violence. How do you explain this?*
3. *Why did the legal issue—whether or not Scopes had broken the law—not remain the focus of the judicial proceedings? Who was responsible for this development?*
4. *How do you think television news would have covered the Scopes trial?*

FURTHER READING

Andrew Sinclair, Prohibition: The Era of Excess *(Boston, 1962), is still one of the best overviews of this topic.* Nativism, Discrimination, and Images of Immigrants, *ed. George E. Pozzetta (New York, 1991) offers numerous essays that show the vast extent to which nativism and anti-immigrant actions have punctuated American history. Kathleen Blee,* Women of the Klan: Racism and Gender in the 1920s *(Berkeley, 1991), is one of numerous recent works that have focused on the second KKK.* Center of the Storm: Memoirs of John T. Scopes *(New York, 1967), by John T. Scopes and James Presley, furnishes an insider's view of the monkey trial. The 1998 Pulitzer Prize for History,* SUMMER FOR THE GODS: The Scopes Trial and America's Continuing Debate Over Science and Religion *(New York, 1997), by Edward J. Larson, presents a very balanced view of the trial and its place in the on-going clash between religion and science in American culture.*

The Origins
of the Cold War

Peter L. Hahn,
Michael J. Hogan, and Bruce Karhoff

Introduction

During World War II the United States and the Soviet Union overcame their traditional discord and cooperated to defeat Germany and Japan. The end of the war in 1945, however, eliminated the original reason for American-Soviet cooperation and opened an era of profound tension between the two victorious allies. The United States and the Soviet Union vied for political and economic influence in a postwar world beset by massive physical destruction, political instability, and vacuums of power in the regions formerly dominated by Germany and Japan. A series of conflicts and crises ensued over issues such as the form of government in Poland, the political and economic orientation of Germany, the level of U.S. and Soviet military involvement in Europe, the control of atomic weapons, and the outcome of civil wars in Greece, China, and Korea. By 1950, the great powers had divided Europe into eastern and western spheres of influence in political, economic, and military matters. Tensions escalated sharply after June 1950, when U.S. forces intervened to repulse a major offensive by Communist North Korea against non-Communist South Korea. Such conflicts caused the Cold War, an American-Soviet confrontation that lasted for nearly fifty years.

SCHOLARS DEBATE THE ORIGINS OF THE COLD WAR

Historians of the early Cold War have engaged in a long and heated debate about its origins. Early accounts by Western historians tended to criticize Soviet actions as provocative and to justify American policies as defensive. In the 1960s and 1970s, by contrast, revisionist historians influenced by the war in Vietnam and the Watergate affair blamed American behavior for much of the tension of the early Cold War. More recently, scholars have moved toward a consensus view that emphasizes mutual responsibility. The essays in this unit illustrate some of these differences of interpretation.

The Soviet Union Blamed for the Cold War

Historian Arthur Schlesinger, Jr., published the following essay in 1967 in response to a series of revisionist accounts on the origins of the Cold War. In portraying the fundamental cause of the Cold War as a difference in principles between the United States and the Soviet Union, Schlesinger acknowledged the revisionist argument that U.S. actions contributed to the conflict. Yet, he implied that the American principles were morally superior and he concluded firmly that Soviet ideology and the nature of Josef Stalin's dictatorship were the key causes of Cold War tensions. Thus, his essay revived the traditional argument that the Soviets were largely responsible for the enduring conflict. Excerpted from Arthur Schlesinger, Jr., "Origins of the Cold War," Foreign Affairs 46 (October 1967): 23–30, 36–43, 45–47, 49–50, 52.

The orthodox American view, as originally set forth by the American government and as reaffirmed until recently by most American scholars, has been that the Cold War was the brave and essential response of free men to communist aggression. . . . The revisionist thesis is very different. In its extreme form, it is that, after the death of Franklin Roosevelt and the end of the Second World War, the United States deliberately abandoned the wartime policy of collaboration and, exhilarated by the possession of the atomic bomb, undertook a course of aggression of its own designed to expel all Russian influence from Eastern Europe and to establish democratic-capitalist states on the very border of the Soviet Union. As the revisionists see it, this radically new American policy—or rather this resumption by Truman of the pre-Roosevelt policy of insensate anti-communism—left Moscow no alternative but to take measures in defense of its own borders. The result was the Cold War. These two views, of course, could not be more starkly contrasting. . . .

One theme indispensable to an understanding of the Cold War is the contrast between two clashing views of world order: the "universalist" view, by which all nations shared a common interest in all the affairs of the world, and the "sphere-of-influence" view, by which each great power would be assured by the other great powers of an acknowledged predominance in its own area of special interest. The universalist view assumed that national security would be guaranteed by an international organization. The sphere-of-interest view assumed that national security would be guaranteed by the balance of power. . . .

In adopting the universalist view, Roosevelt and [Secretary of State Cordell] Hull . . . opposed the sphere-of-influence approach. And here the State Department was expressing what seems clearly to have been the predominant mood of the American people, so long mistrustful of European power politics. . . .

The Kremlin, on the other hand, thought *only* of spheres of interest; above all, the Russians were determined to protect their frontiers, and especially their border to the west, crossed so often and so bloodily in the dark course of their history. . . . The history of Russia had been the history of invasion, the last of which was by now horribly killing up to twenty million of its people. . . .

Excerpts from "Origins of the Cold War" by Arthur Schlesinger, Jr., reprinted from *Foreign Affairs,* October 1967. Copyright © 1967 by the Council on Foreign Relations, Inc.

Chatting on the grounds of Livadia Pal Yalta, Crimea, Russia are Prime Minister Winston Churchill, President Roosevelt, and Marshal Joseph Stalin, 19 February 1945. (Courtesy of AP/Wide World Photos.)

It is now pertinent to inquire why the United States rejected the idea of stabilizing the world by division into spheres of influence and insisted on an East European strategy. . . . The first reason is that they regarded this solution as containing within itself the seeds of a third world war. The balance-of-power idea seemed inherently unstable. It had always broken down in the past. It held out to each power the permanent temptation to try to alter the balance in its own favor, and it built this temptation into the international order. . . . The Americans were perfectly ready to acknowledge that Russia was entitled to convincing assurance of her national security—but not this way. "I could sympathize fully with Stalin's desire to protect his western borders from future attack," as Hull put it. "But I felt that this security could best be obtained through a strong postwar peace organization."

Hull's remark suggests the second objection: that the sphere-of-influence approach would, in the words of the State Department in 1945, "militate against the establishment and effective functioning of a broader system of general security in which all countries will have their part." The United Nations, in short, was seen as the alternative to the balance of power. Nor did the universalists see any necessary incompatibility between the Russian desire for "friendly governments" on its frontier and the American desire for self-determination in Eastern Europe. . . .

Third, the universalists feared that the sphere-of-interest approach would be what Hull termed "a haven for the isolationists," who would advocate America's participation in Western Hemisphere affairs on condition that it did not participate in European or Asian affairs. Hull also feared that spheres of interest would lead to "closed trade areas or discriminatory systems" and thus defeat his cherished dream of a low-tariff, freely trading world.

Fourth, the sphere-of-interest solution meant the betrayal of the principles for which the Second World War was being fought—the Atlantic Charter, the Four Freedoms, the Declaration of the United Nations. Poland summed up the problem. Britain, having gone to war to defend the independence of Poland from the Germans, could not easily conclude the war by surrendering the independence of Poland to the Russians. . . . Nor could American liberals in general watch with equanimity while the police state spread into countries which, if they had mostly not been real democracies, had mostly not been tyrannies either. . . .

Fifth, the sphere-of-influence solution would create difficult domestic problems in American politics. Roosevelt was aware of the six million or more Polish votes in the 1944 election; even more acutely, he was aware of the broader and deeper attack which would follow if, after going to war to stop the Nazi conquest of Europe, he permitted the war to end with the communist conquest of Eastern Europe. . . .

Sixth, if the Russians were allowed to overrun Eastern Europe without argument, would that satisfy them? . . .

If the West turned its back on Eastern Europe, the higher probability . . . was that the Russians would use their security zone, not just for defensive purposes, but as a springboard from which to mount an attack on Western Europe. . . .

Thus idealism and realism joined in opposition to the sphere-of-influence solution. The consequence was a determination to assert an American interest in the postwar destiny of all nations, including those of Eastern Europe. . . .

It is now necessary to attempt the imaginative leap and consider the impact of this position on the leaders of the Soviet Union who . . . had reached the bitter conclusion that the survival of their country depended on their unchallenged control of the corridors through which enemies had so often invaded their homeland. They could claim to have been keeping their own side of the sphere-of-influence bargain. . . . [T]hey were even beginning to enlarge underground operations in the Western Hemisphere. But, from their viewpoint, if the West permitted this, the more fools they; and, if the West stopped it, it was within their right to do so. In overt political matters the Russians were scrupulously playing the game. . . .

They would not regard anti-communist action in a Western zone as a *casus belli*; and they expected reciprocal license to assert their own authority in the East. But the principle of self-determination was carrying the United States into a deeper entanglement in Eastern Europe than the Soviet Union claimed as a right. . . . When the Russians now exercised in Eastern Europe the same brutal control they were prepared to have Washington exercise in the American sphere of influence, the American protests, given the paranoia produced alike by Russian history and Leninist ideology, no doubt seemed not only an act of hypocrisy but a threat to security. . . .

So Moscow very probably, and not unnaturally, perceived the emphasis on self-determination as a systematic and deliberate pressure on Russia's western frontiers. Moveover, the restoration of capitalism to countries freed at frightful cost by the Red Army no doubt struck the Russians as the betrayal of the principles for which *they* were fighting. . . .

The Russians thus may well have estimated the Western pressures as calculated to encourage their enemies in Eastern Europe and to defeat their own minimum objective of a protective glacis. . . .

As the Nazi threat declined, so too did the need for coöperation. The Soviet Union, feeling itself menaced by the American idea of self-determination and the borderlands diplomacy to which it was leading, skeptical whether the United Nations would protect its frontiers as reliably as its own domination in Eastern Europe, began to fulfill its security requirements unilaterally.

. . . [T]he Russians emphatically and crudely worked their will in Eastern Europe, above all in the test country of Poland. They were ignoring the Declaration on Liberated Europe, ignoring the

Atlantic Charter, self-determination, human freedom and every-thing else the Americans considered essential for a stable peace. . . .

The Cold War had now begun. It was the product not of a decision but of a dilemma. . . . Each side believed with passion that future international stability depended on the success of its own conception of world order. Each side, in pursuing its own clearly indicated and deeply cherished principles, was only confirming the fear of the other that it was bent on aggression. . . . So the machinery of suspicion and counter-suspicion, action and counter-action, was set in motion. . . .

. . . [The revisionists assume that] there was unquestionably a failure of communication between America and Russia, a misperception of signals and, as time went on, a mounting ten-dency to ascribe ominous motives to the other side. It seems hard, for example, to deny that American postwar policy created genu-ine difficulties for the Russians and even assumed a threatening aspect for them. . . .

But the great omission of the revisionists—and also the funda-mental explanation of the speed with which the Cold War esca-lated—lies precisely in the fact that the Soviet Union was *not* a traditional national state. . . . [It] was a totalitarian state, endowed with an all-explanatory, all-consuming ideology, committed to the infallibility of government and party, still in a somewhat messianic mood, equating dissent with treason, and ruled by a dictator who, for all his quite extraordinary abilities, had his paranoid moments.

Marxism-Leninism gave the Russian leaders a view of the world according to which all societies were inexorably destined to proceed along appointed roads by appointed stages until they achieved the classless nirvana. Moreover, given the resistance of the capitalists to this development, the existence of any non-communist state was *by definition* a threat to the Soviet Union. . . . Stalin and his associates, whatever Roosevelt or Truman did or failed to do, were bound to regard the United States as the enemy, not because of this deed or that, but because of the primordial fact that America was the leading capitalist power. . . .

Stalin, in spite of the impression of sobriety and realism he made on Westerners who saw him during the Second World War, was plainly a man of deep and morbid obsessions and compul-sions. When he was still a young man, Lenin had criticized his rude and arbitrary ways. A reasonably authoritative observer (N. S. Khrushchev) later commented, "These negative characteristics of his developed steadily and during the last years acquired an absolutely insufferable character." His paranoia, probably set off by the suicide of his wife in 1932, led to the terrible purges of the mid-thirties and the wanton murder of thousands of his Bolshevik comrades. "Everywhere and in everything," Khrushchev says of this period, "he saw 'enemies,' 'double-dealers' and 'spies.' " . . . A revisionist fallacy has been to treat Stalin as just another Realpolitik statesman. . . . But the record makes it clear that in the end nothing could satisfy Stalin's paranoia. . . .

An analysis of the origins of the Cold War which leaves out these factors—the intransigence of Leninist ideology, the sinister dynamics of a totalitarian society and the madness of Stalin—is obviously incomplete. It was these factors which made it hard for the West to accept the thesis that Russia was moved only by a desire to protect its security and would be satisfied by the control of Eastern Europe; it was these factors which charged the debate between universalism and spheres of influence with apocalyptic potentiality.

. . . The difference between America and Russia in 1945 was that some Americans fundamentally believed that, over a long run, a modus vivendi with Russia was possible; while the Russians, so far as one can tell, believed in no more than a short-run modus vivendi with the United States.

. . . The Cold War could have been avoided only if the Soviet Union had not been possessed by convictions both of the infallibility of the communist word and of the inevitability of a communist world. These convictions transformed an impasse between national states into a religious war, a tragedy of possibility into one of necessity. . . . [T]he most rational of American policies could hardly have averted the Cold War.

The United States Blamed for the Cold War

In contrast to Arthur Schlesinger's arguments, many historians remain convinced that the United States deserves a substantial portion of the responsibility for the origins of the Cold War. Thomas G. Paterson suggests that actions by President Harry S. Truman triggered the rise of tensions in the late 1940s. According to Paterson, U.S. officials exaggerated the Soviet threat to American interests and formulated a disproportionate response to it. Taken from Thomas G. Paterson, Meeting the Communist Threat: Truman to Reagan *(New York, 1988), 35–50, 53.*

Presidents from Eisenhower to Reagan have exalted Truman for his decisiveness and success in launching the Truman Doctrine, the Marshall Plan, and NATO, and for staring the Soviets down in Berlin during those hair-trigger days of the blockade and airlift. . . . Some historians have gone so far as to claim that Truman saved humankind from World War III. On the other hand, . . . many historians have questioned Truman's penchant for his quick, simple answer, blunt, careless rhetoric, and facile analogies, his moralism that obscured the complexity of causation, his militarization of American foreign policy, his impatience with diplomacy itself, and his exaggeration of the Soviet threat.

Still, there is no denying the man and his contributions. He fashioned policies and doctrines that have guided leaders to this day. He helped initiate the nuclear age with his decisions to annihilate Hiroshima and Nagasaki with atomic bombs and to develop the hydrogen bomb. His reconstruction programs rehabilitated former enemies West Germany and Japan into thriving, industrial giants and close American allies. His administration's search for oil in Arab lands and endorsement of a new Jewish state in Palestine planted the United States in the Middle East as never before. Overall, Truman projected American power onto the world stage with unprecedented activity, expanding American interests worldwide, providing American solutions to problems afflicting countries far distant from the United States, establishing the United States as the pre-eminent nation in the postwar era.

. . . About three months after assuming office, . . . Truman boarded a ship for Europe, there to meet at Potsdam, near Berlin, with . . . Winston Churchill and Josef Stalin. . . . Truman's assertiveness at Potsdam on such issues as Poland and Germany

---

stemmed not only from his forthright personality, but also from his learning that America's scientists had just successfully exploded an atomic bomb which could be used against Japan to end World War II. And more, it might serve as a diplomatic weapon to persuade others to behave according to American precepts. The news of the atomic test's success gave Truman "an entirely new feeling of confidence . . . ," Secretary of War Henry L. Stimson recorded in his diary. . . .

Truman soon became known for what he himself called his "tough method." He crowed about giving Russia's Commissar for Foreign Affairs, V. M. Molotov, a "straight 'one-two to the jaw'" in their first meeting in the White House not long after Roosevelt's death. Yet Secretary Stimson worried about the negative effects of Truman's "brutal frankness," and Ambassador Harriman was skeptical that the President's slam-bang manner worked to America's advantage. Truman's brash, salty style suited his bent for the verbal brawl, but it ill-fit a world of diplomacy demanding quiet deliberation, thoughtful weighing of alternatives, patience, flexibility, and searching analysis of the motives and capabilities of others. If Truman "took 'em for a ride," as he bragged after Potsdam, the dangerous road upon which he raced led to the Cold War. . . .

The United States entered the postwar period, then, with a new, inexperienced, yet bold President who was aware of America's enviable power in a world hobbled by war-wrought devastation and who shared the popular notion of "Red Fascism."
. . . Truman's lasting legacy is his tremendous activism in extending American influence on a global scale—his building of an American "empire" or "hegemony." We can diagree [disagree] over whether this postwar empire was created reluctantly, defensively, by invitation, or deliberately, by self-interested design. But few will deny that the drive to contain Communism fostered an exceptional, worldwide American expansion that produced empire and ultimately, and ironically, insecurity, for the more the United States expanded and drove in foreign stakes, the more vulnerable it seemed to become—the more exposed it became to a host of challenges from Communists and non-Communists alike.

. . . [The war] bequeathed staggering human tragedy, rubble, and social and political chaos. . . . Europe lost more than 30 million dead in the Second World War. . . . Everywhere, armies had trampled farms and bombs had crumbled cities. . . .

. . . [E]conomic, social, and hence political "disintegration" characterized the postwar international system. The question of how this disintegration could be reversed preoccupied Truman officials. Thinking in the peace and prosperity idiom, they believed that a failure to act would jeopardize American interests, drag the United States into depression and war, spawn totalitarianism and aggression, and permit the rise of Communists and other leftists who were eager to exploit the disorder. . . . [The] formidable task of reconstruction drew the United States and the Soviet Union into conflict, for each had its own model for rebuilding states and each sought to align nations with its foreign policy.

Political turmoil within nations also drew America and Russia into conflict, for each saw gains to be made and losses to be suffered in the outcome of the political battles. Old regime leaders vied with leftists and other dissidents in state after state. . . . When the United States and the Soviet Union meddled in these politically unstable settings in their quest for influence, they collided—often fiercely.

The collapse of old empires also wrenched world affairs and invited confrontation between America and Russia. Weakened by the war and unable to sustain colonial armies in the field, the imperialists were forced to give way to nationalists who had long worked for independence. . . . Decolonization produced a shifting of power within the international system and the emergence of new states whose allegiances both the Americans and Russians avidly sought.

With postwar economies, societies, politics, and empires shattered, President Truman confronted an awesome set of problems that would have bedeviled any leader. He also had impressive responsibilities and opportunities, because the United States had escaped from World War II not only intact but richer and stronger. America's abundant farmlands were spared from the tracks of marching armies, its cities were never leveled by bombs, and its factories remained in place. During the war, America's gross national product skyrocketed and every economic indicator, such as steel production, recorded significant growth. . . . To create the American-oriented world the Truman Administration desired, and to isolate adversaries, the United States issued or withheld loans (giving one to Britain but not to Russia), launched major reconstruction programs like the Marshall Plan . . . and offered technical assistance through the Point Four Program [U.S. aid to

Third World countries]. . . . American dollars and votes also dominated the World Bank and International Monetary Fund, transforming them into instruments of American diplomacy.

The United States not only possessed the resources for reconstruction, but also the implements of destruction. The United States had the world's largest Navy, floating in two oceans, the most powerful Air Force, a shrinking yet still formidable Army, and a monopoly of the most frightening weapon of all, the atomic bomb. . . .

Because of America's unusual postwar power, the Truman Administration could expand the United States sphere of influence beyond the Western Hemisphere and also intervene to protect American interests. But this begs a key question: Why did President Truman think it necessary to project American power abroad, to pursue an activist, global foreign policy unprecedented in United States history? The answer has several parts. First, Americans drew lessons from their experience in the 1930s. While indulging in their so-called "isolationism," they had watched economic depression spawn political extremism, which in turn, produced aggression and war. Never again, they vowed. . . . Americans felt compelled to project their power, second, because they feared, in the peace-and-prosperity thinking of the time, economic doom stemming from an economic sickness abroad that might spread to the United States, and from American dependency on overseas supplies of raw materials. To aid Europeans and other peoples would not only help them, but also sustain a high American standard of living and gain political friends. . . .

Strategists spoke of the shrinkage of the globe. . . . Airplanes could travel great distances to deliver bombs. Powerful as it was, then, the United States also appeared vulnerable, especially to air attack. . . . To prevent such an occurrence, American leaders worked to acquire overseas bases in both the Pacific and Atlantic, thereby denying a potential enemy an attack route to the Western Hemisphere. Forward bases would also permit the United States to conduct offensive operations more effectively. . . .

These several explanations for American globalism suggest that the United States would have been an expansionist power whether or not the obstructionist Soviets were lurking about. . . . As the influential National Security Council Paper No. 68 (NSC-68) noted in April 1950, the "overall policy" of the United States was "designed to foster a world environment in which the American system can survive and flourish." This policy "we would probably pursue even if there were no Soviet threat."

Americans, of course, did perceive a Soviet threat. . . . Their harsh Communist dogma and propagandistic slogans were not only monotonous; they also seemed threatening because of their call for world revolution and for the demise of capitalism. . . .

The Soviet Union, moreover, had territorial ambitions. . . . To Truman and his advisers, the Soviets stood as the world's bully, and the very existence of this menacing bear necessitated an activist American foreign policy and an exertion of American power as a "counterforce."

But Truman officials exaggerated the Soviet threat, imagining an adversary that never measured up to the galloping monster so often depicted by alarmist Americans. Even if the Soviets intended to dominate the world, or just Western Europe, they lacked the capabilities to do so. The Soviets had no foreign aid to dispense; outside Russia Communist parties were minorities; [and] the Soviet economy was seriously crippled by the war. . . . The Soviets lacked a modern navy, a strategic air force, the atomic bomb, and air defenses. Their wrecked economy could not support or supply an army in the field for very long, and their technology was antiquated. . . .

Why then did Americans so fear the Soviets? Why did the Central Intelligence Agency, the Joint Chiefs of Staff, and the President exaggerate the Soviet threat? The first explanation is that their intelligence estimates were just that—estimates. The American intelligence community was still in a state of infancy. . . .

Truman officials also exaggerated the Soviet threat in order "to extricate the United States from commitments and restraints that were no longer considered desirable." For example, they loudly chastised the Soviets for violating the Yalta agreements; yet Truman and his advisers knew the Yalta provisions were at best vague and open to differing interpretations. . . .

Another reason for the exaggeration: Truman liked things in black and white. . . . Nuances, ambiguities, and counterevidence were often discounted to satisfy the President's preference for the simpler answer or his pre-conceived notions of Soviet aggressiveness. . . . American leaders also exaggerated the Soviet threat because it was useful in galvanizing and unifying American public opinion for an abandonment of recent and still lingering "isolationism" and support for an expansive foreign policy. . . . The military particularly overplayed the Soviet threat in order to persuade Congress to endorse larger defense budgets. . . .

Still another explanation for why Americans exaggerated the Soviet threat is found in their attention since the Bolshevik Revolution of 1917 to the utopian Communist goal of world revolution, confusing goals with actual behavior. . . .

Why dwell on this question of the American exaggeration of the Soviet threat? Because it over-simplified international realities by under-estimating local conditions that might thwart Soviet/Communist successes and by over-estimating the Soviet ability to act. Because it encouraged the Soviets to fear encirclement and to enlarge their military establishment, thereby contributing to a dangerous weapons race. Because it led to indiscriminate globalism. Because it put a damper on diplomacy; American officials were hesitant to negotiate with an opponent variously described as malevolent, deceitful, and inhuman. They especially did not warm to negotiations when some critics were ready to cry that diplomacy, which could produce compromises, was evidence in itself of softness toward Communism.

Exaggeration of the threat also led Americans to misinterpret events and in so doing to prompt the Soviets to make decisions contrary to American wishes. For example, the Soviet presence in Eastern Europe, once considered a simple question of the Soviets' building an iron curtain or bloc after the war, is now seen by historians in more complex terms. The Soviets did not seem to have a master plan for the region and followed different policies in different countries. . . . The Soviets did not have a firm grip on Eastern Europe before 1948. . . .

American policies were designed to roll the Soviets back. The United States reconstruction loan policy, encouragement of dissident groups, and appeal for free elections alarmed Moscow, contributing to a Soviet push to secure the area. . . .

Another example of the exaggeration of the Soviet threat at work is found in the Truman Doctrine of 1947. Greece was beset by civil war, and the British could no longer fund a war against Communist-led insurgents who had a considerable non-Communist following. On March 12, Truman enunciated a universal doctrine: It "must be the policy of the United States to support free peoples who are resisting attempted subjugation by armed minorities or by outside pressures." Although he never mentioned the Soviet Union by name, his juxtaposition of words like "democratic" and "totalitarian" and his references to Eastern Europe made the menace to Greece appear to be the Soviets. But there was and is no evidence of Soviet involvement in the Greek civil war. . . .

The story of Truman's foreign policy is basically an accounting of how the United States, because of its own expansionism and exaggeration of the Soviet threat, became a global power. Truman projected American power after the Second World War to rehabilitate Western Europe, secure new allies, guarantee strategic and economic links, and block Communist or Soviet influence. He firmly implanted the image of the Soviets as relentless, worldwide transgressors with whom it is futile to negotiate. Through his exaggeration of the Soviet threat, Truman made it very likely that the United States would continue to practice global interventionism years after he left the White House.

Questions

1. *What were the United States's objectives for the international order after World War II? What aims did the Soviet Union pursue? What issues arose as a result of the conflict in the two powers' ambitions?*
2. *How did the United States define its security interests? How did the Soviet Union define its security interests? Was there any room for accommodation or compromise between the two powers?*
3. *Did the Cold War result primarily from American or Soviet actions, policies, and principles? Which side should be blamed for the Cold War, or was it unavoidable? Were opportunities to diminish tensions missed by either side, or was the tension inevitable?*

THE CONTEMPORARY DEBATE OVER THE COLD WAR

The documents printed in this section shed light on several dimensions of the early Cold War. They illustrate some of the ideas that gave birth to the United States's policy of containment of the Soviet Union and the evolution of that policy from 1946 to 1950. They also reveal some of the opposition to this policy on the American side and provide a glimpse of the Soviet view of global affairs in general and of the Truman Doctrine of 1947 in particular. Collectively, the records printed below demonstrate the multilayered and constantly changing dynamics of the early Cold War conflict.

Stalin Suggests that Conflict Is Inevitable

On February 9, 1946, Soviet leader Josef Stalin delivered a public address in which he blamed World War II on international capitalism and celebrated Soviet contributions to the defeat of Germany. Published during a time of mounting East-West tensions over territorial issues in Eastern Europe and the Middle East, the speech provoked substantial concern in the United States that Stalin was mobilizing his people for conflict—possibly even war—with the West. Excerpted from Text of a Speech Delivered By J. V. Stalin at an Election Rally in Stalin Electoral Area, Moscow, February 9, 1946 *(Washington, 1946), 3, 5–8, 13–15.*

Comrades!

. . . It would be wrong to think that the Second World War was a casual occurrence or the result of mistakes of any particular statesmen, though mistakes undoubtedly were made. Actually, the war was the inevitable result of the development of world economic and political forces on the basis of modern monopoly capitalism. Marxists have declared more than once that the capitalist system of world economy harbors elements of general crises and armed conflicts and that, hence, the development of world capitalism in our time proceeds not in the form of smooth and even progress but through crises and military catastrophes.

The fact is, that the unevenness of development of the capitalist countries usually leads in time to violent disturbance of equilibrium in the world system of capitalism, that group of capitalist countries which considers itself worse provided than others with raw materials and markets usually making attempts to alter the situation and repartition the "spheres of influence" in its favor by armed force. The result is a splitting of the capitalist world into two hostile camps and war between them.

. . . And so, what are the results of the war?

There is one chief result in which all other results have their source. This result is that in the upshot of the war our enemies were defeated and we, together with our Allies, emerged the victors. We concluded the war with complete victory over the enemies. That is the chief result of war. . . . In order to grasp the great historic importance of our victory we must examine the thing more concretely.

And so, how is our victory over our enemies to be understood? . . .

Our victory means, first of all, that our Soviet social order has triumphed, that the Soviet social order has successfully passed the ordeal in the fire of war and has proved its unquestionable vitality.

. . . Second, our victory means that our Soviet state system has triumphed, that our multinational Soviet State has stood all the trials of war and has proved its vitality.

. . . Third, our victory means that the Soviet armed forces have triumphed, that our Red Army has triumphed, that the Red Army bore up heroically under all the trials of war, utterly routed the armies of our enemies and came out of the war as a victor.

. . . The war showed that the Red Army is not a "colossus with feet of clay," but a first-class contemporary army with fully mod-

Reprinted from *Information Bulletin:* Embassy of the Union of Soviet Socialist Republics, Washington, D.C., March 1946.

ern armaments, highly experienced commanding personnel and high moral and fighting qualities. It must not be forgotten that the Red Army is the army that utterly routed the German army which but yesterday was striking terror into the armies of the European states.

. . . Now a few words about the Communist Party's plans of work for the immediate future. As is known these plans are set forth in the new Five-Year Plan which is shortly to be endorsed. The principal aims of the new Five-Year Plan are to rehabilitate the ravaged areas of the country, to restore the prewar level in industry and agriculture, and then to surpass this level in more or less substantial measure. To say nothing of the fact that the rationing system will shortly be abolished *(stormy, prolonged applause)*, special attention will be devoted to extending the production of consumer goods, to raising the living standard of the working people by steadily lowering the prices of all goods *(stormy, prolonged applause)*, and to the widespread construction of all manner of scientific research institutions *(applause)* that can give science the opportunity to develop its potentialities. *(Stormy applause.)*

. . . As regards the plans for a longer period ahead, the Party means to organize a new mighty upsurge in the national economy, which would allow us to increase our industrial production, for example, three times over as compared with the prewar period. . . .

In conclusion, allow me to thank you for the confidence you have shown me *(prolonged, unabating applause. Shout from the audience: "Hurrah for the great captain of all victories, Comrade Stalin!")* in nominating me to the Supreme Soviet. You need not doubt that I shall do my best to justify your trust.

Kennan Warns of Russian Expansion

Alarmed by Stalin's speech, the State Department instructed its leading Soviet expert, George F. Kennan, chargé d'affaires at the U.S. embassy in Moscow, to assess the speech's significance and to predict future Soviet behavior. Kennan replied by sending the so-called long telegram, a secret cable that summarized the principles of Soviet foreign policy, anticipated substantial Soviet efforts to expand political and economic influence around the world by overt and covert methods, and suggested peaceful

but firm U.S. resistance to such expansionism. Kennan's arguments,
which he also published under a pseudonym in Foreign Affairs *in July*
1947, formed the basis of President Truman's policy of containment of
the Soviet Union. Excerpted from U.S. Department of State, Foreign
Relations of the United States, 1946 *(Washington, 1969), 6:697–99,*
701–9.

Basic Features of Post War Soviet Outlook, as Put Forward by Official Propaganda Machine, Are as Follows:

(a) USSR still lives in antagonistic "capitalist encirclement" with
which in the long run there can be no permanent peaceful coexistence. As stated by Stalin in 1927 to a delegation of American
workers:

> "In course of further development of international
> revolution there will emerge two centers of world signifi-
> cance: a socialist center, drawing to itself the countries
> which tend toward socialism, and a capitalist center,
> drawing to itself the countries that incline toward capital-
> ism. Battle between these two centers for command of
> world economy will decide fate of capitalism and of com-
> munism in entire world."

(b) Capitalist world is beset with internal conflicts, inherent in
nature of capitalist society. These conflicts are insoluble by means
of peaceful compromise. Greatest of them is that between England
and US.

(c) Internal conflicts of capitalism inevitably generate wars.
Wars thus generated may be of two kinds: intra-capitalist wars
between two capitalist states, and wars of intervention against
socialist world. Smart capitalists, vainly seeking escape from inner conflicts of capitalism, incline toward latter.

(d) Intervention against USSR, while it would be disastrous to
those who undertook it, would cause renewed delay in progress
of Soviet socialism and must therefore be forestalled at all costs.

(e) Conflicts between capitalist states, though likewise fraught
with danger for USSR, nevertheless hold out great possibilities for
advancement of socialist cause, particularly if USSR remains mili-
tarily powerful, ideologically monolithic and faithful to its
present brilliant leadership.

. . . So much for premises. To what deductions do they lead from standpoint of Soviet policy? To following:

(a) Everything must be done to advance relative strength of USSR as factor in international society. Conversely, no opportunity must be missed to reduce strength and influence, collectively as well as individually, of capitalist powers.

(b) Soviet efforts, and those of Russia's friends abroad, must be directed toward deepening and exploiting of differences and conflicts between capitalist powers. If these eventually deepen into an "imperialist" war, this war must be turned into revolutionary upheavals within the various capitalist countries.

(c) "Democratic-progressive" elements abroad are to be utilized to maximum to bring pressure to bear on capitalist governments along lines agreeable to Soviet interests.

(d) Relentless battle must be waged against socialist and social-democratic leaders abroad. . . .

Background of Outlook

Before examining ramifications of this party line in practice there are certain aspects of it to which I wish to draw attention.

First, it does not represent natural outlook of Russian people. . . . But party line is binding for outlook and conduct of people who make up apparatus of power—party, secret police and Government—and it is exclusively with these that we have to deal.

Second, please note that premises on which this party line is based are for most part simply not true. Experience has shown that peaceful and mutually profitable coexistence of capitalist and socialist states is entirely possible. . . .

Nevertheless, all these theses, however baseless and disproven, are being boldly put forward again today. What does this indicate? It indicates that Soviet party line is not based on any objective analysis of situation beyond Russia's borders: that it has, indeed, little to do with conditions outside of Russia; that it arises mainly from basic inner-Russian necessities which existed before recent war and exist today.

At bottom of Kremlin's neurotic view of world affairs is traditional and instinctive Russian sense of insecurity. Originally, this was insecurity of a peaceful agricultural people trying to live on vast exposed plain in neighborhood of fierce nomadic peoples. To this was added, as Russia came into contact with economically advanced West, fear of more competent, more powerful, more highly organized societies in that area. . . . For this reason they have always feared foreign penetration, feared direct contact between Western world and their own, feared what would happen if Russians learned truth about world without or if foreigners learned truth about world within. And they have learned to seek security only in patient but deadly struggle for total destruction of rival power, never in compacts and compromises with it. . . .

Projection of Soviet Outlook in Practical Policy on Official Level

. . . (a) Internal policy devoted to increasing in every way strength and prestige of Soviet state: intensive military-industrialization; maximum development of armed forces; great displays to impress outsiders; continued secretiveness about internal matters, designed to conceal weaknesses and to keep opponents in dark.

(b) Wherever it is considered timely and promising, efforts will be made to advance official limits of Soviet power. . . .

(c) Russians will participate officially in international organizations where they see opportunity of extending Soviet power or of inhibiting or diluting power of others. . . .

(d) Toward colonial areas and backward or dependent peoples, Soviet policy, even on official plane, will be directed toward weakening of power and influence and contacts of advanced Western nations, on theory that in so far as this policy is successful, there will be created a vacuum which will favor Communist-Soviet penetration. . . .

Basic Soviet Policies on Unofficial, or Subterranean Plane . . .

Agencies utilized for promulgation of policies on this plane are following:

1. *Inner central core of Communist Parties in other countries . . . tightly coordinated and directed by Moscow. . . .*
2. *Rank and file of Communist Parties. . . . no longer even taken into confidence about realities of movement. . . .*
3. *A wide variety of national associations or bodies which can be dominated or influenced. . . . These include: labor unions, youth*

leagues, women's organizations, racial societies, religious societies, social organizations, cultural groups, liberal magazines, publishing houses, etc.

4. *International organizations which can be similarly penetrated through influence over various national components. Labor, youth and women's organizations are prominent among them. . . .*

It may be expected that component parts of this far-flung apparatus will be utilized . . . as follows:

(a) To undermine general political and strategic potential of major western powers. Efforts will be made in such countries to disrupt national self confidence, to hamstring measures of national defense, to increase social and industrial unrest, to stimulate all forms of disunity. . . . Here poor will be set against rich, black against white, young against old, newcomers against established residents, etc.

(b) On unofficial plane particularly violent efforts will be made to weaken power and influence of Western Powers of [*on*] colonial backward, or dependent peoples. On this level, no holds will be barred. . . .

(c) Where individual governments stand in path of Soviet purposes pressure will be brought for their removal from office. . . .

(d) In foreign countries Communists will, as a rule, work toward destruction of all forms of personal independence, economic, political or moral. . . .

(e) Everything possible will be done to set major Western Powers against each other. . . .

(f) In general, all Soviet efforts on unofficial international plane will be negative and destructive in character, designed to tear down sources of strength beyond reach of Soviet control. . . . The Soviet regime is a police regime par excellence, reared in the dim half world of Tsarist police intrigue, accustomed to think primarily in terms of police power. This should never be lost sight of in gauging Soviet motives. . . .

Practical Deductions from Standpoint of U S Policy

In summary, we have here a political force committed fanatically to the belief that with US there can be no permanent *modus vivendi*, that it is desirable and necessary that the internal harmony of our society be disrupted, our traditional way of life be destroyed, the international authority of our state be broken, if Soviet power is to be secure. . . . This is admittedly not a pleasant picture. Problem of how to cope with this force in [is] undoubtedly greatest task our diplomacy has ever faced and probably greatest it will ever have to face. . . . I would like to record my conviction that problem is within our power to solve—and that without recourse to any general military conflict. And in support of this conviction there are certain observations of a more encouraging nature I should like to make:

(1)   *Soviet power . . . does not take unnecessary risks. . . . For this reason it can easily withdraw—and usually does—when strong resistance is encountered at any point. Thus, if the adversary has sufficient force and makes clear his readiness to use it, he rarely has to do so. . . .*

(2)   *Gauged against Western World as a whole, Soviets are still by far the weaker force. Thus, their success will really depend on degree of cohesion, firmness and vigor which Western World can muster. . . .*

(3)   *Success of Soviet system, as form of internal power, is not yet finally proven. . . .*

(4)   *All Soviet propaganda beyond Soviet security sphere is basically negative and destructive. It should therefore be relatively easy to combat it by any intelligent and really constructive program.*

For these reasons I think we may approach calmly and with good heart problem of how to deal with Russia. . . . [B]y way of conclusion, following comments:

(1)   *Our first step must be to apprehend, and recognize for what it is, the nature of the movement with which we are dealing. . . .*

(2)   *We must see that our public is educated to realities of Russian situation. . . .*

(3)   *Much depends on health and vigor of our own society. World communism is like malignant parasite which feeds only on diseased tissue. . . .*

(4)   *We must formulate and put forward for other nations a much more positive and constructive picture of sort of world we would like to see than we have put forward in past. . . .*

(5)   *Finally we must have courage and self-confidence to cling to our own methods and conceptions of human society. After all, the greatest danger that can befall us in coping with this problem of*

Soviet communism, is that we shall allow ourselves to become like those with whom we are coping.

KENNAN

Wallace Questions Containment

Not all American officials approved of President Truman's policy of firm containment of the Soviet Union. In an address delivered September 12, 1946, in New York City, Secretary of Commerce Henry A. Wallace publicly encouraged Truman to reduce tensions with the Soviets through accommodation and compromise and thereby avoid a catastrophic military conflict. Truman rejected such advice and within weeks of Wallace's address fired him from the cabinet. Selected from Vital Speeches of the Day 12 *(October 1, 1946): 738–40.*

Tonight I want to talk about peace—and how to get peace. Never have the common people of all lands so longed for peace. Yet, never in a time of comparative peace have they feared war so much.

Up till now peace has been negative and unexciting. War has been positive and exciting. Far too often, hatred and fear, intolerance and deceit have had the upper hand over love and confidence, trust and joy. Far too often, the law of nations has been the law of the jungle; and the constructive spiritual forces of the Lord have bowed to the destructive forces of Satan.

During the past year or so, the significance of peace has been increased immeasurably by the atom bomb, guided missiles and airplanes which soon will travel as fast as sound. Make no mistake about it—another war would hurt the United States many times as much as the last war. We cannot rest in the assurance that we invented the atom bomb—and therefore that this agent of destruction will work best for us. He who trusts in the atom bomb will sooner or later perish by the atom bomb—or something worse.

I say this as one who steadfastly backed preparedness

Excerpt from "The Way to Peace," speech by Henry A. Wallace, as it appeared in *Vital Speeches of the Day*, Vol. XII, No. 24, City News Publishing Company, October 1, 1946.

throughout the Thirties. We have no use for namby-pamby pacifism. But we must realize that modern inventions have now made peace the most exciting thing in the world—and we should be willing to pay a just price for peace. If modern war can cost us $400 billion, we should be willing and happy to pay much more for peace. But certainly, the cost of peace is to be measured not in dollars but in the hearts and minds of men.

The price of peace—for us and for every nation in the world—is the price of giving up prejudice, hatred, fear, and ignorance.

. . . I plead for an America vigorously dedicated to peace—just as I plead for opportunities for the next generation throughout the world to enjoy the abundance which now, more than ever before, is the birthright of man.

To achieve lasting peace, we must study in detail just how the Russian character was formed—by invasions of Tartars, Mongols, Germans, Poles, Swedes, and French; by the czarist rule based on ignorance, fear and force; by the intervention of the British, French and Americans in Russian affairs from 1919 to 1921; by the geography of the huge Russian land mass situated strategically between Europe and Asia; and by the vitality derived from the rich Russian soil and the strenuous Russian climate. Add to all this the tremendous emotional power which Marxism and Leninism gives to the Russian leaders—and then we can realize that we are reckoning with a force which cannot be handled successfully by a "Get tough with Russia" policy. "Getting tough" never bought anything real and lasting—whether for schoolyard bullies or businessmen or world powers. The tougher we get, the tougher the Russians will get.

. . . We most earnestly want peace with Russia—but we want to be met half way. We want cooperation. And I believe that we can get cooperation once Russia understands that our primary objective is neither saving the British Empire nor purchasing oil in the Near East with the lives of American soldiers. . . .

The real peace treaty we now need is between the United States and Russia. On our part, we should recognize that we have no more business in the *political* affairs of Eastern Europe than Russia has in the *political* affairs of Latin America, Western Europe and the United States. . . .

As for Germany, we all must recognize that an equitable settlement, based on a unified German nation, is absolutely essential to any lasting European settlement. This means that Russia must be assured that never again can German industry be converted into military might to be used against her—and Britain, Western Europe and the United States must be certain that Russia's Germany policy will not become a tool of Russian design against Western Europe.

The Russians have no more business in stirring up native communists to political activity in Western Europe, Latin America and the United States than we have in interfering in the politics of Eastern Europe and Russia. We know what Russia is up to in Eastern Europe, for example, and Russia knows what we are up to. We cannot permit the door to be closed against our trade in Eastern Europe any more than we can in China. But at the same time we have to recognize that the Balkans are closer to Russia than to us—and that Russia cannot permit either England or the United States to dominate the politics of that area.

. . . We are still arming to the hilt. Our excessive expenses for military purposes are the chief cause for our unbalanced budget. If taxes are to be lightened we must have the basis of a real peace with Russia—a peace that cannot be broken by extremist propagandists. . . .

Russian ideas of social-economic justice are going to govern nearly a third of the world. Our ideas of free enterprise democracy will govern much of the rest. The two ideas will endeavor to prove which can deliver the most satisfaction to the common man in their respective areas of political dominance. But by mutual agreement, this competition should be put on a friendly basis and the Russians should stop conniving against us in certain areas of the world just as we should stop scheming against them in other parts of the world. Let the results of the two systems speak for themselves.

Meanwhile, the Russians should stop teaching that their form of communism must, by force if necessary, ultimately triumph over democratic capitalism—while we should close our ears to those among us who would have us believe that Russian communism and our free enterprise system cannot live, one with another, in a profitable and productive peace.

Under friendly peaceful competition the Russian world and the American world will gradually become more alike. The Russians will be forced to grant more and more of the personal freedoms; and we shall become more and more absorbed with the problems of social-economic justice.

Russia must be convinced that we are not planning for war

against her and we must be certain that Russia is not carrying on territorial expansion or world domination through native communists faithfully following every twist and turn in the Moscow party line. But in this competition, we must insist on an open door for trade throughout the world. There will always be an ideological conflict—but that is no reason why diplomats cannot work out a basis for both systems to live safely in the world side by side.

The Truman Doctrine

President Truman's handling of an early 1947 crisis in Greece reflected his resolve to deal firmly with the Soviet Union. In February 1947, British officials explained to Truman that financial troubles would compel them to suspend their support of the monarchy of Greece, which was resisting an internal revolt by leftists. In a personal appearance at a joint session of Congress on March 12, Truman portrayed the rebellion in Greece as evidence of covert Soviet expansionism and vowed to resist it with massive financial assistance to the government in Athens. He also planned to provide aid to Turkey to encourage it to resist Soviet pressures for territorial and political concessions. Congress endorsed the president's policy, commonly called the Truman Doctrine, by allocating some $400 million in assistance to the two Mediterranean states. Truman's address, excerpted below, appears in Public Papers of the Presidents of the United States: Harry S. Truman, 1947 *(Washington, 1963), 176–80.*

The gravity of the situation which confronts the world today necessitates my appearance before a joint session of the Congress. The foreign policy and the national security of this country are involved. One aspect of the present situation, which I present to you at this time for your consideration and decision, concerns Greece and Turkey.

The United States has received from the Greek Government an urgent appeal for financial and economic assistance. . . . [A]ssistance is imperative if Greece is to survive as a free nation.

I do not believe that the American people and the Congress wish to turn a deaf ear to the appeal of the Greek Government. . . . The very existence of the Greek state is today threatened by the terrorist activities of several thousand armed men, led by Communists, who defy the government's authority at a number of points, particularly along the northern boundaries. . . .

. . . [T]he Greek Government is unable to cope with the situation. The Greek army is small and poorly equipped. It needs supplies and equipment if it is to restore authority to the government throughout Greek territory. Greece must have assistance if it is to become a self-supporting and self-respecting democracy. The United States must supply this assistance. . . .

President Harry S. Truman. (Courtesy of The Library of Congress.)

Greece's neighbor, Turkey, also deserves our attention. The future of Turkey as an independent and economically sound state is clearly no less important to the freedom-loving peoples of the world than the future of Greece. . . . Turkey now needs our support.

. . . I am fully aware of the broad implications involved if the United States extends assistance to Greece and Turkey, and I shall discuss these implications with you at this time.

One of the primary objectives of the foreign policy of the United States is the creation of conditions in which we and other nations will be able to work out a way of life free from coercion. This was a fundamental issue in the war with Germany and Japan. . . . At the present moment in world history nearly every nation must choose between alternative ways of life. The choice is too often not a free one.

One way of life is based upon the will of the majority, and is distinguished by free institutions, representative government, free elections, guarantees of individual liberty, freedom of speech and religion, and freedom from political oppression.

The second way of life is based upon the will of a minority forcibly imposed upon the majority. It relies upon terror and oppression, a controlled press and radio, fixed elections, and the suppression of personal freedoms.

I believe that it must be the policy of the United States to support free peoples who are resisting attempted subjugation by armed minorities or by outside pressures. I believe that we must assist free peoples to work out their own destinies in their own way. I believe that our help should be primarily through economic and financial aid which is essential to economic stability and orderly political processes.

... If Greece should fall under the control of an armed minority, the effect upon its neighbor, Turkey, would be immediate and serious. Confusion and disorder might well spread throughout the entire Middle East. Moreover, the disappearance of Greece as an independent state would have a profound effect upon those countries in Europe whose peoples are struggling against great difficulties to maintain their freedoms and their independence while they repair the damages of war.... The seeds of totalitarian regimes are nurtured by misery and want. They spread and grow in the evil soil of poverty and strife. They reach their full growth when the hope of a people for a better life has died.

We must keep that hope alive.

The free peoples of the world look to us for support in maintaining their freedoms. If we falter in our leadership, we may endanger the peace of the world—and we shall surely endanger the welfare of this Nation.

Soviets Denounce the Truman Doctrine

On March 14, 1947, the day after Truman's speech to Congress, the Moscow newspaper Izvestiia *printed a broadside of the Truman Doctrine that likely reflected official Soviet thinking. The statement suggested that neither Greece nor Turkey was threatened by external forces and that American aid would lead to American domination of both states. Abridged from* Izvestiia, *with English translation provided by Dr. Kurt Schultz of the staff of* The Russian Review.

On 12 March, U.S. President H. Truman addressed a message to Congress in which he requested $400 million for urgent aid to Greece and Turkey, and permission to send American civilian and military personnel to these countries and to provide "specially selected" Greek and Turkish personnel with training and instruction by Americans.

To justify his proposal, Truman declared that Greece's economic and political situation was desperate, and that England could no longer take care of the Greeks. "England," said Mr. Truman, "faces the necessity of reducing and liquidating its obligations in several parts of the world, including Greece."

Turkey, for its part, needs America's "immediate assistance." It is true that Turkey, unlike Greece, did not suffer from the Second World War, but she needed England's and America's financial aid, said Truman, "for implementing the modernization necessary to maintain her national integrity." And since the British government, "due to its own difficulties," is in this case not able to extend financial or other assistance to the Turks, then the United States, in Truman's opinion, "must" extend that assistance.

And thus the American Congress is asked to promptly sanction two "good deeds": to save Greece from internal disorders and to pay for the costs of "modernizing" Turkey, upon which, allegedly, her very existence depends.

There can be no doubt that the Tsaldaris administration's tearful pleas to the USA for help is clear evidence of the bankruptcy of Greece's internal political regime, which in Truman's address is portrayed flatteringly. What is key here is not only and not so much the mercenary Greek monarchists and their allies, who are being politely portrayed to American congressmen as the direct descendants of the legendary defender of Thermopylae, Tsar Leonid.

It is well known that the real masters of Greece have been and remain British military authorities. British troops have been on Greek territory since 1944. On Churchill's initiative, England took upon itself the responsibility for "stabilizing" political conditions in Greece. English authorities have not only assisted in perpetuating and nurturing the rule of reactionary and anti-democratic forces in Greece, showing at the same time an extreme indifference to and even supporting people who actively and consciously cooperated with the Germans. All the political and economic activities of every manner of coalition and short-lived Greek gov-

---

Excerpted from *Izvestia*, March 14, 1947, translated by Dr. Kurt Schultz.

ernments have been carried out under close English control and direction.

The result of this is now before us: complete bankruptcy. English troops have not brought peace and tranquillity to a tortured Greece. The Greek people have been cast into the abyss of new sufferings, hunger, and poverty. Instead of subsiding, the civil war is acquiring ever more fierce forms.

Has not the presence of foreign troops on Greek territory actually contributed to this sad situation? Doesn't England, which declared itself to be Greece's guardian, bear the responsibility for its ward's bankruptcy?

The American president's message skirts these perfectly natural questions. The reason for such delicacy is understandable: the United States does not wish to criticize English policy because it intends to follow the English example. No wonder the *Times* of London warmly welcomed Truman's address, while the *Daily Telegraph* noted that his speech "fully justifies English policy in Greece." It is clear from Truman's speech that the United States does not plan to change the course set by British policy in Greece. But in light of this, one cannot expect better results.

The American government has no intention whatsoever of dealing with the Greek question in a fashion that one might expect of a member of the United Nations that is concerned about the fate of another of its members. Clearly no one in Washington wishes to consider the obligations the U.S. government accepted with regard to the UN. Showing unusual nervousness, Truman didn't even consider it necessary to wait for the results of the work of a special commission of the Security Council that had been sent to Greece to investigate the situation on the spot. In vain, the American president remembered that "the United States took upon itself the leading role in creating the United Nations." In any event, it wasn't worth remembering this in order to now declare his desire to act through the head of the United Nations, not taking into account the existence of the international organization and forgetting that in New York there meets a continually active international organ—the Security Council.

Truman has ignored both the international organization as well as the sovereignty of Greece. Indeed, what will remain of Greek sovereignty when "American military and civilian personnel" are sitting on the head of the Greek government and when these "personnel" begin to run the show with the help of their 250 million American dollars? The sovereignty and independence of Greece above all else will be the victims of such peculiar "defense." The Greek people, who have been engaged in a heroic struggle for their independence and freedom, do not deserve this sort of attention. If this is what Messrs. Tsaldarises aim for, then so much the worse for them, since they're the ones who have led Greece into this situation.

The ever-suffering Greek people are now threatened with the replacement of one "master"—England—with another "master"—the United States of America. It is impossible to conceal American pretensions to American predominance in Greece by justifying those pretensions as defense of the freedom and independence of the Greek people.

American arguments for assisting Turkey are based on the existence of a threat to the integrity of Turkish territory, even though no one or nothing is threatening Turkey's integrity.

American "aid" to Turkey is clearly directed toward subordinating that country as well to U.S. control, after which point it will be impossible even to talk about independent domestic and foreign Turkish policy, since that policy will be under the control of American imperialism. Some American commentators are openly speaking of this. Walter Lippmann frankly points out in the *New York Herald Tribune* that the American "alliance with Turkey" would give the United States a "strategic position that is incomparably more favorable than any other from which to exercise authority in the Middle East." And the *New York Times*, commenting upon Truman's message to Congress, bombastically proclaims the advent of "the age of American responsibility."

But, the question arises, what else is this monopolistic "American responsibility" but a screen for expansionist plans?

Arguments that the U.S.A. "is obliged to save" Greece and Turkey from the expansion of so-called "totalitarian states" is not new. Hitler also relied on the Bolsheviks when he wanted to pave the way for his conquests. Now they want to subordinate Greece and Turkey, and they are trying to conceal their expansionist plans by raising a racket about "totalitarian states." This is even more attractive given that the United States is elbowing non-totalitarian Britain out of yet another one or two countries.

Mr. Truman's address could not help but attract the attention of the broad public in both the U.S.A. and abroad. One cannot say that it has not met serious criticism even within the circles of the

249

U.S. Congress. A group of 13 American congressmen tried to talk Truman out of making the address before he delivered it. As the Democratic Senator Taylor declared, "We would be disgusted by a proposal to vote for rendering financial aid to a monarchist government that is persecuting those who fought against the Nazis."

Another Democratic Senator, Johnson, expressed the same thought: "I wholeheartedly sympathize with giving food as aid, without political aims, but the president made no distinction between food and bullets, and that is the reason for my disappointment. I am not sympathetic to the dispatch of our military personnel to Greece and Turkey even as advisers. Military aid to Turkey and Greece could lead to military intervention in other parts of the world. I am ready to give millions in support of aid to hungry people, but not one cent for helping rotting monarchies."

The Democratic Senator Pepper declared that "Truman's recommendation, made without any consultation with the United Nations, constitutes a threat to the UN and lays unknown obligations upon the United States." Also characteristic was the observation of the chairman of the House of Representatives' Budget Committee, the Republican Knudson, who said that "the supporters of Truman's program apparently will not be satisfied until the United States goes bankrupt." Henry Wallace came out with a sharply negative judgment of Truman's address, as did several other leading American figures.

Before us is yet another intrusion by the United States into the affairs of another state. The pretensions of the United States to leadership in international affairs are growing along with the appetite of the interested American circles. But American leaders, operating in new historical circumstances, are not taking into account that the old methods of colonizers and hard-headed politicians have outlived their age and are doomed to failure.

This is the main weakness of Mr. Truman's address.

NSC-68 and the Enduring Cold War

American-Soviet tensions provoked by the Truman Doctrine were exacerbated in 1948-49 by such other Western initiatives as the Marshall Plan, the North Atlantic Treaty Organization, and by the communist coup d'etat in Czechoslovakia and the Soviet blockade of Berlin. In 1949, when Communists seized power in China after a long civil war and when the Soviets successfully tested an atomic device years before Western experts anticipated they would, American concerns escalated sharply. U.S. officials conducted a major re-examination of foreign policy and produced a top secret planning document called NSC-68. The document attributed to Moscow a concerted plan of global conquest and proposed a massive increase in U.S. defense preparations to deter Soviet aggression and thereby create opportunities to weaken the Soviet Union through political and economic means. Drafted in April 1950, NSC-68 was approved by President Truman as an official policy document after the outbreak of the Korean War in June. Excerpted from U.S. Department of State, Foreign Relations of the United States, 1950 *(Washington, 1977), 1:237–38, 240–41, 243–44, 263, 272, 282, 285–87, 292.*

During the span of one generation, the international distribution of power has been fundamentally altered. For several centuries it had proved impossible for any one nation to gain such preponderant strength that a coalition of other nations could not in time face it with greater strength. The international scene was marked by recurring periods of violence and war, but a system of sovereign and independent states was maintained, over which no state was able to achieve hegemony.

Two complex sets of factors have now basically altered this historical distribution of power. First, the defeat of Germany and Japan and the decline of the British and French Empires have interacted with the development of the United States and the Soviet Union in such a way that power has increasingly gravitated to these two centers. Second, the Soviet Union, unlike previous aspirants to hegemony, is animated by a new fanatic faith, antithetical to our own, and seeks to impose its absolute authority over the rest of the world. . . .

. . . [A]ny substantial further extension of the area under the domination of the Kremlin would raise the possibility that no coalition adequate to confront the Kremlin with greater strength could be assembled. It is in this context that this Republic and its citizens in the ascendancy of their strength stand in their deepest peril.

The issues that face us are momentous, involving the fulfill-ment or destruction not only of this Republic but of civilization itself. . . . The fundamental purpose of the United States . . . is to assure the integrity and vitality of our free society, which is founded upon the dignity and worth of the individual. . . . The fundamental design of those who control the Soviet Union and the international communist movement is to retain and solidify their absolute power, first in the Soviet Union and second in the areas now under their control. In the minds of the Soviet leaders, however, achievement of this design requires the dynamic exten-sion of their authority and the ultimate elimination of any effec-tive opposition to their authority. . . . Thus unwillingly our free society finds itself mortally challenged by the Soviet system. No other value system is so wholly irreconcilable with ours, so impla-cable in its purpose to destroy ours, so capable of turning to its own uses the most dangerous and divisive trends in our own society, no other so skillfully and powerfully evokes the elements of irrationality in human nature everywhere, and no other has the support of a great and growing center of military power. . . .

In a shrinking world, which now faces the threat of atomic warfare, it is not an adequate objective merely to seek to check the Kremlin design, for the absence of order among nations is becom-ing less and less tolerable. This fact imposes on us, in our own interests, the responsibility of world leadership. . . .

The Kremlin is able to select whatever means are expedient in seeking to carry out its fundamental design. . . . We have no such freedom of choice, and least of all in the use of force. Resort to war is not only a last resort for a free society, but it is also an act which cannot definitively end the fundamental conflict in the realm of ideas. . . .

Practical and ideological considerations therefore both impel us to the conclusion that we have no choice but to demonstrate the superiority of the idea of freedom by its constructive application, and to attempt to change the world situation by means short of war in such a way as to frustrate the Kremlin design and hasten the decay of the Soviet system.

. . . It is quite clear from Soviet theory and practice that the Kremlin seeks to bring the free world under its dominion by the methods of the cold war. . . .

Four possible courses of action by the United States in the present situation can be distinguished. They are:

a. Continuation of current policies . . . ;

b. Isolation;

c. War; and

d. A more rapid building up of the political, economic, and military strength of the free world than provided under *a*, with the purpose of reaching, if possible, a tolerable state of order among nations without war and of preparing to defend ourselves in the event that the free world is attacked.

. . . [Choice D] is the only course which is consistent with progress toward achieving our fundamental purpose. . . . It is necessary to have the military power to deter, if possible, Soviet expansion, and to defeat, if necessary, aggressive Soviet or Soviet-directed actions of a limited or total character. . . .

A program for rapidly building up strength and improving political and economic conditions will place heavy demands on our courage and intelligence; it will be costly; it will be dangerous. But half-measures will be more costly and more dangerous, for they will be inadequate to prevent and may actually invite war. Budgetary considerations will need to be subordinated to the stark fact that our very independence as a nation may be at stake.

A comprehensive and decisive program . . . would probably involve:

(1) *The development of an adequate political and economic frame-work for the achievement of our long-range objectives.*

(2) *A substantial increase in expenditures for military purposes. . . .*

(3) *A substantial increase in military assistance programs, designed to foster cooperative efforts, which will adequately and efficiently meet the requirements of our allies. . . .*

(4) *Some increase in economic assistance programs and recognition of the need to continue these programs until their purposes have been accomplished.*

(5) *A concerted attack on the problem of the United States balance of payments. . . .*

(6) *Development of programs designed to build and maintain confidence among other peoples in our strength and resolution, and to wage overt psychological warfare calculated to encourage mass defections from Soviet allegiance and to frustrate the Kremlin design in other ways.*

(7) *Intensification of affirmative and timely measures and operations by covert means in the fields of economic warfare and political and psychological warfare with a view to fomenting and supporting unrest and revolt in selected strategic satellite countries.*
(8) *Development of internal security and civilian defense programs.*
(9) *Improvement and intensification of intelligence activities.*
(10) *Reduction of Federal expenditures for purposes other than defense and foreign assistance, if necessary by the deferment of certain desirable programs.*
(11) *Increased taxes.*

. . . The Soviet Union is currently devoting about 40 percent of available resources . . . to military expenditures. . . . In an emergency the Soviet Union could increase the allocation of resources to these purposes to about 50 percent, or by one-fourth.

The United States is currently devoting about 22 percent of its gross national product . . . to military expenditures. . . . In an emergency the United States could devote upward of 50 percent of its gross national product to these purposes (as it did during the last war), an increase of several times present expenditures for direct and indirect military purposes and foreign assistance. . . .

The threat to the free world involved in the development of the Soviet Union's atomic and other capabilities will rise steadily and rather rapidly. For the time being, the United States possesses a marked atomic superiority over the Soviet Union which . . . inhibits aggressive Soviet action. This provides an opportunity for the United States, in cooperation with other free countries, to launch a build-up of strength which will support a firm policy directed to the frustration of the Kremlin design. . . .

The whole success of the proposed program hangs ultimately on recognition by this Government, the American people, and all free peoples, that the cold war is in fact a real war in which the survival of the free world is at stake. . . . The prosecution of the program will require of us all the ingenuity, sacrifice, and unity demanded by the vital importance of the issue and the tenacity to persevere until our national objectives have been attained.

Questions

1. What was the fundamental nature of American-Soviet conflict in the late 1940s? How extensively did the worldviews of the two powers differ?
2. Was the Truman Doctrine an American effort to preserve the independence of Greece and Turkey, or an American quest to gain dominance over both countries?
3. Were the policy prescriptions in NSC-68 valid, in your judgment, on the basis of circumstances facing the United States in 1950?
4. On the basis of these documents, which power do you think was most accountable for the Cold War?

FURTHER READING

Traditional histories of the early Cold War include Herbert Feis, From
Trust to Terror: The Onset of the Cold War, 1945–1950 *(New York,
1970); Hugh Thomas,* Armed Truce: The Beginnings of the Cold
War, 1945–1946 *(New York, 1987); and Randall B. Woods and Howard
Jones,* Dawning of the Cold War: The United States, Quest for
Order *(Athens, Georgia, 1991). For revisionist accounts, see Gar
Alperovitz,* Atomic Diplomacy: Hiroshima and Potsdam *(New
York, 1965); Lloyd C. Gardner,* Architects of Illusion: Men and Ideas
in American Foreign Policy, 1941–1949 *(Chicago, 1970); Thomas G.
Paterson,* Soviet-American Confrontation: Postwar Reconstruction
and the Origins of the Cold War *(Baltimore, 1973); and Joyce and
Gabriel Kolko,* The Limits of Power: The World and United States
Foreign Policy, 1945–1954 *(New York, 1972). Post-revisionist and
synthetic works are Melvyn P. Leffler,* A Preponderance of Power:
National Security, the Truman Administration, and the Cold War
(Stanford, 1992); James Gormly, The Collapse of the Grand Alliance,
1945–1948 *(Baton Rouge, 1987); and John Lewis Gaddis,* The United
States and the Origins of the Cold War, 1941–1947 *(New York,
1972). On specific aspects of U.S. policy, see Bruce Cumings,* The
Origins of the Korean War, *vol. 2:* The Roaring of the Cataract,
1947–1950 *(Princeton, 1990); Michael J. Hogan,* The Marshall Plan:
America, Britain, and the Reconstruction of Western Europe,
1947–1952 *(New York, 1987); and Lawrence Kaplan,* The United
States and NATO: The Formative Years *(Lexington, Kentucky,
1984).*

Anti-Communism at Home: The Second Red Scare and the Problems of Internal Security in a Democracy

William R. Childs

INTRODUCTION

Inextricably tied to the emergence of the Cold War was the Second Red Scare. For about a decade, beginning in earnest in 1947, Americans used many public and private institutions, from White House agencies and congressional committees to local and state groups, to investigate alleged "un-American" activities of Americans in many walks of life. Especially targeted for investigation were artists, intellectuals, teachers, and public servants, but privately employed citizens did not escape the feverish search for "subversives." The assumption was that people who held Communist or "left-leaning" political ideas or associated with those who did threatened the internal security of the nation. The phenomenon was part of the ideological battle between democratic capitalism and communism that shaped the Cold War.

While part of the early years of the Cold War, the Second Red Scare was not a new phenomenon in the United States, nor did it die out after its most vocal supporter, Senator Joseph McCarthy (R-Wisconsin), was censured by the Senate in the mid-1950s. Nineteenth-century Americans generally opposed Communist ideals, and politicians employed "communism" as an invective. In the early twentieth century, conservatives blamed the labor problem on Communist influences. The Soviet revolution of 1917 and other contemporary revolutions in Europe formed a backdrop for the First Red Scare in 1919 and 1920. Tying labor unrest to assumed Communist and subversive influence, rather than to the economic problems that really caused them, federal, local, and state officials rounded up hundreds of supposed radicals, violated their civil rights, but deported very few suspects. (This episode prompted the birth of the modern civil liberties movement.) Some states even required teachers to sign loyalty oaths as a requirement of employment. In the 1930s, fearful that Communist and fascist activity abroad was infiltrating American society, Congress established the House Committee on Un-American Activities (HUAC), which became a key institutional foundation of the Second Red Scare. Even after McCarthy's demise in the mid-1950s, anti-communism at home did not die out. Its legacies underlay the emergence of the John Birch Society in the late 1950s and, most significantly, informed foreign policymaking until the late 1980s, particularly the war in Vietnam.

The Second Red Scare and the riddles it poses—why it occurred, how it evolved, and the effects it had on society then and later—have caught the attention of numerous historians and social commentators. Contrary to the general perception that the virulent actions of Senator Joseph McCarthy inaugurated the scare (taking advantage of a situation already under way), the Second Red Scare grew out of long-held American principles interacting with new realities (little understood at the time) in the postwar world. It evolved into an hysteria in which zealots, as well as simple, scared people living and working in both the public and private sectors, violated with impunity basic American values.

On one level, the Second Red Scare grew from identifiable roots. The postwar world seemed so different from the world of 1939. For the second time in a generation, the United States had played a reluctant role in the world arena. After World War II, however, America was clearly the largest economic and military power. Drawing on its intellectual heritage, American power seemed to demand a world leadership role. Because the Allies had fought the last war in large measure to ensure democracy and because the other great superpower, the Soviet Union, promoted non-democratic ideals, the United States was thrust into an unaccustomed position as a superpower. Uncertainty about the future, especially about the use of nuclear capabilities, complicated America's assumption of world leadership. Especially in 1949 when the Soviets exploded an atomic bomb and the Chinese Communists won their civil war, foreign events lent a sense of urgency to America's new position. The combined tension from these events, along with American antipathy toward communism, clearly underlay the emergence of the Second Red Scare.

On another level, the Second Red Scare represented the extremes to which American politics could sometimes evolve. (The rise of the Second Ku Klux Klan in the 1920s is another example.) The scare was fueled in part by domestic politics (with Republicans out of power since 1933) and by power struggles between Congress and the president. Evidence of subversive activity at home existed, but it was not extensive. When coupled with events abroad, however, these few unconnected episodes convinced some Americans that a widespread subversive conspiracy was under way at home. Politicians like Richard Nixon and, most notoriously, Joseph McCarthy took advantage of the uncertain times to promote their and their party's political fortunes.

The Second Red Scare was a phenomenon much more sweeping in its reach and effects than was the First Red Scare. The "witch hunts" (a reference to the Salem witch trials of the 1690s) lasted much longer than the anti-radical movement of 1919–20. The targets were more numerous, not just avowed radicals and public servants, but anybody (including athletes, washroom attendants, and tenants in public housing) could be subjected to the inquisitions of politicians and bosses. The prosecuting institutions were more extensive in coverage: not only the Department of Justice, but also other executive branch agencies, congressional committees, and many local groups (school boards, librarians, and patriotic groups, especially the American Legion) joined the hunt for subversives and non-patriotic citizens. Unlike the First Red Scare, during the Second Red Scare, large numbers of everyday Americans and the media, including radio and the nascent television industry, supported the crusade against alleged Communist subversive activity, either by actively participating in the witch hunts or by simply watching silently.

Anti-communism at home as played out during the Second Red Scare, while based in historically understandable intersections of long-held passions, the new world realities of an ideological Cold War, and domestic politics, nonetheless should be remembered as a period during which guilt by association, blacklisting, self-incrimination, and lack of due process—all things Americans

*had opposed for nearly two centuries—became commonplace oc-
currences. Paradoxically, the movement to rid the country of "un-
American" thinking and action resulted in "American" patriots
engaging in activities that violated basic American civil liberties.
The state of American politics underscored the use of government
institutions as Americans tried to deal with the problem of internal threats in a democracy.*

Two Views of HUAC and the Origins of the Second Red Scare

The Second Red Scare involved many more institutions, public and private, than did the First Red Scare. One of the key institutions was HUAC—the House Committee on Un-American Activities. Established by Congress in the 1930s to investigate fascist and Communist influence in the United States, HUAC became a centerpiece of the Second Red Scare by 1947.

The following two essays offer divergent views of HUAC's purpose and what it symbolized for Americans. Each author has a different perspective of why the Cold War existed, and, using many of the same people and ideas, each author develops a unique argument. Generally, Garry Wills does not believe that a real internal threat to American security existed, but William F. Buckley, Jr., does. Mr. Wills takes a broad historical view of the issues, while Mr. Buckley focuses more narrowly on the criticisms of HUAC.

Scoundrel Time

Hollywood became an especially easy target for those who believed communism was threatening American society from within. Hollywood promoted the war effort through its stars and its movies; Tinseltown was central to American culture at mid-century. Many scriptwriters were members of the Communist Party USA in the 1930s, although most left the party after only a short time. While some Hollywood writers and artists were politically sympathetic with communism or values on the "left" of the political spectrum, many others in the film industry were in fact apolitical—at least until 1947, when HUAC first targeted them for investigation.

Journalist and historian Garry Wills presents a scathing analysis of the origins and evolution of HUAC and the Second Red Scare in his "Introduction" to the memoirs of Lillian Hellman, one of America's greatest playwrights. Scoundrel Time *recounts the background to her confrontation with HUAC in the spring of 1952. Hellman's interview came during HUAC's second investigation of Hollywood. Wills reveals why the "McCarthy era" is misnamed and offers incisive analyses of why and how the Second Red Scare became central to American culture. The essay is compelling for its one-sidedness—Wills dismisses the possibility that anti-communism at home was directed at a real threat. He argues that the crusade emanated from an intersection of historical ideological beliefs, Americans' place in the world community after the recent total war of World War II, and contemporary domestic political conflicts. Abridged from Garry Wills, introduction to* Scoundrel Time *by Lillian Hellman (Boston, 1976), 3–13, 17–19, 21.*

IN 1952 PLAYWRIGHT Lillian Hellman was summoned to testify on her putatively un-American activities before the congressional committee charged with maintaining our Americanism. That was the year when Joseph McCarthy, at the top of his power, was re-elected to the Senate; but she did not appear before his Senate committee. She was summoned by a committee of the lower house—the one which, by its power and long life, became *the* committee of the Cold War period: the House Committee on Un-American Activities (HUAC). For roughly a third of this century the Committee brooded over its ever-growing files, testimony, and reports. Its time of greatest power began in 1948, with its "breaking" of the Hiss case. But as early as 1947 it had declared its wide mandate by posing ideological tests for American artifacts, beginning with the movies.

One movie, made in 1944, especially disturbed Committee members. They called for expert testimony on the film from novelist Ayn Rand, and she quickly identified the work's major flaw: it showed Russians smiling. "It is one of the stock propaganda tricks of the Communists, to show these people smiling." Since

Russian propaganda shows Russians smiling, and this American film showed Russians smiling, this American film was part of the Russians' propaganda effort. It is the kind of logic for which Miss Rand is famous, and it dazzled the congressional students who had summoned her in 1947 to instruct them. Richard Nixon was one of her pupils that day. . . . Only Representative John McDowell had some reservations:

Movie poster from 1950 advertising "I Married a Communist." (Courtesy of Archive Photos.)

> McDowell: Doesn't anybody smile in Russia anymore?
> Rand: Well, if you ask me literally, pretty much no.
> McDowell: They don't smile?
> Rand: Not quite that way, no. If they do, it is privately and accidently. Certainly, it is not social. They don't smile in approval of their system.

Miss Rand, a screenwriter, must have put some odd directions in her scripts—like: "Smile accidently, not socially."

Robert Taylor played the lead in *Song of Russia*. . . . Just three years after he made the movie, and two days after Miss Rand condemned it, he was subpoenaed to meet the charge of trafficking in Russian smiles. He was properly contrite:

> [Committee Counsel] Robert Stripling: Mr. Taylor, have you ever participated in any picture as an actor which you considered contained Communist propaganda?
> Taylor: I assume we are now referring to *Song of Russia*. I must confess that I objected strenuously to doing *Song of Russia* at the time it was made. I felt that it, to my way of thinking, at least, did contain Communist propa-

ganda . . . I don't think it should have been made. I don't think it would be made today.

Why, if he recognized the Communist propaganda, did Mr. Taylor make the movie? Because the chief of movie propaganda in the federal government's Office of War Information had asked him to—we were portraying a brave ally, smiling along with us in the war on Hitler. So why, if he was responding to his own government's request, *recant*? Because one is supposed to anticipate changes in the government's line, agree with the new and reject the old, grateful for the opportunity to repent. . . .

It was a humiliating little crawl men were learning, that early after World War II. Mr. Taylor even brought names [of people he had *heard* might be Communists]. . . . That put them among those he would, personally, blacklist:

> Stripling: You would refuse to act in a picture in which a person whom you considered to be a Communist was also cast, is that correct?

> Taylor: I most assuredly would, and I would not even have to know that he was a Communist. This may sound biased. However, if I were suspicious of a person being a Communist with whom I was scheduled to work, I am afraid it would have to be him or me, because life is a little too short to be around people who annoy me as much as these fellow travelers and Communists do. . . .

[Wills then notes that Taylor testified that Hollywood pictures should be made only for entertainment and not used for propaganda. After Chairman J. Parnell Thomas prompted him, however, Taylor reversed course.]

> J. Parnell Thomas: Mr. Taylor, are you in favor of the motion picture industry making anti-Communist pictures, giving the facts about Communism?

> Taylor: Congressman Thomas, when the time arrives—and it might not be long—when pictures of that type are indicated as necessary, I believe the motion picture industry will and should make anti-Communist pictures. . . .

By 1947 the House Committee on Un-American Activities had been in existence for almost a decade. But it had been a shabby and backstreet operation, specializing in anti-Semitic and racial insinuations under two Southern Democrats as chairmen (Martin Dies and John S. Wood). Respectable Congressmen avoided it. . . .

But things began to change in 1947. The off-year election of the preceding year had created the first Republican Congress in sixteen years and it seemed to presage the defeat of Harry Truman in 1948. A Republican chairman (J. Parnell Thomas) and chief counsel (Robert Stripling) led the Committee now, and a bright new Congressman like Richard Nixon could see that anxiety over Communism made the Committee a place of opportunity instead of ignominy. A newly aggressive Truman had launched the Cold War in the spring of 1947 with his plan to "rescue" Greece and Turkey. Simultaneously he introduced a new loyalty program, extending investigation to all federal employees (a standard not even imposed in wartime). . . . Another House committee (Appropriations) launched an attack on ten State Department employees as loyalty risks—and Secretary [of State] George Marshall dismissed them all without a hearing. . . .

Republican Senator Richard M. Nixon looks through a magnifying glass at microfilms of state department papers with House on Un-American Activities investigator Robert L. Stripling during the 1950s. (Courtesy of AP/Wide World Photos.)

The McCarthy era does not date from 1950, when Joseph McCarthy made his first charges. It dates from 1947, from the joint efforts of Truman, Attorney General Tom Clark, and J. Edgar Hoover. They gave the House Un-American Activities Committee its weapons—the lists it could use on witnesses, the loyalty program for which it could demand ever stricter enforcement, the presumption that a citizen is disloyal until proved loyal, the denial of work to any man or woman who would not undergo such a proving process. . . .

What made the machinery turn so readily in 1947, launching our vast effort at institutional suspicion and self-policing? . . . [T]here was an equation of Russia, as a national enemy, with "the Axis" of World War II. . . . [T]here was an equation of Russia with Communism—as there had been an equation of Germany, Italy, and even Japan with Fascism in the World War. A nation at war with *ideas* must use ideas as weapons—and the federal government has charge of the national arsenal. Hollywood must be censored politically if the nation was to be protected ideologically.

A nation only partly demobilized by 1947 was very happily, and at once, remobilized. Why? Because of an external threat? Partly, to be sure. But Russia, heavily crippled by the war, still lacking nuclear weaponry, was not a credible threat to our existence then—surely not the kind of threat that would justify so extensive a program of self-defense. Russia's military power did not justify the emergency measures of 1947, including a loyalty program that exceeded even wartime stringencies. Russia was an ideological threat, not a military one; a threat to "Americanism" more than to America—and opposition was made more total because the threat was more subtle. Still, the model for total war was the crusade against Fascism, which was recast as a propaganda ("cold") war of threat and suspicion against Communism. . . .

Ideology played its part—give the Red-baiters their due: America has never loved socialism. . . . Americans feared "Bolshies" from 1917 on, but they did not have the instruments for a large-scale investigation or purge. The notorious Palmer Raids had to rely on a small force of federal marshals and an uncooperative Labor Department. But after World War II we had a bloated and ideologized FBI, the congressional committees, an internal security program, a worldwide intelligence operation, and the will to make our Truth prevail. Our postwar world began, instead of ending, with a bang, and we did not intend to whimper. Instead, we bullied. . . .

One reason the World War enmities could be so quickly revived, with a new focus on Russia, was the depth of America's understanding of herself as always at odds with alien doctrine. We boast that the nation was brought into being by dedication to a *proposition*, in Lincoln's phrase. We date the country's inception not from the actual inauguration of constitutional government but from the declaration of our principles thirteen years earlier. An element in America's sense of mission has always been the belief that close foreign ties might sully the purity of republican doctrine, a fear expressed by Jefferson himself. It was not enough to be America in citizenship or residence—one must be American in one's thoughts. There was such a thing as Americanism. And lack of right thinking could make an American citizen un-American. The test was ideological. That is why we had such a thing as an Un-American Activities Committee in the first place. Other countries do not think in terms of, say, Un-British Activities as a political category. But ours was the first of the modern ideological countries, born of revolutionary doctrine, and it has maintained a belief that return to doctrinal purity is the secret of national strength for us. . . .

It is unfortunate that McCarthyism was named teleologically, from its most perfect product, rather than genetically—which would give us Trumanism. By studying "McCarthyism" in terms of Joseph McCarthy's own period of Red-baiting (1950–1954), a number of scholars have called the disease an imbalance between Congress and the Executive. . . . It is true that the Executive opposed investigative committees by McCarthy's time; but in 1947 the President not only cooperated with these committees, but gave them the means to grow powerful. . . . In March of 1947, when Truman issued his executive order for loyalty tests, he designated HUAC files as an official source of evidence on employees' ties.

HUAC and Its Critics

In sharp contrast to Garry Wills, William F. Buckley, Jr. argues that the threat of communism to American ideals and the American way of life was a real one. Indeed, Buckley wrote his essay in 1961, well after the "McCarthy" period had ended. Buckley, a well-known and respected conservative critic, improved the quality and influence of the National Review while he was its editor. Although Buckley believes HUAC was misnamed, he believes its work was important to the future of the nation. In an introductory essay to a book of essays that defends the existence of HUAC, Buckley takes on some of the criticisms of HUAC's work. Buckley, like Wills, mentions Lincoln and Jefferson, but Buckley utilizes their names and their beliefs differently. Selected from William F. Buckley, Jr., and the editors of National Review, The Committee and Its Critics: A Calm Review of the House Committee on Un-American Activities *(Chicago, 1962) 14–23, 25–26, 32–33.*

It seems as though we must go through it all again. For in the past few years, for complex reasons, we are back to something that resembles the general indifference to the problem of Communist subversion which beset us during the immediate postwar years. There are differences, notably the general agreement on the fact of Soviet intransigence. But along with it goes the fixed conviction, so frequently avowed by our governors of opinion, that the threat is exclusively "external," that those who talk of an "internal" threat are at best deluded, at worst suffering from paranoia; that therefore the existence of a Congressional committee devoted to the internal dimension of the Soviet threat is at best an affront upon reality, at worse a continuing agent of confusion. And quite apart from the irrelevance of such an agency in the present situation, they reason, we should oppose its existence because it does positive damage to our way of life, and belies our implicit commitment to the idea of the free society.

These are important criticisms . . . [based upon] a number of common premises. One is that the Soviet world threat is real, a noncontroversial assumption held in common by the entire spectrum of non-Communist opinion in this country. But we go further to say that in the final analysis, the distinction between the internal and external threat is unreal: that the scope of the Communist effort transcends the conventional boundaries, and that therefore the conventional vocabulary is anachronistic. Thus—we reason—the activities of the Congressional investigating committee cannot be detached from the activities of the CIA, or the FBI; or, even, those of the Pentagon, the United States Information Agency, some of the foreign aid agencies, or any of the manifold enterprises whose common purpose is to ensure the security of the Republic.

Even if that assumption is accepted, we are left with residual problems which anyone concerned with the preservation of freedom must face up to. Assume the need for an all-out response to the Communist threat, and excuses can be made for reordering the entire structure of American life. We often hear the rhetorical cry for a "total" response to the Communist challenge. And no doubt the American people, if it proved necessary, would make "any sacrifice whatever," to use the phrase of President Kennedy, to survive the threat. But after all, that is rhetoric. We are free men, and we accept impositions upon our freedom only as they prove necessary. We do not want to sacrifice a single freedom which we need not sacrifice in order to safeguard the Republic. We fight, after all, not only for the future, but for the here and now. The Communists may, before they are done with us, force us into a garrison state, a government-managed economy, the suspension of civil liberties—the totalist response. But the best instincts of American freemen demand that we stay as free as we can possibly stay, consistent with the stability of the ship of state. It is wrong to sacrifice a single freedom heedlessly. We are, as a people, generally agreed that we must tax ourselves hideously to maintain our armed services; that we must pay the bill of the CIA and of the USIA, and, to the extent necessary, of foreign aid, military and economic, for our allies. We accept conscription—that drastic curtailment of liberty which is, in its generic form, proscribed by the Constitution under the name of involuntary servitude. We accept a Federal Bureau of Investigation which (albeit with decorum) necessarily traffics in tapped telephones, secret informants, and all that grimy business that goes against the grain of a people who value highly the importance of privacy. The question has arisen in serious quarters whether we ought also to accept a House Committee on Un-American Activities.

The purpose of this . . . [essay] is to crystallize the arguments against the Committee and to analyze them in the light of our dual commitment to our national defense and to our free society. . . . [Buckley reminds the readers that he and the other contributors, as conservatives, vigilantly resist the accumulation of power in the government.]

It is in this context that we seek to illuminate a number of questions. . . . The principal questions are: (1) Does HUAC . . . perform licitly? (2) Does it perform a necessary function? (3) Does it harmonize with our free institutions? And (4), if not, should it be abolished? Or should our free institutions move over far enough to accommodate it? . . .

. . . [Buckley then responds to specific criticisms by the Kenyon (College) Council to Abolish the House Committee on Un-American Activities.] HUAC is *not* merely a fact-finding body. It is also an *evaluative* body—a factor of considerable importance. And . . . it *has*, and has had for several years, a special set of rules. . . . In fact it is the first Congressional committee to adopt formal rules of procedure.

Professor B. . . . is against HUAC because it is engaged in *"stigmatizing unpopular ideas and intimidating those who believe or express such ideas."* . . . It may be that in going after Jones [a generic target] the Committee falsely attributed pro-Communism to him—but that is a different charge from the one Professor B makes. The difference is between an honest mistake on the part of the Committee, whether caused by sloppiness or stupidity, and a conscious, hypocritical abuse of HUAC's implicit mandate. . . .

[The Committee has investigated the Ku Klux Klan, thus proving it is not focused solely on people and views on the left of the political spectrum.] . . . Not only are witnesses entitled by the Committee's rules to counsel, meetings have even been suspended when witnesses appeared without counsel. . . .

. . . [I]t seems to me that on at least one important theoretical point, the Committee's critics are correct. . . . [How] is anyone to say, and on what authority, what is an un-American activity? . . .

. . . [E]very country has its own traditions and even, broadly speaking, consensus—with reference to which an anthropologist or historian can responsibly, even if a little arbitrarily, generalize that this custom or that, this innovation or that, is un-American, or un-French, or un-Iroquois. Certainly it should be safe to say that a call for the abolition of the monarchy in England would be un-English—to say it as a plain, observable, empirically and historically verifiable fact. But it is quite another thing to say that a royal commission should be established to persecute those who hold to such un-English views on the monarchy. It might indeed be held that to charge a royal commission with devising the means to discourage even concededly un-English activities, is in itself an un-English thing to do, so that whereas we are agreed that anti-monarchist agitation is un-English, so is it un-English to proscribe antimonarchist agitation. . . .

We should, I think, reject . . . [the] notion that a dynamic and changing society, which governs itself pragmatically, and is continually experiencing and assimilating the disorderly demands of history, cannot therefore responsibly decide what is and what is not un-national. It is all too clear that many national ideas change and that what is un-American today was not necessarily un-American yesterday, nor will be tomorrow. But the historically unimpeachable fact that a people's customs and traditions and mores change perceptibly, does not commit a society to the doctrine that it should hold lightly its current commitments. . . .

. . . Even granting the intellectual validity of the effort to distinguish the "American" from the "un-American" at any particular point in time, this is not a game Congress should play. When the professors are mistaken, the mischief is limited to the influence they exercise. Not so with Congress. In time of emergency Congress may exercise emergency powers, and declare implicitly what is and isn't un-American—it has done this every time it passes a conscription law. . . . But I agree that Congress should proceed very reluctantly to act as fugleman [leader] for what-is, an what-isn't American, or what-is or what-isn't un-American. . . .

Accordingly, I deplore the Committee's name. I believe we should have a standing House Committee on Communist Activities. I believe the durability and resourcefulness of the Communist movement justifies, as a matter of efficiency and economy, the use of a standing committee, as opposed to an *ad hoc* committee. I'd like to see such a committee die the day after the Communist threat ends, but so would I like to see the Armed Services Committee die the day after we can cease to worry about the possible needs for armed services. Meanwhile, the Communists exist, they continue to do mischief, we have yet to find perfect legislative instruments for combating them, they are an integral part of the international Communist conspiracy and must be engaged by the agency entrusted by the Constitution to provide for the common defense—so then let us have the Committee, but let us make a sensible concession to right-minded critics who fear the loose, omnipotent rubric. . . .

. . . [Another charge] is that the Committee's work has by and large been done by self-seeking vulgarians, ignorant of or indifferent to the decent restraints of power. . . . On the abstract question, anyone would agree: if better men can be found to run the Committee, we are all for finding them. If better men can be found to run the White House, we are all in favor of finding *them*, too. The House of Representatives elects its own captains, and that is the way it will probably continue to be. . . .

The profoundest question at issue is whether the open society can tolerate an unassimilable political minority if it is in league with great and powerful and hostile foreign forces; specifically, whether the open society can tolerate Communists-at-large. The answer one most often hears at centers of elevated thought is a complacent pooh-pooh—based on the conspiracy's admittedly small membership. Another response, more congruent with reality, some of us believe, focuses not on the exiguous membership of the Communist Party, but on its capacity, considering always its great international resources and contemporary concentrations of power, to do irreparable damage. . . . One of our problems is our enslavement to abstractions. . . . Our Republic was forged on the assumption—to be sure, explicitly skeptical—that nearly all points of view are, if not equally honorable, at least equally tolerable. Yet even Jefferson lifted himself up from some of his abstractions about the free society far enough to denounce some of his contemporaries and their views as "swinish," and to consider tampering with the judiciary in order to diminish their influence. Lincoln arrived painfully at the conclusion that some points of view were intolerable. These were men who, notwithstanding their devotion to the generally useful principle of freedom for dissenters, even for conspiratorial dissenters, acknowledged, with their pragmatic turn of mind, that requirements of reality transcend at the margin the abstract imperatives of the free society. . . . The tragedy is that at this moment, when the State is so gravely threatened, we find ourselves frozen in inaction by lofty and otherworldly pronouncements. . . . It is nothing short of preposterous willingly to tolerate an active conspiracy in our midst: and if the Constitution is not, as presently understood, resilient enough to cope with the contemporary requirements of survival, then the Constitution should be modified, as it has been before. . . . [HUAC] writhes under the dilemma, and needs understanding and help from those who, desiring the perpetuation of freedom, will realize . . . that "a nation may be placed in such a situation that the majority must either impose disabilities or submit to them, and that what would, under ordinary circumstances, be justly condemned as persecution, may fall within the bounds of legitimate self-defense."

Questions

1. *How do Wills and Buckley define "American" and "un-American"? How does each author explain why HUAC existed? What do you think?*
2. *Why does Wills believe the era should be labelled "Trumanism," and not "McCarthyism"? Do you agree with Wills? Why or why not?*
3. *According to Wills, how was HUAC different in 1952 than it had been in 1947? Why did HUAC focus on Hollywood?*
4. *How does Buckley (implicitly) deal with Wills's argument that "politics" had much to do with the evolution of HUAC?*
5. *In the final analysis, do you think a congressional committee should have been dealing with "un-American" activities? with "Communist" activities?*

INTERNAL SECURITY: TRUMAN, POLITICS, AND INDIVIDUAL RIGHTS

In 1946 in response to public and political pressures, President Harry S. Truman established a Temporary Commission on Employee Loyalty. The following year, he put into effect a permanent program, the Federal Loyalty and Security Program, known by the acronym "FELP" (Federal Employee Loyalty Program). Of the nearly four million federal employees and prospective employees investigated during Truman's presidency, 378 were dismissed or denied employment. Another 2,000, however, left their government jobs under clouds of suspicion. No cases of espionage were discovered.

The following documents chronicle the unfolding of the internal security program in the late 1940s and early 1950s from the president's perspective. In the political realm, the documents reveal not only the contests between Republicans and Democrats but also the growing conflict between Congress and the executive branch for power to direct domestic and foreign policies. They also reveal that fear of possible subversion of the internal security of the nation, along with politics, overwhelmed the constitutional provisions protecting civil liberties.

Truman's successor, Dwight D. Eisenhower, revamped the internal security program and, in the process, actually removed more employees than did Truman. By the mid-1950s, however, individuals in the press and in all three branches of government—the executive, the judicial, and the legislative—began to expose violations of civil liberties within the internal security programs. Steps were taken to control the processes that had trampled Americans' rights.

Directive on the Need for Maintaining the Confidential Status of Employee Loyalty Records, March 15, 1948

Note how this directive deals both with maintaining the confidentiality of employees' records and with the power struggle between the executive and legislative branches of government. Abridged from Public Papers of the Presidents of the United States: Harry S. Truman . . . *January 1 to December 31, 1948 (Washington, 1964), 181–82.*

Memorandum to all officers and employees in the executive branch of the Government:

The efficient and just administration of the Employee Loyalty Program, under Executive Order No. 9835 of March 21, 1947, requires that reports, records, and files relative to the program be preserved in strict confidence. This is necessary in the interest of our national security and welfare, to preserve the confidential character and sources of information furnished, and to protect Government personnel against the dissemination of unfounded or disproved allegations. It is necessary also in order to insure the fair and just disposition of loyalty cases.

For these reasons, and in accordance with the long-established policy that reports rendered by the Federal Bureau of Investigation and other investigative agencies of the executive branch are to be regarded as confidential, all reports, records, and files relative to the loyalty of employees or prospective employees (including reports of such investigative agencies), shall be maintained in confidence, and shall not be transmitted or disclosed except as required in the efficient conduct of business.

Any subpoena or demand or request for information, reports, or files of the nature described, received from sources other than those persons in the executive branch of the Government who are entitled thereto by reason of their official duties, shall be respectfully declined, on the basis of this directive, and the subpena or demand or other request shall be referred to the Office of the President for such response as the President may determine to be in the public interest in the particular case. There shall be no relaxation of the provisions of this directive except with my express authority.

This directive shall be published in the Federal Registry.

HARRY S. TRUMAN

NOTE: On the same day the White House released a statement concerning the President's directive. The statement traced the development from Washington's day of the principle that the President may refuse to divulge or permit the divulgence of confidential information outside the executive branch. Among the precedents cited was a letter from Attorney General [Robert H.] Jackson, dated April 30, 1941, refusing to furnish certain FBI reports to the House Committee on Naval Affairs. Stating that the letter was written with the approval and at the direction of President Roosevelt, the Attorney General said that disclosure of the reports could not do otherwise than seriously prejudice law enforcement. "Counsel for a defendant or prospective defendant could have no greater help than to know how much or how little information the Government has, and what witnesses or sources of information it can rely on." The Attorney General added that the courts had repeatedly held that they would not and could not require the Executive to produce such papers when in the opinion of the Executive their production is contrary to the public interest.

Address in Oklahoma City, September 28, 1948

During his reelection campaign, Truman summarized his views on the politics of internal security. Note how politics intertwines with anticommunism. Excerpted from Public Papers of the Presidents of the United States: Harry S. Truman . . . *January 1 to December 31, 1948 (Washington, 1964) 609–14.*

Here in Oklahoma City, in the heart of the nation, I consider it appropriate to discuss a subject of great importance to all Americans—the relationship of communism to our national security.

I should like the American people to consider the damage that is being done to our national security by irresponsible persons who place their own political interests above the security of the Nation.

I regret to say that there are some people in the Republican Party who are trying to create the false impression that communism is a powerful force in American life. These Republicans know that this is not true.

The time has come when we should take a frank and earnest look at the record about communism and our national security.

First, let me remind you of a few basic facts which are often overlooked.

Our country is strong enough to resist and overcome all the forces of communism—and it will remain so.

Our Government is not endangered by Communist infiltration. It has preserved its integrity—and it will continue to do so.

The FBI and our other security forces are capable, informed, and alert—and will remain so.

I am going to give you the hard facts which prove what I have said.

The Republicans ought to realize that their failure to deal with the big practical issues of American life, such as housing, price control, and education, is too plain to be hidden by any smoke screen. They ought to realize that their reckless tactics are not helping our national security; they are hurting our national security.

I am forced to the conclusion that Republican leaders are thinking more about the November election than about the welfare of this great country.

I charge that the Republicans have impeded and made more difficult our efforts to cope with communism in this country.

I charge that they have hindered the efforts of the FBI, which has been doing wonderful work in protecting the national security.

I charge that the Republicans have attempted to usurp the constitutional functions of the Federal grand juries and of the courts.

I charge that they have not produced any significant information about Communist espionage which the FBI did not already have.

I charge the Republicans with having impaired our Nation's atomic energy program by their intemperate and unjustified attacks on our atomic scientists.

I charge them with having recklessly cast a cloud of suspicion over the most loyal civil service in the world.

I charge them with having trampled on the individual freedoms which distinguish American ideals from totalitarian doctrine.

I charge finally that, in all this, they have not hurt the Communist Party one bit.

They have helped it.

The fact of the matter is that the Republican Party is unwittingly the ally of the Communists in this country. . . .

The greatest danger to us does not come from communism in the United States. The greatest danger has been that communism might blot out the light of freedom in so much of the rest of the world that the strength of its onslaught against our liberties would be greatly multiplied. To meet this danger, my administration has moved vigorously to aid the democratic governments of foreign nations in maintaining the independence and freedom of their peoples.

In spite of considerable opposition from the Republican rank and file in both Houses of Congress, I urged, and the Congress finally approved, programs for economic aid to free nations.

These programs, which began with the Truman Doctrine and the Marshall plan, have made it possible for many nations to stand with us in opposition to Communist encroachment throughout the world. . . .

And while we worked to strengthen democracy in the world, my administration worked with equal vigor to strengthen democracy at home. For we know that this is the best way to kill communism at its roots.

People who are well-fed, well-clothed, well-housed, and whose basic rights are protected, do not become victims of communism.

With this object in mind, I repeatedly presented a legislative program to the Congress.

Among the big elements in that program were:

Inflation control, to stabilize the cost of living;

Housing, not merely for the privileged and the rich, but also for the people of average and low income;

Adequate medical care for millions of our people who are not getting it now;

Improvement in our educational facilities, to reduce illiteracy, and to raise the entire level of American life;

An increase in minimum wages;

An extension of social security to large groups not now covered, and an increase in benefits to the aged, to the crippled, and to widows, mothers, and children.

But what happened to this program to strengthen American democracy?

It ran into a reactionary Republican Congress—the 80th—and there it was stopped dead.

The truth is, the Democratic Party has been leading the fight to make democracy effective and to wipe out communism in the United States.

Long before these Republicans started their Communist talk for political purposes, my administration was engaged in a direct attack on subversive organizations and persons in the United States.

We worked at it every day—and not just before elections. We continued to work at it, and just not before election.

A part of our effort has been to make sure that Communists and other disloyal persons are not employed by the Federal Government.

I want to tell you about that. I want to tell you some things that you have not heard from the Republicans.

Since 1939 the employees of the Government have been required to swear under oath that they are not Communists. That means that there is not one single employee of the Federal Government who is an admitted Communist.

Nevertheless, we all know that Communists are trained to lie. There is no doubt that they, as well as other disloyal persons, have tried to worm their way into the Government service.

So, in 1947, I set up the employee loyalty program to require an individual check on all Federal employees and to discharge them if they were found to be Communists, or if there were other reasonable grounds for doubting their loyalty.

This was a real program to meet a real situation, and it was worked out by competent people who had the facts and understood how the Federal Government actually works.

At the start, the Congress delayed the program for months through slowness in making appropriations, and when it did come through, when the appropriation did come through, it was much less than I had requested. The Republicans at that time said the program was too elaborate.

Now, in an election year, they say it is not elaborate enough. That is Republican consistency.

This program meant the checking of over 2 million Federal employees. I gave the FBI complete charge of this part of the program. And they have handled their job with such efficiency that all present employees have now been checked.

The FBI check showed that the loyalty of 99.7 percent of all Federal workers was not even questionable.

The remaining three-tenths of one percent represented every last instance in which the FBI found any shred of unchecked loyalty information about any Federal employee. It even included employees who were the victims of accusations by malicious, anonymous persons. Each of these employees was investigated intensively by the FBI from their first birthday to the present time.

The results of the FBI loyalty investigations have been turned over to loyalty boards in the agencies which employ these persons involved. The review of these FBI investigations by the loyalty boards has shown that the large majority of these three-tenths of one percent are good, loyal Americans. . . .

Only in the case of about one in 6,000 Government employees has loyalty been found doubtful. That's an amazing record. It is proof of the vigilance of the Government that so small a number of disloyal men and women have been able to work their way into Federal jobs.

Certain Republicans have been shouting for faster action. They seem to want us to fire employees, without hearings, on the basis of unsupported charges. They resent the democratic safeguards of the loyalty program.

Those safeguards are a vital part of the program. The American sense of justice demands for every man a right to defend himself against accusations, the right to a fair hearing, the right to counsel, and the right of appeal. . . .

We have been concerned, not merely with Communists in the Government, but with Communists in the United States of America, wherever they are.

Evidence of Soviet espionage has been presented to a special Federal grand jury which even now is in session in New York City. The FBI has been quietly and efficiently assembling this evidence for several years. The evidence was being presented to the grand jury long before the Republican congressional committees began their recent hearings. Now these committees are trying to win credit for digging up evidence. They are trying to cash in on the work of the FBI, and to usurp the functions of the grand jury and the Federal courts.

Grand jury deliberations, of course, must be confidential. So must the work of the FBI. But the House Un-American Activities Committee doesn't care about that. By its irresponsible publicity, this committee has already done damage to the work of the FBI and other security agencies. Through its press-agent stunts for political ends, this committee has made confidential information available to the intelligence services of foreign countries. And with reckless disregard for the Bill of Rights, this committee has injured the reputations of innocent men by spreading wild and false accusations.

This committee has also deprived the Government of the services of a number of atomic scientists, who are so badly needed to enable this Nation to maintain its leadership in the field of atomic energy. Recently, eight of the most eminent scientists in this country pointed this out as a danger to our national security. . . .

. . . On the basis of evidence collected by the FBI and submitted to the grand jury, twelve top Communist leaders will go to trial in New York on October 15. We have prosecuted and we shall prosecute subversive activities wherever we find them. But we must have real evidence. We cannot use speeches of Republican politicians as evidence.

NOTE: The President spoke at 4 p.m. from the grandstand at the Oklahoma State Fairgrounds. The address was carried on a nationwide radio broadcast.

Letter to the Chairman, Civil Service Commission, on the Administration of the Federal Employee Security Programs, August 8, 1952

The various internal security programs had not operated in a way that protected civil liberties. Note Truman's response to the discovery that the balance between internal security and individual rights had shifted against the latter. Taken from Public Papers of the Presidents of the

United States: Harry S. Truman . . . *January 1, 1952 to January 20, 1953 (Washington, 1966), 513–14.*

Dear Mr. Chairman:

On July 14, 1951, I requested the National Security Council to make an investigation of the administration of Federal employee security programs relating to the denial of employment and the suspension and removal of employees in the interest of national security. Pursuant to that request, a study was made by the Interdepartmental Committee on Internal Security. Its report, prepared in collaboration with the staff of the Civil Service Commission, has been submitted to me by the National Security Council.

This report recommends that certain uniform standards and procedures be established to apply to all agencies where employee security programs are in effect. It also recommends that provision be made for Civil Service Commission review of agency decisions in security risk cases.

In addition, the Interdepartmental Committee on Internal Security, in transmitting its report to the National Security Council, called attention to the confused situation which exists by reason of there three general programs dealing with the denial of employment and the suspension and separation of Government employees. These general programs were described by the Committee as relating to loyalty, security, and suitability under civil service regulations, respectively, and the Committee pointed out that it is extremely difficult if not impossible to draw clear lines of demarcation among them. In order to eliminate this confusion, the Committee recommended that a study be made to effect a single general program covering eligibility for employment in the Federal service, whether on grounds of loyalty, security, or suitability. It is my understanding that the Civil Service Commission agrees with this proposal.

I have given considerable thought to the recommendations contained in this report. I have concluded that the most desirable action at this time would be to merge the loyalty, security, and suitability programs, thus eliminating the overlapping, duplication, and confusion which apparently now exist. It is my understanding that the status of the incumbent employees loyalty program is now so advanced that there would be little or no obstacle to accomplishing this from the standpoint of the future needs of that phase of the loyalty program. Accordingly, I should like for the Civil Service Commission to take the necessary steps to provide me with a plan for combining the three existing programs into one at the earliest practicable date. To achieve this end, I am directing all Executive departments and agencies to cooperate fully with the Commission and to furnish the Commission with such personnel and other assistance as it may require.

Pending action to merge the existing three programs, it does not seem advisable to issue an Executive Order establishing uniform standards and procedures comprising an over-all Government employee security program, with provision for Civil Service Commission review of agency decisions. Such an Executive Order would presumably have only temporary effect, since it would be superseded shortly by the new program I am requesting the Commission to prepare. I believe we can utilize our efforts most effectively by going straight to what we regard as the best solution.

In the meantime, however, departments and agencies having employee security programs should reexamine their procedures in the light of the findings and recommendations of the Interdepartmental Committee. The Committee's report contains a great deal of worthwhile material which should provide valuable guidance for those responsible for the formulation and administration of personnel security procedures, and which should assist them in assuring adequate procedural safeguards for the protection of all personnel who are subject to employee security programs.

I am sending copies of this letter and the report of the Interdepartmental Committee on Internal Security to the heads of all Executive departments and agencies.

Sincerely yours,

HARRY S. TRUMAN

[The Honorable Robert Ramspeck, Chairman of the Civil Service Commission]

NOTE: "A Report by the Interdepartmental Committee on Internal Security on the Government Employee Security Program as Submitted to the President by the National Security Council" (35 pp., plus indexes, processed) was released with the President's letter.

Memorandum on the Secretary of State's Recommendation in the Case of John Carter Vincent, January 3, 1953

The process revealed in this letter ruined the personal careers of State Department employees John Carter Vincent, John P. Davies, Jr., and John S. Service. The damage went beyond the personal, however, for their removals (and those of others) stripped the State Department of expertise on Southeast Asia. This void contributed to ineffective policymaking in that area of the world for the next two decades. Selected from Public Papers of the Presidents of the United States: Harry S. Truman . . . January 1, 1952 to January 20, 1953 *(Washington, 1966), 1110–11.*

Memorandum to the Secretary of State:

I have read your memorandum of today concerning the case of John Carter Vincent. I think the suggestions which you make are well taken and I authorize and direct you to proceed in the manner which you have outlined.

HARRY S. TRUMAN

NOTE: The text of the Secretary of State's memorandum to the President follows:

MEMORANDUM FOR THE PRESIDENT

Subject: Case of John Carter Vincent

I have recently been advised by Chairman Bingham of the Loyalty Review Board that a panel of the Loyalty Review Board has considered the case of Mr. John Carter Vincent, a Foreign Service Officer with class of Career Minister. Chairman Bingham also advises me that while the panel did not find Mr. Vincent guilty of disloyalty, it has reluctantly concluded that there is reasonable doubt as to his loyalty to the Government of the United States. Chairman Bingham further advises me that it is therefore the recommendation of the Board that the services of Mr. Vincent be terminated.

Such a recommendation by so distinguished a Board is indeed serious and impressive and must be given great weight. The final responsibility, however, for making a decision as to whether Mr. Vincent should be dismissed is that of the Secretary of State. . . .

In the first place, I note a statement that the panel has not accepted or rejected the testimony of Mr. Budenz that he recalls being informed by others that Mr. Vincent was a Communist and under Communist discipline. The panel also states that it does not accept or reject the findings of the Committee on the Judiciary of the Senate with respect to Mr. Vincent and the Institute of Pacific Relations or the findings of the Committee with respect to the participation of Mr. Vincent in the development of United States policy towards China in 1945. The panel, however, proceeds to state that, although it has not accepted or rejected these factors, it has taken them into account. I am unable to interpret what this means. If the panel did take these factors into account, this means that it must have relied upon them in making its final determination. Yet I am unable to understand how these factors could have played a part in the final determination of the panel if these factors were neither accepted nor rejected by the Board.

This is not merely a point of language. It is a point of real substance. It is difficult for me to exercise the responsibility which is mine under the law with the confusion which has been cast as to the weight which the panel gave to the charges of Mr. Budenz or the findings of the Senate Committee. . . .

[Acheson continues to analyze the panel's memo.]

"The panel notes Mr. Vincent's studied praise of Chinese Communists and equally studied criticism of the Chiang Kai-shek Government throughout a period when it was the declared and established policy of the Government of the United States to support Chiang Kai-shek's Government."

Mr. Vincent's duty was to report the facts as he saw them. It was not merely to report successes of existing policy but also to report on the aspects in which it was failing and the reasons therefore. If this involved reporting that situations existed in the administration of the Chinese Nationalists which had to be corrected if the Nationalist Government was to survive, it was his duty to report this. If this involved a warning not to underestimate the combat potential of the Chinese Communists, or their contribution to the war against Japan, it was his duty to report this. . . .

The great majority of reports which Mr. Vincent drafted were reviewed and signed by Ambassador Gauss, an outstanding expert in the Far East. Ambassador Gauss has made it crystal clear that in his mind the reports drafted by Mr. Vincent were both accurate and objective.

I do not exclude the possibility that in this or in any other case a board might find that the reports of an officer might or might not disclose a bias which might have a bearing on the issue of his loyalty. But in so delicate a matter, affecting so deeply the integrity of the Foreign Service, I should wish to be advised by persons thoroughly familiar with the problems and procedures of the Department of State and the Foreign Service. . . .

The memorandum from Mr. Bingham indicates that the Board also took into account "Mr. Vincent's failure properly to discharge his responsibilities as Chairman of the Far Eastern Subcommittee of State, War and Navy to supervise the accuracy or security of State Department documents emanating from that Subcommittee." . . . The reference to the accuracy of the State Department documents emanating from that Committee is obscure. In any case, while it might be relative to Mr. Vincent's competence in performing his duties, it does not seem to me to have any bearing on the question of loyalty.

The report finally refers to Mr. Vincent's association with numerous persons "who, he had reason to believe," were either Communists or Communist sympathizers. This is indeed a matter which, if unexplained, is of importance and clearly relevant. It involves inquiry as to whether this association arose in the performance of his duties or otherwise. It further involves an inquiry as to the pattern of Mr. Vincent's close personal friends and whether he knew or should have known that any of these might be Communists or Communist sympathizers.

All these matters raised in my mind the necessity for further inquiry. This further inquiry was made possible by the documents in this proceeding which you provided me upon my request. I find upon examining the documents that the recommendation made by the panel of the Loyalty Review Board was made by a majority of one, two of the members believing that no evidence had been produced which led them to have a doubt as to Mr. Vincent's loyalty. In this situation, I believe that I cannot in good conscience and in the exercise of my own judgment, which is my duty under the law, carry out this recommendation of the Board. I do not believe, however, that in the exercise of my responsibility to the Government, I can or should let the matter rest here. I believe that I must ask for further guidance.

I, therefore, ask your permission to seek the advice of some persons who will combine the highest judicial qualifications of weighing the evidence with the greatest possible familiarity of the works and standards of the Department of State and the Foreign Service, both in reporting from the field and making decisions in the Department. . . .

DEAN G. ACHESON
Secretary of State

Questions

1. *Describe the biases involved in using these sources. What other sources should you check to be balanced in your research?*
2. *From these documents, how would you assess Truman's character and personality?*
3. *Do these documents convince you that there was a real threat to internal security in the late 1940s and early 1950s? How do these documents suggest that politics was more instrumental in creating the hysteria of the Second Red Scare than any actual threat to internal security?*
4. *One of the tensions running through these documents is whether the White House or Congress should be responsible for maintaining internal security. What do you think?*

FURTHER READING

Victor S. Navasky's Naming Names *(New York, 1980) is a compelling account of some of the people who had to decide between protecting themselves and their families or protecting their friends.* The Committee and Its Critics: A Calm Review of the House Committee on Un-American Activities *(New York, 1962) by William F. Buckley, Jr., and the editors of* National Review *is an attempt by conservative commentators to wrestle with the criticisms leveled at HUAC, some of which appeared to support conservative causes. Michal R. Belknap,* Cold War Political Justice: The Smith Act, the Communist Party, and American Civil Liberties *(Westport, Connecticut, 1977) shows how both the prosecutors and the defendants used the trial of leaders of the Communist Party USA to further their own political agendas and how, in the process, First Amendment rights were greatly constricted. Alan D. Harper in* The Politics of Loyalty: The White House and the Communist Issue, 1946–1952 *(Westport, Connecticut, 1969) places Truman's actions within the broader context of politics and domestic events and the federal bureaucracy. John G. Adams in* Without Precedent: The Story of the Death of McCarthyism *(New York, 1983) outlines the rise to power of Joseph McCarthy and incisively chronicles the infamous Army-McCarthy hearings, which eventually exposed McCarthy's real nature to the American people. Arthur Miller's* The Crucible: A Play in Four Acts *(New York, 1953) is a play about the Salem witch trials that clearly reflects the insidiousness of the contemporary McCarthy era. See also the essays on the Red Scare, Civil Liberties, and the Loyalty Program in* The Harry S. Truman Encyclopedia, *ed. Richard S. Kirkendall (Boston, 1989).*

The debate continues in the late twentieth century with several interesting volumes. Richard Gid Powers, Not Without Honor: The History of American Anticommunism *(New York, 1998) presents a neoconservative view, while Ellen Schrecker,* Many Are the Crimes: McCarthyism in America *(Boston, 1998) argues that new evidence of actual subversive activity occurring in the 1940s and 1950s does not excuse the acts of political repression engaged in by many politicians.* The Haunted Woods: Soviet Espionage in America in the Stalin Era *(New York, 1999), by Allen Weinstein and Alexander Vassiliev, utilizes previously unknown files in the Soviet archive to suggest that*

Soviet spying was more widespread in the U.S. than we have heretofore recognized. To date, however, other historians have not been able to check these sources.

Race Relations, 1890–1915: Booker T. Washington and W. E. B. Du Bois

Christopher Waldrep

INTRODUCTION

White racism in America deepened after the end of Reconstruction. In 1866 and 1875 Congress had enacted bold and pioneering civil rights legislation that promised to end discriminatory laws and guarantee equal access to hotels, restaurants, and transportation. By the end of the nineteenth century, however, white Americans pulled back from the promise of Reconstruction. The Supreme Court snuffed out the 1875 Civil Rights law when it ruled that Congress had no power to end segregation in privately owned public accommodations. Despite the Fifteenth Amendment's pledge of voting rights, southern states ruthlessly eliminated black voters from their voting rolls after 1890.

In the midst of this legal discrimination, whites laced their popular culture with vicious and ugly racist insults directed at African Americans. Even "objective" and "neutral" science seemed to favor the white race. Scientists "discovered" that blacks had smaller brains than whites and therefore could never equally compete with persons of European descent. Historians praised the merits of slavery and decried the blunders of Reconstruction. Social Darwinists insisted that those at the top of society deserved to be there, having achieved their position through "natural selection." Similarly, those at the bottom of society had earned their place through their shortcomings.

As black Americans plunged into this deep racial abyss, they struggled to find a new strategy to cope with changed conditions. In 1895 Booker T. Washington suggested a dramatic new approach that backed away from the confrontational tactics favored by abolitionists like Frederick Douglass. Washington proposed making few public demands on whites. In Washington's view, blacks should better themselves, hoping to become worthy of equality. W. E. B. Du Bois first agreed with Washington and then sharply turned in a different direction. Du Bois eventually became Washington's harshest critic, demanding change through protest and direct action.

Washington and Du Bois had strikingly different biographies. Booker Taliaferro Washington was born a slave on James Burrough's farm in western Virginia. Slaves often did not know their birthdays, but Washington probably entered the world in 1856. He never knew his father. After emancipation, Washington worked in a salt mine before attending Hampton Normal and Agricultural Institute. Washington received an industrial education at Hampton where he fell under the spell of General Samuel Chapman Armstrong, head of the school. Armstrong promoted thrifty and industrious living. He had never believed in Reconstruction egalitarianism and ran his school convinced that the "great party of freedom" was over. Washington internalized Armstrong's conservatism.

While Washington experienced slavery first hand, William E. B. Du Bois came from Great Barrington, Massachusetts. Born on 23 February, 1868, Du Bois spent his youth blissfully unaware of racial prejudice. He attended Fisk, Harvard, and the University of Berlin, becoming the first African American to earn a Ph.D. from Harvard in 1896. Despite his education, Du Bois could only land a job teaching Latin and Greek at Ohio's Wilberforce College. He next went to the University of Pennsylvania and then moved to Atlanta University. While in Atlanta Du Bois learned of the brutal Sam Hose lynching. As whites sold fragments of Sam Hose's bones for a quarter and bits of his liver for a dime, Du Bois decided he could not remain a detached, objective academic in the face of such horrors. In 1899, the year white Georgians burned Sam Hose alive, Du Bois began an intellectual journey that took him away from academia.

By the early twentieth century many thought these two remarkably different men had framed the debate for African Americans. Washington advocated accommodation; he and his followers did not criticize whites' racism. Claiming that African Americans had been loyal to whites through slavery, he promised they would now be faithful to their white employers, "without strikes or labour wars." Washington instructed black people to be satisfied with common labor. "It is at the bottom of life we must begin and not at the top." Washington sought to protect for black people their families and their rights to an education while surrendering their political rights and free access to public places. Under Washington's leadership, blacks would no longer demand the right to vote; they would accept disfranchisement just as they accepted segregation.

Du Bois proposed meeting white racism with a militant response. He called for protest against all forms of inequality, civil, political, and economic. In language designed to challenge Washington, Du Bois announced himself unwilling to apologize for the insults of whites or submit to their oppression. Washington hoped black and white Americans could unify, albeit with each race in its proper "place." Du Bois, by contrast, urged black people to pursue the genius of their own culture, assimilating with their own color, not with whiteness.

MODERN ASSESSMENTS OF WASHINGTON AND DU BOIS

Modern scholars have carefully examined the split between Washington and Du Bois. Some emphasize the ultimate goal of equality shared by both men. In this view, Washington and Du Bois differed only on superficialities, not substantive issues. Others argue that Washington and Du Bois represented truly different ideologies. The deeper question, though, involves the effectiveness of Washington's strategy compared with that urged by Du Bois. That question remains important even today.

Boss of Black America

David Howard-Pitney's The Afro-American Jeremiad *contrasts Booker T. Washington unfavorably with the great abolitionist Frederick Douglass. Born a slave in Maryland, Douglass had escaped to become a distinguished orator and author, chastising whites for their racism. After the Civil War, Douglass demanded government-protected economic opportunities for black Americans as well as the right to vote and other political rights. While he admires Douglass's courage, Howard-Pitney characterizes Washington as "underhanded" and "ruthless" and observes that Washington reversed Douglass's more aggressive message. Instead of challenging white America, Washington studiously avoided deploring the misdeeds of white racists. His public statements steered clear of condemnation and protest. Howard-Pitney also condemns Washington for monopolizing power. Between 1895 and his death in 1915, Howard-Pitney writes, Washington was the undisputed "Boss of Black America." The following excerpt is from David Howard-Pitney,* The

Afro-American Jeremiad: Appeals for Justice in America (*Philadelphia, 1990*), 61-67.

Washington . . . built up an impressive organizational and personal power base. His control over the flow of philanthropic monies to blacks became absolute. After 1901, he also became prime distributor of blacks' remaining patronage in the Republican Party, serving as unofficial race advisor to President Theodore Roosevelt. He expanded his institutional base in the black community by holding annual national Negro Farmer Conferences at Tuskegee and by founding a Negro Business League with chapters across the country. American presidents visited and praised the Tuskegee Institute. Washington attended dinner at the White House, socialized with millionaires, and had tea with the Queen of England.

Washington used means foul and fair to create what became known among his critics as the "Tuskegee Machine." Always the epitome of modest deference before whites, Washington was dictatorial with black subordinates and ruthless in suppressing opponents. So complete was his patronage power that virtually no black school, institution, or individual had much chance of securing financing without the recommendation of Booker T. Washington. Washington readily used this power to control events and crush black resistance at his will. The legendary "Wizard of Tuskegee" employed a battery of covert underhanded methods to punish and ruin his enemies. From the start of his Tuskegee years, Washington had discredited rival black educators with Alabama legislators by fabricating and spreading unfavorable rumors about them. Later, he regularly made quiet contributions to black newspapers to ensure favorable editorial comment and coverage of his activities. Organizations that he deemed disloyal he had infiltrated with spies. These are but some of the means by which he established and maintained himself as the most powerful black person in America.

In his political pursuits, Washington skillfully invoked and manipulated messianic myths dear to both black and white Americans. Indeed, he was his era's most influential source of Afro-American messianic rhetoric.

Booker T. Washington, the founder of Tuskeegee Institute and sometimes called "the most powerful black man in America." (Courtesy of Library of Congress.)

Washington suggested that blacks possessed the "soft," non-threatening messianic virtues of (1) servanthood and altruism, (2) humility and meekness, and (3) patient suffering under adversity. One of his leading themes was the "gospel of service." He urged blacks to serve others both as a religious obligation ("Christ said he who would become greatest of all must become servant of all") and as a practical way of gaining an economic foothold in society. "The whole problem of the Negro," he claimed, "rests . . . upon . . . whether he makes himself . . . of indispensable service to his neighbor."

He habitually portrayed blacks' lowly temporal conditions in messianic imagery. For example, he noted that the building first used as a classroom at Tuskegee Institute had been a henhouse and a stable. Thus blacks at Tuskegee's birth, like Jesus, had found no room for their needs save a humble stable. When it came time to raise their own buildings, the students and staff had to learn to make bricks, which Washington later compared with the task of "the Children of Israel . . . making bricks without straw" for Pharaoh. Like the Hebrews of the Bible, Afro-Americans faced hard tasks before they would reach the Promised Land.

Washington often invoked the suffering servant motif that associates undeserved suffering and oppression with redemptive power. Like most blacks, Washington discerned redemptive value in the paradoxical ordeal of slavery. Holding that American slavery "was a great curse to both races," he nonetheless believed that Providence had used the experience to provide blacks with what they most needed for social survival and salvation. America had brought Afro-Americans knowledge of Christianity and English and familiarity with the world's greatest civilization, the Anglo-Saxon. Blacks had entered America as heathens and chattel with no language, he contended, yet had left slavery as Christians and American citizens "speaking the proud Anglo-Saxon tongue." Moreover, the "plantation school" had taught blacks just those work skills now needed by the race in order to develop and prosper. Thus Washington could declare that slavery "in the providence of God . . . laid the foundation for the solution of the problem that is now before us."

Washington portrayed blacks as Christlike to disarm whites and reassure them of black nonaggression. He stressed those gentler traits commonly associated with black messianism to counter the dangerous white stereotype of blacks as rapacious beasts, a popular racial image among whites that spread widely after the Civil War. Negrophobes pictured blacks as such a threatening menace that the severest repression and terror was required to subdue it. Against the rising popularity of this white image, Washington appealed to contrary stereotypes of blacks that invested Afro-Americans with submissive "feminine" and Christian virtues. Blacks, like women, were widely thought to possess an innate religious sensibility and were viewed as naturally meek, devout, unselfish, and inclined to serve and nurture others.

In his 1895 Atlanta address, Washington called blacks "the most patient, faithful, law abiding, and unresentful people that the world has ever seen." When later asked by whites whether lynchings might arouse blacks to violent response, he answered, "No . . . God did not put very much combativeness into our race. Perhaps it would have been better for us if we had not gone licking the hand that had beaten us. But that is the way of our race."

Washington skillfully strummed white Southern heartstrings by playing on their nostalgic myth of the faithful, contented slave. "We have proved our loyalty to you in the past, in nursing your children, watching by the sick-bed of your mothers and fathers and often following them with tear-dimmed eyes to their graves," he told whites, adding that blacks were still "ready to lay down our lives, if need be, in defense of yours." He raised a traditional image of blacks, that of "Sambo," a laughable character with incorrigible but petty faults such as theft and laziness but who was essentially good-natured, harmless, and childlike. Washington liberally sprinkled his talks to whites with humorous stories about sly, lazy, chicken-stealing "darkies," evidently hoping that images of blacks as either Christ or Sambo would counter their image as rebellious beasts requiring violent white domination.

Washington, as had Douglass, posited the universal superiority of Anglo-Saxon, especially Anglo-American culture, and firmly fixed blacks' future within it. Anglo-Saxon civilization was continually demonstrating its superiority through vigorous global expansion, he believed. Indeed, Washington differed from his white compatriots only in his insistence on the cultural, not biological, determinants of Anglo-Saxonism. He maintained that all English-speaking people belonged to that civilization and mission; it was slavery's silver lining that Afro-Americans had received the English tongue and been grafted onto Anglo-American culture. Anglo-Americans had a mission to the world, he affirmed, and blacks, by virtue both of their Americanness and distinctiveness, were a specially covenanted people within the American nation.

Washington always professed to believe in "a proud and great future" for blacks, and he urged blacks to keep faith in themselves and their millennial destiny. He spoke of his work "in putting a new spirit into our people," of inspiring them "with the idea that they *can* . . . they *will* make progress, and fulfill their mission *in this great republic.*"

The key was the more complete adoption of American middle-class values and behavior. The mission of black people was to perfect themselves as Americans, thereby helping America perfect itself. Their qualities of unselfish service and spirituality were widely considered lacking in the overly hard, "masculine" Anglo-Saxon race that was characterized by material acquisitiveness and competitive, ruthless individualism. The spiritual virtues of Afro-Americans were needed for the fuller Christianization and democratization of the nation. Providence had brought blacks to America, he contended, so "that the stronger race may imbibe a lesson from the Negroes, patience, forbearance, and childlike . . . trust in God." "These eight million of my people have been placed here" that the "white man may have a great opportunity to uplift himself" by the unselfish Christlike act of "lifting up this unfortunate race." By cooperating to further each other's moral and material development, black and white Americans would redeem each other, and together found "the new heaven and new earth." By struggling toward economic equality with other Americans, blacks would hasten the day when all Americans would do right by each other "citizen to citizen" and "Christian to Christian." And "if the Negro, who has been oppressed and denied his rights in a Christian land, can help the whites of the North and South to rise, to be the inspiration of their rising," Washington claimed, the Negro "will see in it recompense for all that he has suffered in the past."

Washington's racial nationalism was complementary but subordinate to his general American faith. This can be seen clearly in his attitude regarding Afro-American involvement with Africa. On the one hand, Washington held that Afro-Americans had a duty to assist in elevating Africans. While it was never his main priority, he accepted his responsibility as a black leader to promote worldwide racial progress. He forged important pan-African ties, sending American missionaries to Liberia and Togoland to found schools patterned on Tuskegee and spread the gospel of industrial education. The same program of agricultural and vocational training and self-help that Afro-Americans were starting to follow, he felt, could redeem black people everywhere. In 1906, he advocated founding an organization for social improvement in Africa, declaring, "I believe all the peoples of the earth may hope to find their task and place" in world progress and that each nationality's distinctiveness "should be preserved . . . for the special service they are able to perform." American efforts to spread Christian industrial education in Africa, he believed, would do much "to secure the future of what is, whatever its faults, one of the most useful races the world has ever known."

But despite his peripheral pan-African interests, Washington was foremost an American nationalist. Insofar as he conceived Afro-Americans' messianic duty extending to Africa, it was as advanced bearers of civilization to backward Africans in desperate need of reformation along Western lines. Afro-Americans, in his view, possessed a special destiny as a result of their ties to America, not Africa. Thus, it was those blacks providentially incorporated into America, he stressed, who "are constantly returning to Africa as missionaries to enlighten those who remained in the Fatherland."

Above all, Washington was an inveterate foe of Afro-American emigration to Africa or migration from the South to black enclaves in the American West or elsewhere. Afro-Americans' destiny, he unswervingly held, would one day be realized right where they were, in America and the South. "I see no way out of the Negro's present condition in the South by returning to Africa," Washington said, rejecting Bishop Henry Turner's call for emigration to Africa. To the contrary, it was in the South that "the great body of our people live, and where their salvation is to be worked out." Blacks need not look afar for the Promised Land, Washington asserted; they were already in it if they would but grasp the opportunities around them.

Washington filled the role of a Moses figure, exhorting blacks to keep the American covenant with its promise of economic success and social salvation. "The pillar of fire" that would lead them out of their current economic wilderness was the myth of the self-made individual. In America, he preached, every person rose or fell in direct proportion to individual effort and ability. The measure was the impersonal marketplace. Circumstances of birth were irrelevant, he maintained, since America promised that everyone who worked hard could become a prosperous middle-class individual, and this promise was abundantly available to all.

The self-made hero was mythically recreated in Washington's best-selling 1901 autobiography, *Up from Slavery*. A loose account of his life, it was an artistic arrangement of the facts into a compelling telling of the American myth of the self-made individual. The work descended from a long line of popular American self-help autobiographies, most notably that of Benjamin Franklin. The contemporary dime novels of Horatio Alger were also a great influence. Alger wrote a stream of popular novels in the late nineteenth century around the same "rags-to-riches" plot: A plucky poor boy, through character and determination, rises to a position of wealth and prominence in the fluid American social structure. *Up from Slavery* is strung along the line of an Alger novel. It chronicles Washington's rise from slavery's degrading depths to a pinnacle of fame and success. Washington could even top Alger's heroes, since they had all had the starting advantage of white skins, which deprived them of a rise from the *very* bottom. He rejoiced at having had this additional hurdle in life, declaring that "mere connection with what is known as a superior race will not permanently carry an individual forward unless he has individual worth," just as blackness "will not finally hold an individual back if he possesses intrinsic, individual worth." "It means a great deal," he reflected, "to start off on a foundation which one had made for one's self."

By ceaseless application and self-improvement, Washington rose to wealth and position in America—indeed, anyone who does so *must* rise, he stressed. Although he often acknowledges timely assistance from well-placed people, there is an air of inevitability about his success in this morality play which says, in effect, you can't keep a good man down. The power of right living and positive thinking is invincible, a social metaphysic that Washington made explicit in the book's "Last Words." Here he confessed that "my whole life has largely been one of surprises," but then concluded, "I believe that any man's life will be filled with constant, unexpected encouragements . . . if he makes up his mind to do his level best every day of his life." In Washington's view, the marketplace offered a fair competitive field in which demonstrated merit determined the outcome. In America's marketplace, if not in its social-civil sphere, prejudice had no role or effect.

Booker T. Washington's well-polished image as the black American self-made man confirmed Gilded-Age America's favorite image of itself. A more flattering, comforting picture of American society was scarcely possible. America truly was the land of unlimited promise and opportunity. Here no inherited, artificial social barriers kept individuals from going as far as merit could take them. More than any Alger novel, more than the examples of such self-made white millionaires as Andrew Carnegie, Washington's story proved that the American myth was true. America works, Washington showed in *Up from Slavery*—even for a black man.

Clashing Temperaments

David Levering Lewis traces the roots of the Washington-Du Bois fight to issues of style more than ideology. Like Du Bois, Washington promoted black rights, he just did so secretly. Washington's 1895 speech sealed a clever bargain with whites, promising obsequious behavior in exchange for limited educational opportunities and physical safety. Washington's arrangement failed only when radically racist whites displaced the conservatives with whom Washington had negotiated his deal. White racism hardened after President Rutherford Hayes withdrew federal troops from southern capitals and the Supreme Court declared unconstitutional congressional efforts to protect the rights of black Americans. These decisions amounted to a federal withdrawal from the South and encouraged white southerners in their racism. An economic depression in 1892 and 1893 forced white workers to compete for jobs once held by blacks, discouraging white charity across racial lines. Du Bois challenged Washington after becoming frustrated with this new generation of white racists not because of faults in the original pact. Lewis also writes that cultural dissimilarities divided the two leaders and helps account for their differences. The following excerpt is from David Levering Lewis, W. E. B. Du Bois: Biography of a Race, 1868-1919 *(New York, 1993), 257-263.*

The joke about Washington, that he never met a white man he didn't like, was precisely that—a joke. His gift (one Du Bois neither possessed nor wanted) was almost never to show his dislikes. The stakes were too high. If Ms. Calhoun of Cambridge and Mr. Washington *Bee* deplored his placatory pronouncements, it was because they had never experienced the white-sheeted fury engendered by a lack of obsequiousness. Less than a year after the Atlanta speech had made Washington a household name, the governor of Alabama had figuratively slapped him down in public. Apparently riled up by the proud manner in which the African-American customs collector of Wilmington, North Carolina, had delivered an otherwise Tuskegee-correct commencement address, Governor William C. Oates had torn up his prepared

---

Excerpts from *W.E.B. DuBois: Biography of a Race, 1886–1919*, 1993 Henry Holt & Company.

W. E. B. Du Bois, Washington's chief critic and founder of the National Association for the Advancement of Colored People (NAACP). (Courtesy of the Library of Congress.)

speech and given the Tuskegee assembly a red-faced dressing down. "I want to give you niggers a few words of plain talk and advice," he spluttered. "You might as well understand that this is a white man's country, as far as the South is concerned, and we are going to make you keep your place. Understand that." The Wizard rose, calling for prayer, and promptly terminated the proceedings. The etiquette of race relations was no less touch and go in the North. His boldest public moment, when he lectured white America on its civil rights obligations to black America at the 1898 Chicago Peace Jubilee, had practically been erased from the record when the Associated Press simply omitted his words. Washington complained to a white newspaper editor who had heard alarming accounts of it, that, "in a portion of my address which was not sent out, " he had said nothing more radical than that "the Negro be given every opportunity in proportion as he makes himself worthy."

Taught by such rebukes that there were no percentages in publicly advocating more than the right of African-Americans to live and work within the scheme ordained by the rich and powerful South and North, Washington increasingly moderated his moderation—the duties of the race rather than the rights it was denied were tirelessly, anecdotally emphasized. "When it gets down to hard pan," he told his northern mainstay T. Thomas Fortune, "it is hard to give an individual or race influence that it does not intrinsically possess." To his credit, whenever pinned down about fundamental rights, Washington, in statements usually cast in the negative and balanced on the faults of both races, declined to renounce outright the protections under the Fourteenth and Fifteenth Amendments of the Constitution. "I do not favor the Negro's giving up anything which is fundamental and which has been guaranteed to him by the Constitution," he stated on one notable occasion. "It is not best for him to relinquish his rights; nor would his doing so be best for the Southern white man." But it was quiet diplomacy and practical deeds that mattered. He came to expect the same approach from others, sincerely believing and publicly advising that what men and women said about racial injustice was more often that not unwise and, in any case, less important than what they did. The Wizard's white ghostwriter and future Chicago University sociologist Robert Park recalled that, after fifteen minutes or more ticking off firsthand instances of racial cruelty in the South, his new employer calmly interrupted to suggest that Park spend his time figuring out what to do about them.

Although only a few influential white men and women within the Tuskegee inner circle knew of it at the time, historians have now unearthed the Wizard's impressive record of secret civil rights maneuverings. "Pitchfork Ben" Tillman, Tom Watson, James Vardaman, and the South's other redneck populists went to their graves never suspecting that much of the organized resistance to the extinction of the African-American as a civil being originated in the upstairs study of Tuskegee's principal. Having spoken directly to the Louisiana legislature about voting rights in 1898, he worked behind the scenes to raise legal fees from wealthy whites in an unsuccessful effort to test the constitutionality of Louisiana's grandfather clause in the courts. He played the same covert role three years later in his own state of Alabama, failing again with the legislature, but doggedly lobbying and funneling monies for a legal assault on the state's new disfranchisement clauses. He reached out to the antidisfranchisement forces in Maryland, where, for a change, they were strong enough to win. Court battles against Pullman car discrimination on the railroads in Tennessee, Georgia, and Virginia had his full if invisible backing—usually through the screen of the Afro-American Council. Lawyers fighting racial exclusion from juries in Alabama and Texas looked to him for a portion of their retainers. He savored a rare victory in a hard-fought, infamous case involving Alonzo Bailey, a dirt-poor Alabama farmer forcibly returned to his white employer's farm, having had the cheek to leave owing twenty dollars. The U.S. Supreme Court, grown somnolent in matters involving the rights of black people and laborers, finally roused itself to outlaw peonage (enslavement by contract), although the apparent technicalities were such that the court was unable to find a remedy for Mr. Bailey's specific predicament. Hardly surprising, then, that less than a month after seeking endorsement for the assistant superintendency in the District of Columbia, a furious Du Bois was writing Washington about hauling the Southern Railway before the Interstate Commerce Commission for its refusal to sell him a sleeping berth on account of race.

Being leader of his race was more than a notion, Washington must often have thought, sighing, off the record, that in a two-year period he "spent at least four thousand dollars in cash, out of my own pocket . . . in advancing the rights of the black man." But if all the machination, manipulation, and dissembling had had no higher purpose than the mere physical survival of black people in the South, as well as the greater glory of Tuskegee Institute, Booker Washington's program would not have been so much tragic as pathetic. If he was the Machiavelli of the Black Belt, the Wizard of Tuskegee, like his Renaissance precursor, dreamed of noble ends even as he schemed ignobly. As his biographer discloses, Washington believed—and he had to believe it absolutely—that he personified the Faustian bargain into which his people had entered with the best elements of the white South and the wealthiest elements of the white North. The deal had been sealed at Atlanta in 1895: in exchange for docility in politics and discipline in work (and not even a whisper of social equality), African-Americans in the South were guaranteed due process in law, book learning for life's routines, and the opportunity to prosper economically, while the North, released from any moral, political, and constitutional duty to meddle, would provide money and personnel to make Henry Woodfin Grady's New South dream a reality.

The deal was struck with the survivors of the old planter class and the allied new class of bankers, mill owners, railroad vice-presidents, mine owners, and furnishing merchants who had reclaimed the South from Reconstruction. Heterogeneous in background and disputatious in politics, they were variously called "Redeemers" or "Bourbons" or "Conservatives." Until the early 1890s, what had united them was a strategy (masterfully implemented by the likes of Mississippi senator Lucius Quintus Lamar and South Carolina governor Wade Hampton) of using poor black people to control poor white people and their rising cousins. By poll taxes, residency requirements, literacy laws, stuffed ballot boxes, and a host of discriminatory devices, the conservatives had tilted the electoral process heavily in their favor, disfranchising as many as a fourth of the white males who otherwise could have voted in many of the states of the former Confederacy. Twice as many if not more African-Americans were excluded in the same way—and by stronger measures ranging from economic reprisals to vigilante mayhem. Reliable estimates put the number of African-Americans in the South still voting by the early 1890s near 40 percent. Yet for many lower-class whites for whom the ballot had been an obstacle instead of a passport to advancement, this was far too many. For other whites determined to hold on to power or to challenge it, the rump African-American vote remained a temptation and, not infrequently, a trump card. "The greatest danger that threatens Democratic supremacy in the South," a leading white newspaper warned in 1883, "is that the 'out' faction always gravitates toward the Negro and secures his aid to rout the 'ins.'" With the economic downturn beginning in the late 1880s, this situation had become volatile, with hardscrabble white people mobilizing behind Populist candidates and formerly quiescent black people awakening to their new balance-of-power opportunities. Overproduction had driven cotton from its 1870 high of twenty-nine cents a bale to five cents by 1890, threatening to drag Bourbon hegemony down with it. This had always been the white supremacist's nightmare, one inherent in southern politics so long as the African-American survived as a voter; and now loomed the even greater specter of a black and white coalition of empowered farmers.

It did not happen, and ten years after Booker Washington famously spoke in Atlanta, the nightmare and the specter were fast receding from the southern white consciousness. Where 130,344 African-Americans had been registered voters in Louisiana in 1896, 5,320 remained on the rolls four years later. After 1900, there were some 3,000 registered voters in Alabama out of a black male voting-age population of 181,471. Constitutional conventions in one southern state after another had, by 1910, "counted the Negro down and out," as one politician put it. Poor white people no longer needed to battle against Bourbon rule shored up by the Negro. The conservatives no longer needed dread biracial coalitions of taxing and regulating farmers. And so it became the task of the Wizard of Tuskegee to sanction what in any case he had absolutely no power to prevent—to sell it as a bargain, a compromise, and accommodation; to denounce and renounce the so-called Reconstruction experiment and hold out seductive prospects of a distant but realizable racial parity based on the unifying dollar rather than the divisive ballot. "Harmony will come in proportion as the black man gets something the white man wants," he preached. "Any movement for the elevation of the Southern Negro in order to be successful, must have to a certain extent the cooperation of the Southern whites. They control the government and own the property."

But the fatal flaw in the bargain was that the conservatives who controlled the legislatures in the 1895 South were even then losing power or being forced to share more of it with the rising radicals. The courtly squires of antebellum days—the Haygoods, Currys, Hamptons, and Lamars (even Governor Oates who gave the Tuskegee dressing-down)—were in retreat across Dixie before the Vardamans, Aycocks, Heflins, and Tillmans. Conservative disfranchisement, historian Joel Williamson has written, had been "marked by a willingness to leave the best of the blacks enfranchised and, conversely, to disfranchise the worst of the whites." Vardaman of Mississippi, his lustrous brown hair flying, spoke plainly for the radicals: "I am just as opposed to Booker Washington as a voter with all his Anglo-Saxon reinforcements, as I am to the coconut-headed, chocolate-colored, typical little coon, Andy Dotson, who blacks my shoes every evening." As these men and their followers captured the statehouses, the margin of maneuver for African-Americans would dwindle almost to nothing, not only in the political sphere but also in practically every other arena.

But it was not at first the unraveling of the politics of accommodation that outraged Du Bois and the small number of mostly northern, urban, and college-educated men and women soon to be known as the Talented Tenth. Washington's stratagem had seemed plausible enough—at least for a time—as a political approach to race relations. But its cultural dimensions dismayed and finally alienated those African-Americans (like Du Bois, Towns, Hope, Trotter, Chicago social reformer Ida Wells-Barnett, and others) for whom higher education was not merely a passport to social and professional standing but the master key to collective empowerment as well. When the Great Accommodator derided Latin and philosophy and French on platforms across the country, Du Bois felt mocked in the very center of his considerable self-significance. "The proud fop with his beaver hat, kid gloves, and walking cane" was the bane, said Washington, of the practical black men of goodwill intent upon spreading the gospel of industrial education in the South. "I believe dis darkey am called to preach," the punch line of another of the Wizard's platform favorites, colorfully reinforced the stereotype of shiftless Negroes ever ready to dodge useful labor. Increasingly, it seemed to Du Bois, darky jokes were giving way to jokes about high-falutin' city types. Du Bois and his peers might agree with Washington that a dollar in hand was worth far more to most of their people than a box seat at the opera, but they bridled when the Wizard suggested that higher degrees were a cover for distinguished indolence.

Interestingly, the Wizard gave Hampton students their 1898 commencement marching orders just as Du Bois returned to Fisk for the first time in ten years on a similar mission. Echoing Washington, he told Fiskites that African-Americans must grow into "a source of strength and power instead of a menace and a burden to the nation." "Captains of industry" were desperately needed. Du Bois stressed repeatedly on that day that a great variety of educations and occupations had to be fostered. But if all honest labor was essential, his "Careers Open to College-Bred Negroes" made it clear that Fisk men and women were not meant to be Pullman porters. "Even the higher branches of house-service . . . and the great field of skilled labor" were to be left to the skilled graduates of our "great industrial schools," he advised. They must understand that Fisk was special, that they were destined to go forth to sound the trumpet awakening their "dark historic race." With old classmate Proctor on the dais, Du Bois recalled his exaltation ten commencement mornings past. Winding up on an elitist note that Washington would never have played at Hampton or Tuskegee, he commanded, "Remember next that you are gentlemen and ladies, trained in the liberal arts and subjects in that vast kingdom of culture that has lighted the world from its infancy and guided it through bigotry and falsehood and sin." Du Bois's concept of a saving elite took another step toward completion that morning.

In the role of educator, then Washington was becoming too much for Du Bois to bear. Conflict hung over both men like heavily seeded clouds, although the year 1901 seemed to be passing with a fair prospect of no cloudburst until *Up From Slavery* appeared. The March edition of the *Atlantic Monthly* carried Du Bois's scholarly, historical evaluation of the work of the Freedman's Bureau. In June, another piece of Black Belt scholarship, "The Negro As He Really Is," appeared in *World's Work*. That same month saw his very favorable *Harper's Weekly* article on the accomplishments of the Tuskegee conferences, further indication of social scientist Du Bois seemingly too busy for the passions and distractions of partisanship. Meanwhile, *Up From Slavery*, ghostwritten by Max Bennett Thrasher, a white Vermont newspaperman and released by Doubleday, Page and Company in late February, was a stupendous success. "Negro" was rendered in upper case (almost unprecedented for a major publishing house). The story was vintage American: faith in God and hard, hard work overcoming bleakest adversity. The cast of edifying characters included an unlettered, devoted mother, aristocratic and kindly white families, the white matron who admitted him to Hampton after a parlor-sweeping examination, father-figure General Armstrong and his "gospel of the tooth-brush," the visionary ex-slave, Lewis Adams, who negotiated Tuskegee's existence, Washington's self-sacrificing wives, and good friend Andrew Carnegie.

Questions

1. *Between 1895 and 1915 Booker T. Washington was the most important black man in America. What do you think were his principal positive achievements? What were the negative consequences of his strategy? Do his achievements cover the costs of his approach?*

2. *Washington shaped his strategy in a time of horrible racial violence and legally sanctioned racism. Could Du Bois's strategy of confrontation have worked in such a time?*

3. *Any historical figure necessarily reflects the time within which he or she lives. Yet great and powerful personalities can influence the course of history. How important were Washington and Du Bois in shaping events in their time?*

4. *The disagreement between Washington and Du Bois was a particular historical event at a unique point in time. Yet their quarrel is often used to characterize choices between accommodation and resistance black Americans must make at any time in history, even today. To what extent does the split between Washington and Du Bois still shape African-American intellectual thought today?*

THE DEBATE BETWEEN WASHINGTON AND DU BOIS

Du Bois and Washington criticized each other in many speeches and articles between 1895 and 1915, when Washington died. The most famous texts in the feud are Washington's 1895 Atlanta speech and Du Bois's 1903 article criticizing Washington in Souls of Black Folk, *both of which follow. Washington's speech and Du Bois's essay represent two sides in a battle of ideas, but in another sense all these documents mark different points in Du Bois's intellectual journey. Du Bois initially agreed with Washington and always supported calls for thrift and self-discipline. By 1903 he had come to the position he took in* Souls of Black Folk *and in 1905 he helped write the "Declaration of Principles," an open challenge both to white racism and to Washington's accommodationist stance. Tensions between Washington and Du Bois developed because Washington remained true to his program of industrial education (and disparaged higher education for African Americans) while Du Bois changed his mind. In addition, Du Bois also resented the control Washington exercised over white charity. Washington had the power to see that philanthropic monies did not go to the black colleges he disliked.*

Washington's Speech at the Atlanta Exposition

In 1895, the year Washington delivered his famous speech at Atlanta, raging crowds of white southerners publicly burned, mutilated, castrated, hanged, shot, and tortured at least eighty-nine men, women, and children. The numbers of blacks lynched by whites reached unprec-

edented levels in the 1890s. Such terrorism convinced not just Washing-
ton, but many blacks, of the need for a new strategy. When Washington
delivered his speech at the Atlanta Exposition, formally called the Cotton
States and International Exposition, whites hailed his solution to the race
problem. After all, they blamed their own violence on their victims. If
only blacks would not commit crimes, many whites argued, the lynching
problem would disappear. Washington proposed what came to be called
the Atlanta Compromise: blacks would stop making political demands in
exchange for curbs on white violence. The mostly white audience, gath-
ered at the exposition to promote business prosperity and progress,
responded to Washington's speech enthusiastically. The ex-governor of
Georgia rushed across the stage to clasp Washington's hand. President
Grover Cleveland sent Washington a congratulatory telegram. The fol-
lowing speech is excerpted from The Booker T. Washington
Papers: Volume 3, 1889-95, *ed. Louis R. Harlan (University of Ilinois*
Press, 1974), 583-87.

Mr. President and Gentlemen of the Board of Directors and
Citizens: One-third of the population of the South is of the Negro
race. No enterprise seeking the material, civil, or moral welfare of
this section can disregard this element of our population and
reach the highest success. I but convey to you, Mr. President and
Directors, the sentiment of the masses of my race when I say that
in no way have the value and manhood of the American Negro
been more fittingly and generously recognized than by the managers of this magnificent Exposition at every stage of its progress.
It is a recognition that will do more to cement the friendship of the
two races than any occurrence since the dawn of our freedom.

Not only this, but the opportunity here afforded will awaken
among us a new era of industrial progress. Ignorant and inexperienced, it is not strange that in the first years of our new life we
began at the top instead of at the bottom; that a seat in Congress or
the state legislature was more sought than real estate or industrial
skill; that the political convention or stump speaking had more
attractions than starting a dairy farm or truck garden.

A ship lost at sea for many days suddenly sighted a friendly
vessel. From the mast of the unfortunate vessel was seen a signal,
"Water, water; we die of thirst!" The answer from the friendly
vessel at once came back, "cast down your bucket where you are."
A second time the signal, "Water, water; send us water!" ran up
from the distressed vessel, and was answered, "Cast down your

bucket where you are." And a third and fourth signal for water was answered. "Cast down your bucket where you are." The captain of the distressed vessel, at last heeding the injunction, cast down his bucket, and it came up full of fresh, sparkling water from the mouth of the Amazon River. To those of my race who depend on bettering their condition in a foreign land or who underestimate the importance of cultivating friendly relations with the Southern white man, who is their next-door neighbour, I would say: "Cast down your bucket where you are"—cast it down in making friends in every manly way of the people of all races by whom we are surrounded.

Cast it down in agriculture, mechanics, in commerce, in domestic service, and in the professions. And in this connection it is well to bear in mind that whatever other sins the South may be called to bear, when it comes to business, pure and simple, it is in the South that the Negro is given a man's chance in the commercial world, and in nothing is this Exposition more eloquent than in emphasizing this chance. Our greatest danger is that in the great leap from slavery to freedom we may overlook the fact that the masses of us are to live by the productions of our hands, and fail to keep in mind that we shall prosper in proportion as we learn to dignify and glorify common labour, and put brains and skill into the common occupations of life; shall prosper in proportion as we learn to draw the line between the superficial and the substantial, the ornamental gewgaws of life and the useful. No race can prosper till it learns that there is as much dignity in tilling a field as in writing a poem. It is at the bottom of life we must begin, and not at the top. Nor should we permit our grievances to overshadow our opportunities.

To those of the white race who look to the incoming of those of foreign birth and strange tongue and habits for the prosperity of the South, were I permitted I would repeat what I say to my own race, "Cast down your bucket where you are." Cast it down among the eight millions of Negroes whose habits you know, whose fidelity and love you have tested in days when to have proved treacherous meant the ruin of your firesides. Cast down your bucket among these people who have, without strikes and labour wars, tilled your fields, cleared your forests, builded your railroads and cities, and brought forth treasures from the bowels of the earth, and helped make possible this magnificent representation of the progress of the South. Casting down your bucket among my people, helping and encouraging them as you are doing on these grounds, and to education of head, hand, and heart, you will find that they will buy your surplus land, make blossom the waste places in your fields, and run your factories. While doing this, you can be sure in the future, as in the past, that you and your families will be surrounded by the most patient, faithful, law-abiding, and unresentful people that the world has seen. As we have proved our loyalty to you in the past, in nursing your children, watching by the sick-bed of your mothers and fathers, and often following them with tear-dimmed eyes to their graves, so in the future, in our humble way, we shall stand by you with a devotion that no foreigner can approach, ready to lay down our lives, if need be, in defense of yours, interlacing our industrial, commercial, civil, and religious life with yours in a way that shall make the interests of both races one. In all things that are purely social we can be as separate as the fingers, yet one as the hand in all things essential to mutual progress.

There is no defense or security for any of us except in the highest intelligence and development of all. If anywhere there are efforts tending to curtail the fullest growth of the Negro, let these efforts be turned into stimulating, encouraging, and making him the most useful and intelligent citizen. Effort or means so invested will pay a thousand per cent interest. These efforts will be twice blessed—"blessing him that gives and him that takes."

There is no escape through law of man or God from the inevitable:—

> "The laws of changeless justice bind
> Oppressor with oppressed;
> And close as sin and suffering joined
> We march to fate abreast."

Nearly sixteen millions of hands will aid you in pulling the load upward, or they will pull against you the load downward. We shall constitute one-third and more of the ignorance and crime of the South, or one-third its intelligence and progress; we shall contribute one-third to the business and industrial prosperity of the South, or we shall prove a veritable body of death, stagnating, depressing, retarding every effort to advance the body politic.

Gentlemen of the Exposition, as we present to you our humble effort at an exhibition of our progress, you must not expect overmuch. Starting thirty years ago with ownership here and there in a few quilts and pumpkins and chickens (gathered from miscellaneous sources), remember the path that has led from these to the inventions and production of agricultural implements, buggies, steam-engines, newspapers, books, statuary, carving, paintings, the management of drug stores and banks, has not been trodden without contact with thorns and thistles. While we take pride in what we exhibit as a result of our independent efforts, we do not for a moment forget that our part in this exhibition would fall far short of your expectations but for the constant help that has come to our educational life, not only from the Southern states, but especially from Northern philanthropists, who have made their gifts a constant stream of blessing and encouragement.

The wisest among my race understand that the agitation of questions of social equality is the extremest folly, and that progress in the enjoyment of all the privileges that will come to us must be the result of severe and constant struggle rather than of artificial forcing. No race that has anything to contribute to the markets of the world is long in any degree ostracized. It is important and right that all privileges of the law be ours, but it is vastly more important that we be prepared for the exercise of these privileges. The opportunity to earn a dollar in a factory just now is worth infinitely more than the opportunity to spend a dollar in an opera-house.

In conclusion, may I repeat that nothing in thirty years has given us more hope and encouragement, and drawn us so near to you of the white race, as this opportunity offered by the Exposition; and here bending, as it were, over the altar that represents the results of the struggles of your race and mine, both starting practically empty-handed three years ago, I pledge that in your effort to work out the great and intricate problem which God has laid at the doors of the South, you shall have at all times the patient, sympathetic help of my race; only let this be constantly in mind, that, while from representations in these buildings of the product of field, of forest, of mine, of factory, letters, and art, much good will come, yet far above and beyond material benefits will be that higher good, that, let us pray God, will come, in a blotting out of sectional differences and racial animosities and suspicions, in a determination to administer absolute justice, in a willing obedience among all classes to the mandates of law. This, coupled with our material prosperity, will bring into our beloved South a new heaven and a new earth.

SOULS OF BLACK FOLK

In 1895 Du Bois had no quarrel with Washington's message. But within a few years the same white racist brutalities that confirmed Washington in his policy, convinced Du Bois to change course. By 1903, Du Bois had written a collection of essays critical of the Washington strategy. He published these writings in a book titled Souls of Black Folk, *a publication that has been called the most important work on race relations since* Uncle Tom's Cabin. Souls of Black Folk *contains fourteen essays, nine of which had already appeared in such journals as* Atlantic Monthly *and* World's Work. *But Du Bois revised and reworked every essay, adding new material and rewriting the endings. Lyrical, ironic, and magisterial,* Souls of Black Folk *challenged Washington directly. As Du Bois himself put it, after its publication he knew he could never get a job at Tuskegee. Du Bois had in effect declared war on the most powerful black man in America. The following is from W. E. B. Du Bois,* The Souls of Black Folk *(New York, 1994), 30-35.*

Mr. Washington represents in Negro thought the old attitude of adjustment and submission; but adjustment at such a peculiar time as to make his programme unique. This is an age of unusual economic development, and Mr. Washington's programme naturally takes an economic cast, becoming a gospel of Work and Money to such an extent as apparently almost completely to overshadow the higher aims of life. Moreover, this is an age when the more advanced races are coming in closer contact with the less developed races, and the race-feeling is therefore intensified; and Mr. Washington's programme practically accepts the alleged inferiority of the Negro races. Again, in our own land, the reaction from the sentiment of war time has given impetus to race-prejudice against Negroes, and Mr. Washington withdraws many of the high demands of Negroes as men and American citizens. In other periods of intensified prejudice all the Negro's tendency to self-assertion has been called forth; at this period a policy of submission is advocated. In the history of nearly all other races and peoples the doctrine preached at such crises has been that manly self-respect is worth more than lands and houses, and that a people who voluntarily surrender such respect, or cease striving for it, are not worth civilizing.

Public lynchings, as depicted in this photograph, and other atrocities committed by whites against blacks greatly influenced both Du Bois and Washington in their very different responses to racism in American society. (Courtesy of the University of North Carolina Press.)

In answer to this, it has been claimed that the Negro can survive only through submission. Mr. Washington distinctly asks that black people give up, at least for the present, three things,—

First, political power,
Second, insistence on civil rights,
Third, higher education of Negro youth,—

and concentrate all their energies on industrial education, the accumulation of wealth, and the conciliation of the South. This policy has been courageously and insistently advocated for over fifteen years, and has been triumphant for perhaps ten years. As a result of this tender of the palm-branch, what has been the return? In these years there have occurred:

1. The disfranchisement of the Negro.
2. The legal creation of a distinct status of civil inferiority for the Negro.
3. The steady withdrawal of aid from institutions for the higher training of the Negro.

These movements are not, to be sure, direct results of Mr. Washington's teachings; but his propaganda has, without a shadow of doubt, helped their speedier accomplishment. The question then comes: Is it possible, and probable, that nine millions of men can make effective progress in economic lines if they are deprived of political rights, made a servile caste, and allowed only the most meagre chance for developing their exceptional men? If history and reason give any distinct answer to these questions, it is an emphatic *No*. And Mr. Washington thus faces the triple paradox of his career:

1. He is striving nobly to make Negro artisans business men and property-owners; but it is utterly impossible, under modern competitive methods, for workingmen and property-owners to defend their rights and exist without the right of suffrage.
2. He insists on thrift and self-respect, but at the same time counsels a silent submission to civic inferiority such as is bound to sap the manhood of any race in the long run.
3. He advocates common-school and industrial training, and depreciates institutions of higher learing; but neither the Negro common-schools, nor Tuskegee itself, could remain open a day were it not for teachers trained in Negro colleges, or trained by their graduates.

This triple paradox in Mr. Washington's position is the object of criticism by two classes of coloured Americans. One class is spiritually descended from Toussaint the Savior, through Gabriel, Vesey, and Turner, and they represent the attitude of revolt and revenge; they hate the white South blindly and distrust the white race generally, and so far as they agree on definite action, think that the Negro's only hope lies in emigration beyond the borders of the United States. And yet, by the irony of fate, nothing has more effectually made this programme seem hopeless than the recent course of the United States toward weaker and darker peoples in the West Indies, Hawaii, and the Philippines,—for where in the world may we go and be safe from lying and brute force?

The other class of Negroes who cannot agree with Mr. Washington has hitherto said little aloud. They deprecate the sight of scattered counsels, of internal disagreement; and especially they dislike making their just criticism of a useful and earnest man an excuse for a general discharge of venom from small-minded opponents. Nevertheless, the questions involved are so fundamental and serious that it is difficult to see how men like the Grimkes,

Kelly Miller, J.W.E. Bowen, and other representatives of this group, can much longer be silent. Such men feel in conscience bound to ask of this nation three things:

1. The right to vote.
2. Civic equality.
3. The education of youth according to ability.

They acknowledge Mr. Washington's invaluable service in counselling patience and courtesy in such demands; they do not ask that ignorant black men vote when ignorant whites are debarred, or that any reasonable restrictions in the suffrage should not be applied; they know that the low social level of the mass of the race is responsible for much discrimination against it, but they also know, and the nation knows, that relentless color-prejudice is more often a cause than a result of the Negro's degradation; they seek the abatement of this relic of barbarism, and not its systematic encouragement and pampering by all agencies of social power from the Associated Press to the Church of Christ. They advocate, with Mr. Washington, a broad system of Negro common schools supplemented by thorough industrial training; but they are surprised that a man of Mr. Washington's insight cannot see that no such educational system ever has rested or can rest on any other basis than that of the well-equipped college and university, and they insist that there is a demand for a few such institutions throughout the South to train the best of the Negro youth as teachers, professional men, and leaders.

This group of men honor Mr. Washington for his attitude of conciliation toward the white South; they accept the "Atlanta Compromise" in its broadest interpretation; they recognize, with him, many signs of promise, many men of high purpose and fair judgment, in this section; they know that no easy task has been laid upon a region already tottering under heavy burdens. But, nevertheless, they insist that the way to truth and right lies in straightforward honesty, not in indiscriminate flattery; in praising those of the South who do well and criticising uncompromisingly those who do ill; in taking advantage of the opportunities at hand and urging their fellows to do the same, but at the same time in remembering that only a firm adherence to their higher ideals and aspirations will ever keep those ideals within the realm of possibility. They do not expect that the free right to vote, to enjoy civic rights, and to be educated, will come in a moment; they do not expect to see the bias and prejudices of years disappear at the blast of a trumpet; but they are absolutely certain that the way for a people to gain their reasonable rights is not by voluntarily throwing them away and insisting that they do not want them; that the way for a people to gain respect is not by continually belittling and ridiculing themselves; that, on the contrary, Negroes must insist continually, in season and out of season, that voting is necessary to modern manhood, that color discrimination is barbarism, and that black boys need education as well as white boys.

In failing thus to state plainly and unequivocally the legitimate demands of their people, even at the cost of opposing an honored leader, the thinking classes of American Negroes would shirk a heavy responsibility,—a responsibility to themselves, a responsibility to the struggling masses, a responsibility to the darker races of men whose future depends so largely on this American experiment, but especially a responsibility to this nation,—this common Fatherland. It is wrong to encourage a man or a people in evil-doing; it is wrong to aid and abet a national crime simply because it is unpopular not to do so. The growing spirit of kindliness and reconciliation between the North and South after the frightful differences of a generation ago ought to be a source of deep congratulation to all, and especially to those whose mistreatment caused the war; but if that reconciliation is to be marked by the industrial slavery and civic death of those same black men, with permanent legislation into a position of inferiority, then those black men, if they are really men, are called upon by every consideration of patriotism and loyalty to oppose such a course by all civilized method, even though such opposition involves disagreement with Mr. Booker T. Washington. We have no right to sit silently by while the inevitable seeds are sown for a harvest of disaster to our children, black and white.

First, it is the duty of black men to judge the South discriminatingly. The present generation of Southerners are not responsible for the past, and they should not be blindly hated or blamed for it. Furthermore, to no class is the indiscriminate endorsement of the recent course of the South toward Negroes more nauseating than to the best thought of the South. The South is not "solid"; it is a land in the ferment of social change, wherein forces of all kinds are fighting for supremacy; and to praise the ill the South is to-day perpetrating is just as wrong as to condemn the good. Discriminating and broad-minded criticism is what the South needs,—needs it for the sake of her own white sons and daughters, and for the insurance of robust, healthy mental and moral development.

To-day even the attitude of the Southern whites toward the blacks is not, as so many assume, in all cases the same; the ignorant Southerner hates the Negro, the workingmen fear his competition, the money-makers wish to use him as a laborer, some of the educated see a menace in his upward development, while others—usually the sons of the masters—wish to help him to rise. National opinion has enabled this last class to maintain the Negro common schools, and to protect the Negro partially in property, life, and limb. Through the pressure of the money-makers, the Negro is in danger of being reduced to semi-slavery, especially in the country districts; the workingmen, and those of the educated who fear the Negro, have united to disfranchise him, and some have urged his deportation; while the passions of the ignorant are easily aroused to lynch and abuse any black man. To praise this intricate whirl of thought and prejudice is nonsense; to inveigh indiscriminately against "the South" is unjust; but to use the same breath in praising Governor Aycock, exposing Senator Morgan, arguing with Mr. Thomas Nelson Page, and denouncing Senator Ben Tillman, is not only sane, but the imperative duty of thinking black men.

It would be unjust to Mr. Washington not to acknowledge that in several instances he has opposed movements in the South which were unjust to the Negro; he sent memorials to the Louisiana and Alabama constitutional conventions, he has spoken against lynching, and in other ways has openly or silently set his influence against sinister schemes and unfortunate happenings. Notwithstanding this, it is equally true to assert that on the whole the distinct impression left by Mr. Washington's propaganda is, first, that the South is justified in its present attitude toward the Negro because of the Negro's degradation; secondly, that the prime cause of the Negro's failure to rise more quickly is his wrong education in the past; and, thirdly, that his future rise depends primarily on his own efforts. Each of these propositions is a dangerous half-truth. The supplementary truths must never be lost sight of: first, slavery and race-prejudice are potent if not sufficient causes of the Negro's position; second, industrial and common-school training were necessarily slow in planting because they had to await the black teachers trained by higher institutions,—it being extremely doubtful if any essentially different development was possible, and certainly a Tuskegee was unthinkable before 1880; and, third, while it is a great truth to say that the Negro must strive and strive mightily to help himself, it is equally true that unless his striving be not simply seconded, but rather aroused and encouraged, by the initiative of the richer and wiser environing group, he cannot hope for great success.

In his failure to realize and impress this last point, Mr. Washington is especially to be criticised. His doctrine has tended to make the whites, North and South, shift the burden of the Negro problem to the Negro's shoulders and stand aside as critical and rather pessimistic spectators; when in fact the burden belongs to the nation, and the hands of none of us are clean if we bend not our energies to righting these great wrongs.

The South ought to be led, by candid and honest criticism, to assert her better self and do her full duty to the race she has cruelly wronged and is still wronging. The North—her co-partner in guilt—cannot salve her conscience by plastering it with gold. We cannot settle this problem by diplomacy and suaveness, by "policy" alone. If worse come to worst, can the moral fibre of this country survive the slow throttling and murder of nine millions of men?

The black men of America have a duty to perform, a duty stern and delicate,—a forward movement to oppose a part of the work of their greatest leader. So far as Mr. Washington preaches Thrift, Patience, and Industrial Training for the masses, we must hold up his hands and strive with him, rejoicing in his honors and glorying in the strength of this Joshua called of God and of man to lead the headless host. But so far Mr. Washington apologizes for injustice, North or South, does not rightly value the privilege and duty of voting, belittles the emasculating effects of caste distinctions, and opposes the higher training and ambition of our brighter minds,—so far as he, the South, or the Nation, does this,—we must unceasingly and firmly oppose them. By every civilized and peaceful method we must strive for the rights which the world accords to men, clinging unwaveringly to those great words which the sons of the Fathers would fain forget: "We hold these truths to be self-evident: That all men are created equal; that they are endowed by their Creator with certain unalienable rights; that among these are life, liberty, and the pursuit of happiness."

Declaration of Principles

After publication of Souls of Black Folk, *Du Bois felt isolated and alone, locked in a one-man war against the vast resources of the Tuskegee Machine. In 1905 he assembled twenty-nine educators, lawyers, doctors, ministers, and businessmen in a Canadian hotel. At this meeting, Du Bois launched a campaign for full citizenship rights that challenged Booker T. Washington. Washington dispatched a spy to report on the proceedings and successfully kept news of the meeting from appearing in the black or white press. Nonetheless, Du Bois succeeded in establishing the Niagara Movement which led, in 1909, to the National Association for the Advancement of Colored People or NAACP.*

Assembled in Niagara in 1905, Du Bois and his followers produced the "Declaration of Principles," filled with indignant demands of the sort Washington avoided. Taken from The Complete Published Works of W. E. B. Du Bois, *ed. Herbert Aptheker (Millwood, NY, 1982), 55-58.*

The Niagara Movement
Declaration of Principles
1905

PROGRESS

The members of the conference, known as the Niagara Movement, assembled in annual meeting at Buffalo, July 11th, 12th and 13th, 1905, congratulate the Negro-Americans on certain undoubted evidences of progress in the last decade, particularly the increase of intelligence, the buying of property, the checking of crime, the uplift in home life, the advance in literature and art, and the demonstration of constructive and executive ability in the conduct of great religious, economic and educational institutions.

SUFFRAGE

At the same time, we believe that this class of American citizens should protest emphatically and continually against the curtailment of their political rights. We believe in manhood suffrage; we believe that no man is so good, intelligent or wealthy as to be entrusted wholly with the welfare of his neighbor.

Du Bois (seated on the left) led the Niagara Movement, a meeting of which is pictured above, which led to the founding of the NAACP in 1909. (Courtesy of the Special Collections and Archives, W. E. B. DuBois Library, University of Massachusetts Amherst.

CIVIL LIBERTY

We believe also in protest against the curtailment of our civil rights. All American citizens have the right to equal treatment in places of public entertainment according to their behavior and deserts.

ECONOMIC OPPORTUNITY

We especially complain against the denial of equal opportunities to us in economic life; in the rural districts of the South this amounts to peonage and virtual slavery; all over the South it tends to crush labor and small business enterprises; and everywhere American prejudice, helped often by iniquitous laws, is making it more difficult for Negro-Americans to earn a decent living.

EDUCATION

Common school education should be free to all American children and compulsory. High school training should be adequately provided for all, and college training should be the monopoly of no class or race in any section of our common country.

We believe that, in defense of our own institutions, the United States should aid common school education, particularly in the South, and we especially recommend concerted agitation to this end. We urge an increase in public high school facilities in the South, where the Negro-Americans are almost wholly without such provisions. We favor well-equipped trade and technical schools for the training of artisans, and the need of adequate and liberal endowment for a few institutions of higher education must be patent to sincere well-wishers of the race.

COURTS

We demand upright judges in courts, juries selected without discrimination on account of color and the same measure of punishment and the same efforts at reformation for black as for white offenders. We need orphanages and farm schools for dependent children, juvenile reformatories for delinquents, and the abolition of the dehumanizing convict-lease system.

PUBLIC OPINION

We note with alarm the evident retrogression in this land of sound public opinion on the subject of manhood rights, republican government and human brotherhood, and we pray God that this nation will not degenerate into a mob of boasters and oppressors, but rather will return to the faith of the fathers, that all men were created free and equal, with certain unalienable rights.

HEALTH

We plead for health—for an opportunity to live in decent houses and localities, for a chance to rear our children in physical and moral cleanliness.

EMPLOYERS AND LABOR UNIONS

We hold up for public execration the conduct of two opposite classes of men: The practice among employers of importing ignorant Negro-American laborers in emergencies, and then affording them neither protection nor permanent employment; and the practice of labor unions in proscribing and boycotting and oppressing thousands of their fellow-toilers, simply because they are black. These methods have accentuated and will accentuate the war of labor and capital, and they are disgraceful to both sides.

PROTEST

We refuse to allow the impression to remain that the Negro-American assents to inferiority, is submissive under oppression and apologetic before insults. Through helplessness we may submit, but the voice of protest of ten million Americans must never cease to assail the ears of their fellows, so long as America is unjust.

COLOR-LINE

Any discrimination based simply on race or color is barbarous, we care not how hallowed it be by custom, expediency, or prejudice. Differences made on account of ignorance, immorality, or disease are legitimate methods of fighting evil, and against them we have no word of protest; but discrimination based simply and solely on physical peculiarities, place of birth, color or skin, are relics of that unreasoning human savagery of which the world is and ought to be thoroughly ashamed.

"JIM CROW" CARS

We protest against the "Jim Crow" car, since its effect is and must be to make us pay first-class fare for third-class accommodations, render us open to insults and discomfort and to crucify wantonly our manhood, womanhood and self-respect.

SOLDIERS

We regret that this nation has never seen fit adequately to reward the black soldiers who, in its five wars, have defended their country with their blood, and yet have been systematically denied the promotions which their abilities deserve. And we regard as unjust, the exclusion of black boys from the military and navy training schools.

WAR AMENDMENTS

We urge upon Congress the enactment of appropriate legislation for securing the proper enforcement of those articles of freedom, the thirteenth, fourteenth and fifteenth amendments of the Constitution of the United States.

OPPRESSION

We repudiate the monstrous doctrine that the oppressor should be the sole authority as to the rights of the oppressed.

The Negro race in America stolen, ravished and degraded, struggling up through difficulties and oppression, needs sympathy and receives criticism; needs help and is given hindrance, needs protection and is given mob-violence, needs justice and is given charity, needs leadership and is given cowardice and apology, needs bread and is given a stone. This nation will never stand justified before God until these things are changed.

THE CHURCH

Especially we are surprised and astonished at the recent attitude of the church of Christ—on the increase of a desire to bow to racial prejudice, to narrow the bounds of human brotherhood, and to segregate black men in some outer sanctuary. This is wrong, unchristian and disgraceful to the twentieth century civilization.

AGITATION

Of the above grievances we do not hesitate to complain, and to complain loudly and insistently. To ignore, overlook, or apologize for these wrongs is to prove ourselves unworthy of freedom. Persistent manly agitation is the way to liberty, and toward this goal the Niagara Movement has started and asks the co-operation of all men of all races.

HELP

At the same time we want to acknowledge with deep thankfulness the help of our fellowmen from the abolitionist down to those who to-day still stand for equal opportunity and who have given and still give of their wealth and of their poverty for our advancement.

DUTIES

And while we are demanding, and ought to demand, and will continue to demand the rights enumerated above, God forbid that we should ever forget to urge corresponding duties upon our people:

The duty to vote.
The duty to respect the rights of others.
The duty to work.
The duty to obey the laws.
The duty to be clean and orderly.
The duty to send our children to school.
The duty to respect ourselves, even as we respect others.

This statement, complaint and prayer we submit to the American people, and Almighty God.

Questions

1. *Many African Americans and whites responded enthusiastically to Washington's speech in Atlanta and the program he followed thereafter. How can you account for the success of Washington's appeal?*
2. *Booker T. Washington's program of accommodation and W. E. B. Du Bois's call for militant protest have often been depicted as irreconcilably opposed. Can you identify commonalities in the arguments advanced by Washington and Du Bois or are the two positions hopelessly at odds?*
3. *According to David Howard-Pitney, Washington considered whites "masculine" and blacks "feminine." Can you detect a gendered perspective in Washington's Atlanta speech? In Du Bois's response?*
4. *W. E. B. Du Bois criticized Washington's public record. David Levering Lewis writes that historians have uncovered civil rights gains secretly accomplished by Washington. To what extent does this private record of achievement undermine Du Bois's criticism of Washington's public position?*

FURTHER READING

For a biography of Booker T. Washington, see Louis R. Harlan, Booker T. Washington: The Making of a Black Leader, 1856-1901 *(New York, 1972). There is also a thirteen volume edition of Washington's papers:* The Booker T. Washington Papers, *ed. Louis R. Harlan (Urbana, 1972-85). For Du Bois, see David Levering Lewis,* W. E. B. DuBois: Biography of a Race, 1868-1919 *(New York, 1993). For Du Bois's papers, consult* The Correspondence of W. E. B. Du Bois, *ed. Herbert Aptheker, 3 vols. (Amherst, 1973-78).*

The Rise of the New Right

Michael Kazin

INTRODUCTION

"I find that America is fundamentally a conservative nation," wrote Senator Barry Goldwater, a Republican from Arizona, in 1960. "The preponderant judgment of the American people, especially of the young people, is that the radical, or Liberal, approach has not worked and is not working. They yearn for a return to conservative principles."

At the time, the senator seemed to be claiming far too much for his political persuasion. Such New Deal measures as Social Security and the minimum wage enjoyed great popularity, and the Democrats, under the leadership of John F. Kennedy and Lyndon B. Johnson, were about to enact new federal programs designed to protect the rights of black Americans, finance health care for the elderly, and lift millions of people out of poverty. In 1964, Goldwater suffered a crushing defeat when he ran for president on the Republican ticket.

By the early 1970s, however, the nation had indeed shifted markedly to the right. The Johnson administration had led Americans into a seemingly endless war in Vietnam, while it raised expectations for a "war on poverty" it could not possibly satisfy. Movements of angry young people loudly demonstrated against these policies, portraying the federal government as cruel and dishonest. The radical tone and appearance of many of these protests alienated many white adults in the middle and working classes, who blamed liberals both for civil unrest and for failing to solve the problems that occasioned it. Gradually, a growing conservative movement captured the Republican party and learned how to speak to these popular discontents.

The rise of the New Right owed much of its success to a handful of conservative opinions that were fast becoming conventional political wisdom: antipoverty programs do not help the poor; taxes should always be lowered; "preferential treatment" for minorities is wrong; business is overregulated; and the size of government ought to be reduced—in every area but the military. From 1968 until the end of the century, no successful candidate for president identified himself as a liberal or dared to question the mistrust of "big government" and the faith in "law and order" and "traditional values" that conservatives like Goldwater had long been promoting. Why and how did this political sea change occur? The readings that follow should help you answer that question.

THE REVOLT OF MIDDLE AMERICA

To gain influence, conservatives had to develop a critique of liberalism and a different vision for how the nation should be run. They also had to alter an image of themselves, set during the Great Depression, as reactionaries who championed big business and cared little for the interests and opinions of ordinary working Americans. To accomplish these tasks, conservatives were aided by the blunders of their opponents (both liberals and radicals) and the growth and prosperity of the Sun Belt region (the southern tier of the U.S.) where federal power was increasingly unpopular. At the same time, conservatives began to borrow from "populist" figures whose racist views they had previously disdained. Sociologist Jonathan Rieder examines how the Right remade itself during the quarter-century after World War II. Taken from "The Rise of the 'Silent Majority'" in The Rise and Fall of the New Deal Order, 1930–1980, *ed. Steve Fraser and Gary Gerstle (Princeton, 1989), 243–66.*

Jonathan Rieder: Excerpts from "The Rise of the 'Silent Majority'"

Introduction: Populist Conservatism

The New Deal collapsed in the 1960s. Baldly put, in need of qualification, this is the key truth, the essential condition, of our recent political life. The popular coalition that sustained the New Deal through postwar prosperity and McCarthyism burst into its

From "The Rise of the 'Silent Majority'" in *The Rise and Fall of the New Deal Order, 1930–1980*, ed. Steve Fraser and Gary Gerstle, (Princeton, 1989), copyright © 1989 Princeton University Press, 243–66.

constituent shards. The early years of the decade sounded a note of high liberal promise. By the end of the decade, liberalism was in full rout, with the Democratic party embroiled in internal warfare and the Republicans ascendant. At the time, Lyndon Johnson's defeat of Barry Goldwater in 1964 was widely interpreted as proof that a conservative ideologue could not achieve victory in America. In truth, the outlines of Reagan's popular victory may be glimpsed in shadowy form in the Goldwater debacle.

The travail of the Democrats, and its corollary, the Right's return from the fringes of national political life, involved many things. Most tangibly, this coming unstuck of the New Deal alliance could be seen at the level of architecture, of broken form: millions of voters, pried loose from their habitual loyalty to the Democratic party, were now a volatile force, surging through the electoral system without the channeling restraints of party attachment. This does not mean that they immediately underwent some ideologically profound conversion; it does mean that they were now available for courting. And the Republicans courted them. In the presidential elections from 1968 through 1984, the Democrats won only once, and that was in 1976 with a candidate who disavowed New Deal themes, embraced budget balancing, and ran against a Republican party discredited by Watergate.

No less important than this institutional volatility was the middling status of the voters who helped produce it. Of course, certain segments of that vast and eclectic American middle, split in countless ways by region and income, religion and ethnicity, had warmed to the Republicans for a long time. But now in the 1960s and its aftermath, conservatives and Republicans found a responsive audience among once-Democratic constituencies: southerners, ethnic Catholics in the Northeast and Midwest, blue-collar workers, union members, even a sprinkling of lower-middle-class Jews. Out of this maelstrom of defection there emerged a new social formation, Middle America.

Middle America did not really exist as a popular term before the 1960s. In part, it emerged out of the center's own efforts to name itself. But it also emerged from the efforts of others to capture and beguile it, most notably from the oratorical flourishes of Republicans, reactionaries, and conservatives who had their own ideological projects in mind.

The rhetorical foil to this middle, "limousine liberalism," another coinage of the time, sought to convince the middling classes that liberalism was the special enthusiasm of the well-born and well-placed, that the Democrats decreasingly spoke to and for the vast middle. The reborn right, then, was a populist right, at least in its oratory. This too must be qualified. But it offers an important insight into the Right's recovery, and its vulnerability and fleeting tenure.

Beyond the novel language, the new formation and broken architecture, something more basic was at work in this political upheaval. The language took, because it jibed with the resentments of so many ordinary Americans. The forms broke because they could no longer contain the surging passions of betrayal and resistance. What drew the disparate segments of the middle together was its restorationist impulse, its unhappiness with the directions of change in American life. If there was any single source of displeasure that shook the New Deal coalition to its core, it was the civil rights revolution. Race, however, was only the earliest and most powerful spur to these defections. Later, the Vietnam War cleaved through the Democratic party and hacked it into bits. Other issues like law and order, the revolution in morals, and a corrosive inflation added to disaffection. Whatever the mélange of separate complaints that fed the stream of resentment and complaint, this much is clear: the consequences were immense. At least for a time, they rearranged the basic categories of American political life.

Prelude: The Problem of the Right

Despite a variety of demographic, economic, and institutional changes in American life between 1932 and 1960, it was still possible to argue in the early 1960s that little had changed in thirty years, and that the New Deal remained essentially intact, with some erosions and qualifications. Even at the height of the New Deal, the Democratic majority contained certain vulnerabilities. One potential strain involved the ambiguity of the "liberalism" that sustained the New Deal electorally, and the limited sense in which various working-class fractions could be described as liberal. While Roosevelt had a penchant for high-flown rhetoric, and progressive forces fashioned an idiom of transcendent social purpose, many workers, naturally enough, liked the New Deal mainly for the benefits it bestowed. For them, the New Deal did not represent universalism as much as the particularism of household provision.

Ethnic commitments, and the foreign policy concerns they generated during World War II, further weakened the unity of the New Deal coalition. Above all, isolationism fed a fierce alienation from Democratic liberal internationalism. The Irish opposed Roosevelt's war policy as pro-British intervention. His condemnation of Italy's attack on France—"The hand that held the dagger has plunged it into the back of its neighbor"—stirred public outcry in America's Little Italys. And now for a second time, American entry into a world war risked compromising the good reputation of German-Americans. In the years after the war, these grievances would give rise to a "politics of revenge," to borrow Samuel Lubell's famous phrase, against the Democrats. Similarly, ethnic Catholics from the occupied countries of Eastern Europe—including many Lithuanian, Polish, and Czech Democrats—responded to charges that the party of Roosevelt was soft on communism and had sold out their ancestral homelands at Yalta.

Finally, the progressive policies of the national Democratic party rested anomalously on a racist electoral base of Southern Democrats, who constituted an enclave of white supremacy within the party. However much Southern workers and farmers prized the social legislation of the New Deal, the Southern Democratic party was, by any reckoning, a reactionary force. As a result of the one-party character of the South, the Democratic party contained many "natural" Republicans, awaiting release.

All these vulnerabilities of the Democrats—and others—could be detected at the very start of the New Deal, but they remained low-level tensions that flared episodically. The reactionary right, that remnant of the pre-1929 order that never forgave the New Deal and its "creeping Socialism" for subverting the individualistic verities of "true Americanism," retained its presence in the Midwestern branch of the Republican party. The Right also survived as a force in Congress. As an influence on national policy, however, it was essentially demobilized, and took recourse in a sulking desire for vengeance. It had to accept a bitter truth: the "modern" Republican party was no longer an agency of reactionary restoration. Mainstream Republicans, too, had faced facts: there was no electoral market for ending state benevolence. The conservatism they could muster consisted of a recognition that the innovations of the New Deal were part of the fabric of American life—had become the past that was to be saved. The rejectionists of the Right—not content with modest trimming—

wanted domestic rollback. They were thus truly radical in colloquial parlance. They were radical in another sense: they had ceased to be popular. The masses of ordinary working men and women, at least on average, belonged to the Democrats.

The Right did not cease to imagine the people, and to imagine them as its allies, or its potential allies. It developed a theory of a natural majority, hidden and kept from it. Anticipating the turn of 1960s conservatism toward majoritarian themes, some conservative intellectuals like Willmoore Kendall lauded the "virtuous people."

And still the Right kept seeking ways to return to power. The Truman victory of 1948 underscored the popularity of the New Deal's social policies. Any attack on the Democrats would thus have to be oblique, could not be a headlong defense of "liberty against socialism." The Right had to fight for a popular following on the more auspicious terrain of foreign policy.

More than any other figure, Sen. Joseph McCarthy offered the Right a brief flurry of hope. He developed all the plaints of the nationalist right and added new twists: the sellout of Yalta, the weak moral fiber of New Dealers and their penchant for humiliating appeasement, the loss of Eastern Europe and China, the enfoldment of subversives into the heart of the New Deal. The time was ripe to expand the market for these classic themes. Global developments in the postwar years had deepened the public's anxiety about foreign affairs. Moreover, the implacable anticommunism of the Catholic church, and the problem of the captive nations, sustained a ferocious conservatism among many Catholic Democrats. Presumably, in appealing to these more plebeian constituencies, McCarthy's tough, swaggering style and his pseudo-populist diatribes would prove helpful. His famous Wheeling, West Virginia, speech was laced with seeming class resentment. "It is not the less fortunate, or members of minority groups who have been selling this nation out, but rather those who have had all the benefits the wealthiest nation on earth has had to offer. . . . This is glaringly true of the State Department. There the bright young men who are born with silver spoons in their mouth are the ones who have been worst."

For various reasons, McCarthyism did not rescue the Right. The gap between McCarthy's core constituencies and his popular support never closed. As Michael Rogin has argued, McCarthyism "reflected the specific traumas of conservative Republican

activists—internal Communist subversion, the New Deal, centralized government, left-wing intellectuals, and the corrupting influences of a cosmopolitan society." The market for these themes
remained confined to the Right's traditional base among the
provincial petite bourgeoisie. Among his ethnic plebeian supporters, McCarthy tapped rather straightforward worries about
Korea, the cold war, and communism. On these issues, however,
the two parties did not fundamentally differ. Democrats and
Republicans alike shared in the anti-Communist consensus; the
marginal difference between soft and hard forms of anticommunism was insufficient to stir the public at large.

If anticommunism failed to realign the parties, McCarthy
accomplished two things of moment for this discussion. First, his
success in the polls with Catholic ethnics prefigured "one of the
right's basic post-war strategies for a return to power—the
Catholic/ethnic/blue-collar strategy." The ethnic response to
McCarthy heartened Catholic conservatives like L. Brent Bozell
and William Buckley and highlighted the folly of what Buckley
called "the university crowd." It appeared that openings to the
ethnic working class might be welcome, and more: the status
resentments of petit-bourgeois elites in the hinterland toward the
Eastern Establishment offered an idiom with which to seduce ethnic Democrats. As a result, the Right's commitment to a rhetoric of
plebeian contempt for things effete and patrician deepened. All in
all, McCarthy hurried the movement of the Right toward a conservatism conspicuously more majoritarian than previously.

The second effect of McCarthyism was on the liberal imagination. Simply put, the red scare revealed a dimension of the people
that was frightening. It seemed as if a demonic volk was rising up
to assault established institutions and civil liberties with its
plebiscitary passion. In American historiography, the reconsidera-
tion of populism as an ethnocentric movement fueled by wish fulfillment and status humiliation underlined this change of heart
among many liberals. In less academic quarters, McCarthyism
highlighted the festering ethnic tension within the Democratic
party, in which Jewish liberals decried Catholic authoritarianism
and Catholics reciprocated with charges of Jewish bolshevism.
These mutual recriminations marked more than ethnic squab-
bling; they indicated an important vein of Catholic conservatism
within the Democratic party, as well as the ideological schisms it
was capable of provoking.

McCarthyism broke through the civil rhetorical settlement that kept animosity suppressed and backstage. Once McCarthyism was defeated, those tensions were driven underground, to be whispered sotto voce. But the stylistic war between plebeian and patrician continued as a latent undertheme in the struggle between conservatism and liberalism. During the 1960s it resurfaced with dramatic intensity.

Southern Insurgency

An ideological party of right-wing reaction could not rouse the middle-income classes from their self-absorbed, acquisitive mood in the 1950s. The Right's broadsides against the Warren Court and sociological jurisprudence fell on deaf ears. That same indifference befell the Right's apocalyptic vision of communism, its pure form of laissez-faire, its indictment of the permissive society. Nor did the public show much appetite for a more respectable corporate-style conservatism. Despite the running down of liberal energies, depression-vintage tensions between the classes, while muted and diminishing, remained. Lower- and working-class Americans supported welfare state measures more vigorously than did upper-middle- and upper-class voters, and they linked their economic fate to the Democratic party. In addition, ingrained Democratic loyalty, no matter how ritualized, tended to keep the electorate from considering more conservative alternatives. Even when Democrats did vote for a particular Republican, say for Eisenhower, they did not alter their basic political identities and sympathies.

Even the inertia of old partisan habits did not survive the social crisis that erupted across America between 1960 and 1972. The exodus of habitual Democrats from the party began earliest in the South. In the presidential election of 1948, Truman's initiatives on civil rights spurred a Dixiecrat secession led by Strom Thurmond. The quickening assault on white supremacy by Supreme Court decisions, the civil rights movement, and Democratic liberals eventually led to the collapse of the Democratic party in the white South. In the early 1960s, Republican strategists developed Operation Dixie, the precursor to the Southern Strategy that envisioned a new Republican majority founded on the conservatism of the West, the South, and the heartland. By 1980, the Republicans had essentially fulfilled this vision of political geography.

Racial resentment was not the sole cause of these defections, nor was it only a cause. It also was a condition for defections on other grounds. Anything that broke the hold of Democratic loyalty, as only the racial liberalism of the national party could, freed conservative-leaning Democrats to embrace the Republican party. Already in the 1950s, a stream of upper-middle-class business and professional types had begun to flow to the Republicans. In metropolitan areas like Shreveport, Augusta, and Jackson, Donald Strong concluded, "They're acting like Yankees! The prosperous folk of Richmond, Charleston, and Dallas voted just like their economic counterparts in Syracuse, Indianapolis, and Cleveland." In a sense, racial turmoil in the South did not overthrow the class axis of the New Deal but simply completed it, albeit on terms favorable to Republicans.

The emotional edge of Southern defections in the 1960s came from more tawdry racial passions. The effort to dismantle the South's caste system catalyzed a politics of massive resistance that redounded to the Republicans' benefit. Barry Goldwater, the Republican candidate in 1964, seemed a good bet to capitalize on white resistance. His defense of states rights came from a Jeffersonian fear of federal power, not from heartfelt racialist ideology, but the South did not mind. One of eight senators who had voted against the Civil Rights Act of 1964, he appealed directly to segregationists alienated by Johnson's civil rights efforts. Although Goldwater's reactionary politics were repudiated in a Democratic victory of landslide proportions, he won stunning victories in the Deep South. Unlike the Republicanism of the 1950s, his support was distributed across the classes, among lower-income whites as well as those in the upper social strata.

Goldwater's brand of reactionary Republicanism met the requirements of preserving the racial order, but it had its shortcomings. In the absence of racial struggle, it was too steeped in Sunbelt individualism to entice disprivileged Southern workers and farmers, especially up-country whites in the Deep South outside the Black Belt counties. For those elements, George Wallace was the true talisman of order. As governor of Alabama, Wallace defied a court order to integrate the University of Alabama, placing himself in front of federal marshals and vowing, "I will never submit to an order of the federal court ordering the integration of the schools." He quickly became a hero of Southern nullification.

Wallace frankly defended the Southern way of life: "I don't believe in the social and educational mixing of the races."

Heir to one strain of the Southern populist tradition, Wallace heralded "this average man on the street, this man in the textile mill, this man in the steel mill, this barber, this beautician, the policeman on the beat, they're the ones, and the little business-man—I think those are the mass of people that are going to support a change on the domestic scene." A former Golden Gloves boxer with a tough and gritty mien, Wallace jabbed at the fancy people, the Eastern Establishment, the cultural sophisticates who allegedly disdained the values of the common people. "We are going to show them in November that the average American is sick and tired of all those over-educated Ivory-tower folks with pointed heads looking down their noses at us." As rebuttal to such imputed slights, he proffered a raw version of linguistic democracy: "Being from Alabama, we didn't know what it means when the head recapitulator of Maryland said that they were going to recapitulate the vote. . . . We still don't know what reca-pitulate means, but I'll tell you this, when anyone says he is going to recapitulate on you, you better watch out, because they're fix-ing to do something to you." As Kevin Phillips put it, "Wallace was the personification of the poor white Deep South. His Dixie crowds roared every time Wallace brandished a *New York Times* clipping which sneered at his wife's dime store job."

Wallace matched his rhetoric with a vigorous economic liber-alism. As a state legislator and as governor he championed pro-gressive legislation in housing and health. His electoral vehicle, the American Independent party, affirmed a classical New Deal position on social policy. It called for increases in Social Security and affirmed the government's obligation to ensure health care for the economically vulnerable. Despite the South's long-stand-ing hostility to organized labor and the pervasive regional sup-port for the right-to-work laws, the AIP applauded "the great trade organizations" and the right to collective bargaining.

As the 1960s unfolded, Wallace's average men and women in the street fumed over other grievances besides race, and Wallace ministered to them as well. The Vietnam War expanded, and the country, and the Democratic party, divided into camps of hawks and doves. In addition, protests against the war raised emotional debates about the limits of dissent, the meaning of patriotism, and the loyalty of demonstrators. Speaking to those who chafed at the ambiguities of limited war, Wallace, and his running mate Curtis Lemay, prescribed a solution in the manly mode: do not cut and run; bomb the Communists back to the Stone Age. Wallace's calls for using the same forcefulness against domestic enemies drew an equally sympathetic hearing. In good Southern fashion, Wallace's supporters prized military courage and sacrifice. As they saw it, patriotism demanded a simple, unreflective loyalty. They did not cotton to abstract notions of the right of dissent, especially when the people doing the protesting were privileged college students exempt from the draft who donned scruffy, hippy garb and waved Vietcong flags. As a result, they cheered when Wallace cast protesters beyond the pale of the loyally opposed, rendering them as shameful cowards and traitors.

This struggle over patriotism reflected a broader cultural struggle between the forces of moral tradition and modernist liberation. Both were lodged in the Democratic party. Wallace's followers were disproportionately unlettered and provincial; they clung to fundamentalist and Baptist forms of faith. As they peered out at America in the 1960s, they saw an upsurge of sexual immorality, the decline of the work ethic, disrespect for authority. Demands for women's liberation threatened to blur the primal distinctions between men and women. Worse still, for some, they evoked a satanic violation of biblical prescriptions. The mobilization of fundamentalist Christians was only in its infancy, but throughout the 1970s, Supreme Court decisions on abortion and the tax status of religious schools shook fundamentalist ministers out of their quiescence. As Democratic platforms heralded the Equal Rights Amendment, a politicized ministry, and the larger New Right movement that prodded it, discovered in Wallace supporters a responsive audience for their fulminations against moral decline.

For all these racial, moral, and patriotic infamies, Wallace offered relief. He promised to restore law and order to America, and would not let squeamishness or finicky concerns about due process stand in the way. "Hell, we got too much dignity in government," Wallace told his true believers. "What we need is some *meanness*. You elect one of those steel-workers guvnuh, you talk about a revolution—damn, there'd be shootin' and tearin' down and burnin' up and killin' and bloodlettin' sho nuff." His stump oratory was tinged with hints of retaliatory violence against traitors and wreckers. He excelled at using the hecklers who showed up at his rallies, baiting them and driving his supporters to a higher pitch of emotion. In Marshall Frady's words, "Wallace had invoked, had discovered a dark, silent, brooding mass of people whom no one—the newspapers, the political leaders, the intellectuals—no one but Wallace had suspected were there."

The power of this populist conservative movement of the Southern middling classes showed itself in the 1968 presidential election. The force of racial reaction and populist passion blasted away the Democratic hold on the South. Classical New Deal Democrat Hubert Humphrey took only 30 percent of the vote; in the Deep South, a rising number of black votes barely pushed him to the 20-percent level. But this was no obvious Valhalla for the Republicans. Their effort to build on the Goldwater breakthrough ran smack into Wallace and his American Independent party. Wallace and Republican candidate Richard Nixon split the rest of the Southern vote down the middle, each taking 34 percent. Wallace won the Deep South. Nixon and the Republicans won the Outer South. Nixon held the more privileged, better educated, economic conservatives. Less often were Nixon voters members of pietistic Protestant sects, and they did not evince the high levels of commitment to segregation. . . .

But populist conservatism had its limits. No matter how much the Right tried to encompass Wallace and Goldwater within the same category, they did not fit. Wallace's attack on bureaucrats and liberals, his revilement of an intrusive national state, formed a contingent opposition to specific bureaucrats and judicials who were transforming the Southern way. The "conservatism" of Wallace voters was spotty and suspect in other respects. "Country and Western Marxism," Chilton Williamson dubbed it in the *National Review.* "To the Nashville Station" was how Kevin Phillips captured the ambiguous drift of the "conservative" movement. Wallace's people did not feel at home in a Republican party that still was the organ of establishment conservatism. In 1976, Carter constructed a biracial populist coalition in the South; in 1982, in the midst of the recession, Southern workers flocked back to the Democrats. Finally, Wallace came at the midpoint of racial transition. Once the shocks of the 1960s were through, racial politics lost their corrosive edge. The gradual coming of black power to the South, and the growing acceptance among whites that the civil rights revolution could not—and in many cases, should not—be reversed, marked a change of heart in the 1970s. . . .

Revolt in the North

At the start of the 1960s, the bitter passions of race seemed very much a Southern affair. The ferocity of resistance could still be considered a regional aberration. It soon became clear that the North could not achieve immunity from the struggle for racial justice. The complex forces that kept blacks subordinate in the North lacked the clarity of the evil of the Southern caste system, which also meant that the limits of liberal reform, and the ambiguous entanglement of race, ethnicity, and class, surfaced more quickly in the North.

The racial discontent that marked the 1969 mayoral race in New York City and the behavior of blue-collar ethnic Democrats in a Philadelphia industrial suburb in 1968 struck Walter Dean Burnham as a historic break with New Deal routine. Far more ominous than the break itself was its character—a proto-fascist revolt of the little man, animated by fearful resentment. This was populism with a vengeance, literally; it was not the populism of optimistic reform but the populism of Poujade and the petite bourgeoisie. That the Weimar analogy could issue forth from one of America's savviest electoral analysts marked just how far the country, and the North most spectacularly, had traveled toward racial conflict in barely half a decade. New York City, crucible of New Deal liberalism and bastion of Jewish tolerance, seemed a paradoxically apt symbol of this unhappy development, and more than a few conservatives savored that fact.

The most flamboyant indication of the threat of the civil rights movement to the Democratic party in the North occurred during the presidential primaries in 1964, when George Wallace did amazingly well—between 30 percent and 45 percent of the vote—in strongly Democratic blue-collar precincts in Milwaukee, Baltimore, and Cleveland. Wallace had not minced words. His boast that he would make race the basis of politics across the nation credited his own powers too fulsomely, but the general point held. Wallace prefigured things to come, in more eclectic, and less reactionary, form. In the congressional elections of 1966, white backlash against Great Society liberalism was in full force throughout the country. As the decade advanced, backlash spread from the working class to the middle class, from Catholic enclaves to Jewish ones, from the provincial, vindictive reaches of the center up into its more genteel, democratic quarters.

The motives behind resistance may be so transparent as to require little accounting. Unabashed racism played its considerable part. And as Burnham indicates, the frustrations of a squeezed lower-middle class could easily yield to the most vindictive and paranoid intimations.

Accurate as far as it goes, the diagnosis of racism or populism fails to grasp the complexity of racial resentment. Backlash was a disorderly affair that contained democratic, populist, genteel, conspiratorial, racist, humanistic, pragmatic, and meritocratic impulses. Simply put, the middle was too diverse, the grievances it suffered too varied, to be captured in a single category.

Escalation in part followed from certain structural limitations of liberal reform. Blacks in the North still had much work to do in achieving basic constitutional rights and fighting white supremacy, but class issues—of poverty, of jobs, of inequality—prevailed over strictly caste ones, and demanded other solutions. A stance of racial neutrality, of equal opportunity, would not immediately benefit the members of the lumpen classes, especially during a time of economic transition. As black demands ran up against the limits of liberalism, frustration spurred the search for alternatives: affirmative action, community control of schools, welfare rights, racial quotas, model cities programs, busing, reparations, political mobilization of the black masses, black pride. Each of these remedies surpassed the existing level of moral legitimacy and political acceptability.

Opposition to compensatory efforts sprang from the self-interest of vulnerable whites, whose hold on middle-class status was precarious. Integration threatened white ethnic monopolies on labor markets, the civil service, unions, and municipal power. More specifically, for disprivileged whites in high-tax states like California and New York, the fiscal levies of a spiraling welfare bill seemed like confiscatory exactions on their meager resources. Busing for racial integration heightened primal anxieties about children's safety and futures. Philadelphia plans in the construction industry, like court-ordered affirmative action programs elsewhere, often reserved a certain percentage of jobs for blacks, thereby reducing the number of jobs available for whites.

Such policies gradually yielded a diffuse sense among many traditional Democratic ethnic workers that they had become the victims of "reverse discrimination." This was more than a proxy for racist animosity. Unemployed carpenters might yell, "Those quotas and Philadelphia plans made us angry. They should create plans to help both sides. Create jobs, but don't take from one to give the other and create bitterness." Former supporters of the early civil rights movement argued that blacks wanted to get ahead, "they *should* get ahead. But not on my kid's back. Blacks are taking advantage." As the lament suggests, "reverse discrimination" also formed an ethical critique of the remedies advanced by liberals, the judiciary, and blacks. As well as a psychic economy and a political economy of backlash, there was a moral economy of backlash.

Policies that seemed to give special privileges to blacks and exempt them from the rigors of competition scandalized whites. This is not to say that Northern Democratic workers were pristine Lockeans. Even more than the Protestant working and middle classes of the South and Sunbelt, Jewish and Catholic Democrats came from familistic and communal cultures, and had benefited greatly from the welfare state. But they were also partisans of earning, self-reliance, and the work ethic. Their own historic experience, and the mythologies that surrounded it, sustained a great faith in, even a romance of, bootstrapping. Even whites sympathetic to black suffering often responded to compensatory policies with indignation, an emotion born of violated justice. One spokesman for aggrieved white ethnics rejected the claim by an NAACP official that whites had to pay the price for all those years of slavery: "But I ask you, who will pay the Jews for two thousands [sic] years of slavery? Who will compensate the Italians for all the ditches they dug?"

The whole tenor and turn of the black movement after the mid-1960s offended no less than the remedies it championed. Its militancy, the increasingly forceful and even violent tone of its demands, the spread of black nationalism through the Northern ghettos—these frightened and offended provincial workers, many of whom little understood the historical brutalization of blacks in America and the assaults on culture and identity that accompanied it. The Watts riot of 1965, during which images of blacks crying "Burn, baby, burn" flickered across white television sets, marked a turning point in the white perception of the black movement. In a great reversal, white support for black demands, which had been steadily growing through the early 1960s, dropped precipitously. The proportion of whites who believed the civil rights movement was proceeding too fast rose in tandem.

This spiral upward in black anger and militancy had a certain ironic quality that escaped white workers. Every display of white reluctance and meanness frustrated the desire of blacks for moderation, and disillusionment then pushed them toward higher levels of militancy, and eventually black nationalism. If the universal vision of integration gave way to the particularism of racial separatism, defensive whites unwittingly helped call forth the very nationalist excess they reviled.

In ways that Americans did not always appreciate, these apparent arguments about race and remedy were often displaced conflicts of class. In the minds of many white ethnics, ghetto rioting fused with the street crime practiced by a dispirited segment of the black underclass. The white view that quotas were a way to get ahead without paying one's dues merged with popular resentment of welfare "giveaways" to poor blacks. The dislike of welfare drew force from a broader perception of the ghetto as a place of incivility, where the cult of pleasure triumphed over all moral restraint and striving. Little in their culture focused the attention of provincial ethnic Democrat on the sociological causes of drug addiction, illegitimate births, male sexual irresponsibility, and female-headed households. Their moral traditionalism stoked contempt for transgression, which added a powerful overlay of virtue and vice to the fundamental cleavage of race and class already dividing two crucial elements of the Democratic coalition.

The final ingredient in this volatile mix of race, morality, ethnicity, and class was proximity. The historical patterns of migration and settlement were such that millions of Northern Democratic workers lived near black ghettos, and the black underclass loomed as a powerful physical presence. Integration was not a remote abstraction. It was freighted with a vivid and brutal particularity. When white ethnics of modest means thought about integration of schools and neighborhoods, they did not envision encounters with blacks in general but with the quite specific blacks who lived near them, who seemed morally and physically dangerous. Countless ethnic neighborhoods had undergone rapid racial change, and many of those formerly white enclaves had become seamy ghettos. To hard-pressed workers, whose major investment was tied up in their home and community, the prospect of integrated schools and residences raised the prospect of jeopardy, racial engulfment, tipping.

None of the tangible threats of the underclass unsettled whites as much as crime. Black street crime soared in the 1960s, and as black protest devolved into ghetto rioting, both fortified the white perception that poor blacks were a malevolent lot who resorted to illegitimate means to get what they wanted. "Crime in the streets" catapulted to the very top of the list of pressing issues by the mid-1960s, and created a market for conservative politicians who would restore "law and order." Demagogues often inflamed popular fears about crime. The phrase functioned for some as a code word for racism; when would-be avengers recited the phrase, some listeners heard a commitment to satisfy their fantasies of reprisals against blacks. But the phrase also spoke to more practical fears of physical safety shared by the racially generous and vindictive alike.

As James Sundquist has well summarized, fear of crime tended to blend with a host of other moral anxieties: "In the public's perception, all these things merged. Ghetto riots, campus riots, street crime, anti-Vietnam marches, poor people's marches, drugs, pornography, welfarism, rising taxes, all had a common thread: the breakdown of family and social discipline, of order, of concepts of duty, of respect for law, of public and private morality. If Northern ethnic Democrats were not Bible-thumping pietists after the fashion of Southern fundamentalists and evangelicals, they were moral traditionalists. Just as they affirmed the verities of patriotic duty, they grieved over flagrant homosexuality, the apparent decline in respect for authority, the feminist revolution with its blurring of the boundaries between men's and women's places. On all these issues, many middle-income Democrats saw liberal fellow Democrats as their moral adversaries.

Each of the varied issues that grew up around the controversies of race (especially), life-style, and foreign policy became points of complaint and conflict with their own consequences. Together, they had a cumulative effect that was more diffuse but no less critical. They added to a growing sense of alienation among many white Democrats of modest means who felt betrayed by the direction of change. The political system seemed unfairly stacked against them. Increasingly, they saw other factions dominating the Democratic party with an agenda that did not include room for white ethnic concerns.

No small part of this sense of danger and dispossession flowed from the perception by the middle-income classes of a growing chasm between themselves and the regnant version of liberalism. This sense of difference transformed the folk imagery of liberalism. In the popular mind, liberalism acquired a variety of invidious connotations. No longer did it suggest a vision of transcendent justice or the support of vulnerable working people. Liberalism meant taking the side of blacks, no matter what; dismissing middle-class plaints as racism; handcuffing the police; transferring resources and sympathy from a vulnerable middle class to minorities; rationalizing rioting and dependency and other moral afflictions as "caused" by the environment or its justifiable response to oppression. Liberalism appeared to them as a force inimical to the working and lower-middle classes, assaulting their communities, their sense of fairness, their livelihood, their children, their physical safety, their values.

The Democrats in Disarray

By the late 1960s, the issues of race, Vietnam, and life-style had changed the political climate of the entire nation, not just of the South. Restive forces had broken free of the party restraints that once enveloped them. With that institutional breakdown, there emerged a new civic culture, or, more precisely, a culture of incivility. Tension between rival groups now yielded to outright feuding, and unabashed denunciation replaced private grumbling.

One sign of the grass-roots revolt against liberalism was the emergence of new champions of the white working and lower-middle classes. Republicans saw a chance here to expand their sway, but conservative Democrats abounded who articulated the passions of provincial reaction. Mario Procaccino in New York City, Mayor Sam Yorty in Los Angeles, Frank Rizzo in Philadelphia, and Louise Day Hicks in Boston developed a politics that was essentially the geopolitics of local community. They spoke to white concerns about busing, tipping neighborhoods, crime in the streets, scatter-site low-income housing, judicial leniency, the safety of schools, white flight, and the death penalty. The style of the politics was even more striking than its substantive themes. These leaders affected a vulgar speaking style that was unembarrassed in its vow to protect white interests; no genteel inhibitions kept them from lambasting black leaders and "limousine liberals." Unafraid of appearing tough and racist, at times they reveled in their "bad-boy," outlaw identity, embodied in their willingness to resort to disrespectable, illegal, even violent, means to protect white power.

For all the vividness of these local saviors, developments in the cities were only a microcosm of the organizational implosion of the Democratic party at the national level. The mobilization of blacks, programmatic liberals, antiwar protesters, and women brought volatile new forces into the party that disturbed the existing balance of power. As the white Democratic electorate split into reactionary, traditionalist, and left-liberal wings, disputes about race and Vietnam produced intense feuding between liberal, "regular," and conservative elites. Antiwar Democrats, who demanded withdrawal from Vietnam, squared off against hawkish boosters of the war—cold war liberals, powerful unionists, and machine leaders. Speaking for many New Deal traditionalists, Hubert Humphrey during the 1972 Democratic primaries tagged George McGovern as a proponent of three A's: "Acid, Abortion, and Amnesty."...

The Democrats' disquiet was an open invitation to their rivals. From the moment of its appearance, Republicans sought to capitalize on popular grievance. A party whose image was dominated by country-club Republicanism, Eastern Establishment patricians, and corporate conservatism could not sharpen those resentments into a barbed electoral weapon. But the institutional work of transforming the Republican party into a vehicle for such a mission had been proceeding for some time. The efforts of conservative strategists to move the party toward a Sunbelt strategy in the early 1960s was part of this effort to oust liberal Republicans and seize control of the party. As the 1960s unfolded, they came to see that the Southern Strategy might have Northern applications.

Organizational succession was necessary to produce a version of populist conservatism, but it was only a condition of success, not a guarantee. To refashion Republican identity around more populist-sounding themes also required cultural work, the refinement of a new kind of political rhetoric. In 1964, even as he plied the waters of the Southern Strategy, Goldwater had targeted his appeal to "the Silent Americans" at Northern ethnic workers. Although he had some success with Northern Catholics in racially tense urban precincts in the Midwest and Northeast, Goldwater's opening to Northern ethnics mainly went unheeded. The appeal was premature. The racial and social crisis had not advanced sufficiently to weaken party ties and make the demand for law and order resonate. The question thus remained for conservatives, how to entice Democratic ethnics, whose material circumstances and cultural traditions sustained a rival sensibility, with the language of Republican fundamentalism? Narrative trickery alone would not build a market among traditional Democratic constituencies, and neither would self-congratulatory calls to silent and forgotten Americans.

What doctrinal grudges, cultural alienation, and finely honed argument had not yet achieved for conservatives, the turbulence of the times finally accomplished. In the years after the Goldwater debacle, the idiom of populist conservatism was repeated and refined, and always with growing resonance. The idiom acquired high and low, genteel and vulgar, incarnations. Not only Republicans mouthed its pieties. Wallace spouted his vindictive variant. Democrats experimented with their versions in local and state elections. It was the core of Ronald Reagan's oratory, and his successful gubernatorial bid. At the end of the decade, this language even entered the presidency as its official motif.

Elections during this period frequently seemed like cockfights or slugfests; the voters affirmed not the goal of corrective equilibrium but their own irreconcilable desires. In 1968, the country was racked by antiwar protest, political assassination, and urban conflagration. Throughout the campaign, Republican candidate Richard Nixon appealed to the middle, ever mindful of the chance to reap a windfall among working- and middle-class Catholics. Garry Wills has well described Nixon's ingenious appeal to the middle-American belief in striving. "Nixon's success was not offered in Miami as a theme for mere self-congratulations. It was a pledge to others, a pledge that he would not rob them of the fruits of their success." Nixon declared, "In a time when the national focus is concentrated upon the unemployed, the impoverished and the dispossessed, the working Americans have become the forgotten Americans. In a time when the national rostrums and forums are given over to shouters and protestors and demonstrators, they have become the silent Americans. Yet they have a legitimate grievance that should be rectified and a just cause that should prevail."

Democrats and Republicans alike could not afford to ignore the threat of George Wallace, who had taken his campaign beyond the South and turned it into a national social movement on the American Independent party line. As the election neared, it seemed as if Wallace might deny both major parties a majority. Democratic unionists were shocked to find strong support for him among Democratic workers in usually loyal unions. "The death of his old adversary, Martin Luther King, came like a miracle. The riots it touched off meant that the 1968 campaign would be fought on Wallace's chosen ground. The theme would be his theme: law and order." This time, in contrast with 1964, Wallace did not run as an unreconstructed segregationist but couched his racialist concerns in more sublimated form.

Wallace's support in the polls of 23 percent fell by half on election day; his stronger showing in the South was balanced by a lower figure in the other regions. Countless workers who admired Wallace or saw him as a fitting vehicle for their protest shied from wasting their vote on a third-party chimera. Despite that, Wallace did well among Catholics in northeastern locales where racial violence had recently erupted. Among New Jersey Catholics, he took between 10 and 15 percent of the vote. In New York City, Wallace captured almost 10 percent of the vote in Catholic assembly districts, reaching 15 percent in lower-middle-class Irish districts; he drew support from Italian and Irish policemen, firemen, bus drivers, and sanitation workers. Wallace ran strongly in blue-collar ethnic strongholds in racially polarized Flint, Michigan, Cleveland, Ohio, and Gary, Indiana.

Nixon also made inroads in traditionally Democratic working- and middle-class communities. Nixon's appeal was pure simplicity: he heralded a less malevolent version of Wallace's crusade against 1960s liberalism. If Wallace offered rollback, Nixon suggested containment. . . .

The power of the racial and social issues did not abate during Nixon's presidency. In the face of continuing black and antiwar dissent, Nixon and his vice-president, Spiro Agnew, went on the attack. As Jonathan Schell recounted it, the president was building a political consensus around the Silent Majority. Increasingly, he believed the principal institutions of American life—including the Supreme Court, Congress, the foundations, television, and the press, all of them in sway to the left-liberal ideology—"were impeding his communion with the new majority, and were thereby thwarting the majority's will." The task, then, was "to clear away this noisy, willful minority impediment." The appeal to Middle America took on a more vindictive edge, as the line between the virtuous middle and demonic outsiders—blacks, liberals, antiwar protesters—was drawn with increasing sharpness.

Nineteen seventy-two marked the culmination of the party system of the 1960s. The Democratic nominating process produced in George a candidate who came to personify all the forces that were anathema to the interests and ideals of the middle-income classes. His pledge to get down on his hands and knees to obtain peace from North Vietnam violated popular taboos on humiliating appeasement. He supported busing, amnesty for draft evaders, and abortion rights, all the while repudiating the death penalty. His widely misinterpreted plan for a Demogrant, a plan to give every American family one thousand dollars, reinforced an impression of fiscal extravagance.

Nixon defeated McGovern in a rout, as the Democrat won only the single state of Massachusetts. Among countless conservative Democratic leaders, including many champions of alienated working-class ethnics, the seeming "radicalism" of the "prairie populist" sparked rebellious rump committees of Democrats and Independents for Nixon. The Teamsters', Longshoremen's, and Construction Workers' unions rallied to the president. As always, ideological preferences alone did not produce the pattern of defection; Nixon's stimulation of a preelection economic boom also motivated Democrats to leave their party. In addition, the rate of defection from the Democrats was a function of conservative views on Vietnam, the use of force to quell college demonstrations, amnesty for draft dodgers, and legalization of marijuana. Nixon received a majority of white working-class votes. And of the preponderantly Democratic voters attracted to Wallace in 1968, nearly 80 percent voted for Nixon.

Questions

1. *How did McCarthyism both aid and limit the growth of the Right?*
2. *What role did George Wallace play in the rise of a populist conservatism? Did he appeal solely to racial resentments?*
3. *Why did the Democrats fail to respond effectively to the discontent of ordinary white Americans?*
4. *Do contemporary conservatives still portray themselves as the representatives of "Middle America"? Does that term carry the same meaning it did during the 1970s? How would you define its opinions and interests today?*

CONSERVATIVES ARGUE
FOR THEIR CAUSE

Conservatives in the 1960s came from diverse backgrounds of region, class, and educational background. Some engaged in intellectual combat—putting forth philosophical concepts of "liberty" and "constitutional government" distinct from those that animated liberal thinkers and policy-makers. Others on the Right spoke bluntly to the anger of "middle Americans," promising to remove the perceived causes of their discontent. The two kinds of rhetoric clashed, but each was valuable in giving conservatives a sense that they might control the nation's future.

The Creed of the Young Right

In September 1960, a small group of conservatives, most of whom were or had recently been college students, founded Young Americans for Freedom (YAF) at the family estate in Sharon, Connecticut, of editor and writer William F. Buckley. YAF quickly grew into the largest group of non-party political activists on the nation's campuses (a position it held until 1965). Many of its activists went on to influential positions in the 1964 Goldwater campaign and in the campaigns and presidential administrations of Richard Nixon and Ronald Reagan. The Sharon Statement was YAF's pithy declaration of beliefs. Taken from http://www.yaf.com/sharon.shtml.

From "The Rise of the 'Silent Majority'" in *The Rise and Fall of the New Deal Order, 1930–1980*, ed. Steve Fraser and Gary Gerstle, (Princeton, 1989), copyright © 1989 Princeton University Press, 243–66.

The Sharon Statement
Young Americans for Freedom
Adopted in conference at Sharon, Connecticut, on 11 September 1960.

In this time of moral and political crises, it is the responsibility of the youth of America to affirm certain eternal truths.
We, as young conservatives, believe:

That foremost among the transcendent values is the individual's use of his God-given free will, whence derives his right to be free from the restrictions of arbitrary force;

That liberty is indivisible, and that political freedom cannot long exist without economic freedom;

That the purpose of government is to protect those freedoms through the preservation of internal order, the provision of national defense, and the administration of justice;

That when government ventures beyond these rightful functions, it accumulates power, which tends to diminish order and liberty;

That the Constitution of the United States is the best arrangement yet devised for empowering government to fulfill its proper role, while restraining it from the concentration and abuse of power;

That the genius of the Constitution—the division of powers—is summed up in the clause that reserves primacy to the several states, or to the people, in those spheres not specifically delegated to the Federal government;

That the market economy, allocating resources by the free play of supply and demand, is the single economic system compatible with the requirements of personal freedom and constitutional government, and that it is at the same time the most productive supplier of human needs;

That when government interferes with the work of the market economy, it tends to reduce the moral and physical strength of the nation; that when it takes from one man to bestow on another, it diminishes the incentive of the first, the integrity of the second, and the moral autonomy of both;

That we will be free only so long as the national sovereignty of the United States is secure; that history shows periods of freedom are rare, and can exist only when free citizens concertedly defend their rights against all enemies;

That the forces of international Communism are, at present, the greatest single threat to these liberties;

That the United States should stress victory over, rather than coexistance with, this menace; and

That American foreign policy must be judged by this criterion: does it serve the just interests of the United States?

George Wallace and the "Average Man on the Street"

In 1968, American society seemed to be unraveling at a rapid pace. Radical students were occupying administration buildings at Columbia and other universities to protest the war in Vietnam. Young black activists in urban ghettos were calling for revolution; some began training for guerrilla warfare. That summer, demonstrations against the Democratic Convention in Chicago turned violent, when police attacked young people who had gathered to jeer both them and the incumbent party whose meeting they protected. In this environment, millions of voters were eager to listen to politicians who advocated stern measures to ensure "law and order"—and a new breed of militant conservatives stepped into the breach.

George C. Wallace (1919–1998) was one of the scrappiest, most skillful campaigners the modern South produced. An amateur boxing champion in his youth, he began his political career after World War II as a New Deal Democrat who underplayed racial divisions. But, as governor of Alabama from 1963 to 1967, he became a flamboyant defender of segregation and a prominent scourge of the civil rights movement. When these stances proved popular among many whites in the North as well as the South, Wallace decided to launch an independent campaign for the presidency in 1968. He won almost 14 percent of the vote. Here is part of a speech Wallace gave at Madison Square Garden in New York City that October. Notice how Wallace responds to left-wing hecklers in the crowd. The speech is reprinted in History of U.S. Political Parties. Volume IV: 1945–1972, The Politics of Change, *ed. Arthur M. Schlesinger, Jr. (New York, 1973), 3491–94.*

George C. Wallace:
Speech at Madison Square Garden,
October 24, 1968

Well, thank you very much ladies and gentlemen. Thank you very much for your gracious and kind reception here in Madison Square Garden. I'm sure that the *New York Times* took note of the reception that we've received here in the great city of New York. I'm very grateful to the people of this city and this state for the opportunity to be on the ballot on November 5, and as you know we're on the ballot in all 50 states in this union. This is not a sectional movement. It's a national movement, and I am sure that those who are in attendance here tonight, especially of the press, know that our movement is a national movement and that we have an excellent chance to carry the great Empire State of New York.

I have a few friends from Alabama with me and we have a number of others who were with us last week, but we have with us Willie Kirk, past president of Local 52, United Association of Plumbers and Pipefitters.

Well, I want to tell you something. After November 5, you anarchists are through in this country. I can tell you that. Yes, you'd better have your say now, because you are going to be through after November 5, I can assure you that.

I have also with me W. C. Williamson, business manager of Local 52, UAPP, Montgomery, Alabama, and R. H. Low, president of the Mobile Building and Construction Trades Council and business manager of Local 653 Operating Engineers.

And, you came for trouble, you sure got it.

From *History of U.S. Political Parties. Volume IV: 1945–1972, The Politics of Change,* ed. Arthur M. Schlesinger, Jr., (New York, 1973), 3491–94.

Alabama Governor George Wallace. (Courtesy of Getty Images.)

And we have R. H. Bob Low, president of the MBC—We—why don't you come down after I get through and I'll autograph your sandals for you, you know?

And Charlie Ryan, recording secretary of the Steam Fitters Local 818, New York City. We have been endorsed in Alabama by nearly every local in our state: textiles workers, paper workers, steel workers, rubber workers, you name it. We've been endorsed by the working people of our state.

Regardless of what they might say, your national leaders, my wife carried every labor box in 1966, when she ran for governor of Alabama in the primary and the general election. And I also was endorsed by labor when I was elected governor in 1962.

Now, if you fellows will—I can drown—listen—if you'll sit down, ladies and gentlemen, I can drown that crowd out. If you'll just sit down, I'll drown 'em out—that—all he needs is a good haircut. If he'll go to the barbershop, I think they can cure him. So all you newsmen look up this way now. Here's the main event. I've been wanting to fight the main event a long time in Madison Square Garden, so here we are. Listen, that's just a preliminary match up there. This is the main bout right here. So let me say again as I said a moment ago, that we have had the support of the working people of our state. Alabama's a large industrial state, and you could not be elected governor without the support of people in organized labor.

Let me also say this about race, since I'm here in the state of New York, and I'm always asked the question. I am very grateful for the fact that in 1966 my wife received more black votes in Alabama than did either one of her opponents. We are proud to say that they support us now in this race for the presidency, and we would like to have the support of people of all races, colors, creeds, religions, and national origins in the state of New York.

Our system is under attack: the property system, the free enterprise system, and local government. Anarchy prevails today in the streets of the large cities of our country, making it unsafe for you to even go to a political rally here in Madison Square Garden, and that is a sad commentary. Both national parties in the last number of years have kowtowed to every anarchist that has roamed the streets. I want to say before I start on this any longer, that I'm not talking about race. The overwhelming majority of all races in this country are against this breakdown of law and order as much as those who are assembled here tonight. It's a few anarchists, a few activists, a few militants, a few revolutionaries, and a few Communists. But your day, of course, is going to be over soon. The American people are not going to stand by and see the security of our nation imperiled, and they're not going to stand by and see this nation destroyed, I can assure you that.

The liberals and the left-wingers in both national parties have brought us to the domestic mess we are in now. And also this foreign mess we are in.

You need to read the book "How to Behave in a Crowd." You really don't know how to behave in a crowd, do you?

Yes, the liberals and left-wingers in both parties have brought us to the domestic mess we are in also to the foreign policy mess we find our nation involved in at the present time, personified by the no-win war in Southeast Asia.

Now what are some of the things we are going to do when we become president? We are going to turn back to you, the people of the states, the right to control our domestic institutions. Today you cannot even go to the school systems of the large cities of our country without fear. This is a sad day when in the greatest city in the world, there is fear not only in Madison Square Garden, but in every school building in the state of New York, and especially in the City of New York. Why has the leadership of both national parties kowtowed to this group of anarchists that makes it unsafe for your child and for your family? I don't understand it. But I can assure you of this—that there's not ten cents worth of difference with what the national parties say other than our party. Recently they say most of the same things we say. I remember six years ago when this anarchy movement started, Mr. Nixon said: "It's a great movement," and Mr. Humphrey said: "It's a great movement." Now when they try to speak and are heckled down, they stand up and say: "We've got to have some law and order in this country." "We've got to have some law and order in this country." They ought to give you law and order back for nothing, because they have helped to take it away from you, along with the Supreme Court of our country that's made up of Republicans and Democrats.

It's costing the taxpayers of New York and the other states in the union almost a half billion dollars to supervise the schools, hospitals, seniority and apprenticeship lists of labor unions, and businesses. Every year on the federal level we have passed a law that would jail you without a trial by jury about the sale of your own property. Mr. Nixon and Mr. Humphrey, both three or four weeks ago, called for the passage of a bill on the federal level that would require you to sell or lease your own property to whomsoever they thought you ought to lease it to. I say that when Mr. Nixon and Mr. Humphrey succumb to the blackmail of a few anarchists in the streets who said we're going to destroy this country if you do not destroy that adage that a man's home is his castle, they are not fit to lead the American people during the next four years in our country. When I become your president, I am going to ask that Congress repeal this so-called open occupancy law and we're going to, within the law, turn back to the people of every state their public school system. Not one dime of your federal money is going to be used to bus anybody any place that you don't want them to be bussed in New York or any other state.

Yes, the theoreticians and the pseudo-intellectuals have just about destroyed not only local government but the school systems of our country. That's all right. Let the police handle it. So let us talk about law and order. We don't have to talk about it much up here. You understand what I'm talking about in, of course, the City of New York, but let's talk about it.

Yes, the pseudo-intellectuals and the theoreticians and some professors and some newspaper editors and some judges and some preachers have looked down their nose long enough at the average man on the street: the pipe-fitter, the communications worker, the fireman, the policeman, the barber, the white collar worker, and said we must write you a guideline about when you go to bed at night and when you get up in the morning. But there are more of us than there are of them because the average citizen of New York and of Alabama and of the other states of our union are tired of guidelines being written, telling them when to go to bed at night and when to get up in the morning.

I'm talking about law and order. The Supreme Court of our country has hand-cuffed the police, and tonight if you walk out of this building and are knocked in the head, the person who knocks you in the head is out of jail before you get in the hospital, and on Monday morning, they'll try a policeman about it. I can say I'm going to give the total support of the presidency to the policemen and the firemen in this country, and I'm going to say, you enforce the law and you make it safe on the streets, and the president of the United States will stand with you. My election as president is going to put some backbone in the backs of some mayors and governors I know through the length and breadth of this country.

You had better be thankful for the police and the firemen of this country. If it were not for them, you couldn't even ride in the streets, much less walk in the streets, of our large cities. Yes, the Kerner Commission Report, recently written by Republicans and Democrats, said that you are to blame for the breakdown of law and order, and that the police are to blame. Well, you know, of course, you aren't to blame. They said we have a sick society. Well, we don't have any sick society. We have a sick Supreme Court and some sick politicians in Washington, that's who's sick in our country. The Supreme Court of our country has ruled that you cannot even say a simple prayer in a public school, but you can send obscene literature through the mail, and recently they ruled that a Communist can work in a defense plant. But when I become your president, we're going to take every Communist out of every defense plant in the United States, I can assure you.

Goldwater Was Right!

Phyllis Schlafly (1924–) has been a conservative activist since she was a high-school student in Illinois. In 1964, she wrote a best-selling book, A Choice Not an Echo, *calling for the Republican party to nominate a principled conservative for president. She then went on to campaign against détente with the USSR, ratification of an equal rights amendment to the Constitution, and extending anti-discrimination laws to homosexuals. In the following column, published in June 1998, Schlafly argues that Barry Goldwater, who had recently died, was vital to the success of the modern Right. The selection, entitled "The Legacy of Barry Goldwater," can be found at the website,* <www.eagleforum.org/column/1998/June98/98-06-10.html>.

The Legacy of Barry Goldwater

It is unlikely that any nominee for President who was not elected ever had the lasting influence on American politics that Barry Goldwater did. Unlike other defeated presidential candidates, he will never be just a footnote in the history books.

That's because Barry Goldwater was the undisputed original leader of the modern conservative movement. And that movement has been the dominant political reality since 1980.

It is hard to overestimate the importance of Barry Goldwater to the conservative movement. If there hadn't been a Barry Goldwater, there wouldn't have been a Ronald Reagan.

In 1964, the liberal establishment ridiculed Goldwater as a reactionary behind the times. We can now recognize that he was a man ahead of the times. He started the relay race against all odds in the 1960s, and Ronald Reagan carried the flag over the finish line to victory in the 1980s.

When Goldwater walked onto the political stage, most politicians sought the label liberal. Conservative was a sort of an epithet that took political courage to accept.

By the time Michael Dukakis ran for President in 1988, the L word had become a Scarlet Letter. Today, most politicians of all

From the Phyllis Schlafly Column, June 1998, by Phyllis Schlafly, *(www.eagleforum.org/column/1998/June98/98-06-10.html)*, published by The Eagle Trust Funds, 1998.

Phyllis Schlafly leading a rally against passage of the Equal Rights Amendment. (Courtesy of AP/Wide World Photos.)

parties and persuasions proclaim that they are conservative (whether they are or not).

Today, a dozen presidential aspirants are waiting in the wings, hoping they will feel a draft. Barry Goldwater is one of the very few men ever really drafted. He did not seek the heavy mantle of leadership. He was drafted by a movement seeking a leader who would never compromise with or accommodate the liberals.

Goldwater was authentic, and what you saw was what you got. His political positions and agenda came from his personal convictions, not from reading the polls. He was willing to stand alone against the good ol' boys club known as the U.S. Senate.

Goldwater was so refreshingly honest. Bill Clinton's first comment, on learning of Goldwater's passing, summed it up. "He was truly an American original. I never knew anybody like him." No doubt Clinton thinks an honest politician is a curiosity, perhaps something to be encased for display in the Smithsonian.

To calculate how far we've descended from Goldwater's honesty, ask yourself, Where are the Republicans today who have the candor to say about Clinton, as Goldwater said about Richard Nixon, "He was the most dishonest man I ever met" and "Nixon can go to China and stay there."

Goldwater was not a complex man, but his legacy is complex. First, his book "The Conscience of a Conservative" defined the conservative agenda as limited, constitutional government, lower taxes, a superior national defense, individual freedom and responsibility. He plotted the route to get there by reducing the size of government, promoting freedom not welfare, and repealing laws, not passing new ones.

Second, he attracted Mainstreet Americans by the millions into the conservative movement. Commentators may not have recognized his ideology as populist, but his movement definitely was. His supporters believed that their participation in politics could actually make public policy and elect candidates.

Third, by proclaiming from the start that he offered "a choice not an echo," Goldwater made his supporters understand who their enemy was. That enemy was the liberal, eastern Rockefeller Republicans who, every four years from 1936 through 1960, had inflicted the Republican Party with a presidential candidate who "me-too-ed" the Democrats on the fundamental issues of big federal spending and an interventionist foreign policy.

It was the second and third elements of his movement that brought down on his head the orchestrated wrath and venom of the liberal establishment and their friends in the media, as well as of the Lyndon B. Johnson campaign.

At the 1964 Republican National Convention in San Francisco, Nelson Rockefeller launched the word missiles against Goldwater that have remained explosive to this day. Rockefeller labelled Goldwater an "extremist" and taunted his delegates as outside the "mainstream" of politics. Goldwater fielded the smear with dignity: "Extremism in the defense of liberty is no vice."

It was truly remarkable that, despite the intensity of the 1964 anti-Goldwater invective, 27 million Americans voted for him anyway. That trial by fire transformed conservatives from Americans who just read books about what's wrong with America into politically active warriors.

The 27 million who withstood Big Media's vitriol in 1964 kept the faith, and they grew into the 54 million mighty majority that validated the Reagan Revolution in 1984. Conservative Republicans today are looking for a leader who will pickup where Ronald Reagan left off and assure the permanence of the Goldwater legacy.

The Vision of Ronald Reagan

The 1980 election of Ronald Wilson Reagan (1911–) to the presidency owed more to the failed policies (both foreign and domestic) of his predecessor, Jimmy Carter, than to the popularity of his conservative principles. But Reagan, a former movie star and governor of California, was the most engaging speaker the American Right had ever known, and his election was the culmination of decades of activism and advocacy by the conservative movement. In the following speech, given just two months after he entered the White House, Reagan outlines the philosophy that will govern his administration. The address was given to an audience of fellow conservatives. Taken from Ronald Reagan, "Remarks at the Conservative Political Action Conference Dinner," March 20, 1981, from Public Papers of the President: Ronald Reagan, 1981 *(Washington, GPO, 1982), 275–79.*

Remarks at the Conservative PoliticalAction Conference Dinner, March 20, 1981

It's been said that anyone who seeks success or greatness should first forget about both and seek only the truth, and the rest will follow. Well, fellow truthseekers, none of us here tonight—contemplating the seal on this podium and a balanced budget in 1984—can argue with that kind of logic. For whatever history does finally say about our cause, it must say: The conservative movement in 20th century America held fast through hard and difficult years to its vision of the truth. And history must also say that our victory, when it was achieved, was not so much a victory of politics as it was a victory of ideas, not so much a victory for any one man or party as it was a victory for a set of principles—principles that were protected and nourished by a few unselfish Americans through many grim and heartbreaking defeats.

Now, you are those Americans that I'm talking about. I wanted to be here not just to acknowledge your efforts on my behalf, not just to remark that last November's victory was singularly your victory, not just to mention that the new administration in Washington is a testimony to your perseverance and devotion to principle, but to say, simply, "Thank you," and to say those

President Ronald Reagan delivers a speech in 1982. (Courtesy of Photo Researchers.)

words not as a President, or even as a conservative; thank you as an American. I say this knowing that there are many in this room whose talents might have entitled them to a life of affluence but who chose another career out of a higher sense of duty to country. And I know, too, that the story of their selflessness will never be written up in Time or Newsweek or go down in the history books.

You know, on an occasion like this it's a little hard not to reminisce, not to think back and just realize how far we've come. The Portuguese have a word for such recollection—*saudade*—a poetic term rich with the dreams of yesterday. And surely in our past there was many a dream that went aglimmering and many a field littered with broken lances.

Who can forget that July night in San Francisco when Barry Goldwater told us that we must set the tides running again in the cause of freedom, and he said, "until our cause has won the day, inspired the world, and shown the way to a tomorrow worthy of all our yesteryears"? And had there not been a Barry Goldwater willing to take that lonely walk, we wouldn't be here talking of a celebration tonight.

But our memories are not just political ones. I like to think back about a small, artfully written magazine named National

Review, founded in 1955 and ridiculed by the intellectual establishment because it published an editorial that said it would stand
athwart the course of history yelling, "Stop!" And then there was
a spritely written newsweekly coming out of Washington named
Human Events that many said would never be taken seriously,
but it would become later "must reading" not only for Capitol
Hill insiders but for all of those in public life.

How many of us were there who used to go home from meetings like this with no thought of giving up, but still find ourselves
wondering in the dark of night whether this much-loved land
might go the way of other great nations that lost a sense of mission and a passion for freedom? . . .

Our goals complement each other. We're not cutting the budget
simply for the sake of sounder financial management. This is only a
first step toward returning power to the States and communities,
only a first step toward reordering the relationship between citizen
and government. We can make government again responsive to
people not only by cutting its size and scope and thereby ensuring
that its legitimate functions are performed efficiently and justly.

Because ours is a consistent philosophy of government, we
can be very clear: We do not have a social agenda, separate, separate economic agenda, and a separate foreign agenda. We have one
agenda. Just as surely as we seek to put our financial house in
order and rebuild our nation's defenses, so too we seek to protect
the unborn, to end the manipulation of schoolchildren by utopian
planners, and permit the acknowledgement of a Supreme Being in
our classrooms just as we allow such acknowledgements in other
public institutions.

Now, obviously we're not going to be able to accomplish all
this at once. The American people are patient. I think they realize
that the wrongs done over several decades cannot be corrected
instantly. You know, I had the pleasure in appearing before a Senate
committee once while I was still Governor, and I was challenged
because there was a Republican President in the White House
who'd been there for several months—why we hadn't then corrected everything that had been done. And the only way I could
think to answer him is I told him about a ranch many years ago that
Nancy and I acquired. It had a barn with eight stalls in it in which
they had kept cattle, and we wanted to keep horses. And I was in
there day after day with a pick and a shovel, lowering the level of
those stalls, which had accumulated over the years. *[Laughter]* And

I told this Senator who'd asked that question that I discovered that you did not undo in weeks or months what it had taken some 15 years to accumulate.

I also believe that we conservatives, if we mean to continue governing, must realize that it will not always be so easy to place the blame on the past for our national difficulties. You know, one day the great baseball manager Frankie Frisch sent a rookie out to play center field. The rookie promptly dropped the first fly ball that was hit to him. On the next play he let a grounder go between his feet and then threw the ball to the wrong base. Frankie stormed out of the dugout, took his glove away from him and said, "I'll show you how to play this position." And the next batter slammed a line drive right over second base. Frankie came in on it, missed it completely, fell down when he tried to chase it, threw down his glove, and yelled at the rookie, "You've got center field so screwed up nobody can play it." [Laughter]

The point is we must lead a nation, and that means more than criticizing the past. Indeed, as T. S. Eliot once said, "Only by acceptance of the past will you alter its meaning."

Now, during our political efforts, we were the subject of much indifference and often times intolerance, and that's why I hope our political victory will be remembered as a generous one and our time in power will be recalled for the tolerance we showed for those with whom we disagree.

But beyond this, beyond this we have to offer America and the world a larger vision. We must remove government's smothering hand from where it does harm; we must seek to revitalize the proper functions of government. But we do these things to set loose again the energy and the ingenuity of the American people. We do these things to reinvigorate those social and economic institutions which serve as a buffer and a bridge between the individual and the state—and which remain the real source of our progress as a people.

And we must hold out this exciting prospect of an orderly, compassionate, pluralistic society—an archipelago of prospering communities and divergent institutions—a place where a free and energetic people can work out their own destiny under God.

I know that some will think about the perilous world we live in and the dangerous decade before us and ask what practical effect this conservative vision can have today. When Prime Minister Thatcher was here recently we both remarked on the sudden, overwhelming changes that had come recently to politics in both our countries.

At our last official function, I told the Prime Minister that everywhere we look in the world the cult of the state is dying. And I held out hope that it wouldn't be long before those of our adversaries who preach the supremacy of the state were remembered only for their role in a sad, rather bizarre chapter in human history. The largest planned economy in the world has to buy food elsewhere or its people would starve.

We've heard in our century far too much of the sounds of anguish from those who live under totalitarian rule. We've seen too many monuments made not out of marble or stone but out of barbed wire and terror. But from these terrible places have come survivors, witnesses to the triumph of the human spirit over the mystique of state power, prisoners whose spiritual values made them the rulers of their guards. With their survival, they brought us "the secret of the camps," a lesson for our time and for any age: Evil is powerless if the good are unafraid.

That's why the Marxist vision of man without God must eventually be seen as an empty and a false faith—the second oldest in the world—first proclaimed in the Garden of Eden with whispered words of temptation: "Ye shall be as gods." The crisis of the Western world, Whittaker Chambers reminded us, exists to the degree in which it is indifferent to God. "The Western world does not know it," he said about our struggle, "but it already possesses the answer to this problem—but only provided that its faith in God and the freedom He enjoins is as great as communism's faith in man."

This is the real task before us: to reassert our commitment as a nation to a law higher than our own, to renew our spiritual strength. Only by building a wall of such spiritual resolve can we, as a free people, hope to protect our own heritage and make it someday the birthright of all men.

There is, in America, a greatness and a tremendous heritage of idealism which is a reservoir of strength and goodness. It is ours if we will but tap it. And, because of this—because that greatness is there—there is need in America today for a reaffirmation of that goodness and a reformation of our greatness.

The dialog and the deeds of the past few decades are not sufficient to the day in which we live. They cannot keep the promise of tomorrow. The encrusted bureaucracies and the engrained procedures which have developed of late respond neither to the minority or the majority. We've come to a turning point. We have a decision to make. Will we continue with yesterday's agenda and yesterday's failures, or will we reassert our ideals and our standards, will we reaffirm our faith, and renew our purpose? This is a time for choosing.

I made a speech by that title in 1964. I said, "We've been told increasingly that we must choose between left or right." But we're still using those terms—left or right. And I'll repeat what I said then in '64. "There is no left or right. There's only an up or down:" up to the ultimate in individual freedom, man's age old dream, the ultimate in individual freedom consistent with an orderly society—or down to the totalitarianism of the ant heap. And those today who, however good their intentions, tell us that we should trade freedom for security are on that downward path.

Those of us who call ourselves conservative have pointed out what's wrong with government policy for more than a quarter of a century. Now we have an opportunity to make policy and to change our national direction. All of us in government—in the House, in the Senate, in the executive branch—and in private life can now stand together. We can stop the drain on the economy by the public sector. We can restore our national prosperity. We can replace the overregulated society with the creative society. We can appoint to the bench distinguished judges who understand the first responsibility of any legal system is to punish the guilty and protect the innocent. We can restore to their rightful place in our national consciousness the values of family, work, neighborhood, and religion. And, finally, we can see to it that the nations of the world clearly understand America's intentions and respect for resolve.

Now we have the opportunity—yes, and the necessity—to prove that the American promise is equal to the task of redressing our grievances and equal to the challenge of inventing a great tomorrow.

This reformation, this renaissance will not be achieved or will it be served, by those who engage in political claptrap or false promises. It will not be achieved by those who set people against people, class against class, or institution against institution. So, while we celebrate our recent political victory we must understand there's much work before us: to gain control again of government, to reward personal initiative and risk-taking in the marketplace, to revitalize our system of federalism, to strengthen the private institutions that make up the independent sector of our society, and to make our own spiritual affirmation in the face of those who would deny man has a place before God. Not easy tasks perhaps. But I would remind you as I did on January 20th, they're not impossible, because, after all, we're Americans.

This year we will celebrate a victory won two centuries ago at Yorktown, the victory of a small, fledgling nation over a mighty world power. How many people are aware—I've been told that a British band played the music at that surrender ceremony because we didn't have a band. *[Laughter]* And they played a tune that was very popular in England at the time. Its title was "The World Turned Upside Down." I'm sure it was far more appropriate than they realized at that moment. The heritage from that long, difficult struggle is before our eyes today in this city, in the great halls of our government and in the monuments to the memory of our great men.

It is this heritage that evokes the images of a much-loved land, a land of struggling settlers and lonely immigrants, of giant cities and great frontiers, images of all that our country is and all that we want her to be. That's the America entrusted to us, to stand by, to protect, and yes, to lead her wisely.

Fellow citizens, fellow conservatives, our time is now. Our moment has arrived. We stand together shoulder to shoulder in the thickest of the fight. If we carry the day and turn the tide, we can hope that as long as men speak of freedom and those who have protected it, they will remember us, and they will say, "Here were the brave and here their place of honor."

Thank you.

Questions

1. Based on his speech, how did Wallace's criticism of the government differ from that of the Sharon Statement or of President Reagan? Was the difference one of style or of conviction?
2. Why did Wallace argue that "the average man on the street" was the best protector of "law and order" in the late 1960s? How did he turn hecklers into examples of the problem?
3. Which qualities of leadership did Schlafly find in Goldwater? Are these qualities as important to a president as to the leader of a movement?
4. To what degree do contemporary conservatives adhere to the principles in the Sharon Statement? Try to account for the changes that have taken place in the ideology of the Right.
5. How did Ronald Reagan portray his philosophy as that of a majority of Americans? Do you agree that it was? Is it accurate to say that his liberal opponents worshipped a "cult of the state"?
6. Compare the rhetorical style of George Wallace and Ronald Reagan. Why did most people consider the latter to be the more persuasive communicator?

FURTHER READING

For the ideas and national leaders of the postwar right, see George Nash, *The Conservative Intellectual Movement in America Since 1945* (New York, 1976); Paul Gottfried, *The Conservative Movement* (Boston, 1993); Robert A. Goldberg, *Barry Goldwater* (New Haven, 1995); Dan T. Carter, *The Politics of Rage* (New York, 1995), a study of George Wallace; Lou Cannon, *President Reagan: The Role of a Lifetime* (New York, 1991); and the relevant chapters in Michael Kazin, *The Populist Persuasion: An American History* (rev. ed., Ithaca, 1998). On the grassroots insurgency that politicians both responded to and fueled, see Jonathan Rieder, *Canarsie* (Cambridge, Mass., 1985); Ronald P. Formisano, *Boston Against Busing* (Chapel Hill, 1991); and Lisa McGirr, *Suburban Warriors* (New York, forthcoming), a study of the Right in Orange County, California.

The Environmental Movement

Austin Kerr and Terence Kehoe

INTRODUCTION

The environmental movement that emerged in the 1960s and early 1970s built upon previous efforts to conserve and protect America's natural resources and to control the harmful health effects of concentrated urban living and various industrial processes. At the end of the nineteenth century, the closing of the American frontier and the legacy of unrestrained development in ravaged areas, such as the depleted forests of the Upper Great Lakes region, inspired some influential public figures to push for an expanded government role in decisions affecting natural resources. Conservationists such as Theodore Roosevelt and Gifford Pinchot, the first head of the U.S. Forest Service, wanted to bring America's resources under the authority of experts in the federal government so that rational planning could ensure the most efficient use and continued benefits of natural resources for all Americans.

During the same period, the steady push of settlement and the increasingly urban character of American life generated a desire among some citizens to preserve as much of the landscape as possible in its natural, unspoiled state. Preservationists such as John Muir, the founder of the Sierra Club, believed that natural areas possessed an intrinsic value and attached a spiritual significance to wilderness. The preservationist attitude clashed with the views of conservationists, who wanted to efficiently exploit natural areas for their economic value. While the two groups sometimes cooperated to achieve common objectives, their different perspectives increasingly brought them into direct conflict with one another. In 1901, Muir and his allies attempted to block efforts to transform the beautiful Hetch-Hetchy Valley in California's

Yosemite Park into a reservoir for the population of San Francisco. In the end, the needs of the city won out over the desire to preserve the majesty of the valley.

The public health movement of the Progressive Era also represented an effort to tame the excesses of industrial capitalism. In this case, public health reformers focused on improving the urban environment. Politicians, physicians, civic organizations, and other groups worked to impose controls on industrial pollution and improve sanitation practices with the goal of eradicating disease and improving the general quality of city life. These activities also included efforts to improve the safety of industrial workers exposed to various toxic and hazardous substances on the job.

The concerns and objectives of the conservationists became institutionalized through the continuing activities of the Forest Service, the Army Corps of Engineers, and other government agencies. The national park system represented the greatest legacy of the preservationists. Public health reformers achieved their greatest successes in improving urban sanitation practices, while having much less of an impact on industrial practices. But in spite of their considerable gains, none of these reform movements could claim anywhere near the popular, sustained support of the later environmental movement.

The environmental movement that bloomed in the 1960s drew support from a much broader cross section of the American public than these earlier movements and prompted many citizens to question deep-rooted assumptions about the benefits of economic growth and humankind's relationship to the natural environment. While the leadership of the organized environmental movement—especially at the national level—remained overwhelmingly white, male, and affluent, poll after poll demonstrated that Americans from all groups shared a broad consensus about the desirability of preserving and protecting the natural environment. The environmental movement achieved significant and lasting political power; in response to popular concerns about the environment and various forms of activism, governments at all levels enacted new laws and created new agencies designed to ensure greater protection of the environment.

Since 1980, the environmental movement has become more diverse. Minority groups and working-class Americans have become more involved in environmental issues as they attempt to protect their communities from the health dangers posed by nearby hazardous waste dumps and industrial plants that generate toxic compounds. In addition, so-called radical environmentalists have criticized mainstream organizations, such as the Sierra Club, for their willingness to compromise with the forces of development and their unwillingness to challenge seriously what the radicals perceive as the inherent flaws of modern industrial society.

The Emergence and Evolution of the Environmental Movement

Historians are often concerned with explaining why things happened. This question is particularly important in understanding significant social movements. In the first reading, Samuel Hays links the emergence of environmentalism to the increasing standard of living in post-1945 America. According to Hays, new "environmental values" were closely linked to the widespread search for a greater quality of life that extended beyond material possessions. Kirkpatrick Sale then describes the splintering of the environmental movement in recent years and the growing diversity of voices within the movement. During the 1980s, community activists and radical environmentalists criticized the major environmental organizations for their failure to address adequately the environmental health concerns of working-class and minority communities and their willingness to accept incremental reform and play by the traditional rules of interest group politics. The critics of mainstream environmentalism eventually founded organizations of their own that attempted to move beyond the limitations of the established environmental groups.

Environmentalism and the Affluent Society

Abridged from Samuel P. Hays, in collaboration with Barbara D. Hays, Beauty, Health, and Permanence: Environmental Politics in the United States, 1955–1985 *(Cambridge, England, 1987), 2–5, 22–28.*

The Transformation of Values

Environmental concerns were rooted in the vast social changes that took place in the United States after World War II. Although some beginnings can be identified in earlier years, only after the war did they become widely shared social phenomena. . . . The expansion of this interest brought it to the forefront of public life. This began with a rapid growth in outdoor recreation in the 1950s, extended into the wider field of the protection of natural environments, then became infused with attempts to cope with air and water pollution and still later with toxic chemical pollutants. Such activity was hardly extensive prior to World War II; afterward it was a major public concern.

Two observations help to identify the historical timing of the environmental concern. One is the transition from an older stress on efficient development and use of material resources such as water, forests, and soils known as the conservation movement, which took place in the first four decades of the twentieth century. Conservation gave way to environment after World War II amid a rising interest in the quality of life beyond efficiency in production. The two tendencies often came into conflict as resources long thought of as important for their material commodities came to be prized for their aesthetic and amenity uses. Rivers, forests, wetlands, and deserts were seen as valuable in their natural state as part of a modern standard of living; it was maintained that some such areas should be left undeveloped and undisturbed. This preposterous notion was difficult if not impossible to accept to those whose preferences were rooted in an older time. Many clashes between older commodity and newer environmental values occurred in the Environmental Era. World War II is a convenient dividing line between the old and the new values.

Evolving environmental values were closely associated with rising standards of living and levels of education. These changed markedly after the war. Personal real income grew and the percentage of Americans with college education increased. The social context within which environmental values flourished was two-

---

fold: younger people and the more educated. With each level of age from younger to older, environmental interest fell; and with each level of education from elementary school to college degree, it rose. The advancing edge of demographic change included an advancing interest in environmental objectives. Quality of life as an idea and a focus of public action lay at the heart of what was new in American society and politics; environmental affairs were an integral element.

Several aspects of these changes are worth keeping in mind. . . . One is that they can be thought of as part of a history of consumption rather than of the history of production. They arose not out of the way in which people carried out an occupation and earned income, but out of the kind of life that income made possible and the ways in which people chose to express their new standards of living.

At one time income was spent largely to purchase necessities, and in the third decade of the twentieth century that was extended to the capacity to acquire conveniences that lightened the tasks of normal living. But with rising incomes something beyond necessities and conveniences now lay within the reach of many; they can be called amenities. Associated with home and leisure, with recreation and the "good life," these came to involve considerable choice because spending was not dictated by necessity or convenience. A general direction to the new opportunities emerged that came to be described as quality of life. Sales analysts in private business were particularly attuned to such changes as they identified diverse markets to be supplied with new goods and services. Environmental quality was an integral part of this new search for a higher standard of living.

These changes did not come to all sectors of American society in the same degree or at the same time. There were the older and the newer, those adhering to previously dominant values and those searching out more recently emerging ones. Although age was often the dividing line, there were also geographical variations. New England and the Pacific Coast were among the leading sectors of change, whereas the South moved much more slowly. In between were the Mountain West and the Midwest. These regional differences could be identified in many realms of new cultural values from the changing role of women to self-expression to environmental interests.

Several writers have attempted to analyze the social roots of environmental affairs in a more limited fashion. They emphasize

President Theodore Roosevelt and naturalist John Muir at Yosemite Valley, California. (Courtesy of Corbis Images.)

factors on the periphery of American society rather than central to it, or the capacity of a few leaders of environmental organizations to manipulate the attitudes of their members or the public so as to create imaginary problems.

All this seems rather complex and contrived; public interest in environmental affairs is far simpler. It stems from a desire to improve personal, family, and community life. The desires are neither ephemeral nor erratic; they are evident in many nations, first in the advanced industrial and consumer societies and then in more recent years in those of middle and even earlier stages of development. They express human wants and needs as surely as do demands for better housing, more satisfying leisure and recreation, improved household furnishings, better health, and a greater sense of well-being. We customarily associate these with human "progress," which normally is accepted as a fundamental concern unnecessary to explain away in other terms. An interest in the environmental quality of life is to be understood simply as an integral part of the drives inherent in persistent human aspiration and achievement. . . .

The Search for Environmental Amenities

The most widespread source of emerging environmental interest was the search for a better life associated with home, community, and leisure. A new emphasis on smaller families developed, allowing parents to invest their limited time and income in fewer children. Child rearing was now oriented toward a more extended period of childhood in order to nurture abilities. Parents sought to provide creative-arts instructions, summer camps, and family vacations so as to foster self-development. Within this context the phrase "environmental quality" would have considerable personal meaning.

It also had meaning for place of residence. Millions of urban Americans desired to live on the fringe of the city where life was less congested, the air cleaner, noise reduced, and there was less concentrated waste from manifold human activities. In the nineteenth century only the well-to-do could afford to live some distance from work. Although streetcars enabled white-collar workers to live in the suburbs and work downtown, blue-collar employees still could not pay the cost of daily transportation. But the automobile largely lifted this limitation, and after World War II blue-collar workers were able to escape the industrial community as a place of residence. Still, by the 1970s as many as one-third of urban Americans wished they could live farther out in the countryside.

The search for a higher quality of living involved a desire for more space both inside and outside the home. Life in the city had been intensely crowded for urban dwellers. Often the street in front of the house had constituted the only available open space. Moving to the suburbs reflected a desire to enjoy a more natural setting, but it also evidenced the search for nature beyond the metropolitan area in the parks and woodlands of the countryside. This desire increased with the ease of access to rural areas by means of the automobile. The state-parks movement of the 1920s expressed the demand by city dwellers for places in which to enjoy the countryside on the weekend or during summer vacations.

There was also the desire to obtain private lands in the countryside so as to enjoy nature not found in the city. In the 1960s and 1970s the market for vacation homesites boomed. Newspaper advertisements abounded with phrases that signaled the important values: "by a sparkling stream," "abundant wildlife," "near the edge of a forest road," "200 feet of lakefront," "on the edge of a state forest."

This pursuit of natural values by city dwellers led to a remarkable turnabout in the attitudes of Americans toward natural environments. These had long been thought of as unused wastelands that could be made valuable only if developed. But after World War II many such areas came to be thought of as valuable only if left in their natural condition. Forested land, once thought of by many as dark, forbidding, and sinister, a place to be avoided because of the dangers lurking within, now was highly esteemed.

Wetlands, formerly known as swamplands, fit only for draining so that they could become productive agricultural land, were valued as natural systems, undisturbed and undeveloped. Similar positive attitudes were expressed for the prairies of the Midwest, the swamps of the South, and the pine barrens of the East. For many years wild animals had been seen as a threat to farmers and others. Little concern had been shown for the sharp decline even in the deer population, let alone among the bear and bobcat. Yet by the 1960s and 1970s predators, as well as deer, small mammals, and wild turkey, had assumed a positive image for many Americans, and special measures were adopted to protect them and increase their numbers.

Close on the heels of these changes in attitude were new views about western deserts. The desert had long been thought of as a forbidding land where human habitation was impossible and travel was dangerous. The desert hardly figured in the debate over the Wilderness Act of 1964. But by the late 1970s this had changed. The increased popularity of nature photography had brought home the desert to the American people as a place of wonder and beauty. By 1976 western deserts had been explored and identified by many Americans as lands that should be protected in their natural condition.

Environmental Health and Well-being

The search for greater health and well-being constituted an equally significant element of the drive for environmental quality. Such concerns had firm roots in the earlier public-health movement, which emphasized the social conditions that gave rise to health problems. Improvements in water quality all but eliminated typhoid fever and other waterborne bacterial ailments while parasitic and viral diseases such as malaria and yellow fever were brought under control by sanitary measures. The discovery and widespread use of antibiotics after World War II limited the adverse effects of secondary infections. Such measures greatly reduced human suffering and prolonged life. But they also emphasized new causes of illness, many of them environmental.

As tuberculosis declined, other lung problems such as emphysema and cancer received more attention. The Tuberculosis Association changed its name to the American Lung Association to reflect the new emphasis; it became especially concerned with smoking as a cause of lung cancer and air pollution as a cause of pulmonary problems. Exposures formerly associated with infectious diseases now were found to be responsible for more deep-seated problems. Asbestos, for example, once had been thought of primarily as a cause of asbestosis, a pulmonary condition. Many lung problems arising from exposure to asbestos could not be treated with antibiotics and were found to be cancer.

Cancer received particular attention, as its incidence seemed to increase. By the late 1970s one-fourth of all living Americans would contract cancer during their lifetime, and two-thirds of these would die from it. The long latency period between exposure and the appearance of cancer created a sense of peril that made the disease more dramatic. At the same time, cancer was identified with either personal habits, such as smoking and diet, or environmental pollutants in air and water.

The new concerns for environmental health also focused on the workplace. Occupational dangers to workers had long been thought of mainly as posed by physical factors such as machinery. Increasingly the workplace was seen as an environment in which the air itself could transmit harmful substances to cause diseases in workers. Recognition of this danger came only slowly. Much of it awaited evidence accumulated from long-term studies of the relationship between occupational exposure and disease.

The concern for environmental health was primarily an urban phenomenon. The incidence of cancer was twice as high in cities as in the rural countryside, a difference attributed to the impact of urban pollution. The chemical products involved in manufacturing, increasing with each passing year after World War II, seemed especially to affect urban people adversely. The extensive use of the automobile in cities also posed continuing pollution threats. And studies of indoor air identified health hazards in offices and households.

Although older waterborne diseases had been controlled through chlorination and disinfection of drinking-water supplies, the rapid accumulation of newer chemical pollutants in the nation's rivers and its underground water generated new health concerns. Synthetic organic compounds, as well as heavy metals from industry, were discovered in many drinking-water sources. The disposal of industrial toxic wastes constituted an even more pervasive concern; they were often injected underground, but just as frequently they were disposed of in landfills from which they leaked into water supplies.

The increasing emphasis on environmental health arose from a rising level of expectations about health and well-being. As life expectancy increased, the average American could look forward to a decade or more of active life after retirement. As the threat of infectious disease decreased, fear of sudden death or disability from polio, secondary infections from simple surgical procedures such as appendectomies, or other dangers declined sharply. All this led to a new focus in health associated more with expectations of well-being than with fear of death. There was a special interest in the quality of life of elderly people. An increasing portion of the population became concerned about preventive health care, showing interest in physical fitness, food and diet, and protection from exposure to environmental pollutants. This marked innovation in ideas about personal health was an important element in the expanding concern for one's environment as a critical element in well-being.

The Ecological Perspective

Ecological objectives—an emphasis on the workings of natural biological and geological systems and the pressures human actions placed on them—were a third element of environmental concern. Whereas amenities involved an aesthetic response to the environment, and environmental health concerned a choice between cleaner and dirtier technologies within the built-up environment, ecological matters dealt with imbalances between developed and natural systems that had both current and long-term implications. These questions, therefore, involved ideas about permanence.

The term "ecology" had long referred to a branch of biology that emphasized study of the interaction of living organisms with their physical and biological environment. Popular ecology in the 1960s and 1970s went beyond that scientific meaning. One heard of the impact of people on "the ecology." Professional ecologists disdained this corruption of the word as they had used it. Popular use involved both a broad meaning, the functioning of the biological and geological world, and a narrower one, the disruption of natural processes by human action, as well as the notion that the two, natural systems and human stress, needed to be brought into a better balance.

The popular ecological perspective was reflected in the ecology centers that arose in urban areas. Initially these grew out of the recycling movement—the collection of paper, glass, and tin cans for reprocessing. These centers drew together people who wished to help solve the litter problem and thus to enhance the aesthetic quality of their communities. But soon the concept of recycling seemed to spill over into larger ideas about natural cycles, a traditional ecological theme, and to human action to foster such processes. Ecology centers often expanded their activities into community organic gardens, nutrition and food for better health, and changing life-styles to reduce the human load on natural resources and natural systems.

An ecological perspective grew from the popularization of knowledge about natural processes. These were ideas significant to the study of ecology, but selected and modified by popular experience rather than as a result of formal study. An increasing number of personal or media encounters with the natural world gave rise to widely shared ideas about the functioning of biological and geological systems and the relationship of human beings to them.

Even before World War II, the problem of deer overpopulation on the north rim of the Grand Canyon, or imbalances between the numbers of deer and food in the cutover forestlands of Pennsylvania, Michigan, Wisconsin, and Minnesota, had popularized knowledge about predator-prey and food-population relationships. Overgrazing by cattle and sheep on the western range sparked discussions in the media of the problem of stress in plant communities in which, through overuse, the more vulnerable plants gave way to the hardier, reducing the variety of species. This conveyed the ideas that species diversity had evolved in the process of natural succession, that the number and diversity of species were reduced under population pressures, and that the capacity of ecological systems to sustain human use without major changes were limited.

The threat of toxic chemicals diffused throughout the biological world led to the spread of knowledge in the 1960s about biological and chemical cycles. Transported through the atmosphere, falling into water and on land, chemicals were absorbed by plants, eaten by animals and then by humans. With each step in that food chain they increased in concentration. Media coverage in the late 1950s and early 1960s of radioactive fallout from atomic testing increased awareness of these processes. The most dramatic example was radioactive cesium, which was absorbed by lichens in the Arctic, eaten by reindeer and in turn by Alaskan Eskimos and Laplanders, at each step increasing in concentration in fatty tissues.

The public encounter with pesticides drove home ideas about the accumulation of toxic materials in the food chain. These persistent pesticides found their way into water to be taken up by small fish that were eaten by larger fish, and then by birds to produce weakened eggshells and reduced hatching. Rachel Carson's book *Silent Spring*, published in 1962, spread the word about the problem; even more influential was a widely reported administrative proceeding about DDT in Wisconsin in 1968 and 1969.

New Strands of Environmentalism

Abridged from Kirkpatrick Sale, The Green Revolution: The American Environmental Movement, 1962–1992 *(New York, 1993), 57–68.*

As the environmental majors expanded their Washington operations, a process that would continue for the next decade, two other important dimensions were added to (or became more note-

Excerpts from *The Green Revolution: The American Environmental Movement, 1962–1992* by Kirkpatrick Sale. Copyright © 1993 by Kirkpatrick Sale. Reprinted by permission of Hill & Wang, a division of Farrar, Straus & Giroux, Inc.

worthy in) the movement: grass-roots activism and radical environmentalism.

Some part of environmentalism had always been primarily local, simply because many of the problems—nuclear plants, waste dumps, factory emissions—were local. But with the eighties, and the growing feeling that official Washington was unresponsive and environmental Washington preoccupied, grass-roots organizations proliferated; Peter Borrelli, editor of . . . *Amicus* magazine, estimated that some 25 million people were involved one way or another at the local level by 1987–88. With the passion of people whose lives were intimately affected and an energy fired by what came to be called the NIMBY (Not in My Backyard) syndrome, these groups made themselves heard by both state and city agencies and local corporations, often with telling effect. "Today the action is bottom-up," Borrelli noted, "since it is at the local level that laws and programs set in place over the last two decades are implemented"—or, just as often, not. It was just such action that led to the passage of Proposition 65 in California in 1985, an anti-toxic initiative against state agricultural and chemical industries, the first successful environmental initiative since 1972.

The grass-roots response was often much tougher and less compromising than those of national organizations, both because the local activists did not have large disparate constituencies to worry about and because they had, literally, to live with the decisions made. "If someone's worried about the health of their children," as one activist put it, "they won't be convinced by appeals to 'political pragmatism.'" Or as Barry Commoner saw it:

> The older national environmental organizations in their Washington offices have taken the soft political road of negotiation, compromising with the corporations on the amount of pollution that is acceptable. The people living in the polluted communities have taken the hard political road of confrontation, demanding not that the dumping of hazardous waste be slowed down but that it be stopped.

Grass-roots organizations also had a broader reach and, in usually undeveloped ways, a somewhat deeper perception than the nationals tended to have. Minority groups of all kinds and many blue-collar neighborhoods were drawn to environmental activism out of some local need—particularly because they were often targets of undesirable and dangerous projects that affluent communities resisted—whereas the majors were made up largely of white and more affluent staffs and constituencies. Women, too, were disproportionately represented in both membership and leadership of local groups, often housewives with little previous activism but a number who were veterans of various protests of the sixties. And because such people were in the trenches, as it were, they tended to have much less reverence either for the assurances of officialdom or for the pronouncements of experts, all of which they treated with a healthy distrust, and they were much less inclined to believe in the inevitable worth of economic growth or the unquestioned right of corporations to make decisions affecting local social and environmental affairs.

The most impressive evidence of grass-roots power came with the hottest issue of the decade, toxic waste. Largely at the instigation of Lois Gibbs, a housewife whose effective leadership of the residents of the Love Canal neighborhood brought her national attention, a Citizens' Clearinghouse for Hazardous Wastes was formed in 1981 to coordinate and assist the work of local groups. By the fall of 1986 it had a network of 1,300 groups, two-thirds of them begun after 1984, when news of the evacuation of dioxin-infested Times Beach and the explosion at the chemical plant in Bhopal was prominent in the media; by the end of the decade it reported working with no fewer than 7,000. Organized around such issues as groundwater contamination from landfills, dumping of industrial chemicals and heavy metals, and new incinerators for municipal garbage, such groups energized many people who had been politically inactive and exerted their power with letter-writing campaigns, town meetings, door-to-door canvassing, and even demonstrations and civil disobedience. With encouragement, information, and advice from the Clearinghouse—for example, on up-to-the-minute alternatives for sewage treatment that could win over reluctant town boards—many of the locals were able to gain substantial concessions or outright victories, usually to the surprise of their high-powered antagonists. One indication of the alliance's effect is that since the Love Canal crisis in 1978, no new hazardous-waste dumps have been established in America. "Not because they're illegal," Lois Gibbs is careful to point out, "but because people have lobbied at the grass roots.". . .

The second new dimension of the eighties, radical environmentalism, was similarly decentralized and often emerged in similar reaction to the nationals, but it was usually inspired by people with considerable political experience, much of it tinged by the insights of the sixties and often informed by years of work inside the mainstream movement. Their causes and their tactics, not to mention their styles and rhetoric, grew directly out of opposition to what they saw as the reformism and the "cooptation" of the mainstream at a time when the perils seemed to be multiplying and the national leadership unresponsive. Among the charges that they leveled was that the old organizations were too legalistic ("You should never support a piece of legislation," said Dave Foreman, radicalized after a decade of suit-and-tie lobbying in Washington, "you should always be asking for more"); too professional ("You've got a new group of bureaucratic professionals," asserted Lorna Salzman, a onetime . . . activist in New York, "who are not in it for a cause but because it's a 'public interest' highfalutin *job*"); and too limited ("The reform environmentalists have no program and no vision," argued George Sessions, a professor of philosophy at Sierra College, "they're about on the level of the penal establishment").

The emergence of this new breed and their criticism of the majors were serious enough to prompt Michael McClosky, director of the Sierra Club from 1969 to 1985 and its subsequent chairman, to send a confidential memo to his board of directors in January 1986 warning of the "new, more militant" environmentalists. "They are people who do not hesitate to criticize the main players such as the Sierra Club," he wrote, but their target is larger, to change "the relationship of individuals to society and the ways in which society works." The question they pose to the movement is "whether it is wise to work within the context of the basic social, political, and economic institutions to achieve stepwise progress, or whether prime energies must be directed at changing those institutions." And he added: "They're just utopian. We may be 'reformist' and all, but we know how to work within the context of the institutions of the society—and they're just blowing smoke."

Not quite smoke. The new radicals could sometimes be more vociferous than they were coherent, sometimes let frustrations lead them into actions insufficiently planned, sometimes were trapped into taking positions in public without having done

393

enough homework—in short, showed the failings of any large group of disparate people acting in the public arena against the status quo. But in the decade of the eighties they made their mark.

Despite differences, sometimes substantial, what generally united the radical environmentalists was an underlying criticism of the dominant anthropocentric Western view of the world and a feeling that the transition to an ecological or biocentric view had to be made with all possible speed, with active and dramatic prodding if necessary. Such a sensibility was deeply ecological, in that it understood the true interdependence of species and their habitats (and the necessarily limited role of the human among them), and deeply radical too, in that it demanded a profound change in the values and beliefs of industrial society from the bottom up. Altogether, in the words of philosopher George Sessions, "it shows us that the basic assumptions upon which the modern urban-industrial edifice of Western culture rests are erroneous and highly dangerous. An ecologically harmonious paradigm shift is going to require a *total* reorientation of the thrust of Western culture."

Among the expressions of this new radicalism, four overlapping tendencies stand out.

Bioregionalism, the idea that the earth is to be understood as a series of life territories defined by topography and biota rather than by humans and their legislatures, was the first to take root in America. It imagined human societies organized on the lines of empowered bioregions, expressing such values as conservation and stability rather than exploitation and progress, cooperation and diversity rather than competition and uniformity, and decentralism and division rather than centralization and mono-culture; as one early formulation put it, "the bioregional movement seeks to re-create a widely shared sense of regional identity founded upon a renewed critical awareness of and respect for the integrity of our natural ecological communities."

The movement itself began in California in the late 1970s and by the mid-1980s it encompassed some sixty local organizations: some were explicit bioregional councils, as in the Ozarks, the Kansas prairie, the Hudson Valley, and the Northwest; some, such as the National Water Center in Arkansas and Friends of the Trees in Washington State, had the specialized interests their names implied; some, including those in Appalachia, the Columbia River valley, the San Francisco Bay area, and Cape Cod, published regular magazines on bioregional themes. The first of a series of biannual continental congresses, designed to set policies on environmental issues and establish movement-wide links, was held in the Ozarks in 1984, since then followed by meetings in Michigan, British Columbia, Maine, and Texas.

Deep ecology, originally formulated by Norwegian philosopher Arne Naess in the seventies, was brought to the United States primarily by George Sessions and sociologist Bill Devall, who co-authored its first popular account in 1984. Standing in contrast to what Naess termed the "shallow environmentalism" of most of the movement, deep ecology stressed such points as: ecological equality, the right of every species to existence and survival and with equal "intrinsic value" regardless of its importance for humans; the diversity and abundance of all life forms, which should not be reduced by humans except "to satisfy vital needs"; the sharp reduction of human population so that other species may not only survive but have sufficient habitat to thrive; the preservation of the wilderness as a pristine habitat valuable in its own right; and the self-realization of humans through lower levels of consumption and resource use. Complicated as they were, such ideas quickly gained a following in the United States—and elsewhere in the world, including Canada, Australia, and Northern Europe—and proved especially influential among both radical activists and academic philosophers, no mean feat. . . .

Ecofeminism, a synergistic blend of sixties-style feminism with eighties-style ecology, placed its emphasis on the connections between the domination and exploitation of women and the domination and exploitation of nature, both seen as products of a male-dominated society. Inspired in part by two books, Susan Griffin's *Woman and Nature* in 1978 and Carolyn Merchant's *The Death of Nature* in 1980, ecofeminism sought to go beyond the limits of earlier feminist ideologies, particularly by raising issues that set women in a context wider than just the economic. "Why is it that women and nature are associated, and vilified in our culture?" asked one early proponent, Ynestra King. "Does the liberation of one depend on the liberation of the other?" It also sought to go beyond what were seen as the limitations of other radicalisms by raising questions about "androcentrism," the male-focused perspective, as the real heart of the eco-crisis and about patriarchy as the central instrument in understanding the Western domination of nature. Like deep ecology, ecofeminism had a considerable following on the campuses, in women's studies and philosophy departments particularly, and inspired a veritable torrent of books and articles in this decade; several ecofeminist conferences were held in these years as well, the largest and most comprehensive at UCLA in the spring of 1987.

The Gaia hypothesis, formulated by British scientist James Lovelock in a small book in 1979, suggested that because the earth was apparently so regulated as to maintain its temperature, its atmosphere, and its hydrosphere with extraordinary precision for millions of years, it could in fact be thought of as a living organism. Immediately popular among many nonscientists as a useful metaphor for thinking about a biocentric earth, the Gaia idea spawned a number of similar analyses (as well as conferences, T-shirts, study groups, and an oceangoing Viking ship), all supporting positions congenial to the radical perspective. Interestingly, the hypothesis was seen to embody perceptions not very different from those of various early tribal peoples, including the American Indians, whose record as model ecologists was being brought to light at about this time; it was characteristic of most Indian mythologies to think of the earth as a single living being and to derive ways of behavior and thought that would ensure its careful, productive existence.

These expressions of radical environmentalism naturally gave rise to a great many organizations in these years, several of which had national importance. Among them:

- Earth First!, the more or less organized expression of the activist side of the new radicalism, was started by Dave Foreman and a handful of other disillusioned operatives from mainstream environmentalism around a campfire in 1980. Designedly formless, without national staff, bylaws, formal incorporation, or even membership, it was simply dedicated to the principle that "in *any* decision consideration for the health of the earth must come first" and that in carrying this out, it should make "no compromise in defense of Mother Earth." Inspired in part by novelist Edward Abbey's 1975 *The Monkey Wrench Gang*, Earth First!ers stood foursquare in defense of wilderness and its biodiversity and made militance a cardinal part of their tactics, soon including guerrilla theater, media stunts, civil disobedience, and, unofficially, "ecotage" (also called "monkey wrenching"): sabotaging bulldozers and road-building equipment on public lands, pulling up survey stakes, cutting down billboards, destroying traps, and, famously, "spiking" trees at random to prevent their being cut and milled. No sure way exists of checking such a figure, but an EF! spokesperson has said that the cost to the nation of such ecotage was $20-$25 million a year.

With such forthright militance, EF! succeeded in attracting a considerable following and by the end of the decade had grown to more than seventy-five chapters in twenty-four states (mostly in the Southwest and on the West Coast) and Mexico and Canada. But it paid a penalty for its success: as Foreman put it, "from one side there are concerted efforts to moderate us, mellow us out, and sanitize our vices; from another side have come efforts to make us radical in a traditional leftist sense; and there are ongoing efforts by the powers that be to wipe us out entirely." Such pressures—including FBI infiltration and a trumped-up federal suit against Foreman and others in July 1989 and a car-bombing of two California activists in May 1990—eventually led to Foreman's dropping out and the group's splintering into several rival groups in the early 1990s. . . .

- Sea Shepherd Conservation Society was started by Paul Watson after he was kicked out of Greenpeace for being too militant; it became the method by which he lived out a vision he had had during a Sioux sweat-lodge rite that he was destined to save the mammals of the ocean, especially whales. With a "navy" consisting of a single ship, he and his crew had dedicated themselves to being the police of the seas, eventually incapacitating at least seven vessels illegally hunting whales, confronting ships illegally fishing with gill nets that trap marine mammals and birds, and taking direct action, not excluding ecotage, to prevent seal hunts in Canada, dolphin slaughter in Japanese waters, and whaling in the North Atlantic. The organization, which has some 15,000 support members, has adopted a slogan of "We don't talk about problems, we act," and it has lived up to it.

Questions

---

1. *What factors explain the rise of the environmental movement, according to Hays? Can you think of other factors that might have played an important role?*
2. *Compare the environmental movement to other reform movements in American history. Is the environmental movement unique in any way?*
3. *Do you believe that the tactics of direct-action environmental groups such as Earth First! are justified?*
4. *How successful has the environmental movement been in the United States?*

ENVIRONMENTALISTS AS CRITICS

In the decades following the end of the Second World War, the material prosperity enjoyed by the majority of Americans made the American standard of living the envy of much of the world. By the early 1960s, however, some influential Americans were beginning to call attention to the negative environmental effects of unrestrained industrial expansion and the wasteful excesses of the consumer society. Despite continuing efforts to present a positive alternative vision of a society in harmony with nature, environmentalists in the United States have made their greatest mark in the role of stern critics of our wasteful, destructive society. In this respect, environmentalism is part of the long tradition of dissent in the United States that has challenged the workings of the capitalist system. The selections that follow question in both explicit and implicit fashion some of the core assumptions that guided the development of American society for generations. As you read these selections, be careful to consider the broader implications of the authors' arguments for individual lifestyles and the role of government in the United States.

The Chemical Threat

One historian called Rachel Carson's book Silent Spring "the Uncle Tom's Cabin of modern environmentalism." Carson's best-selling volume alerted Americans to the dangers of the unrestrained use of pesticides and foreshadowed the environmental movement's obsession with the health dangers of human-made chemicals. Excerpted from Rachel Carson, Silent Spring *(Boston, 1962), 1–3, 5–9.*

THERE WAS ONCE a town in the heart of America where all life seemed to live in harmony with its surroundings. The town lay in the midst of a checkerboard of prosperous farms, with fields of grain and hillsides of orchards where, in spring, white clouds of bloom drifted above the green fields. In autumn, oak and maple and birch set up a blaze of color that flamed and flickered across a backdrop of pines. Then foxes barked in the hills and deer silently crossed the fields, half hidden in the mists of the fall mornings.

Along the roads, laurel, viburnum and alder, great ferns and wildflowers delighted the traveler's eye through much of the year. Even in winter the roadsides were places of beauty, where countless birds came to feed on the berries and on the seed heads of the dried weeds rising above the snow. The countryside was, in fact, famous for the abundance and variety of its bird life, and when the flood of migrants was pouring through in spring and fall people traveled from great distances to observe them. Others came to fish the streams, which flowed clear and cold out of the hills and contained shady pools where trout lay. So it had been from the days many years ago when the first settlers raised their houses, sank their wells, and built their barns.

Then a strange blight crept over the area and everything began to change. Some evil spell had settled on the community: mysterious maladies swept the flocks of chickens; the cattle and sheep sickened and died. Everywhere was a shadow of death. The farmers spoke of much illness among their families. In the town the doctors had become more and more puzzled by new kinds of sickness appearing among their patients. There had been several sudden and unexplained deaths, not only among adults but even among children, who would be stricken suddenly while at play and die within a few hours.

There was a strange stillness. The birds, for example—where had they gone? Many people spoke of them, puzzled and disturbed. The feeding stations in the backyards were deserted. The few birds seen anywhere were moribund; they trembled violently and could not fly. It was a spring without voices. On the mornings that had once throbbed with the dawn chorus of robins, catbirds, doves, jays, wrens, and scores of other bird voices there was now no sound; only silence lay over the fields and woods and marsh.

On the farms the hens brooded, but no chicks hatched. The farmers complained that they were unable to raise any pigs—the

Excerpts from *Silent Spring* by Rachel Carson, published by Houghton Mifflin Company, 1962. Copyright © 1962 by Rachel L. Carson.

Rachel Carson sounded the alarm about the dangers of pesticide use in her 1962 book Silent Spring *and attracted public interest in the growing environmental movement. (Courtesy of AP/Wide World Photos.)*

litters were small and the young survived only a few days. The apple trees were coming into bloom but no bees droned among the blossoms, so there was no pollination and there would be no fruit.

The roadsides, once so attractive, were now lined with browned and withered vegetation as though swept by fire. These, too, were silent, deserted by all living things. Even the streams were now lifeless. Anglers no longer visited them, for all the fish had died.

In the gutters under the eaves and between the shingles of the roofs, a white granular powder still showed a few patches; some weeks before it had fallen like snow upon the roofs and the lawns, the fields and streams.

No witchcraft, no enemy action had silenced the rebirth of new life in this stricken world. The people had done it themselves.

This town does not actually exist, but it might easily have a thousand counterparts in America or elsewhere in the world. I know of no community that has experienced all the misfortunes I describe. Yet every one of these disasters has actually happened somewhere, and many real communities have already suffered a substantial number of them. A grim specter has crept upon us almost unnoticed, and this imagined tragedy may easily become a stark reality we all shall know.

What has already silenced the voices of spring in countless towns in America? This . . . is an attempt to explain.

The history of life on earth has been a history of interaction between living things and their surroundings. To a large extent, the physical form and the habits of the earth's vegetation and its animal life have been molded by the environment. Considering the whole span of earthly time, the opposite effect, in which life actually modifies its surroundings, has been relatively slight. Only within the moment of time represented by the present century has one species—man—acquired significant power to alter the nature of his world.

During the past quarter century this power has not only increased to one of disturbing magnitude but it has changed in character. The most alarming of all man's assaults upon the environment is the contamination of air, earth, rivers, and sea with dangerous and even lethal materials. This pollution is for the most part irrecoverable; the chain of evil it initiates not only in the world that must support life but in living tissues is for the most part irreversible. In this now universal contamination of the environment, chemicals are the sinister and little-recognized partners of radiation in changing the very nature of the world—the very nature of its life. Strontium 90, released through nuclear explosions into the air, comes to earth in rain or drifts down as fallout, lodges in soil, enters into the grass or corn or wheat grown there, and in time takes up its abode in the bones of a human being, there to remain until his death. Similarly, chemicals sprayed on croplands or forests or gardens lie long in soil, entering into living organisms, passing from one to another in a chain of poisoning and death. Or they pass mysteriously by underground streams until they emerge and, through the alchemy of air and sunlight, combine into new forms that kill vegetation, sicken cattle, and work unknown harm on those who drink from once pure wells. As Albert Schweitzer has said, "Man can hardly even recognize the devils of his own creation."

It took hundreds of millions of years to produce the life that now inhabits the earth—eons of time in which that developing and evolving and diversifying life reached a state of adjustment and balance with its surroundings. The environment, rigorously shaping and directing the life it supported, contained elements that were hostile as well as supporting. Certain rocks gave out dangerous radiation; even within the light of the sun, from which all life draws its energy, there were short-wave radiations with power to injure. Given time—time not in years but in millennia—life adjusts, and a balance has been reached. For time is the essential ingredient; but in the modern world there is no time.

The rapidity of change and the speed with which new situations are created follow the impetuous and heedless pace of man rather than the deliberate pace of nature. Radiation is no longer merely the background radiation of rocks, the bombardment of cosmic rays, the ultraviolet of the sun that have existed before there was any life on earth; radiation is now the unnatural creation of man's tampering with the atom. The chemicals to which life is asked to make its adjustment are no longer merely the calcium and silica and copper and all the rest of the minerals washed out of the rocks and carried in rivers to the sea; they are the synthetic creations of man's inventive mind, brewed in his laboratories, and having no counterparts in nature.

To adjust to these chemicals would require time on the scale that is nature's; it would require not merely the years of a man's life but the life of generations. And even this, were it by some miracle possible, would be futile, for the new chemicals come from our laboratories in an endless stream; almost five hundred annually find their way into actual use in the United States alone. The figure is staggering and its implications are not easily grasped—500 new chemicals to which the bodies of men and animals are required somehow to adapt each year, chemicals totally outside the limits of biologic experience.

Among them are many that are used in man's war against nature. Since the mid-1940s over 200 basic chemicals have been created for use in killing insects, weeds, rodents, and other organisms described in the modern vernacular as "pests"; and they are sold under several thousand different brand names.

These sprays, dusts, and aerosols are now applied almost universally to farms, gardens, forests, and homes—nonselective chemicals that have the power to kill every insect, the "good" and the "bad," to still the song of birds and the leaping of fish in the streams, to coat the leaves with a deadly film, and to linger on in soil—all this though the intended target may be only a few weeds or insects. Can anyone believe it is possible to lay down such a barrage of poisons on the surface of the earth without making it unfit for all life? They should not be called "insecticides," but "biocides."

The whole process of spraying seems caught up in an endless spiral. Since DDT was released for civilian use, a process of escalation has been going on in which ever more toxic materials must be found. This has happened because insects, in a triumphant vindication of Darwin's principle of the survival of the fittest, have evolved super races immune to the particular insecticide used, hence a deadlier one has always to be developed—and then a deadlier one than that. It has happened also because . . . destructive insects often undergo a "flareback," or resurgence, after spraying, in numbers greater than before. Thus the chemical war is never won, and all life is caught in its violent crossfire.

Along with the possibility of the extinction of mankind by nuclear war, the central problem of our age has therefore become the contamination of man's total environment with such substances of incredible potential for harm—substances that accumulate in the tissues of plants and animals and even penetrate the germ cells to shatter or alter the very material of heredity upon which the shape of the future depends.

Some would-be architects of our future look toward a time when it will be possible to alter the human germ plasm by design. But we may easily be doing so now by inadvertence, for many chemicals, like radiation, bring about gene mutations. It is ironic to think that man might determine his own future by something so seemingly trivial as the choice of an insect spray.

All this has been risked—for what? Future historians may well be amazed by our distorted sense of proportion. How could intelligent beings seek to control a few unwanted species by a method that contaminated the entire environment and brought the threat of disease and death even to their own kind? Yet this is precisely what we have done. We have done it, moreover, for reasons that collapse the moment we examine them. We are told that the enormous and expanding use of pesticides is necessary to maintain farm production. Yet is our real problem not one of *overproduction*? Our farms, despite measures to remove acreage from production and to pay farmers *not* to produce, have yielded such a staggering excess of crops that the American taxpayer in 1962 is paying out more than one billion dollars a year as the total carrying cost of the surplus-food storage program. And is the situation helped when one branch of the Agriculture Department tries to reduce production while another states, as it did in 1958, "It is believed generally that reduction of crop acreages under provisions of the Soil Bank will stimulate interest in use of chemicals to obtain maximum production on the land retained in crops."

All this is not to say there is no insect problem and no need of control. I am saying, rather, that control must be geared to realities, not to mythical situations, and that the methods employed must be such that they do not destroy us along with the insects.

Questioning the Affluent Society

Stewart Udall served as secretary of the interior under Presidents Kennedy and Johnson and played a major role in shaping national environmental policy during the seminal decade of the 1960s. Excerpted from Stewart L. Udall, The Quiet Crisis *(New York, 1963), vii–viii.*

ONE WEEK last fall two events came to my attention which seemed to sum up the plight of modern man: the first was a press report which indicated the T. S. Eliot, the poet, was a victim of London's latest "killer fog" and lay gravely ill, the second was a call from a preservation-minded citizen of New Hampshire who informed me that Robert Frost's old farm—fixed for all time in memory by the poem "West-running Brook"—was now an auto junk yard.

The coincidence of these two events raised questions in my mind: Is a society a success if it creates conditions that impair its finest minds and make a wasteland of its finest landscapes? What does material abundance avail if we create an environment in which man's highest and most specifically human attributes cannot be fulfilled?

Each generation has its own rendezvous with the land, for despite our fee titles and claims of ownership, we are all brief tenants on this planet. By choice, or by default, we will carve out a land legacy for our heirs. We can misuse the land and diminish the usefulness of resources, or we can create a world in which physical affluence and affluence of the spirit go hand in hand.

History tells us that earlier civilizations have declined because they did not learn to live in harmony with the land. Our successes in space and our triumphs of technology hold a hidden danger: as modern man increasingly arrogates to himself dominion over the physical environment, there is the risk that his false pride will cause him to take the resources of the earth for granted—and to lose all reverence for the land.

America today stands poised on a pinnacle of wealth and power, yet we live in a land of vanishing beauty, of increasing ugliness, of shrinking open space, and of an overall environment that is diminished daily by pollution and noise and blight.

This, in brief, is the quiet conservation crisis of the 1960s.

Attacking Corporate America

During the 1960s, the deteriorating conditions of the Great Lakes became a national symbol of unchecked pollution and environmental degradation. Under the leadership of Walter Reuther, the United Auto Workers (UAW) took a prominent role in calling for greater efforts to halt the decline of the Great Lakes. Taken from a public statement by Robert Johnston, regional director of the UAW, submitted to a federal conference on the pollution of Lake Michigan in February 1968, U.S. Department of the Interior, Federal Water Pollution Control Administration, Proceedings of the Conference in the Matter of Pollution of Lake Michigan and its Tributary Basin *(Washington, 1968), 1333–38.*

The UAW wishes to associate itself at this conference with those who believe that we are in danger of being too late with too little if we are to save Lake Michigan. Fifty years of indifference

---

Excerpts from *Proceedings of the Conference on Pollution of Lake Michigan and Its Tributary Basin*, published by the U.S. Department of the Interior, Federal Water Pollution Control Administration, 1968.

and inaction about Lake Michigan and the Great Lakes has created a problem that can't be solved by old techniques that are comparable to trying to bail out pollution with a bucket. Reliance on such techniques will only result in creating another Dead Sea along the industrial and urban waterfronts of Lake Michigan.

The formula for saving Lake Michigan and the Great Lakes is simple enough. All that is needed is higher anti-pollution standards and the realization of these standards by faster action and rigid enforcement. We believe that the present Federal and State laws are inadequate to secure the enforcement of the anti-pollution measures that are needed. We believe that the present Federal funds, reduced in the proposed new budget, are inadequate to assist cities and States in pure water projects. . . .

The corporations responsible for turning the lakefront into an industrial cesspool reads like a Blue Book of big profit companies in America. United States Steel, Ford Motor Company, Standard Oil, International Harvester, Inland Steel, Republic Steel, Sinclair Refining Company. The Who's Who of Big Business have helped themselves to billions in profits by using the lake water and dumping back pollutants. These same corporations are protesting adequate anti-pollution standards, and dragging their feet under the inadequate enforcement provisions. . . .

The labor movement deserves to be criticized for leaving the corporation polluters alone too long. It isn't enough for a union to get sufficient drinking fountains and hot showers in an auto plant or a steel mill and ignore the fact that the companies are helping kill a great natural resource like Lake Michigan. The lake belongs to union dues payers and the rest of the public, and not to corporations. The labor movement therefore has an obligation to also fight to save the lake. . . .

The corporations certainly can plead poverty about our grievance over Lake Michigan. Corporations in the industrial complex along the lake make several billion in profits annually. They have invested hundreds of millions in the most modern automated equipment and new plants while delaying the installation of effective anti-pollutant systems.

The UAW has welcomed recently the signs of an awakening social conscience on the part of some corporations on such national problems as hard-core unemployment, open housing, and low-cost housing developments. The corporations should also expand their moral obligation to cleaning up Lake Michigan. All these problems have a relationship. Behind the big profit plants on the polluted lake are the poor neighborhoods and the slums enveloped in polluted air and all the increasing social problems of the urban centers. We are either going to clean up Lake Michigan and the slums behind them or the indifference of corporate neglect and public apathy will fan some social firestorms that all the polluted water in the Great Lakes can't put out.

The final solution to pure water, the new sewerage and sanitation systems needed by the cities and the cleaning up of the rivers that dump into Lake Michigan and the Great Lakes, depends upon putting a proper high national and State priority on this crucial problem and allocating adequate funds to solve the problem.

We in the UAW believe that our Nation must remain strong, not only in military hardware, but in social progress. As President Walter Reuther pointed out at our National Pure Water Conference, "We must find a way to spend as much on such basic necessities of life as water and fresh air and social welfare as we do on defense and armaments."

Protecting Working-Class Communities

In 1978, the community of Love Canal near Niagara Falls, New York, received national attention when local citizens and public health authorities connected area health problems to a nearby toxic waste dump. The tactics used by Lois Gibbs and her neighbors to combat this local threat and force government action became the model for other communities across the nation faced with similar problems. The following excerpt is taken from a speech by Gibbs in 1980. Abridged from "'It Does Affect You:' Women at Love Canal and Three Mile Island," ed. Celeste Wesson, Radical America *17 (March–June 1983): 29–32.*

The women of Love Canal are much like myself—housewives, mothers. Most have a high school education. We are lower-

---

Excerpts reprinted from "'It Does Affect You:' Women at Love Canal and Three Mile Island," a speech by Lois Gibbs, as it appeared in *Radical America*, Vol. 17, No. 2–3, March–June 1983. Reprinted by permission of Lois Gibbs.[1]

middle-class families with our biggest investment our home, and our most precious asset our children. The majority did not work but remained home tending to houses, gardens and growing children. Since the Love Canal exposure, this way of life has changed. Women are no longer at home, because it is unsafe; we're not allowed to go near our gardens. The decisions have changed too, from normal everyday questions such as: What are we going to have for dinner? Where are we going on vacation? What color shall we paint the walls? Now the decisions are: How can we afford a new home? Will my baby have leukemia? Will my daughter ever have a normal baby? What will we do with our sick child? We can't move and we can't stay here.

Women prior to the Love Canal disaster were very sort of square, I guess. Women who at one time looked down on people picketing, being arrested and acting somewhat radical are now doing those very things. Now women who would never have volunteered for anything have given up two years of their lives to try to save their families, working in our office, conducting phone surveys, going from door to door. . . .

Many women, especially the active ones, have been faced with another major problem—their marriages. Most of them were homemakers. Dinner was ready at five, laundry was done, and children were properly cared for. Now, in many households, dinner is not ready at five, laundry is not quite done, and the neighbor is taxiing the children around. The husbands are forced to do these things—to be satisfied with hamburgers at McDonald's three times a week, with taking care of the children more. The husbands feel helpless because they cannot protect their families and are also jealous because their wives are now working with other men in the office. The result of all this is stress, which leads to arguments and in many cases divorce. Among families who relocated in August 1978, approximately 40% have ended in separation or divorce. There are pressures and decisions that no normal marriage is subjected to: Will we walk away from our homes and our savings to protect our children? It's easy for you sitting in the audience to say, of course. But think about it. Think about packing the clothes in your closet and walking away to start all over again with nothing—no savings, no furniture, no money, children who are always hungry and ten thousand dollars a year.

The first thing we learned when we started organizing was

how valuable the media can be. We learned what would get us national attention, like our survey on women who became pregnant during the construction of the containment system on the canal proper. During this period there was additional air contamination from open trenches. There were 15 pregnancies during this time. Of the 15, only one normal baby was born. All the rest ended in miscarriages, birth defects or diseased children.

We organized rallies and protests around times when coverage was slow throughout most of the state. We found that numbers, long chemical names and statistics confused people, so we arranged a series—a horror story of the day. One family, in their home, would tell of their problems: a mother would explain how her baby died or had three major birth defects, or a family would reveal that state officials told them not to go into their basement, their son's bedroom or their kitchen because of chemical readings—and then the state would publicly announce there was no problem there. This was very successful and we received a large response. Readers became furious with the government for allowing this to continue.

We also found the media very helpful in pushing the government to do what is right. In August 1979, Governor Carey was running for reelection. We held a public meeting and asked: Where is the Governor? Is he campaigning instead of taking care of the emergency situation in his state? What are his priorities? Two days later Governor Carey visited Love Canal, stood on stage in front of hundreds of people who were screaming "Murderer, help our children," with both men and women crying. Cameras rolled. The whole state watched, so he told everyone that the state would buy their homes at fair market value. Now he was a hero. He was reelected. We found that one thing government cannot stand is a confrontation of men, women and children out in the street protesting and pleading for help in front of the press. . . .

Although Love Canal may be the first, it is definitely not the only real toxic waste problem. Because we have received national media coverage, citizens call us from all over the country. Many of them tell us of wastes buried in their backyards and health problems they believe are not normal. The whole toxic waste issue affects everyone. There are thousands of known poisonous dump sites across the country and many unknown ones. These dump sites are invading our land, air and drinking water, and they must be cleaned up. Because of the cost involved to clean and monitor each site, both government and industry would like to ignore them. Meanwhile, innocent people are being hurt and profits are being made by industry.

The only way to clean up the sites properly and to avoid new Love Canals being built is for people to force the government to implement laws to stop careless disposal of toxic wastes and force industries to clean up their own dumps. We, the taxpayers, should not bear the costs of clean up while the responsible party is sitting back making a profit. The one thing you must understand is that *it does affect you*—you, the taxpayer; you, the consumer; or you, the victim! Unless you have thoroughly checked out your backyard and your drinking water, you are not safe. We never knew about Love Canal when we moved in eight years ago. Your children may move into an unsafe area as we did, unaware and innocent, only to suffer.

Basic Principles of Deep Ecology

Those who adhere to the ideals of deep ecology reject the moderation of "reform environmentalism" and call instead for a complete reorientation of the way in which Western society relates to the natural world. George Sessions and Bill Devall are two of the leading proponents of deep ecology in the United States. Taken from Bill Devall and George Sessions, Deep Ecology: Living as If Nature Mattered *(Salt Lake City, 1985), 65–66, 70.*

Ecological consciousness and deep ecology are in sharp contrast with the dominant worldview of technocratic-industrial societies which regards humans as isolated and fundamentally separate from the rest of Nature, as superior to, and in charge of, the rest of creation. But the view of humans as separate and superior to the rest of Nature is only part of larger cultural patterns. For thousands of years, Western culture has become increasingly obsessed with the idea of *dominance:* with dominance of humans over nonhuman Nature, masculine over the feminine, wealthy and powerful over the poor, with the dominance of the West over non-Western cultures. Deep ecological consciousness allows us to see through these erroneous and dangerous illusions. . . .

Basic Principles

1. The well-being and flourishing of human and nonhuman Life on Earth have value in themselves (synonyms: intrinsic value, inherent value). These values are independent of the usefulness of the nonhuman world for human purposes.
2. Richness and diversity of life forms contribute to the realization of these values and are also values in themselves.
3. Humans have no right to reduce this richness and diversity except to satisfy vital needs.
4. The flourishing of human life and cultures is compatible with a substantial decrease of the human population. The flourishing of nonhuman life requires such a decrease.
5. Present human interference with the nonhuman world is excessive, and the situation is rapidly worsening.
6. Policies must therefore be changed. These policies affect basic economic, technological, and ideological structures. The resulting state of affairs will be deeply different from the present.
7. The ideological change is mainly that of appreciating life quality (dwelling in situations of inherent value) rather than adhering to an increasingly higher standard of living. There will be a profound awareness of the difference between big and great.
8. Those who subscribe to the foregoing points have an obligation directly or indirectly to try to implement the necessary changes.

Notes

1 Lois Gibbs began her 16 years of environmental activism as President of the Love Canal Homeowners Association in 1978. Since then, she has spoken at thousands of confer-

ences and seminars, been featured in hundreds of newspapers, magazines and textbooks, appeared on hundreds of television and radio shows, and been the recipient of numerous awards. Among her many honors are the 1990 Goldman Environmental Prize, *Outsider Magazine's* "Top Ten Who Made a Difference" Honor Roll in 1991, and an honorary Ph.D. from the State University of New York, Cortland College.

Lois has struggled alongside thousands of communities to win environmental justice. As Executive Director, Lois has led CCHW's efforts to provide organizing, training, research, educational and technical assistance services to communities in environmental crisis across the country for the past 13 years.

Questions

1. *Why did* Silent Spring *become such a popular and influential book?*
2. *What tactics do Carson and Gibbs use to appeal to people's emotions? Do these methods get in the way of good public policy or do they promote it?*
3. *How does deep ecology differ from mainstream environmentalism? Can you identify principles of deep ecology in the first four selections? Which of the first four authors is most in tune with the philosophy of deep ecology?*

FURTHER READING

Stephen Fox, John Muir and His Legacy: The American Conservation Movement *(Boston, 1981), places the environmental movement in historical perspective, while John McCormick,* Reclaiming Paradise: The Global Environmental Movement *(Bloomington, Indiana, 1989), surveys the international scene.* American Environmentalism: The U.S. Environmental Movement, 1970–1990, *ed. Riley E. Dunlap and Angela G. Mertig (Philadelphia, 1992), is an excellent source for recent developments. A major new work by Robert Gottlieb,* Forcing the Spring: The Transformation of the American Environmental Movement *(Washington, 1993), offers a useful corrective to much of the scholarship in this field by giving equal attention to urban-industrial health and pollution concerns.*